Estrangement and the
Somatics of Literature

PARALLAX  RE-VISIONS OF CULTURE
AND SOCIETY

Stephen G. Nichols, Gerald Prince, and Wendy Steiner
SERIES EDITORS

Estrangement and the Somatics of Literature

Tolstoy, Shklovsky, Brecht

Douglas Robinson

The Johns Hopkins University Press
Baltimore

© 2008 The Johns Hopkins University Press
All rights reserved. Published 2008
Printed in the United States of America on acid-free paper
9 8 7 6 5 4 3 2 1

The Johns Hopkins University Press
2715 North Charles Street
Baltimore, Maryland 21218-4363
www.press.jhu.edu

Library of Congress Cataloging-in-Publication Data

Robinson, Douglas, 1954–
    Estrangement and the somatics of literature : Tolstoy,
Shklovsky, Brecht / Douglas Robinson.
        p.   cm. — (Parallax, re-visions of culture and society)
    Includes bibliographical references and index.
    ISBN-13: 978-0-8018-8796-3 (hardcover : alk. paper)
    ISBN-10: 0-8018-8796-8 (hardcover : alk. paper)
        1. Alienation (Social psychology) in literature. 2. Tolstoy,
Leo, graf, 1828–1910—Criticism and interpretation.
3. Shklovskii, Viktor Borisovich, 1893–1984—Criticism and
interpretation. 4. Brecht, Bertolt, 1898–1956—Criticism
and interpretation. 5. Criticism—Russia (Federation)—
History. 6. Criticism—German—History. I. Title.
    PN56.A45R63 2008
    809'.9333—dc22   2007033705

A catalog record for this book is available from the
British Library.

Special discounts are available for bulk purchases of this book.
For more information, please contact Special Sales at
410-516-6936 or specialsales@press.jhu.edu.

Contents

Contents

Gestic Transformation 235   Conclusion:
The Somatics of Literature 251

Acknowledgments

I wrote this book while on a Fulbright in Voronezh, Russia, where access to the hard-copy Russian originals of Tolstoy, Shklovsky, and their Russian critics and sources was easier than it might have been in the United States but every other aspect of the research was more difficult. My first thanks go, therefore, to Martha Swan, Lisa Harrison, and Anne Johnson in the Interlibrary Loan office at the University of Mississippi, who obtained for me well over a hundred chapters and articles. Kara Hobson in the Ole Miss English department and my daughters Laura, Sara, and Anna, especially Laura in Finland, helped me get the books I absolutely had to have. Thanks also to my colleagues at Voronezh State University, especially Vyacheslav Borisovich Kashkin and Irina Dobrynina, for helping me get into the university library there, to the consultants at the Russian State Library (the Leninka) in Moscow, and to the Fulbright Program in the Russian Federation (Ed Rosloff, Valentina Gruzintseva, and the others) for a productive year in the country of Tolstoy, Shklovsky, and Il'inskaya, who gave me invaluable help with the other two.

Charles Rougle, my fellow Fulbrighter at Moscow State University that year, read the Russian chapters not just for argumentative coherence but for accuracy on Russian culture and language and Anna Karenina's dreams; thanks also to Svetlana Boym and Caryl Emerson for e-mailing their essays in the then-forthcoming *Poetics Today* special issue on estrangement, guest edited by Professor Boym, and for discussing my project with me. Aleksandr Skidan, in the course of a long conversation in St. Petersburg on Brecht and Shklovsky, got me to write a five-page essay on both for the newspaper he and some friends were putting out, *Chto delat'?/What is to be done?* I ended up deciding not to publish the piece there, but writing it kicked off the writing of the book. Sasha also read some early drafts of chapter 3 and made helpful comments. Thanks to Artyom Magun and David Riff for their comments on the draft of the five-page essay. Michael Denner, editor of *Tolstoy Studies Journal,* in the course of accepting my article version of chapters 1 and 2 for publication pointed me in some useful directions with Tolstoy and Shklovsky; the two external evaluators to whom he sent that manuscript also offered helpful suggestions. Timothy Sergay engaged me in a lively e-mail discussion of issues of translation, Russian literature, and transliteration.

Introduction

This book is in part a comparative study of Russian and German literary-theoretical history, specifically of a single strain of that history associated with the concepts of estrangement and alienation (*Befremdung, Entfremdung, Verfremdung; ostranenie, otchuzhdenie*) and formalist modernism, as well their roots in German Romanticism, Hegel, and Marx. Due to the antithetical impulses driving all of these movements, however, both estrangement and alienation are from the beginning double, contradictory, dialectical: Friedrich von Schlegel's Romantic irony as the familiar and the strange, as openness and disguise, as serious and a joke; Hegel's alienation (*Entfremdung*) as the externalization (*Entäußerung*) of self and the internalization (*Erinnerung* or recollection) of things as "I"; Marx's materialism as saturated with the contradictory tensions of Schlegelian Romanticism and Hegelian Idealism; Viktor Shklovsky and Bertolt Brecht as Hegelian (Shklovsky) and Marxist-Hegelian (Brecht) formalists interested specifically in the psychological impact of form on the phenomenological and/or intellectual (re)construction of a material world. As Stanley Mitchell argues, the "meeting-point" between Shklovsky and Brecht is the European avant-garde in the Weimar period, roughly from the Russian revolution in 1917 to the fascist counterrevolution in 1933—a period during which the cultural axis of artistic experimentation ran from Berlin (Brecht's city) to Moscow (Shklovsky's). As the Stalinist Thermidor increasingly took over in the Soviet Union in the late 1920s and early 1930s, formalism was branded "cosmopolitan" and banned; Shklovsky was subjected to enormous public pressure to recant in the late 1920s, and even twenty and twenty-five years later, in the newly formed German Democratic Republic (GDR), Brecht—given his own theater in East Berlin and officially lionized—also remained somewhat under a cloud as a formalist.

But that history is only one part of the book. Of at least equal importance is the part of my main title that I haven't yet discussed: the somatics of literature. At its simplest and most conventionally salvific, the somatics of literature is mapped out by Lev Tolstoy in his infection theory: literature infects its readers with the author's feelings, which then guide or regulate the readers' behavior for good ("true" moral or Christian literature) or evil ("perverse" modernist celebrations of sex, pride, and ennui).[1] The somatics of literature was not a new idea in Tolstoy, of course; in some sense his theory in *What Is Art?* (1898) simply restated the argument between Plato and Aristotle over the ways in which literature channels shared communal feelings to its audience. Plato argues that literature channels to its audience all the worst, most destructive feelings and so incites the psychological equivalent of political insurrection (*Republic* 605c–606c), Aristotle that literature doesn't just *channel* the feelings of pity and fear but effects their *catharsis* (*Poetics* 1449b24–28). What Tolstoy contributes to the somatic theory of literature is the useful metaphor of infection, which, as we see in chapter 1, helps build a dialectical bridge between the Platonic image of art as the carrier of social disease or disorder (infecting audiences with insurgent feelings and a disinclination to resist or suppress them) and the Aristotelian image of art as the carrier of a cure or therapy for emotional excess (infecting audiences with the excessive feelings *and* their purgation—a dim or distant model for the homeopathic cure the estranging formalists imagine).

One of my primary concerns in the book is to show that formalist modernism, at least as theorized by Shklovsky and Brecht, is not the simple binary opposite to Tolstoy's antimodernist theory of the transfer of pure feeling that it has been taken to be. In his introduction to Benjamin Sher's 1990 English translation of Viktor Shklovsky's *Theory of Prose,* for example, Gerald L. Bruns writes that the Russian formalists defined themselves in opposition to psychology, which is to say in opposition to *persons:* "Structuralism raises itself on an opposition between system and history, structure and event; Russian Formalism defines itself not against history but against psychology . . . the idea here is to foreground the individual text in its intelligibility rather than to reconstruct what lies behind the text in the form of an originating expression or rule" (xii). Formalism, thus, as the reduction of the text to abstract form, depersonalized form, the reduction of literature from *signs* to *things:* "But to make the stone stony is to chip away the inscription someone carved on it; it is to turn signs back into things. Formalist poetry (not to say a good deal of modern writing) does this by foregrounding the materiality of language, disrupting the signifying function in order to free words from the symbolic order that rational people say we construct from them" (xii–xiii). The vagueness of Bruns's metaphor of chipping away the inscription someone carved on the stone allows for the possibility that by "turn signs back into things" he means something like "re-intensify the algebraized or conventionalized or 'significationalized' perception of a thing," which is how I read Shklovsky; but Bruns is heading in exactly the opposite direction, away from psychology, away from perception, away from reader response, indeed away from signification or the symbolic order, in the general direction of language as thing, as object, as matter. The only way I can imagine an author turning a sign into a thing is through the social psychology or phenomenology of literature, the ideologically guided construction of signs *and* things as meaningful phenomena in a world collectively projected and internalized by human readers. Yet for Bruns, as for several earlier generations of depersonalizing structuralist readers of the formalists, this collective "world" or social construct is precisely the personalized dross from which the author seeks to liberate the word-as-thing, the "the symbolic order that rational people say we construct from them," from which the word must be freed as a postsocial or posthuman thing.

The mythic posthuman nonworld conjured up by this depersonalizing metaphor inevitably remains saturated with the sociality from which it is figuratively trying to escape; the metaphor can only activate its vision of a nonworld ideally cleansed of the detritus of human interaction in the reader's imagination if the activation remains incomplete, if that nonworld is brought into being only as a dystopia, an imaginary negation of the social regulation of meaning, not as an "actual" (which is to say, collectively and regulatively experienced) "reality." The depersonalizing imagination nevertheless places its hopes in a self-deactivating activation, a metaphor that collectively cleanses us of metaphorical collectivity, and so leaves us ideally stranded in a world without shared meaning. That depersonalization is not just an extremely widespread psychological disorder but in some sense the modern condition, the capitalist alienation theorized by Rousseau, Hegel, and Marx, and that Viktor Shklovsky explicitly set himself the Hegelian task of discovering in the somatics of literary reader response an *antidote* to that disorder, is thus swept aside by the philosophical symptomatology of the disorder itself. Shklovsky's insistence that literature exists to restore the full-bodied *sensation* of a thing, to generate in the reader the felt experience of the author's making of the thing, is depersonalized as the reduction of signs to *dead* things, material objects beyond the repersonalizing effects of sensation or feeling or experience, which for these alienated critics in some sense never existed in the first place.

To be sure, there is a radically depersonalizing impulse in much modernist avant-garde art (dada, surrealism, constructivism, atonality, etc.) and in the machinic sensibilities of formalism and structuralism in general. The structuralist and poststructuralist readers of the formalists are not simply imagining this. What they *are* imagining, though, I want to argue, is that Viktor Shklovsky is somehow involved in that depersonalizing project—even that, as for the Russian scholar Vadim Rudnev (whose readings of depersonalization in Tolstoy and Shklovsky I examine in chapters 2 and 3), he is at the head of it. Specifically, my brief is that Shklovsky and Brecht, two of the most influential theorists and practitioners of modernist formalism, are not so much depersonalizing structuralist formalists as repersonalizing somatic formalists—or, to put that more complexly, that Shklovsky and Brecht are concerned with depersonalization on *both* sides of the dialectic between infection-as-epidemic and infection-as-cure: that they want to repersonalize their alienated or anesthetized audiences by intensifying and belaboring the aesthetic forms of depersonalization (or estrangement).

The dialectical complexity of this alienation of alienation, this estrangement of estrangement, makes it an excellent test case for a somatics of literature. If Tolstoy's utopian imagination of the smooth literary transfer of shared feeling is born out of a wishful negation of depersonalization, and Shklovsky's and Brecht's utopian imagination of repersonalization is based on the interruption or obstruction of shared feeling, clearly "shared feeling" will have to shuttle both dystopian disorders and utopian cures back and forth across the shifting boundary between the familiar and the strange, the local and the foreign, the "own" and the alien, the conventional and the experimental—a boundary that is continually being created, or at least temporarily stabilized, by the somatic shuttle. By situating the somatics of literature in this dialectical movement between Tolstoy's radically idealized sentimentalism, for which the slightest ironic distance or detachment is the death of art, and the radically idealized depersonalization of modernist formalism and structuralism, for which the slightest felt connection with communal values or conventions is the death of art, I'd like to be able to redistribute the excluded middle between thinking and feeling, between the structuralist and the sentimentalist, between estrangement and empathy. But that project would be quixotic: the exclusion of that middle between thinking and feeling, between mind and body, is too hegemonic an ideosomatic operation to be dislodged by mere argumentation—even if you already disbelieve in it. Along the way I do hope, however, to estrange the binary a little: to increase your discomfort in it to some small degree.

I'll save the details of somatic theory for the chapters, especially chapter 1, but here's a taste: according to Antonio Damasio, what we call the human

xii

mind is a homeostatic (self-regulatory) function of the nervous system aimed at controlling the human organism's internal and external environments, and born specifically out of homeostatic "mappings" of body states. For example, a certain kind of sensation in the abdomen will generate a "hunger" map that will generate thoughts of finding and eating food; a certain different sensation in the abdomen will generate an "illness" map that will generate thoughts of *avoiding* food (and ignoring hunger). A certain sensation of sweating and flushing skin will generate an "overheated" map that will generate thoughts of turning down the heat or opening a window or drinking a cold glass of water—unless accompanied by a "fever" map, which may generate thoughts of piling on clothing and blankets and drinking hot fluids to precipitate therapeutic sweating. "Mind," therefore, is conceived as mental images and strategies built out of maps of body states.

But there are at least two intermediate layers of homeostatic regulation between these reflexive/appetitive body states and mental maps, images, and strategies: what the tradition coming out of William James' *Principles of Psychology* calls *emotions,* states that "move" the body, and *feelings,* which map emotional states. It's possible in James (and in Shklovsky, Brecht, and Damasio, all strongly influenced by James)[2] to *have* an emotion without *feeling* it—as when we are getting irritated but haven't felt the bodily disturbance yet. It's also possible to feel an emotion without thinking it—as when we are seething with irritation, "vaguely" or "unconsciously" feeling the disturbance, but remain mentally convinced that nothing is bothering us. This complex layering of homeostatic response serves important evolutionary functions. Thinking consumes enormous quantities of time and energy, and may therefore be ill suited to certain kinds of decision-making events, such as how to protect yourself from an object hurtling toward your face: you don't *think,* you just duck and throw up an arm. The emotion of fear is at work in that self-protective impulse, but we neither feel nor think the fear: we just act on it. Feeling the fear might retard the self-protective impulse; thinking might paralyze it entirely.

In the hunger scenario of two paragraphs ago, in fact, unfelt emotion sometimes may be at work as well. Having eaten and banished the signals of hunger, our bodies experience the background emotion of pleasure. In humans, that emotion may then also be felt and even thought and voiced—"Mm, that hit the spot!"—but it need not be, and presumably in other mammals is typically not. Note what happens, though, when human homeostatic response generates feelings and then thoughts: we may condition ourselves to patternize the process, to eat when we *expect* to feel hungry, and thus to build a self-regulatory regime around somatically triggered impulses, around "somatic markers" that channel stored (learned, conditioned) behavioral patterns through feelings into guided thought and action. This is the core of Damasio's somatic theory of human behavior: the guidance of thought and action through learned or conditioned bodily signals.

There are, then, roughly three levels of homeostatic guidance generated on top of (as increasingly complex mappings of) emotional response. The first is feelings, which involve both mental representations of body states and the style and speed by which those representations are brought into consciousness: a feeling of pleasure, for example, will typically both generate thoughts or images (verbal or visual mappings) thematically related to the pleasurable emotion and speed up the mode or style of image-generation, rendering it richer, more complex, more abundant. Feelings of pain are more varied than those of pleasure, but a feeling of sadness, for example, generates thoughts or images of loss and slows down and impoverishes the mode or style of image-generation. The style and speed of image-generation are typically associated phenomenologically with "submental" or "bodily" experience, the mental representations with "thoughts" and "ideas," and thus with "mind"; but both emerge homeostatically out of the organism's need to respond appropriately to a body state, often specifically to a body state in relation to an external condition. It should be easy enough to see, for example, how the feeling of pleasure at sexual attraction in a complex human society might generate not only "stop" or "go" signals but complicated strings of cost-benefit analyses (who will this hurt and how badly? can I lie my way out of it? can I survive the hit if I can't lie my way out of it? etc.). So-called higher reasoning ultimately exceeds this sort of cost-benefit analysis, but it emerges evolutionarily as the second level of the human organism's homeostatic self-regulation of emotion.

Out of analytical reasoning, then, emerges the third level: the creation of a mentalized self that organizes the body's experience as "its own." To some extent this function is performed unconsciously by the proprioceptive system, which "tells" us, way beneath the level of our conscious awareness, where the parts of our bodies are. But a mentalized self is a kind of virtual map of the "I" or the "me" that can be radically shrunk to a single brain function ("I have a clear and distinct idea of myself, in as far as I am only a thinking and unextended thing, and as, on the other hand, I possess a distinct idea of body, in as far as it is only an extended and unthinking thing, it is certain that I am entirely and truly distinct from my body, and may exist without it" [Descartes, *Meditations* 6:9]) or extended almost infinitely. For example, I may feel that my car is an extension of my body and that anybody who touches my car touches me—even if I am not in it, even if I do not see the car being touched and only find the scratched paint when I come to it in the morning. I may consider my property lines, or the borders of my country, or even some fairly abstract idea like a specific dogma in my religion, to be part of myself, so that anyone who invades or degrades one of these has violated *me*. We return to this specific topic (the proprioception of the body politic) in chapter 3, but in some sense it is the core topic of the entire book: the (constant re)creation of a floating boundary between "own" and alien, familiar and strange, and the attempt to stabilize that boundary homeostatically by estranging the overfamiliar and familiarizing the overstrange.

This virtual self is a construction, of course, but then so is every thought and feeling, and that does not make them any less valuable to us as guides to coherent action. One influential channel of theoretical depersonalization finds them far less valuable: because selves, thoughts, and feelings are constructs and therefore "not real," this line of thought goes, they are not valuable, are in fact harmful illusions or dead or alien objects. In *Feeling in Theory: Emotion after the "Death of the Subject,"* for example, Rei Terada defines feeling, emotion, and passion through Derrida and de Man as decentered nonsubjectivity, as "represented by traces in a differential network" (45)—which I take to be the poststructuralist depersonalization of ideosomatic regulation as *trans*subjectivity. "We would have no emotions if we *were subjects*" (4), Terada insists, clinging to the tired binarizing objectivist ontology according to which the subject is either real or unreal, alive or dead, and if it can't (mustn't) be the former, we'll have to find a way to take pleasure and passion in the latter. And Fredric Jameson argues that Brecht rejected empathetic identification because such a thing does not exist, because there is no "self" that might identify empathetically with another: "'third-person acting' . . . is the result of a radical absence of the self, or at least the coming to terms with a realization that what we call our 'self' is itself an object for consciousness, not our consciousness itself: it is a foreign body within an impersonal consciousness, which we try to manipulate in such a way as to lend some warmth and personalization to the matter" (53–54). Not only is the self for Jameson a mere construct of consciousness—and therefore, through depersonalized nostalgia for a lost or discredited objectivism, "radically absent"—but consciousness is depersonalized as well, emptied of even the kind of guidance that a socially constructed self, thoughts, or feelings might provide. This is precisely the kind of philosophical position I attempt to undermine with the somatic theory.

Note once again that word *guidance:* the somatic theory is neither essential-ist/biologistic nor behaviorist/mechanistic; it is *constructivist.* Bertolt Brecht wrote in "A Short Description of a New Technique of Acting which Produces an Estrangement Effect" (1940) that "the emotions always have a quite definite class basis; the form they take at any time is historical, restricted and limited in specific ways. The emotions are in no sense universally human and timeless" (145)—and while contemporary neurophysiologists would perhaps not insist so strongly on the "class basis" of affective psychobiology, they wouldn't deny any of this either. Somatic response is not only learned, socially conditioned; it is learned/conditioned through *guided choice.* Philosophically it occupies a complex and extensive middle ground between liberal-rational autonomy and mechanistic conditioned response. It is a social construct that is soft-wired by interpersonal experience into our neural functioning so that it *feels real* and of-fers stabilizing behavioral guidance that also feels real, but that feeling-real is a phenomenology, not a mechanism. Its power to stabilize this behavioral guid-ance gives it the phenomenological feel of a "structure" (Raymond Williams calls it a "structure of feeling" [132]) and indeed makes it the primary channel of ideological (or what I call ideosomatic) group regulation, but it is *guidance,* the guidance of constructivist choice, not robotic programming.

We might, in fact, identify two default excluded-middle assumptions that the somatic theory provokes in binarizing scholars. The first is that, because whatever is not perfectly autonomous (and thus liberal/humanistic/rationalis-tic) must be perfectly mechanistic or robotic (and thus behavioristic), and vice versa, and because whatever is not perfectly social (and thus cultural, ideologi-cal, political, philosophical, etc.) must be perfectly biological (and thus essen-tialist or biologistic), and vice versa, any mention of physiology automatically signals behaviorism and biologizing essentialism. The second is that, because true intellect is perfectly depersonalized or desomatized, "purified" of all feel-ing, any mention of feelings (at least without Terada-style high-theory deper-sonalization) signals liberal humanist sentimentalism.

These assumptions are philosophically and scientifically a good half cen-tury out of date; but then, as Oscar Wilde says of sunsets (313), they do go on. The middle ground between rational autonomy and conditioned response was mapped out by Wittgenstein in the *Investigations* under the rubrics of "being guided" and "following a rule," in the late 1940s and early 1950s; the middle ground between sociology and biology (that in social animals and insects— mammals, birds, ants, honeybees—there is no sociology or biology that is not sociobiology) was first imagined by Warder C. Allee and Alfred E. Emerson and their collaborators in 1949, further developed by William D. Hamilton in 1964, and fully theorized by Edward O. Wilson in 1975. The idea of an integrated psychological system incorporating both feeling and thinking has been around even longer: it was first explored extensively by Aristotle and has since been variously treated by Spinoza and Leibniz, Adam Smith and David Hume, Hegel and Nietzsche, William James and Broder Christiansen, Heidegger and Merleau-Ponty, Austin and Wittgenstein, and many others. *Estrangement and the Somatics of Literature* is the second in a series of three book-length studies of the somatics (respectively) of language, literature, and culture but the first to be published; the first is "The Somatics of Language," the third "Displacement and the Somatics of Postcolonial Culture." In "The Somatics of Language" I trace the history of the somatic *Binärendämmerung* in the philosophy of language from Nietzsche's *Genealogy of Morals* through Heidegger's *Being and Time* (*das Man*) to Lacan, Foucault, Derrida, and Judith Butler, and through Austin's performativity through Butler again to an entire rethinking of the relationship between the body and language, especially perhaps Shoshana Felman's brilliant Lacanian reading of Austin in *The Scandal of the Speaking Body* and Julia Kristeva's Lacanian/Bakhtinian notion of intertextuality as the speaking subject's introjected mother tongue. But there are many other signal explorations of the excluded middle between thinking and feeling that did not find their way into that book. Notions of the interpersonal transmission of emotion through motor mimicry, to some extent anticipated by William Carpenter's work in the nineteenth century, began to be hypothesized and tested by Howard Friedman's nonverbal communication group in the late 1970s and early 1980s and found full articulation in Elaine Hatfield, John T. Cacioppo, and Richard L Rapson's *Emotional Contagion* (1994). Teresa Brennan's *The Transmission of Affect* appeared in 2004, Denise Riley's *Impersonal Passion: Language as Affect* in 2005, the former arguing for the transmission of affect through "chemical entrainment," largely through smell, the latter offering a richly poetic phenomenology of language-as-affect without much in the way of theory—indeed neither book is aware of Damasio or somatic theory, although Brennan, like Damasio, emphasizes the transmission not just of affect but of *evaluative* affect, which shapes and regulates other people's thoughts, feelings, and behavior.[3]

Other Francophone and Anglophone feminists as well, in particular Irigaray, Cixous, and Wittig in French and Griffin and Grosz in English, have done important work in this area. The cyborg theory inspired by Donna Haraway (see Gray) has worked hard to break down the old human-machine binary and thereby the related thinking-unthinking and autonomous-robotic binaries. Cognitive scientists, coming out of Austin and Wittgenstein, have made important contributions to the expansion of this crucial middle ground; the subfield I explored in detail in "The Somatics of Language" was the cognitive kinesthetics of language and metaphor in Lakoff and Johnson. Pierre Bourdieu's theory of *habitus,* grounded as it is in Wittgenstein's "social practices," or *Lebensform,* and Heidegger's *das Man,* has radical implications for the field. The work in the philosophy of the body tracked in Stephen David Ross's *The Gift of Touch* and Gemma Corradi Fiumara's *The Mind's Affective Life,* and anthologized in Donn Welton's *Body and Flesh: A Philosophical Reader,* is another collective attempt to carve out a radical middle ground between the social and the biological, the mental and the physical, the rational and the emotional, the autonomous and the robotic.

That these efforts almost invariably seem to be uphill battles has a good deal to do, I suggest, with the ideosomatic stabilization of behavioral guidance. Despite the deluge of antibinaristic thought in these fields over the past half century, and the unassailable authority of the pioneers in the fields (Hegel, Marx, Nietzsche, James, Freud, Bakhtin, Heidegger) for the century and a half previous, it still *feels right* to binarize thinking and feeling, mind and body, rational autonomy and conditioned response. The radical spirit/flesh dualism of Augustine's medieval Christianity was formative for feudalism, justifying military and economic disregard for the survival or comfort of the material body by situating "true" spiritual reality in a world beyond. The radical mind/body dualism of Rene Descartes, a secularized version of Augustinian dualism, was a powerful sign or signal of social progress in early capitalism, heralding rational scientific and economic *freedom* from the constraints of the body, from the conformative moral pressures of shared feeling, and as Bertolt Brecht goes on to suggest in the "Short Description," "emotions accompanying social progress will long survive in the human mind as emotions linked with interests" (146). This is true even long after the social progress they once accompanied has faded into the past—but, of course, war, economic exploitation, capitalist commodity fetishism, and their concomitant pressures to depersonalize and desomatize are still very much with us today.

Because we live in the body, however, it does seem a reasonable starting assumption that our social learning and volitional guidance are stored in and channeled through the body, in and through what the phenomenological tradition calls the "mindful body," or what I prefer to call the body-becoming-mind. Indeed, barring the existence of a mystical or supernatural realm such as God or "pure reason," where else could they be stored and channeled? The radical late-capitalist depersonalization of the formalist-(post)structuralist theoretical tradition has conditioned many critical theorists in particular not to think about such matters at all, and to regard any mention of the body or biology or feelings therefore as a kind of nagging return of the ideological repressed, the ringing of a particularly annoying alarm clock in the counterhegemonic distance that must be slapped into silence as quickly as possible. By taking a close look at two of the primary progenitors of that tradition, I hope to bring the alarm clock a little closer.

The book is divided into three parts and five chapters, two chapters each in Parts I and II, one long chapter in Part III. I tried to divide Part III into two chapters as well, but "Brecht," the most dialectical thinker of the three I examine, wouldn't let me. The three parts are ordered chronologically: Part I focuses on the period roughly from Tolstoy's spiritual crisis around 1880 to *What Is Art?* in 1898, Part II on Shklovsky's "Art as Device" from its writing in 1916 and its publication in 1917 to its theoretical afterlife up through the rising antagonism against formalism in the Soviet Union in the mid- to late 1920s, Part III on Brecht's theoretical writings from the mid-1920s to his death in 1956.

Part I establishes the critical split between Tolstoy's utopian infection theory (chapter 1) and his own psychological depersonalization (chapter 2)—but it does so by splitting chapter 1 too more or less down the middle, with sections on infection as disease and infection as cure. Since Tolstoy's infection theory is also a rudimentary somatics of literature, I devote the third section of chapter 1 to an introductory discussion of the somatic theory.

Part II is even more sharply divided: chapter 3 is devoted to a close reading of Shklovsky's theory of the estrangement device, chapter 4 to a tracing of Shklovsky's methodological roots in Hegel. The topics of chapter 3 include the Hegelian (dialectical) "thing" in Shklovsky, the homeostatic/proprioceptive problematic of "restoring sensation to life," and the nature of deautomatization; the topics of chapter 4 include Hegel's theories of alienation from the *Phenomenology*, alienated labor from *The System of Ethical Life*, and Romantic form from the *Aesthetics* lectures.

Part III begins with the problem of the etiology of Brecht's estrangement effect, in four sections: Brecht's debt to Shklovsky, Brecht's debt to the German tradition (specifically, in my discussion, to Schlegel and Marx, with a detour through the "demonic" dialectic of Gregory Bateson's double bind), Brecht's response to Mei Lanfang's impromptu performance in Moscow in the spring of 1935 (the complexity of the spatiotemporal dialectic of estrangement), and Brecht's response to theater life in Munich and Berlin in the 1920s and early 1930s (specifically his gradual dialecticization of empathy and estrangement). Emerging out of that discussion of empathy and estrangement, then, I devote section 5 to Brecht's "infection theory" (making stops at Fredric Jameson's depersonalizing reading of Brecht, Raymond Williams's "structures of feeling," William James on emotion and feeling, and Ludwig Wittgenstein's *Lebensform*) and section 6 to Brecht's theory of the *Gestus*.

The overall movement of the argument is toward increased theoretical awareness of and engagement with the problem. In Part I we see Tolstoy historicizing depersonalization but offering a radically dehistoricized (transcendentalized, universalized) solution to it. In Part II we see Shklovsky attempting to historicize the solution as well, to fight depersonalized estrangement with aesthetically enhanced and therefore potentially repersonalizing estrangement, but not getting very far. "Art as Device" is a sketchy manifesto written by a very young man, and his own history (his participation in the civil war, in which he fought on the losing side, his conspiracy against the Bolsheviks and subsequent exile to Germany, and, shortly after his return in 1923, the Thermidor and rise of Stalin and the banning of formalism) made it difficult for Shklovsky to delve more deeply into the problematics of estrangement. Mostly, Shklovsky was temperamentally ill suited to sustained philosophical and practical engagement with the dialectical complexities of estrangement as literary therapy. He was more of a scout than a settler. In Part III we see Brecht, the settler, making the most progress toward an understanding of the dialectic, but even he is constantly falling short, constantly conceptualizing estrangement dialectically only by distinguishing it binarily from empathy. Only toward the end of his short life, in his forties and early fifties, did he begin to build a more capacious dialectical model, a model based on the "infectiousness" of "living together."

PART ONE

Zarazhenie

Tolstoy's Infection Theory

1 ▮ *Tolstoy's Infection*

"It is widely accepted in contemporary Anglo-American aesthetics," Saam Trivedi writes in the opening lines of his 2004 article on Lev Nikolayevich Tolstoy's 1898 aesthetic tract *What Is Art?*, "that, despite Tolstoy's own literary achievements, his 'moralism' about art is a view without much merit. For the most part, I concur with this current consensus about Tolstoy. However, despite the many flaws in his view, I think Tolstoy was on to *something*, after all" (Trivedi, 38). Trivedi's tone of voice can tell us a lot about the socioemotional complexities of a modern response to Tolstoy's essay: Trivedi's decent embarrassment about Tolstoy's "moralism," the awkward stress on "*something*," the carefully modulated defensiveness of that hedging "after all," the nervous quantifiers in "without *much* merit" and "for the *most* part" and "the *many* flaws in his view." "I believe a concept of artist-audience communication similar to what Tolstoy had in mind," Trivedi adds, "can be fleshed out so as to *avoid* the problems that Tolstoy ran into, while reclaiming the insights in his view" (38). Would we need that grim stress on *avoid* if *What Is Art?* did not make us profoundly uneasy?

The problem is, Tolstoy's late work in aesthetics seems to leave admirers of *War and Peace* and *Anna Karenina* nowhere to put their eyes, or the rest of their body language, either. It's not just that Tolstoy's complex psychological understanding of the characters in his novels leads us to expect a better mind at work on the problem of art; it's also that his condemnation of his own novels as bad art sets up a critical feedback loop that undermines Tolstoy's credibility in both directions, as postconversion moral critic of his own novels and as pre-conversion author of those novels. Then, because he has just coached us to disapprove of *him* morally, and of his aesthetic treatise, his condemnation begins to leak moral discreditation in ever-widening circles, undermining our own moral credibility as well. Although most of this is unconscious—operating at the level of what I call somatic guidance—because we neither want our moral credibility undermined nor want our credibility thematized in moral terms, we work to suppress Tolstoy's ideas as infamous or to find some carefully hedged way to praise them.

What makes this leakage or seepage of moral (self-)condemnation from author to reader particularly disturbing in this case is that it is an instance, though not one Tolstoy himself theorized, of the central claim in his book: that art works by the moral infection of feeling from authors to readers. (The apparent problem that a treatise on aesthetics is not art in the strict sense and therefore should not be covered by his infection theory is itself covered by Tolstoy's insistence that art be taken in the broadest possible sense, to include things like parades, jokes, and, presumably, aesthetic treatises.) Precisely because for him all artistic expression is infectious, and what is transferred from author to reader infectiously is feeling, and feeling is the primary channel of morality, Tolstoy must work hard to condemn art that he considers immoral, to prevent its infecting readers with its immoral (hedonistic) feelings—in effect, to quarantine it, to keep readers away from it. "We have the terrible probability to consider that while fearful sacrifices of the labour and lives of men and of morality itself are being made to art, that same art may be not only useless but even harmful" (*What*, 81–82). His moral condemnation of bad art in the book, including his own, is intended as a kind of one-man center for moral disease control, Tolstoy doing his part to stop the epidemic spread of emotional anesthesis or alienation in contemporary society—an epidemic of which he portrays himself too as a carrier, both as a reader and as a writer.[1] Because the wrong kind of art made him morally sick in his youth, he wrote a string of famous novels that infected others and that, unfortunately, continued to infect others even when he was in his late sixties, despite his conversion to a particularly radical form of Rousseauistic Christian asceticism almost two decades before. And, as I try to show in chapter 2, at the writing of *What Is Art?* he was still vulnerable to that infection. He was, in fact, still sick—only relatively symptom-free because he worked so hard to avoid all carriers of the infection, which might have brought about a relapse.

The Disease

The disease Tolstoy diagnoses in *What Is Art?* is an aestheticoreligious version of the proto-Romantic theory of alienation developed by Jean-Jacques Rousseau, the hero of Tolstoy's youth.[2] Ideally, for Rousseau, in alienating (ceding or selling) their natural anarchistic rights to the community in the so-called social contract, humans do not alienate their freedom, which is inalienable ("as each gives himself to all, he gives himself to no one" (*Social*, 139), but exchange it for higher and larger forms of liberty, especially "civil liberty and the proprietorship of all he possesses" (141) and "moral freedom, which alone makes man truly master of himself. For the mere impulse of appetite is slavery, and obedience to a law which we prescribe to ourselves is liberty" (142; see Moore). As Rousseau recognizes, however, this ideal is everywhere trampled in social reality, corrupted by civilization, which he describes in terms of humans' "alienation from nature"—a "nature" that includes a utopian image of God and prelapsarian innocence that Tolstoy was to find powerfully attractive: "Everything is good as it leaves the hands of the Author of things; everything degenerates in the hands of man" (*Emile*, 37). Our basic human "constitution"—what for Rousseau is the *natural* constructedness of the body politic and psychologic—is good, pure, and innocent but is perverted or alienated by social institutions, which enslave it to every manner of vice. For Rousseau this social perversion of the individual's innate goodness comes from the "outside," which suggests a myth of the fall as a primal scene of perversion in which a single private vice is alienated from a single individual, cast out of the individual "inside" into the social "outside," where it propagates itself and becomes "civilization," which then, through its own alienated logic, corrupts and alienates everyone.

That this is a semisecularized version of the Christian myth of the fall should be clear (see Mészáros, 28–33). Compare, for example, Paul's words to the Ephesians: "remember that you were at that time separated from Christ [*choris Christou*, literally 'without Christ'], alienated [*apillotriomenoi < apo* 'away' + *allotrios* 'estranged' < *allos* 'other, another's, foreign, strange, alien'] from the commonwealth [*politeias*] of Israel, and strangers [*ksenoi* 'foreign, alien'] to the covenants of promise, having no hope and without God in the world. But now in Christ Jesus you who once were far off [*makran < makros < mekos* 'long' in space or time, here 'long-distanced'] have been brought near [*eggus*] in the blood of Christ" (Eph. 2:12–13, RSV). As one might expect of a Christian discussion of salvation, Paul's thinking here is radically binary.

In fact, he sets up three separate binary alienation metaphors for the central split between salvation and damnation: self/other (the social binary), local/foreign (the cultural binary), and near/far (the geographical binary). Implicit in all three is that there is a border separating the "good" state of belonging, at-homeness, familiarity, and acceptance, from the "bad" state of alienation, foreignness, and geographical distance, and that the transcendental—transcultural, transhistorical, transgeographical—being of God is not only the figurative home to which the alienated sinner seeks to return but also, via the blood of Christ, the mediator that facilitates the border crossing from there to here, away to home, alienation to hope and promise.

Rousseau's version of this mythology is only semisecular in the sense that, like Hegel and Marx after him, he retains Christianity's ideal of a lost home to which we must somehow strive to return; also like Hegel but unlike Marx, he has no clear idea how that dealienation might be brought about. For Christians, obviously, the solution to alienation is the blood of Jesus, the transcendental mediator who stands at the boundary between home and away, the familiar and the strange, the self and the other and polices traffic between them. For Marx, who secularizes the Judeo-Christian paradisal home as an actual society in which the state has withered away, the solution is radical change in the material conditions of capitalism that generated the alienation in the first place. Tolstoy follows Rousseau here only in his diagnosis of the disease; he considers himself a Christian, but for his cure he is actually closer to Marx than to Jesus, whose divinity and mediatory redemption he rejects.[3] Tolstoy was no revolutionary, certainly (though many actual revolutionaries were inspired by him and came to sit at his feet, and, despite Lenin's disapproval, he was venerated by the Soviet regime), and he despised Marxist materialism for its denial of God.[4] His cure, however, is ultimately materialist, based on the bodily-becoming-mental *infection* of the world's population with moral feelings and values, through art.[5]

Tolstoy's version of Rousseau's diagnosis focuses specifically on the falling away first of the medieval Church from "true" Christianity, then of the European aristocracy, beginning in the Renaissance, from medieval "Church" Christianity. He begins with a nostalgic image of the Middle Ages as a prealienation Golden Age: "The artists of the Middle Ages, vitalized by the same source of feeling—religion—as the mass of the people, and transmitting in architecture, sculpture, painting, music, poetry, or drama, the feelings and states of mind they experienced, were true artists; and their activity, founded on the highest conceptions accessible to their age and common to the entire people—

though for our times a mean art—was nevertheless a true one, shared by the whole community" (130–31). As we see in chapter 4, this vision is close to Hegel's conception of the precapitalist state of simple labor. The problem arose as the educated rich, exposed to widespread corruption in the Church and the "lucidity" of classical antiquity, began to doubt Christianity: "If in externals they still kept to the forms of Church teaching, they could no longer believe in it, and held to it only by inertia and to influence the masses, who continued to believe blindly in Church doctrine and whom the upper classes for their own advantage considered it necessary to support in those beliefs" (131).

This is a myth of the fall, obviously, but it is mostly an intensely historical myth. Modern Europeans fell from Tolstoy's own postconversion faith not in some dim Adamic prehistory but over the period of four or five or six centuries leading up to his own time. Very much like Marx, Tolstoy historicizes the upper classes' failure to convert to true Christianity in terms of the threat that conversion would have posed to their political and economic ascendancy over the masses, and their continued observance of the outward forms of Church Christianity in terms of their desire to protect that ascendancy.

Unlike Marx, however, he is not particularly clear on how or why the upper classes fell away from God and thus into alienation. Tolstoy seems to offer two different epidemiological models of the genesis of this process, which I call the *fake-infectious* and the *perverse-infectious*. The former is his main or "official" model, his normative model, outlined consciously; the latter is mostly rhetorically suppressed but constitutes his fallback model, the one he finds himself applying surreptitiously, behind his own back, as it were.

In the fake-infectious model, religion and art decay and bring about the decay of culture at large, through a *sham* infection, a kind of ghastly theater in which the principals do not actually feel the enlivening infectious power of God or morality or true art but know that they are expected to show the outward signs of feeling that power, so they fake it. The unstated assumption behind this model is that any religion requires real blood in its bloodstream, an actual somatic current from the deity; without that current, a religion comes to rely more and more heavily on reason-based imitations, imitations not just of religious rituals but of the conventional emotional states religion is supposed to generate in believers. Tolstoy repeatedly describes the emotional effects of these false forms of Christianity and European art on their constituents as a nervous excitement, a kind of hypnotic or drugged state. Because he wants to save the notion of the infection or sharing of feelings from one person to another for his *cure* for alienation, however, he insists that this is not a true somatic effect or "in-fect" of art or religion but a rational simulation, a body state audience members deliberately reproduce in themselves mimetically because they know they are supposed to receive both "God" and "art" in a state of exaltation. It is precisely this (ir)rational mimesis of religion's and art's emotional impact that brings about the entropic degeneration of both: rather than channeling the felt infection of "true religion" through their collectivized bodies, Tolstoy insists, Europeans are hypermimetically exhausting their own mimeses of artistic *and* religious receptivity, mimicking with progressively enhanced and therefore ever more intensely alienating exaggeration the outward appearance of a somatic current that they do not feel. The cure for alienation thus conceived can only be a new blast of true religion, a new infusion of that somatic current of joy and spiritual union that only the true Christian—ultimately only Tolstoy himself—can infect us with. Since there is no obvious historical error that European civilization committed that might be rectified in order to get itself back on course, since there is only entropic alienation from God, this model's impulse to return home, to cross back over from the far to the near, from the strange to the familiar, from alienation to "one's own," must come from outside historical time, from an imagined God as a transcendental power.[6]

The perverse-infectious model, on the other hand, is based on the assumption that the alienating disease or disorder of hedonistic secularism is not, as in the fake-infectious model, just a falling away from the true infection, a failure to experience the sharing of feeling and to be enlivened by that feeling, or a repeated attempt to conceal that failure through shamming. Rather, the disorder is infectiously *spread* by hedonistic secular art. Upper-class art since the Renaissance, he hints, including religious art, has been infected with the wrong kind of feelings, specifically pleasure, and specifically the wrong kind of pleasure—pleasure for pleasure's sake, pleasure in beauty as the only moral good, pleasure in the new, pleasure in sexual arousal. This model sets up an implicitly historical agon between rival infections, between infectious moral art and infectious immoral art, and offers as a cure for alienation the power of the true religious infection to overwhelm and banish the alienating power of the perverted infection.[7]

Note that his definition of emotional infection as that which distinguishes true art from fake also includes an implicit warning against fake infection:

> There is one indication that incontrovertibly separates true art from fake: its
> infectiousness. If a person, without any activity on his/her side and without

any change of standpoint, while reading or having heard or seen another person's work, experiences a state of mind that unites him with this person and with other people who also perceive the object of art as he does, then the object evoking that state is an art object. No matter how poetic the object is, no matter how closely it resembles reality, no matter how effective or entertaining it is, it is not an art object unless it evokes in a person that feeling that is totally different from all others, of joy, of spiritual union with another (the author) and with others (hearers or viewers) perceiving the same artistic work. (*Chto*, 148, my translation)

The idealized infection theory, in other words, depends on the exclusion of *doing*: "If a person, without any *activity* on his/her side and without any change of position, while reading or having heard or seen." Any activity at all, including any cognitive awareness or any emotional orientation or motivation, will distort the effect, and render the perceiver incapable of distinguishing true art from fake. By implication, civilization consists precisely of this sort of distorting activity: we are all taught by society to pretend to feel things that we do not feel, and we are infected by society with feelings that distort or pervert the true primeval meaning and function of art. Tolstoy imagines "that feeling that is totally different from all others," therefore, as a utopian Rousseauistic feeling, a noble-savage feeling that is experienced in its pure form only by those hypothetical beings (such as Russian peasants, he hopes or postulates) who have never been perverted by civilization, those who are not pretending never to have been perverted by civilization, and that—more to the point—can be reexperienced by a modern civilized person only through the idealized activity of excluding or subtracting or negating the perverted and pretended activities of estranged and estranging civilization (especially, as we'll see below, "attuning" yourself to a work of art). Only thus can one reachieve that ideal primeval state in which one does not need to change one's standpoint in order to (pretend to) feel infectious joy and spiritual union.

As I say, Tolstoy's motives in suppressing the perverse-infectious theory of alienation rhetorically have something to do with his desire to present aesthetic infection as pure and good—in order, presumably, not to have to explain how the feelings with which the artist infects the audience have been perverted, or, *a fortiori*, how to distinguish between pure and perverted infections. But on a deeper level, his motives are also themselves complex symptoms of the alienation he is diagnosing. According to his own diagnosis, Tolstoy, like others of his class, has been alienated from what he considers true religious feeling; he is anesthetized so that he does not feel *either* infection, either the alienating perverse infection of hedonistic art or the dealienating true infection of moral art. As a result, the outward signs of somatic infection that he sees on other people's bodies seem to him false, rationally simulated, grotesquely entropic mimeses of true somatic response, and he feels driven to present the dealienating infection that he theorizes as a transcendental ideal that he has mostly only heard others talk about, not something he has himself experienced:

> I must say what I think, namely, that people of our circle . . . have never (except in childhood and earliest youth before hearing any discussions on art) experienced that simple feeling familiar to the plainest man and even to a child, that sense of infection with another's feeling—compelling us to joy in another's gladness, to sorrow at another's grief and to mingle souls with another—which is the very essence of art. And therefore these people not only cannot distinguish true works of art from counterfeits, but continually mistake for real art the worst and most artificial, while they do not even perceive works of real art, because the counterfeits are always more ornate, while true art is modest. (226)

Tolstoy only passingly hints that he himself suffers from this disease, in passages like this one: "besides being insufficiently informed in all branches of art, I belong to the class of people whose taste has been perverted by false training. And therefore my old, inured habits may cause me to err, and I may mistake for absolute merit the impression a work produced on me in my youth" (246n). As I show in chapter 2, however, the entire book is a powerful testament to his suffering. His own alienation, inexorably produced by the historical forces he himself is theorizing, makes him unable or unwilling to feel either the spread of alienation through the infectiousness of pleasure or the spread of dealienation through the infectiousness of joy and spiritual union. As a result, he presents the disease (the "is") as an attrition or exhaustion of pleasure, and the cure (the "ought") as a mystical resurgence of pleasure sparked, presumptively, transcendentally by some force that he calls "God" but mostly imagines, through what Martine de Courcel aptly calls his "spiritual autism" (163), arising from within himself (i.e., *not* from others).

But he also finds—or, as he says here, used to find—the impulse to fake the infection arising within himself:

> For a long time I used to attune myself to delight in those shapeless improvisations which form the subject-matter of the works of Beethoven's later period, but I had only to consider the question of art seriously, and to compare the impression I received from Beethoven's later works, with those pleasant, clear, and strong musical impressions which are transmitted, for instance, by

the melodies of Bach (his arias), Haydn, Mozart, Chopin (when his melodies are not overloaded with complications and ornamentation), of Beethoven himself in his earlier period, and above all, with the impressions produced by folk-songs . . . and other such simple, clear, and powerful music, for the obscure, almost unhealthy, excitement from Beethoven's later pieces, which I had artificially evoked in myself, to be immediately destroyed. (222)

He *attuned* himself, so as to evoke artificially the "obscure, almost unhealthy excitement" with which high art is supposed to infect the upper classes. Before his conversion, in other words, he had to create the requisite emotional state internally, by an effort, by altering his standpoint, so as to *seem* to be appropriately infected by the work of art. This self-attuning response to art has now become his implicit model for the fake-infectious emotional response of everybody else in the world. He assumes that everyone who now claims to be "moved" by high art is doing what he used to do: faking it.

That he used to do it himself proves his claim, of course: he's not merely speculating about what people do; he knows for a fact that this is done. Subtextually, however, his argument opens a can of worms. Based solely on his knowledge that he used to attune himself so as to display the appropriate body language of aesthetic infection, how can he be sure (a) that other people do it as well and (b) that he isn't doing it still? His only evidence for the near-universality of these self-attunements, after all, is external body language: it *looks* to him as if others are faking it too, just as he used to do. And yet the methodology of fakery is by definition aimed at the undermining of all such empirical judgments, all such certainty that things are (or even are not) as they seem. Could it be that his demystificatory skepticism is a mere projection of his own earlier fakery, indeed a mere projection of his isolation from the sharing of others' feelings that he now idealizes as the true religious alternative to fakery, and that other people really did delight in late Beethoven and other art that he now wants to condemn as bad?

Note what happens eight years after *What is Art?*—and, more to the point, a quarter century after his "conversion," when everything supposedly changed for him—when his favorite daughter Masha dies at the age of 35. Tolstoy is calm: "Just now, one o'clock in the morning, Masha died. A strange thing. I didn't feel horror or fear or the awareness of anything strange taking place, nor even pity or grief. I seemed to consider it necessary to arouse in myself a special feeling of emotion, grief, and I did so, but at the bottom of my heart I was more composed than I would have been in the case of another person's bad or improper behavior, not to mention my own" (Tolstoy's diary, November 27,

1906; 2:561). At the age of 78, Tolstoy is still attuning himself. He still needs to fake the emotional displays expected by society.

In art, as Tolstoy sees things, the alienating effects are so disastrous that he himself, as he comes out of his spiritual crisis at the end of the 1870s and beginning of the 1880s, swears off writing fiction entirely (and only occasionally and guiltily lapses). Most of *What Is Art?* is a detailed indictment of the disease that has either fake-infected or perverse-infected virtually every artist and every artwork and every artistic trend for the previous two or three centuries—certainly all "high" art, the art that everyone is taught to respect, which has fallen away from religion, morality, and the public good and exists purely for the pleasure of the upper classes and their imitators. The primary signs of infection are (a) the impoverishment of subject matter (all high art is about sex, pride, and ennui, but Tolstoy is mostly worried about the ubiquity in art of sex, nudity, adultery, and general voluptuousness), (b) the exhaustion of form (the relentless quest for the new and the strange causes artists to use up traditional forms like tissues), and (c) the alienation of the artist from his or her audience (the conservatism of the audience seems to demand that the artist stick to the previous generation's trends, a demand that the artist repulses by becoming more and more difficult). He is writing in the mid-1890s, as what we now know as literary modernism (Tolstoy cites Baudelaire, Mallarmé, Verlaine) is just gearing up to overthrow the premodern work of Tolstoy himself and others of his generation, but as we see in the opening sections of chapters 2 and 3, Viktor Shklovsky takes nearly all of his examples of estrangement, which he takes to be the signature strategy of modernism, from Tolstoy's works, and Vadim Rudnev argues that estranged or depersonalized modernism begins in Russia with Pushkin's *Eugene Onegin* (1823–33). In any case, Tolstoy extends his indictment all the way back to the Renaissance.

His conclusion to this assessment of alienation in art once again surreptitiously relies on the perverse-infectious model: "The assertion that art may be good art and at the same time incomprehensible to a great number of people, is extremely unjust, and its consequences are ruinous to art itself; but at the same time it is so common and has so eaten into [*v"yelos' v*] our conceptions, that it is impossible to make sufficiently clear its whole absurdity" (*Chto*, 107–8; *What*, 176). Tolstoy's insistence that this assertion *v"yelos' v nashe predstavlenie* "has eaten into our conception/idea/representation" makes it sound very much like a bacterial infection. And when he considers how the upper classes have kept the masses ignorant, the conclusion that art is being used to infect them with alienation seems unavoidable:

Look carefully into the causes of the ignorance of the masses, and you may see that the chief cause does not at all lie in the lack of schools and libraries as we are accustomed to suppose, but in those superstitions, both ecclesiastical and patriotic, with which the people are saturated, and which are unceasingly generated by all the methods of art. Church superstitions are supported and produced by the poetry of prayers, hymns, painting, by the sculpture of images and of statues, by singing, by organs, by music, by architecture, and even by dramatic art in religious ceremonies. Patriotic superstitions are supported and produced by verses and stories (which are supplied even in schools), by music, by songs, by triumphal processions, by royal meetings, by martial pictures, and by monuments.

Were it not for this continual activity in all departments of art, perpetuating the ecclesiastical and patriotic intoxication and embitterment of the people, the masses would long ere this have attained to true enlightenment. (*What*, 259–60)

The lower classes, in other words, have not simply picked up a few of the bad habits of the upper; they have been systematically (perversely) infected with a strain of the upper-class disease, one designed to keep them superstitious, patriotic, and stupid.

The Cure

Infection

If the disease is spread by art, however, so may be its cure: "Sometimes," Tolstoy writes, "people who are together are, if not hostile to one another, at least estranged [*chuzhdie* 'alien'] in mood and feeling, till perchance a story, a performance, a picture, or even a building, but oftenest of all music, unites them all as by an electric flash, and, in place of their former isolation or even enmity, they are all conscious of union and mutual love" (*Chto*, 158; *What*, 240). Whereas (at least in the suppressed perverse-infectious model) the wrong kind of artistic infection—patriotic or other group-oriented songs that drive wedges between people, for example—estranges people from each other, the right kind of artistic infection unites them:

The chief peculiarity of this feeling is that the receiver of a true artistic impression is so united to the artist that he feels as if the work were his own and not some one else's—as if what it expresses were just what he had long been wishing to express. A real work of art destroys in the consciousness of the receiver the separation between himself and the artist, and not that

> alone, but also between himself and all whose minds receive this work of art.
> In this freeing of our personality from its separation and isolation, in this
> uniting of it with others, lies the chief characteristic and the great attractive
> force of art. (*What*, 228)

The right kind of art, moral art, religious art, channels moral feelings to whole
populations, and it does so in order to transform them without force: this is
the cure. If the upper classes have infected first themselves, through high art,
then the masses, through religious and patriotic art, with the modern disease—alienation, estrangement, depersonalization—then, Tolstoy argues, the
new task for a new kind of art (which is also, he insists, the very oldest kind
of art) must be to infect them with joy and spiritual union, and thereby with
a new social order:

> The feelings with which the artist infects others may be most various—very
> strong or very weak, very important or very insignificant, very bad or very
> good: feelings of love for native land, self-devotion and submission to fate or
> to God expressed in a drama, raptures of lovers described in a novel, feelings
> of voluptuousness expressed in a picture, courage expressed in a triumphal
> march, merriment evoked by a dance, humour evoked by a funny story, the
> feeling of quietness transmitted by an evening landscape or by a lullaby, or
> the feeling of admiration evoked by a beautiful arabesque—it is all art.
>
> If only the spectators or auditors are infected by the feelings which the
> author has felt, it is art. (122–23)

Here, it should be clear, Tolstoy leans toward the perverse-infectious model of
alienation, according to which it is spread by means of bad art, art that infects
audiences with perverted feelings. Elsewhere he argues that those audience
members are *not* infected by the feelings which the author has felt, and the
"art" that does not carry those perverted feelings is therefore not art at all but
counterfeits, imitations, fakes (*poddelki*).

As Gary Jahn argues, Tolstoy's infection theory of art initially emerges out
of the Russian lexicon for the traditional transceiver model of artistic communication: the author transmits a message, which is primarily feeling, through
the medium of the work of art, and that message is received by the perceiver,
Tolstoy's general term for the reader or listener or viewer. What is sent *out*
by the artist is taken *in* by the perceiver. Because what is sent out by the artist is traditionally called *ex-pression*, the Latin roots signifying the "pressing
out" of artistic content (again, for Tolstoy, specifically of feelings), in English
and other Western European languages that use the Latin roots we would
want to describe the artwork's impact on its audience as an *im-pression*. In

Russian, however, which does not use the Latin roots, the in-word takes us in a different imagistic direction: "to express" is *vyrazhat'/vyrazit'*, literally "to strike out(wards)," and since there is no in-version of this, no **vrazhat'/vrazit'* "to strike in(wards)," Tolstoy ends up with a slightly different preposition, *za* (behind or beyond), yielding *zarazhat'/zarazit'*, literally "to strike behind/beyond," and thus "to infect" (the outward-bound opposite of which in English, obviously, is *effect*). For example:

> To evoke in oneself a feeling one has once experienced and having evoked it in oneself then by means of movements, lines, colours, sounds, or forms expressed in words [vyrazhennykh slovami], so to transmit that feeling that others experience the same thing—this is the activity of art.
>
> Art is a human activity consisting in this, that one man consciously by means of certain external signs, hands on to others feelings he has lived through, and that other people are infected [zarazhayutsya] by these feelings and also experience them. (Chto, 65, What, 123; emphasis in original)

"Expressed in words" there is morphologically "struck out in words," the words as blows sent out of the author's brain and fingers and pen and stored on the page as "certain external signs" that will in turn infect readers, or, again morphologically, will "strike behind/beyond" them, the blows that the author sent out onto the page going behind the reader and striking him or her there.

This is clearly, as Michael Denner points out, a violent and aggressive conception of art (284–85); I think it a reasonable suspicion that Tolstoy used these words for art with a strong sense not only of disease but of the violence of disease and the infectious violence of art, its dangerous power to transform us into something else—and therefore of the high stakes in the theory and practice of art, the enormous potential for both evil and good that art contains.

What kind of "feeling" is infectiously carried from author to reader? This is obviously a crucial question for a somatics of literature, and below I offer some contemporary neurophysiological suggestions. For now, though, let's explore (following Jahn) what Tolstoy might have meant by *chuvstvo* (feeling). Is it the same thing as *emotion*? René Wellek seems to think so: in the *History of Modern Criticism* he describes Tolstoy's infection theory of art as "emotionalist" and links it to the theories of Denis Diderot and William Wordsworth (4:282, 291). Tolstoy takes much of his theory of art from Eugène Véron's *L'Esthétique*, which defines art in terms of the expression of emotion; as Tolstoy paraphrases Véron, "Art is the external manifestation, by means of lines, colours, movements, sounds, or words, of emotions felt by man" (*What*, 119). In adapting this theory to his purposes in *What Is Art?*, Tolstoy makes two signal changes.

One is that art is not merely the *expression* of affective materials; it is the expression and infection of those materials, the *transfer* of those materials from author to reader. The other is that, while in paraphrasing Véron he uses the narrower foreign word *emotsiya,* in stating his own theory Tolstoy uses the broader Russian word *chuvstvo* (feeling). What all he meant by *chuvstvo* is clear from the examples he gives in chapter 5 of *What Is Art?* It means not just happiness, sorrow, anger, woe, and terror but also the external expressions of emotion, such as laughter, tears, groans, and sobs, and the deeper physical experiences of health and pain. If feeling arises out of the body and can move the body, it also influences the mind: Tolstoy's examples include decisiveness, amazement, respect, and contentment. As Jahn adds, "It is justifiable to amplify this list of examples still further by saying that even the subject matter usually associated with the purview of thought may pass over into the purview of feeling when it is regarded other than from the point of view of the objective reason. For example, the statement that two plus two equals four belongs basically to the objective reason, but if it becomes an object of hatred, as it does for Dostoevsky's Underground Man, it passes over into the purview of feeling" (62).

The two most significant aspects of feeling for Tolstoy, then, are that it is *infectious* (can be transferred from body to body like a disease) and that it is a channel of behavioral and intellectual *guidance* (shapes how we think and act). It is these two characteristics of feeling that make art, conceived as a feeling transceiver, so powerful and so important for Tolstoy: by channeling feelings to readers, art channels *moral* guidance, for good or evil, which is to say, for psychological health or sickness. As Michael Denner writes, "Etymological arguments aside, Tolstoy makes explicit the psychological violation that goes hand-in-hand with the experience of a work of art in a diary entry from a period of work on an earlier variant of *What Is Art?:* 'One must hone the artistic work so that it penetrates. To hone a work means to make it perfect artistically, in which case it will pierce through the indifference . . . ' In an earlier version of the essay, Tolstoy offers 'hypnotism' as a synonym for infection . . . " (284–85). We will see hypnotism reemerging as a negative synonym for infection in both Tolstoy's final version of the book (see below) and in the drama theory of Bertolt Brecht (see chapter 5). What for Tolstoy is good art for Brecht is bad art, and presumably vice versa, but both men, as well as Viktor Shklovsky, agree on the nature of the depersonalizing disorder that must be cured and, generally speaking, on the nature of the cure that they are calling on literature to perform. Denner describes this cure in Tolstoy, but virtually the same could be said for Shklovsky and Brecht, and we will be exploring those visions in Parts II and III:

> One must not overlook the paramount role art plays in Tolstoy's cosmology. Art is a demiurgic tool: Its function is remaking the individual by exacting an enduring and significant change in his or her psychology, something Tolstoy explicitly addresses when he remarks that the best kind of art, Christian religious art, by evoking "under imaginary conditions" a sense of brotherhood and love essential to Christian teaching, will "train men to experience those same feelings under similar circumstances in actual life; it will lay in the souls of men the rails along which the actions of those whom art educates will naturally pass" . . . We are to understand that art accomplishes an almost physiological change in the mind of the perceiver. Were he writing today, Tolstoy would no doubt replace his train metaphor with something like "art rewires the neural circuits." It would be hard to imagine a more explicit rendering of Stalin's slogan about the artist being the "engineer of the human soul." And, in fact, the Bolsheviks learned much from Tolstoy, and from *What Is Art?* in particular. Consider a characteristic pronouncement by Anatoly Lunacharsky (the USSR's first Commissar of Education) on art from *The Press and Revolution:* "Real art is always ideological. By ideological I mean one stemming from an intense experience which drives the artist . . . towards spiritual expansion, towards rule over souls"—a quote that, *mutatis mutandi* [*sic*], might be drawn from *What Is Art?* (285–86)

Powerful Content, Smooth Form, Sincerity

Most important for the somatic aesthetics of estrangement that others will catch or contract from Tolstoy and build into modernist literary theory and practice, though, is his specific aesthetic program, his series of strategies for creating a literary art that will wield this kind of demiurgic power over the moral psychology of whole populations. Denner traces the evolution of Tolstoy's thinking along these lines through several articles written during the period from his spiritual crisis and "conversion" in the late 1870s up to the writing of *What Is Art?* in the mid-1890s: "On Art" (1889), the "Introduction to S. T. Semyonov's Peasant Stories" (1894), and the "Introduction to the Works of Guy de Maupassant" (1894; all quotations from these three works in the next three paragraphs are taken from Denner, 288).

Essentially, a work of art has to have three qualities to have the desired effect: powerful content, smooth form, and sincerity. The content must be something that "pertains to all of mankind but that is still not wholly understood by it" ("On Art") or something that "the artist reveals from a new side important and necessary for men" ("Semyonov").

The form or craft or technique should be smooth enough not to draw attention to itself, so as to make the "efforts of the artist invisible" ("On Art"), because, as Denner explains, "complicated, belabored form hampers . . . the transference of emotion by making laborious the process of experiencing art" (288). This is an extremely important point to note here because it is precisely where Shklovsky will reverse Tolstoy: belabored form is important for Shklovsky *because* it hampers the transference of feeling and makes laborious the process of experiencing art. This is the post-Romantic key Shklovsky invents for modernist experimentation—and, as we'll see, he takes almost all his examples of this belabored form out of Tolstoy's own writings (which, of course, Tolstoy himself condemned as bad art). Since Shklovsky calls the effect of belabored form *estrangement,* and estrangement is one of the symptoms of depersonalization, Vadim Rudnev argues that Shklovsky's concept and the tradition of modernist literary theory that arises out of it are celebrations and instances of depersonalization—and certainly Tolstoy would have agreed with that part of Rudnev's argument. For Tolstoy, the infectiousness of smooth form makes it an effective homeopathic (infection-against-infection) cure for depersonalization, and belabored form simply blocks the (counter)infective cure and prolongs the disease. For Shklovsky and Brecht, the infectiousness of smooth form is itself a symptom of depersonalization, and belabored form is the homeopathic cure (which is also, it turns out in the end, infectious). What is interesting about these conflicting thematizations of the disease and its cure is that in them symptomatic images of the (psycho/homeo)pathology themselves become infected and carriers of the infection, which they mutate as they infect later generations of readers and writers.

The third criterion for infectious art, sincerity, simply means that the artist feels such a powerful overriding love for what s/he loves and hatred for what s/he hates that his or her feeling "irresistibly grasps and sweeps away the perceiver" ("On Art"). This is so not only because "without sincerity, without a heartfelt connection between the artist and object, the work is not a work of art" ("On Art") but because sincerity "gives force to a work of art and makes it infectious" ("Maupassant"). Tolstoy sums up this last criterion in *What Is Art?*

> I have mentioned three conditions of contagion in art, but they may all be summed up in one, the last, sincerity; that is, that the artist should be impelled by an inner need to express his feeling. That condition includes the

first; for if the artist is sincere he will express the feeling as he experienced it. And as each man is different from every one else, his feeling will be particular for every one else; and the more individual it is—the more the artist has drawn from the depths of his nature—the more sympathetic and sincere it will be. And this same sincerity will impel the artist to find clear expression for the feeling that he wishes to transmit.

Therefore this third condition—sincerity—is the most important of the three. (229–30)

Of course, this discussion is purely aesthetic; it deals only with what makes a work of art powerfully infectious. Tolstoy's eulogistic rhetoric here suggests that he is associating infectious art with *good* art, art that infects the perceiver with good religious moral values, but he really isn't; theoretically, his three criteria for infectious art could be met by bad art, his own included. Shklovsky's analysis suggests that Tolstoy's fiction doesn't meet the criterion of smooth (unbelabored, unestranging) form either, and Tolstoy's own strictures on his fiction, both in *What Is Art?* and in the earlier *Confession* (1882), make it clear that he doesn't consider it to have proceeded from personal sincerity. He was, he says in *A Confession* especially, just trying to become rich and famous. If, in fact, some author were to meet all three criteria in a work dedicated to the infection of readers with evil, rancorous, soul-destroying feelings, it would be truly dangerous—assuming, of course, that Tolstoy was at that moment willing to accept his mostly suppressed conception of the rival perverted infection that spreads depersonalization.

Damasio's Somatic Theory

Tolstoy's metaphor of infection is itself infectious, and many theorists—including Brecht, who mostly loathed it—have found it irresistible in describing the transfer of feelings or somatic guidance from one body to another. The parallels between microbial and somatic transfers are experientially compelling, through what we may call the infectious power of metaphor as "with-across-living" or "in-living" (*soperezhivanie* or *vzhivanie,* respectively, two Russian words for empathy). In other words, because we *feel* about the mimetic somatic transfer more or less as we feel about microbial infection, the similarity of our somatic senses of the two phenomena allows our images of one to leach over into and blend with our images of the other. For many centuries, before Louis Pasteur and Robert Koch demonstrated the germ theory of disease in the mid-nineteenth century, infection was taken to be no transfer at all but rather the spontaneous generation of disease in a body. Up until the discovery in the 1990s of what the U.S.-based Portuguese neurologist Antonio Damasio called the as-if body loop, the almost instantaneous neurological simulation in one body of another body's inward states, we similarly had no empirical evidence that anything was being transferred from one body to the other when everybody in a room started "spontaneously" yawning or laughing or crying, so we assumed there too that no transfer was taking place. To the nonscientist, both processes remain invisible and therefore largely mysterious even today: because we can't see either microbial or somatic infection, we are inclined to discount or discredit both. It requires a radical reeducation process to teach a whole population to take rudimentary preventive steps against bacterial infection, and folk theories of how we catch a cold, for instance, still prevail in many cultures over the microbial explanation (you get chilled, you get wet, air moves through an open window and makes you sneeze). Talk of the somatic mimeticism involved in the contagiousness of yawns or other body states provokes sneers from intellectuals and remarks about "biological mysticism."

I call the somatic theory Damasio's because he has the credentials to back it up—he is M. W. Van Allen Professor of Neurology at the University of Iowa College of Medicine and director of the neurology lab there, and all his claims about somatic markers are research based and published in medical journals—but in fact I began theorizing it independently, in the mid-1980s, and gave my first conference presentation on the somatics of language in 1985. My first published formulation of the theory, based on William James, Ludwig Wittgenstein, and Kenneth Burke, was chapter 1 of *The Translator's Turn,* which appeared the same year (1991) as the Damasio team's first medical publication on the somatic-marker hypothesis.

The Somatic Transfer

The determining criteria for the somatic theory are essentially Tolstoy's for the infection theory—that social feelings be seen as infectious (transferable from body to body) and regulatory (guiding thought and behavior). As Tolstoy writes of the former,

> The activity of art is based on the fact that a man receiving through his sense of hearing or sight another man's expression of feeling, is capable of experiencing the emotion which moved the man who expressed it. To take the simplest example: one man laughs, and another who hears becomes merry;

or a man weeps, and another who hears feels sorrow. A man is excited or irritated, and another man seeing him comes to a similar state of mind. By his movements or by the sounds of his voice a man expresses courage and determination or sadness and calmness, and this state of mind passes on to others. A man suffers, manifesting his sufferings by groans and spasms, and this suffering transmits itself to other people; a man expresses his feeling of admiration, devotion, fear, respect, or love, to certain objects, persons, or phenomena, and others are infected by the same feelings of admiration, devotion, fear, respect, or love, to the same objects, persons, or phenomena. (121)

This is what I call the somatic transfer: a somatic orientation in one body is transferred to another body.[8] Based on sensory evidence, typically visual or aural observation of another person's body, the recipient of the "infection" comes to feel more or less what the other is feeling. The classic case of this infection is the contagious yawn; when someone else yawns, it requires enormous effort not to start yawning oneself. But as Tolstoy indicates, merriment is contagious as well, as are sorrow, excitement, irritation, and other body states. Some people are more susceptible to this infection than others: many men, for example, scoff at such observations, insist that it never happens to them, and attribute it to weak-mindedness or overemotionalism, citing the hypersensitive woman who cries at strangers' funerals or is wracked with anguish at the suffering of a character on a soap opera. I have given up trying to get such scoffers to reflect on the emotional-becoming-mental effort they must exert in order to suppress this sort of empathetic response in their own bodies; they invariably claim that there is nothing to suppress. The somatic transfer for them is simply hogwash—possibly a kind of metaphorical and wholly imaginary extension of grammar, based perhaps on the fact that in English we say "it feels to me as if . . ."

As I say, it was around the same time my first published account of the somatic transfer appeared, in the early nineties, that Damasio's team began to realize that empathy—specifically, the so-called Carpenter Effect, the fact observed by William B. Carpenter in 1874 that we unconsciously tend to mimic other people's body language in our own bodies—is crucial to the somatic theory. At that point several members of the team, headed by Ralph Adolphs, began to investigate it and to publish papers (beginning in 1994) that addressed subjects' ability to *recognize* somatic states in other people's faces. Damasio himself did not deal with the somatic transfer under any title in his books of the nineties; it was not until *Looking for Spinoza* in 2003 that he offered a neurophysiological model for the phenomenon, summarizing the results of the most recent study (2002):[9]

A recent study from Ralph Adolphs speaks directly to the issue of simulated body states. The study was aimed at investigating the underpinnings of empathy and involved more than 100 patients with neurological lesions located at varied sites of their cerebral cortex. They were asked to participate in a task that called for the sort of process needed for empathy responses. Each subject was shown photographs of an unknown person exhibiting some emotional expression and the task consisted of indicating what the unknown person was feeling. Researchers asked each subject to place himself or herself in the person's shoes to guess the person's state of mind. The hypothesis being tested was that patients with damage to body-sensing regions of the cerebral cortex would not be capable of performing the task normally.

Most patients performed this task easily, precisely as healthy subjects do, except for two specific groups of patients whose performance was impaired. The first group of impaired patients was quite predictable. It was made up of patients with damage to visual association cortices, especially the right visual cortices of the ventral occipito-temporal region. This sector of the brain is critical for the appreciation of visual configurations. Without its integrity, the facial expressions in the photographs cannot be perceived as a whole, even if the photos can be seen in the general sense of the term.

The other group of patients was the most telling: It consisted of subjects with damage located in the overall region of the *right* somatosensory cortices, namely, in the insula, SII and SI regions of the right cerebral hemisphere. This is the set of regions in which the brain accomplishes the highest level of integrated mapping of body state. In the absence of this region, it is not possible for the brain to simulate other body states effectively. The brain lacks the playground where variations on the body-state theme can be played.

It is of great physiological significance that the comparable region of the left cerebral hemisphere does not have the same function: Patients with damage to the left somatosensory complex perform the "empathy" task normally. This is one more finding that suggests that the right somatosensory cortices are "dominant" with regard to integrated body mapping. This is also the reason why damage to this region has been consistently associated with defects in emotion and feeling, and with conditions such as anosognosia and neglect, whose basis is a defective idea of the current body state. The right versus left asymmetry in the function of the human somatosensory cortices probably is due to a committed participation of the left somatosensory cortices in language and speech. (116–17)

Another recent study, this one done by a Swedish team at Uppsala University directed by Ulf Dimberg, found that "normal individuals who were viewing photographs depicting emotion immediately and subtly activated the muscular groups of their own faces that would have been necessary for them to make the emotional expressions depicted in the photographs. The individuals were not aware of this mirror-image 'presetting' of their own muscles but electrodes distributed across their faces picked up on electromyographic changes" (Damasio, *Looking,* 117). This is the neurophysiological explanation of the "contagion" or "infection" of feelings or somatic states from one body to another: through empathy we simulate each other's body states, based on seeing or hearing external evidence of those states. Nor is this a voluntary process undergone by especially sensitive people who deliberately project themselves into other people's feelings because they *want* to; it happens to all of us, all the time, except to people with those specific types of brain damage Damasio mentions. It is not just "sensitive" people who yawn or fight the overwhelming impulse to yawn when they see other people yawning; it is virtually everyone. I call this *somatic mimeticism*: the almost instantaneous mimicking of another person's body states in your own, which serves to "infect" you with the other person's feeling.

The Somatic Transfer Through Story

The next step in Tolstoy's infection theory is the extension of this somatic mimeticism to cases in which the other body is not visually or aurally present but simply remembered or imagined through a verbal account:

And it is on this capacity of man to receive another man's expression of feeling and experience those feelings himself, that the activity of art is based.

If a man infects another or others, directly, immediately, by his appearance or by the sounds he gives vent to at the very time he experiences the feeling; if he causes another man to yawn when he himself cannot help yawning, or to laugh or cry when he himself is obliged to laugh or cry, or to suffer when he himself is suffering—that does not amount to art.

Art begins when one person with the object of joining another or others to himself in one and the same feeling, expresses that feeling by certain external indications. To take the simplest example: a boy having experienced, let us say, fear on encountering a wolf, relates that encounter, and in order to evoke in others the feeling he has experienced, describes himself, his condition before the encounter, the surroundings, the wood, his own lightheartedness, and then the wolf's appearance, its movements, the distance between himself and the wolf, and so forth. All this, if only the boy when telling the story again experiences the feelings he had lived through, and infects the hearers and compels them to feel what the narrator had experienced—is art. Even if the boy had not seen a wolf but had frequently been afraid of one, and if wishing to evoke in others the fear he had felt, he invented an encounter with a wolf, and recounted it so as to make his hearers share the feelings he experienced when he feared the wolf, that also would be art. (121–22)

This *narratively* triggered somatic mimesis, obviously central to the somatics of literature, has not been researched by Damasio's team or any other neurologist, but Damasio speculatively incorporates it into his model under the sign of the "as-if body loop":

It also is apparent that the brain can simulate certain emotional body states internally, as happens in the process of turning the emotion sympathy into a feeling of empathy. Think, for example, of being told about a horrible accident in which someone was badly injured. For a moment you may feel a twinge of pain that mirrors in your mind the pain of the person in question. You feel as if you were the victim, and the feeling may be more or less intense depending on the dimension of the accident or on your knowledge of the person involved. The presumed mechanism for producing this sort of feeling is a variety of what I have called the "as-if-body-loop" mechanism. It involves an internal brain simulation that consists of a rapid modification of ongoing body maps. This is achieved when certain brain regions, such as the prefrontal/premotor cortices, directly signal the body-sensing brain regions. The existence and location of comparable types of neurons has been established recently. Those neurons can represent, in an individual's brain, the movements that very brain sees in another individual, and produce signals toward sensorimotor structures so that the corresponding movements are either "previewed," in simulation mode, or actually executed. These neurons are present in the frontal cortex of monkeys and humans, and are known as "mirror neurons." (115)

"An internal brain simulation that consists of a *rapid* modification of ongoing body maps"—so rapid (less than 300 milliseconds) that it may seem simultaneous, and it is based now not on visual or aural evidence but on *story.* You are *told* of the horrible accident, and your body produces a simulation of the victim's pain. This literary extension of empathy or infection depends on a conception of the human brain as capable of organizing *remembered* body maps into a new composite simulation, a complexly (re)constructive mimesis of somatic states not only across the self/other or own/alien boundary but across the past/future boundary as well. Somaticity tends to blur all such boundaries: it is paradigmatically difficult to tell, when feeling an emotion, when "mapping" a body state, whether the feeling is purely one's own or another's as well, and whether it was triggered purely by some event in the present or cotriggered by something in the past. This blurring of boundaries has long been familiar to psychoanalysis—projection, for example, is the externalization of one's own feeling into someone else's body, introjection the internalization of someone else's feeling into one's own, and transference and countertransference are the projection of a past feeling for someone not now present onto the person now present—and a good deal of psychoanalytic ink has been spilled over how to identify the "true" origin of a feeling, how to separate what is yours from what is someone else's, what is past from what is present or being projected into the future.[10] Damasio's model suggests that what is at work in these attempts to sort feelings into "own" or "other's" and "past" or "present" is simply a more complex mapping: as a feeling is a mental map of an emotional state, a psychoanalysis is a verbalized mental map of a feeling or complex of feelings. Each new level of mapping pushes the internal representation of the body state(s) in an increasingly mentalized direction, but because the maps not only grow out of the body states but may alter the states as well, there is no question here of accuracy or objectivity. The boundaries between emotion and feeling and mental image are among those definitively blurred by somaticity. Hence my preference, when writing about somatic phenomena, to use Hegelian "becoming" constructions like body-becoming-mind or emotional-becoming-mental.

Damasio writes of *being told* of a horrible accident, Tolstoy of *being told* the story of an encounter with a wolf: these are oral narrations, obviously, channeled through the spoken word, which, as we see in chapter 4, Hegel analyzes as the rational synthesis of one's own body language (gesture, facial expression, body posture, intonation) and another's "corporeal sign," which would include at the very least the other person's body language, the external signs of internal body states. I've called this cycling or circulating of somaticity back and forth between bodies—each reading and internalizing the other's corporeal signs, simulating the other's body states, and reexternalizing the resulting feelings as new corporeal signs—the *somatic exchange,* and identified it as the primary channel of social regulation (more on that in a moment). The important point to note for now is that it is relatively easy to show how embodied speech, the speaking of what Shoshana Felman calls the "speaking body," channels somaticity from teller to hearer, even in a long chain of such tellings and retellings, as when A tells B about the encounter with the wolf, and B tells C, and C tells D, and something of A's original fear is ultimately transferred to D. Tolstoy wants to argue that *precisely the same* feeling is passed from body to body; having been infected by Bakhtin and Freud, Heidegger and Wittgenstein, Hegel and Schopenhauer and Nietzsche, we may find that we have developed antibodies against such idealized simplicity.

In any case, accepting the theory of somatic transfer as applied to the spoken word, we may be willing to speak of the somatics of the oral tradition or the somatics of drama but reluctant to extend the theory to the written word, and thus to literature. Surely, Derrida's strictures in *Of Grammatology* and elsewhere against the metaphysics of presence should warn us away from any facile equation of speech with writing? Worries like this are themselves conditioned by the metaphysics of presence, by the pre-Kantian notion that we are somehow passively affected by speech, writing, other people, other objects in the world, so that, say, because of their intrinsic natures, the spoken word and the written word will have significantly different effects on us. But contemporary neurophysiology is thoroughly Kantian in its focus on the constitutivity of all human understanding: we construct our worlds out of sense data but also out of everything else that is circulating through our brains, which includes, I'm arguing, much that is circulating through the brains of the groups to which we belong. Tolstoy's infection theory is objectivistic, quasiscientistic, based on the assumption that a feeling exists in one body like a disease and somehow makes the jump across the intervening space to another body, where it burrows in and infects its new host. Damasio's empathy theory is constructivist, based on the assumption that the new host is the active party in the transaction, that we are constantly reaching out to our world creatively and mimetically, seeking out stimuli, which we then convert into something internally meaningful. It doesn't really matter where we find such stimuli—in novels and poems and plays, in critical works, in oral narrations, in the embodied speaking of our friends, in the pattern of a tapestry or a table arrangement, in the sounds of cars in a city street, in the swaying of trees or the crash of thunder—we convert it all, constructively, constitutively, into our own somatic material, as we need it. Another boundary blurred by the somatic theory is that between the spoken and written word; we can distinguish them, obviously, but only by mapping a more analytical layer of understanding onto our somatic mimeses.

Of course, because everyone is doing this all the time and because what we take from others we almost instantaneously convert into internal material for our own constructions, and because we are constantly displaying the results of this constructivity on the surfaces of our bodies as "corporeal signs" for others to internalize and reconstruct, it is simplistic to say that we convert stimuli into something *internally* meaningful; that is only a snapshot of the entire process of the somatic exchange. Ultimately, what we are doing is working collectively to convert random stimuli into a world, complete with sensations, feelings, and intellectual understanding.

Somatic Guidance

The third key element of the somatic theory is the somatic guidance of thought, language, and behavior in general. This is important to Tolstoy because his goal in the promotion of infectious art is to spread not merely feelings but *the right kind* of feelings: moral and religious feelings that will organize audiences' behavior and general spiritual orientation around the "true" Christian doctrine. In chapter 3, we see Viktor Shklovsky theorizing the power of poetry to estrange its readers from estrangement, to have a hypermimetic therapeutic effect: this notion depends, obviously, on something very like Tolstoy's infection theory, the power of art to rearrange the audience's psychology. In chapter 5, we see Bertolt Brecht enlisting Shklovsky's theory of estrangement in a large-scale Marxist conversion project similar in scope and purpose to Tolstoy's, indeed one that, as Michael Denner argues, was powerfully influenced by Tolstoy's project in *What Is Art?*—simply with a different ideology at the core of the new transformative infection.

Damasio does not theorize this sort of collective regulation, except passingly, hinting at it in *Looking for Spinoza* (to which I return below). The basic building block in the theory of the regulatory power of somatic response, though, is his somatic-marker hypothesis, the theory he has worked longest and hardest to establish. The Damasio team's research began with a group of patients with damage to the ventral-tegmental area of their brains, an area known to be involved in the regulation of feeling. What the researchers found, though, was that ventral-tegmental damage had a mysterious adverse effect on reasoning capacities—specifically, the ability to prioritize and hierarchize, especially in practical decision making, as at work when you have to decide which are the most pressing jobs and do them first. The ventral-tegmental patients were unable to do this and so found it nearly impossible to keep a job. Yet they passed all the standard psychological tests for reasoning ability with no difficulty and so found it nearly impossible to convince doctors and insurance companies to grant them disability benefits.

The somatic-marker hypothesis that Damasio and his team developed to explain this suggests that in normal people rational decision making is guided at a very rough level by somatic signals or markers, measurable by a skin-conductance meter such as a polygraph machine, and that this somatic marking of behavioral options makes it possible for us to sort through extremely complex alternatives and make a "rational" choice. The kind of cool, unemotional reasoning process that has been idealized by philosophers for centuries is in fact physiologically impossible because the human brain is incapable of holding in working memory more than a handful of the complex variables that contribute to a rational decision. This is why we have developed externalizing strategies for this sort of rational process: we make lists of pros and cons, for example, in essence storing on paper what we have observed and decided thus far, so that it doesn't simply drop out of working memory and become lost to us. The storage capacity of our attention and working memory is extremely limited; we reach our limits quickly and either learn to rely on ancillary strategies like taking notes or give up in frustration.

Or, as Damasio argues, we rely on somatic markers, which are programmed by experience into the ventral-tegmental areas of our brains. This is not, in other words, a purely biologistic (in the sense of "mechanistic") theory; Damasio is hypothesizing that the ventral-tegmental area of the brain stores what we have learned about life and signals it to us somatically, which is to say, through our social emotions. This ability is what the team's ventral-tegmental patients have lost. They, in effect, reason on the model of the great rationalist philosophers: coolly, without emotional support. As a result, they lose track of what they have already decided and what they have previously learned about the consequences of this or that course of action, and either make rash, impetuous, more or less random decisions with destructive consequences, or flounder about in vacillating confusion, unable to decide at all.

To illustrate his hypothesis, in *Descartes' Error* Damasio imagines a typically complex practical decision-making situation, so complex that it defies our ability to hold all the overlapping variables in our memories at once: as the owner of a business, you must decide whether to meet with a potential client who is also your best friend's worst enemy. You badly need the money, but you also need the friendship of this close person. How do you decide? Damasio writes,

> The key components unfold in our minds instantly, sketchily, and virtually simultaneously, too fast for the details to be clearly defined. But now, imagine that *before* you apply any kind of cost/benefit analysis to the premises, and before you reason toward the solution of the problem, something quite important happens: When the bad outcome connected with a given response option comes into mind, however fleetingly, you experience an

unpleasant gut feeling. Because the feeling is about the body, I gave the phenomenon the technical term *somatic* state ("soma" is Greek for body); and because it "marks" an image, I called it a *marker*. Note again that I use somatic in the most general sense (that which pertains to the body) and I include both visceral and nonvisceral sensation when I refer to somatic markers.

What does the *somatic marker* achieve? It forces attention on the negative outcome to which a given action may lead, and functions as an automated alarm signal which says: Beware of danger ahead if you choose the option which leads to this outcome. The signal may lead you to reject, *immediately,* the negative course of action and thus make you *choose among other alternatives.* The automated signal protects you against future losses, without further ado, and then allows you to choose from among fewer alternatives. There is still room for using a cost/benefit analysis and proper deductive competence, but only *after* the automated step drastically reduces the number of options. Somatic markers may not be sufficient for normal human decision-making since a subsequent process of reasoning and final selection will still take place in many though not all instances. Somatic markers probably increase the accuracy and efficiency of the decision process. Their absence reduces them. This distinction is important and can easily be missed. The hypothesis does not concern the reasoning steps which follow the action of the somatic marker. In short, *somatic markers are a special instance of feelings generated from secondary emotions.* Those emotions and feelings *have been connected, by learning, to predicted future outcomes of certain scenarios.* When a somatic marker is juxtaposed to a particular future outcome the combination functions as an alarm bell. When a positive somatic marker is juxtaposed instead it becomes a beacon of incentive. (*Descartes',* 173–74)

The phenomenon Damasio is describing is familiar to all of us, of course: we say "I've got a bad feeling about this," or "This feels good to me," or "My gut tells me not to do this," and act accordingly. Or we ignore the gut feeling and regret it later, telling ourselves and our friends, "I *knew* there was something wrong with him from the beginning, I could feel it, but I told myself to be reasonable, not to act on some wild hunch, and look at me now." We do tend to call somatic markers hunches, gut instincts, and intuitions, and to develop policies for responding to those markers when we feel them, like "always act on your gut instinct, it knows something you don't," or "look before you leap" (a proverb encouraging additional cost/benefit reasoning after a somatic marker has been felt).[11] People who seem not to have such hunches tend to make us uneasy; they seem somehow less human, like machines. And, as Damasio's team has demonstrated through two decades of research, people who lack the neurological ability to send themselves such somatic markers really are lost in the world, unable to function normally. They cannot hold a job; it is difficult for them to maintain friendships; they seem to function "blindly," randomly, without the kind of socio-emotional guidance the rest of us feel.

Was Tolstoy one of these people? Might he have suffered damage to his ventral-tegmental area and been unable to regulate his own behavior and cognition somatically? I don't know. It's possible—but perhaps extreme. Chapter 2 details evidence from *A Confession* and *What Is Art?* that in formulating his theories of things, including of his own "conversion," he did not receive adequate guidance from his feelings and had to rely much more heavily than most of us do on his analytical reason; but, sketchy as this evidence is, speculative as my reading of the evidence is, it would appear to point to something other than the kind of ventral-tegmental dysfunction that Damasio has studied. Tolstoy may have experienced somatic guidance but weakly and sporadically, or he may have been able to guide his own behavior and cognition somatically but unable to experience such guidance from other people, empathetically, or what he himself calls infectiously. Or his ability to be infected by other people's feelings may simply have been weak and sporadic. It may also be that he was physiologically capable of experiencing both kinds of somatic guidance, from within and from without, but psychologically incapable of letting himself feel it—it may, for whatever reason, have been a nightmarish feeling for him. I do believe strongly that Tolstoy suffered from some degree or type of somatic dysfunction; just what degree, or what type, however, I will not venture to guess.

Ideosomatic Regulation

The next step beyond each individual's reliance on somatic markers to regulate his or her own decision-making process comes out of the integration of the somatic-marker hypothesis with the somatic transfer, which I call somatic mimeticism or the somatic exchange. If I'm five years old and my own somatized experience does not tell me whether it's a good idea to climb up on the roof, I can start climbing, and then let the shocked and horrified cries of disapproval and dismay from my parents guide me into climbing back down before I hurt myself. Moving to a foreign country, I can gradually let the collectivized somatics of the new culture resocialize me to a new set of values, through the somatic transfer of regulatory feelings (approval and disapproval, through approving and disapproving corporeal signs) from the locals to me and my increasing willingness to win their approval by entering into the regulatory social exchange with them. If I am tempted to cheat on my spouse or leave my spouse for a lover, I may be able to impose collectivized regulation on my own behavior by summoning up a projected mental image of my spouse's future face (or my parents' or friends' faces) when she or he or they hear what I've done.

I can also resist this. The somatic theory is not behavioristic, not based on an assumed robotization of stimulus and response; it is, as I say, constructivist, based on each individual's guided but nonetheless creative response to regulatory pressure. Some people live abroad for decades and never adapt their thinking, speaking, feeling, and acting to the local values because their resistance—based typically on their childhood socialization to what were once local and current but are now "foreign" and "past" values—is too strong. Because each individual's creative response to regulatory pressure is often in large part preconscious, guided by emotional-becoming-mental pressures that have not yet quite become mental enough to yield self-awareness, the somatic theory is sometimes casually equated with behaviorism. But, as in Freud's theory of preconscious behavior, somatic resistance to regulatory pressure can always be ratcheted up through the generation of new cognitive mappings of body states, which is to say, through awareness, through conscious articulation.

Damasio has only recently begun to consider this sociological extension of his theory. In *Looking for Spinoza,* for example, he notes that because somatic markers are specifically *social* feelings, their disruption or disablement at an early age typically makes the child unresponsive to social guidance, not just punishment and reward but somatic mimeticism of all kinds. Thus while adults who suffer traumatic damage to their prefrontal regions do not display social emotions, they at least *know* the social conventions intellectually and can conform to some extent to social norms; children who suffer such trauma early in life usually grow up incorrigible. Damasio gives this example in *Looking for Spinoza:*

> The very first patient we studied with this condition was twenty when we met her. Her family was comfortable and stable, and her parents had no history of neurological or psychiatric disease. She sustained head injury when she was run over by a car at age fifteen months, but she had recovered fully within days. No behavioral abnormalities were observed until age three when her parents noted she was unresponsive to verbal and physical punishment. This differed remarkably from the behavior of her siblings who went on to become normal adolescents and young adults. By fourteen her behavior

was so disruptive that her parents placed her in a treatment facility, the first of many. She was academically capable yet routinely failed to complete her assignments. Her adolescence was marked by failure to comply with rules of any sort and frequent confrontations with peers and adults. She was verbally and physically abusive to others. She lied chronically. She was arrested several times for shoplifting and stole from other children and from her own family. She engaged in early and risky sexual behavior and became pregnant at eighteen. After the baby was born, her maternal behavior was marked by insensitivity to the child's needs. She was unable to hold any job due to poor dependability and violation of work rules. She never expressed guilt or remorse for inappropriate behavior or any sympathy for others. She always blamed others for her difficulties. Behavioral management and psychotropic medication were of no help. After repeatedly placing herself at physical and financial risk, she became dependent on her parents and on social agencies for both financial support and oversight of her personal affairs. She had no plans for the future and no desire to become employed. (153)

With the breakdown of social emotion-management in the prefrontal ventromedial region, Damasio explains, "the experience of pain, which is part of punishment, becomes disconnected from the action that caused the punishment, and thus *there will not be a memory of their conjunction for future use;* likewise for the pleasurable aspects of reward" (155). This observation leads Damasio to imagine a world without the conformative somatic marking of social emotions and thus (negatively) to reenvision ethics as channeled somatically:

In a society deprived of such emotions and feelings, there would have been no spontaneous exhibition of the innate social responses that foreshadow a simple ethical system—no budding altruism, no kindness when kindness is due, no censure when censure is appropriate, no automatic sense of one's own failings. In the absence of the feelings of such emotions, humans would not have engaged in a negotiation aimed at finding solutions for problems faced by the group, e.g., identification and sharing of food resources, defense against threats or disputes among its members. There would not have been a gradual build-up of wisdom regarding the relationships among social situations, natural responses, and a host of contingencies such as the punishment or reward incurred by permitting or inhibiting natural responses. The codification of rules eventually expressed in systems of justice and sociopolitical organizations is hardly conceivable in those circumstances, even assuming that the apparatus of learning, imagination, and reasoning could be otherwise intact in the face of emotional ravages, a most unlikely possibility. With the natural system of emotional navigation more or less disabled, there would not have been a ready possibility of fine-tuning the individual

to the real world. Moreover, the possibility of constructing a fact-based social navigation system, independently of the missing natural system, appears
unlikely. (157)[12]

My terms for the individual and social regulation of decision making
through somatic markers are *idiosomatic* (idiosyncratically somatic) and *ideosomatic* (ideologically somatic). Such is the nature of the ideosomatic regulation
of social behavior, however, that the only way we can normally distinguish idiosomatic response from ideosomatic is through conflicting signals: if a course
of action feels right on the inside but receives massive regulatory disapproval
signals from the group, the resulting somatic dissonance may lead the subject to identify the internal impulse as idiosomatic and to reflect on whether
that impulse is strong enough to warrant (counterideosomatic) resistance to
ideosomatic pressures.

2 ▎ *Tolstoy's Estrangement*

Tolstoy has a dual role to play in this book: as a theorist of artistic infection and thus of the somatics of literature (my topic in chapter 1), and as a literary exemplar of estrangement (my topic here in chapter 2). Estrangement as a literary device was first theorized by Viktor Shklovsky in 1917, and chapter 3 is devoted to a detailed discussion of that theory, but as critics invariably note, almost all of Shklovsky's examples come from Tolstoy, which makes Tolstoy a kind of honorary godfather of estrangement.

Estrangement Of/From

Estrangement Of

Perhaps the most interesting tracking of Shklovsky's citations of Tolstoy is Carlo Ginzburg's in "Making Things Strange: The Prehistory of a Literary Device."[1] Ginzburg argues specifically that Tolstoy learned his strategy of estrangement from Marcus Aurelius, a writer he admired enormously. "Marcus Aurelius was interested in self-instruction, not in introspection. His favorite verbal mood was the imperative. 'Efface imagination!' he wrote over and over, using a word—φαντασία—that was part of the Stoics' technical vocabulary. According to Epictetus, the slave-philosopher whose ideas had a profound impact on Marcus Aurelius, the obliteration of wrong imaginations was a necessary step toward a right perception of things, hence toward virtue" (10). Every time something became attractive to him, he would ask "*has this the mastery of me?*" (quoted in Ginzburg, 10). Nor is it enough for Marcus Aurelius merely

34

to examine every attraction and seek to undermine it. "We must also learn to look at things from a distance . . . Through the immensity of time and the multiplicity of people, we will realize the irrelevance of our own existence" (11). And further,

> A search for the causal principle is also part of the Stoic program aimed at a right perception of things:
>
>> Surely it is an excellent plan, when you are seated before delicacies and choice foods, to impress upon your imagination [φαντασία] that this is the dead body of a fish, that the dead body of a bird or a pig; and again, that the Falernian wine is grape juice and that robe of purpose a lamb's fleece dipped in a shellfish's blood; and in matters of sex intercourse, that it is attrition of an entrail and a convulsive expulsion of mere mucus. Surely these are excellent imaginations [φαντασίαι], going to the heart of actual facts and penetrating them so as to see the kind of things they really are. You should adopt this practice all through your life, and where things make an impression which is very plausible, uncover their nakedness, see into their cheapness, strip off the profession on which they vaunt themselves . . .
>
> This extraordinary passage inevitably strikes the twentieth-century reader as an early example of estrangement. The label is fully justified. Tolstoy had a deep admiration for Marcus Aurelius and, in his old age, edited an anthology of universal wisdom in calendar form that included more than fifty passages from Marcus Aurelius's reflections. But I would like to suggest that even Tolstoy's uncompromising approaches to law, ambition, war, and love were deeply indebted to Marcus Aurelius. Like a horse, like a child, Tolstoy looked at human conventions and institutions as strange, opaque phenomena, thereby stripping them bare of their conventional meanings. Things unveiled themselves to his passionate and detached gaze "as they really are," to use Marcus Aurelius's phrase. (11)

And Ginzburg goes on to detail numerous other corroborating and reinforcing models for Tolstoy's approach to the world, especially his deep grounding in the Enlightenment tradition of Voltaire and Montaigne, both of whom Ginzburg reads as heavily indebted to Marcus Aurelius as well.

The interesting question that Ginzburg begs in his wonderfully detailed and useful essay, however, is the obvious one of causality or influence: whether (a) Tolstoy learned to estrange the ordinary world by reading Marcus Aurelius and his followers, as he argues, so that estrangement was a mere *literary device,* a gimmick that Tolstoy used powerfully but, in terms of his own psychic makeup, fairly superficially; whether (b) estrangement was instead an *infec-*

tion that Tolstoy picked up from his reading in these authors, and thereafter something that he could not help but infect others with; or whether, finally, (c) Tolstoy was powerfully attracted to these writers because he was already estranged from the ordinary world, infected by estrangement through some other channel, and simply found himself powerfully drawn to these estrangers as to a kindred spirit. In the rest of this chapter I argue for (c); it seems to me that Tolstoy's estranging devices in his fiction and nonfiction alike arise not out of literary emulation but out of some deeper idiosomatic dysfunction.

Look, for example, at these two fairly typical passages from *A Confession*, and decide whether Tolstoy is consciously using literary devices in them:

> My mental condition presented itself to me in this way: my life is a stupid and spiteful joke someone has played on me. Though I did not acknowledge a "someone" who created me, yet such a presentation—that someone had played an evil and stupid joke on me by placing me in the world—was the form of expression that suggested itself most naturally to me.
>
> Involuntarily it appeared to me that there, somewhere, was someone who amused himself by watching how I lived for thirty or forty years: learning, developing, maturing in body and mind, and how, having with matured mental powers reached the summit of life from which it all lay before me, I stood on that summit—like an arch-fool—seeing clearly that there is nothing in life, and that there has been and will be nothing. And he was amused. (19)

> But again and again, from various sides, I returned to the same conclusion that I could not have come into the world without any cause or reason or meaning; I could not be such a fledgling fallen from its nest as I felt myself to be. Or, granting that I be such, lying on my back crying in the high grass, even then I cry because I know that a mother has borne me within her, has hatched me, warmed me, fed me, and loved me. Where is she—that mother? If I have been deserted, who has deserted me? I cannot hide from myself that someone bore me, loving me. Who was that someone? Again "God"? (63)

What seems typical of *A Confession* about both passages is that Tolstoy tries *not* to set up his estranging metaphors as literature, as a device, but rather to present everything he writes as the naked postliterary truth. He seems to be pleading with us to understand that, to the extent that the obvious literary devices in the passages—the stupid and spiteful joke, the spiteful joker in whom he does not believe, even the summit of his life (which modulates into an actual place to stand), the arch-fool, the fledgling on its back in the grass—*are* literary devices, they are not *current* literary devices, not tricks he is playing in the present (late 1870s) to pull the wool over the reader's eyes. Rather, they are past devices, past images and ideas that occurred to him back in the throes of his crisis, before his conversion, back when he was still a novelist dedicated to illusionary effects, effects whose memory images he is now presenting as truthfully, sincerely, and straightforwardly as he possibly can.

He is at some pains from this point in his life onwards to set up a tidy binary between the lying novelist he was before his conversion and the humble truthteller he has become since. Still, not much has changed in him, as is evident from the end of *A Confession,* written in 1882 and appended to the book just before publication. He tells of a recent dream in which he is first lying in bed, half slipping off, and then begins to discover that he is hanging at an unimaginable height over a terrifying abyss: "And I felt that from fear I was losing my last supports, and that my back was slowly slipping lower and lower. Another moment and I should drop off" (82). And now we recognize the story: it's an oneiric recurrence of the "Eastern fable" he told back in chapter 4 (20–21), about a traveler who, chased by a wild beast on a vast plain, climbs down a deep well to escape and finds nothing to support himself but a tiny twig; at the bottom of the well, he spies a dragon, maw gaping. As he dangles from that twig, slipping toward the dragon but afraid to climb for fear of the beast above him, two mice nibble at the twig, and his only consolation is two drops of honey on one of the twig's leaves. In the earlier chapter, Tolstoy worked that fable into a powerful parable of his sense of his situation at the time: the two drops of honey, for example, came to represent his family and his writing. Like a good novelist, he is returning to one of the most powerful metaphors of his story so far and reframing it: "And then it occurred to me that this cannot be real. It is a dream. Wake up! I try to arouse myself but cannot do so. What am I to do? What am I to do? I ask myself, and look upwards" (82–83). And of course what he sees above him this time is no enraged wild beast but God, who is supporting him by a sling and an unsupported but nonetheless stable pillar, and he wakes up. End of book. God has miraculously been transformed from a beast on a plain into a voice in the sky saying, "See that you remember."

Of course, it's also a *dream,* from which he wakes up, like Anna Karenina on the morning of her death. And the dream returns him, in the midst of his supposed contentment as an honorary peasant believer in a dereligionized God, to the terror and despair he felt for all those years leading up to his conversion. He is, in other words, still feeling not only the same hopelessness from which God has supposedly saved him, but the same estrangement from what he desperately wants to believe are "normal" (truthful, pedestrian, peasantlike) modes of perception. He still can't help but see everything in its aspect of the strange. And he still can't help but frame his straightforward story—masterfully, in fact—with parables and dreams.

Estrangement From

Estrangement is everywhere present in *A Confession,* on the verbal surface of the work as well as in its metaphors. Some form of the word *strange*—*strannyi* "strange", *stranno* "strangely", *strannost'* "strangeness"—appears twelve times in the book; thirteen if you count the *stranniki,* literally "strangers," the pilgrims or wandering saints he mentions in chapter 10 who renounced all property and, begging for food and lodging, traveled from monastery to monastery in quest of an ideal society. (Tolstoy himself longed to become one of these *stranniki,* and in a sense his dream came true in the last days of his life, when he set off wandering at the age of 82 and died at a railway station.) One of Tolstoy's recurring refrains throughout the book is *kak ni stranno* "how [is it] not strange," which Aylmer Maude renders "strange as it now seems" or "strange as it was":

> Strange, incredibly incomprehensible as it now seems to me that I could, while reasoning about life, overlook the whole life of mankind that surrounded me on all sides; that I could to such a degree blunder so absurdly as to think that my life, and Solomon's and Schopenhauer's, is the real, normal life, and that the life of the milliards is a circumstance undeserving of attention—strange as this now is to me, I see that so it was. (*Ispoved',* 32; *Confession,* 45–46)

> And strange as much of what entered into the faith of these people was to me, I accepted everything, and attended the services, knelt morning and evening in prayer, fasted, and prepared to receive the Eucharist: and at first my reason did not resist anything. (*Ispoved',* 48, *Confession,* 67)

Another is that it seemed strange then but now makes perfect sense:

> It was terribly strange, but is now quite comprehensible. (*Ispoved',* 7; *Confession,* 11)

> I continued to fulfil the rites of the Church and still believed that the doctrine I was following contained the truth, when something happened to me which I now understand but which then seemed strange. (*Ispoved',* 52; *Confession,* 73)

Tolstoy also uses the Russian words for *alien* (*chuzhoy, chuzhdyi*) several times, and Maude translates one of them with *strange:*

As long as I was not living my own life but was borne on the waves of some other life [*chuzhaya zhizn'* "alien life"]—as long as I believed that life had a meaning, though one I could not express—the reflection of life in poetry and art of all kinds afforded me pleasure: it was pleasant to look at life in the mirror of art. (*Ispoved'*, 15; *Confession*, 22)

But though I made all possible concessions, and avoided all disputes, I could not accept the faith of these people [educated Christians]. I saw that what they gave out as their faith did not explain the meaning of life but obscured it, and that they themselves affirm[ed?] their belief not to answer that question of life which brought me to faith, but for some other aims alien to me [*chuzhdikh mne tseley*]. (*Ispoved'*, 38; *Confession*, 54)

I say that that search for God was not reasoning, but a feeling, because that search proceeded not from the course of my thoughts—it was even directly contrary to them—but proceeded from the heart. It was a feeling of fear, orphanage, isolation in a strange land [*chuvstvo strakha, sirotlivosti, odino-chestva sredi vsevo chuzhogo*, literally, "in the midst of everything alien"], and a hope of help from someone. (*Ispoved'*, 43–44; *Confession*, 62)

What one expects from a conversion narrative couched in terms of the strange-and-alien and the homey-and-familiar, of course, is a radical *conversion* from one to the other: my preconversion life seemed familiar back then but now, from across the critical divide of my spiritual crisis and conversion, seems strange; what seemed impossibly strange and alien before I found God now feels familiar, like home. I was estranged and alienated then; I am home now, surrounded by my own, my family and everything familiar. But this is precisely what Tolstoy cannot give us. The feeling of estrangement and alienation besets him at every stage of his life, as a child, as a young unmarried and debauched man, as a middle-aged married man, during his long spiritual crisis and the several years of his conversion, and for the remaining decades of his life, till he runs away from home at 82 and dies of pneumonia at a random railway station. What specifically besets him at every juncture is the experience of the strange-becoming-familiar and the familiar-becoming-strange, the abrupt and disorienting bidirectional transvaluation of (de)familiarization, a shifting feeling of estrangement as becoming-familiar in its becoming-strangeness and of familiarity as becoming-strange in its becoming-familiarity.[2]

To him the fact that he did not find his youthful way of life strange is strange. The intensification of his estrangement at the onset of his midlife crisis is strange: "So I lived; but five years ago something very strange began to happen to me. At first I experienced moments of perplexity and arrest of life, and though I did not know what to do or how to live; and I felt lost and became dejected. But this passed and I went on living as before" (15). To the extent that we can call his conversion a conversion and isolate a single moment at which it occurred, that moment too is strange: "And strange to say the strength of life which returned to me was not new, but quite old—the same that had borne me along in my earliest days" (65). His love for the peasants is strange: "the strange physical affection I have for the real laboring people" (46). And his postconversion life, which he works hard to depict as happy and healthy and balanced and familiar, bringing him a sense of rightness that he has never experienced before, is also estranging: "But this argument, justifying in my eyes the queerness [*strannost*] of much on the ritual side of religion, did not suffice to allow me in the one great affair of life—religion—to do things which seemed to me questionable. With all my soul I wished to be in a position to mingle with the people, fulfilling the ritual side of their religion; but I could not do it. I felt that I should lie to myself and mock at what was sacred to me, were I to do so" (*Ispoved'*, 49; *Confession*, 69).

Tolstoy's estrangement is never just one thing, one subjective take on the world, one psychological state. It is constantly in motion across the liminal distance between self and other, own and alien, here and there, inner and outer, past and present. Things become strange to him when other people find his behavior strange, or when he finds their behavior strange, or when he finds it strange that no one finds his or someone else's behavior strange. Estrangement is a hollowing out of the feeling of the fullness of life, a leakage outward of all joy and peace and acceptance, but it is also a source of control, an advantage, an edge. Because he is the Martian who cannot fit in with human society, he feels bereft but also superior, isolated but also in command; his alienation from community certainly gives him an edge as a writer, as he finds it the most natural thing in the world to depict the vast complexity of human life—including the very naturalness of this feeling for him—in its aspect of the strange. His so-called conversion is a conscious decision to stop living through these arrogant estranging contradictions, to become a rough uneducated unthinking peasant believer with all the overdetermined Rousseauistic simplicity that "peasant" signifies for him—but he can't do it. His will is not sufficient to the task. The peasants' superstitions and rituals seem absurd to him, alien, strange; he knows he, too, is strange to them, in his peasant garb and his proud humility, his pretend sincerity.

Tolstoy's Depersonalization

All this suggests that estrangement for Tolstoy, so far from being a mere literary device that he used to great effect in his fiction, was a debilitating psychological disorder—what the psychiatric community refers to as *depersonalization*. But before we begin to psychoanalyze Tolstoy, let's first review the signal events in his life.

Tolstoy's Life

Tolstoy's mother, Mariya Nikolayevna Tolstaya, née Princess Volkonskaya, whose own mother died when she was a toddler, died shortly after giving birth to Lev's baby sister when he was eighteen months old. Apparently sensing that her end was near, she asked that her children be brought to her; little Lev, who had recently been weaned from his mother's breast, was terrified at the sight of his mother and ran screaming from her. His father Nikolay Il'yich Tolstoy died of pulmonary tuberculosis when Lev was nine, and the children were sent to live with their aunt in Kazan'; Tolstoy's bouts with depression began shortly after. As he grew into adulthood, he devised radical Franklinesque "improvement" regimens and then castigated himself furiously when he was unable to meet his own requirements. Sexuality was particularly fraught with guilt and self-recrimination—a pattern that was to continue until his early seventies, when his sex drive finally diminished. Bored and depressed in law school, he flunked out, then managed to stave off depression by joining the army and fighting in Chechnya; it returned when he was discharged.

In his mid-thirties he married 18-year-old Sof'ya Andreyevna Behrs, and for ten years the joys of married life and fatherhood—five children between 1863 and 1871—sustained him, although the children's increasing monopolization of their mother's time and energy began to threaten his precarious peace of mind. With Sof'ya's help, he worked on *War and Peace,* which exhilarated him at first but soon began to exhaust him. Upon finishing the novel in 1869, he set out on a journey to the remote province of Penza to buy some property, but en route he underwent an anxiety crisis of devastating proportions, what has come to be called the Arzamas horror (*arzamassky uzhas*)—and no matter what he did, the horror would not leave him, even after his return home. Over a two-year period beginning shortly after his return, three of his children and several other close relatives died. Desperate and suicidal, he decided to write another big novel and began *Anna Karenina,* which he worked on from 1872 to 1879. Depression plagued him throughout the rather sporadic writing of the novel, and when it was finished his greatest spiritual crisis yet began. He decided to give up literary creation, which he declared not only useless but actively harmful. The "conversion" he underwent at this time, recorded in *A Confession,* seemed to cure his suicidal tendencies but did not give him peace of mind; he became rigid, dogmatic, controlling, even more violently disgusted with sexuality and women (but no less libidinous) than he had been before, and still depressed. He longed to become a true ascetic and was encouraged in this in later life by his disciple Vladimir Grigoryevich Chertkov, whose manipulative war for control of the master's legacy against an increasingly hysterical and suicidal (and equally manipulative) Sof'ya plagued Tolstoy's last years of life.

Finally at the age of 82, in 1910, deciding he could not stand the uproar of his household any longer, Tolstoy took off with his Slovak doctor and fled to the convent where his sister Mariya was cloistered. There he heard that his wife had attempted to commit suicide shortly after he left and (this was Chertkov's lie) that Sof'ya knew where he was and was coming to collect him. Torn between guilt and a desire not to hurt his wife further and a fear that she would find him, he and his retinue boarded a train at random. On the train his temperature started climbing, so his Slovak doctor insisted that they get off at the tiny station of Astapovo, where, a few days later, in the midst of a media circus, he died of pneumonia.

Psychoanalysis

So what was wrong with him?

Let me begin by registering a protest against the approach I am taking in this chapter. In "Tolstoy's Aesthetics" Caryl Emerson lodges an animus against psychoanalytical readings of Tolstoy, beginning with that offered by William James while Tolstoy was still alive and continuing on through books like Daniel Rancour-Laferriere's *Tolstoy on the Couch* (1998) and articles like Annie Anargyros-Klinger's "The Thread of Depression Throughout the Life and Works of Leo Tolstoy" (2002). "As provocative as these studies can be," Emerson writes, "the feeling remains that it is not for us to interrogate and reduce to system the inexhaustible creative energy of Leo Tolstoy.[3] What is seemly to investigate, in my view, is how Tolstoy strove to stimulate a sense of artistic productivity and receptivity in others" (249). I agree that if a psychoanalytical reading of Tolstoy were no more than the "reduction to system" of his creativity, it would indeed be meretricious. What I want to argue, however, is that the many contradictions in Tolstoy's late religious and aesthetic works make little sense without an analysis of his psychological disorder—what Richard Gustafson calls the "stranger" in him, his emotional isolation from other people.

Another way of charting the differences between Emerson's approach and mine is that we track different lines of influence from Tolstoy into twentieth-century thought and to that end highlight different aspects of *What is Art?* Emerson reads him as anticipating the humanistic psychologies of Erich Fromm and Abraham Maslow, and so seeks to normalize Tolstoy, to give pride of place to his idealized theory of the humanistic exchange of feelings between artist and audience—what Rimvydas Šilbajoris calls the ways in which for Tolstoy "art is not something that *is* but something that *happens* between the artist and his audience" (18; see also Barran 9–12). Since I want here to read him as anticipating the modernist estrangement theories of Viktor Shklovsky and Bertolt Brecht, I seek instead to denormalize him, to explore the ways in which his often contradictory idealization of the utopian exchange of feelings grows out of his inability to experience that exchange himself and thus out of his need to imagine it by "remote control," as it were, by guessing at its collectivized emotional contours intellectually.

So let us begin with William James, who in *The Varieties of Religious Experience* calls Tolstoy's disorder "religious melancholy":

> Religious melancholy must be cast in a more melting mood. Tolstoy has left us, in his book called My Confession, a wonderful account of the attack of melancholy which led him to his own religious conclusions. The latter in some respects are peculiar; but the melancholy presents two characters which make it a typical document for our present purpose. First it is a well-marked case of anhedonia, of passive loss of appetite for all life's values; and second, it shows how the altered and estranged aspect which the world assumed in consequence of this stimulated Tolstoy's intellect to a gnawing, carking questioning and effort for philosophic relief. (149)

Building on James, the French Freudian psychoanalyst Annie Anargyros-Klinger offers a diagnosis of melancholic depression tending toward depersonalization, probably triggered first by the traumatic scene at Tolstoy's mother's deathbed (compounded by the fact that he had just been weaned from her breast). "For Karl Abraham," Anargyros-Klinger writes, "'the psychic life of the melancholic always revolves around their mother,'" and she situates Tolstoy's intense misogyny and loathing of sex in his relationship with the maternal imago, "a source of arousal and anxiety" that "instilled in him a femininity that threatened his integrity" (412). This is also the source of his moral masochism, "the superego mercilessly judging the ego identified with the object: his mother" (412). Reading the scene in *Anna Karenina* where Vronsky, having seduced Anna, entertains fantasies of murder—"There was something awful and revolting at the memory of what had been bought at this fearful price of shame. But in spite of all the murderer's horror before the body of his victim, he must hack it to pieces, hide the body, must use what he had gained by his murder" (quoted in Anargyros-Klinger, 410)—she suggests that "Tolstoy may have remained fixated at a primitive oral stage with its succession of cannibalistic fantasies that were extremely alarming in terms of their destructive taking over of the object. The presence in him of the dead object, faecalised, formed a psychic pole of attraction and fascination due to the libidinal stimulation linked to the original trauma. Thus the eroticized image of his mother and the fantasy of murder were linked into a single obsession" (412). Falling in love with Sof'ya "provided a kind of narcissistic refueling" (410) that enabled him to sublimate his contradictory urges through writing, "transforming a part of his sexual libido into narcissistic libido" (414), which "formed an element of internal cohesion and stability for the ego" (414).

But writing proved to be psychically dangerous for him; he was insufficiently protected against the revelations of his own inner impulses opened by the telling of fictitious stories, rendering the sublimation unstable: "A destructive flood of impulses unacceptable to the ego caused a fear of loss of the self. He was thus compelled toward defence mechanisms of a psychotic nature—splitting and projection—which were not able to protect him from the fear of death and self-accusations and never managed to relieve his guilt" (411). We know that Tolstoy's characters were modeled so closely on actual people he knew that his family and friends would discuss the parallels. So, in terms of Tolstoy's own infection theory, we might suggest that when he wrote, an overwhelming flood of other people's feelings was channeled (perverse?-) infectiously through his body into his characters and that this flooding of shared feeling caused a fear of loss of the self. According to Anargyros-Klinger, then, he defended against this threat of psychosis by "converting," not just to ascetic Christianity (no sex) but to an antiliterary moralism (no writing fiction):

> For a time, sublimation through writing acted on the partial drives, inhibited their aim, displaced and desexualized, relieving the feeling of a haunting and dreadful guilt.

... The fantasies that inspired him retain the marks of primary processes that will be perceived by the reader, contributing to the emotion aroused through reading.

But Tolstoy had not yet managed to establish a sufficiently protective distance through his writing. He sometimes felt threatened within by what emerged from him in certain moments of inspiration.

It is possible that the prospect of this unconscious fantasy breaking into the ego, brought about by writing, added to the "unspeakable anxieties" that appeared after writing *War and Peace* and contributed to drying up Tolstoy's creativity, which was perceived as a vital danger, a threat to the ego. Numerous passages in Tolstoy's two major novels reveal in him a disposition towards a state of depersonalisation that encouraged the emergence of images and thoughts from the preconscious, the thinly veiled expression of forbidden desires. At the time when the depression manifested itself, he had to block the path of these forbidden desires at all costs. And in order to do this he had to give up writing. (416–17)

Depersonalization

Depersonalization has been a recognized medical condition since Ludovic Dugas identified it in 1898 and is now considered the third most common psychiatric symptom, affecting at least 70 percent of the population at some point. It has also been called the "Alice in Wonderland" disease and compared philosophically to existentialism, Buddhism, and positivist science, but there is little that is wonderful, philosophical, religious, or scientific about it. It is characterized by a pervasive sense of strangeness, foreignness, unreality, not-rightness—the sense not only that the sufferer has just passed over into a strange world but that the sufferer him- or herself is strange, estranged from self, from thought, from feeling. It takes different forms: sometimes it dissolves into a feeling of numbness, even of nothingness, as if the sufferer were emotionally dead; other times, as in Tolstoy's crises of the 1870s, it explodes into a full-blown kaleidoscopic panic attack, akin in its disorientations to schizophrenia. As Vadim Rudnev describes the disorder, "From the physiological point of view, depersonalization most often appears as the brain's answer to a sharp emotional shock by way of an increased secretion of endorphins, which anesthetize consciousness. From the point of view of the behavioral strategy of consciousness, depersonalization appears as a powerful defense against stress. The *locus classicus* of depersonalization is when after the sudden loss of a loved one the person seems to become 'petrified,' to lose all affect" (55; all translations from Rudnev's Russian are my own). Noting that Levi-Strauss called myth a mechanism for the destruction of all oppositions, especially that between life and death, Rudnev adds that "it is clear why depersonalization is not just a symptom of illness but a powerful defense against reality, an anesthesia, albeit a doleful one. The sufferer from depersonalization falls into the special world of myth, among the basic characteristics of which is the absence of logical binary thought ('it's all the same to me'). Of course this is a special 'lackluster world' " (56–57). Other psychoanalytical terms for this state include desomatization (Krystal), somatic or somatoform dissociation (Scaer, 104; Nijenhuis), and derealization (Mollon). As Allan Schore summarizes the affect-neurological research,

> Kohut's "depleted" self characterizes an organismic state of dysregulated parasympathetic hypoarousal, dissociation, and excessive energy conservation, subjectively experienced as an implosion of the self, wherein there is not enough energy in the brain/mind/body system to form the interconnections responsible for coherence. This would be clinically manifest as an anaclitic depression that accompanies a state of conservation-withdrawal marked by high levels of dissociation (see Weinberg 2000, on right-hemisphere deficiency and suicide). In this condition there is a simultaneous loss of both modes of self-regulation, interactive regulation and autoregulation. The former would be subjectively experienced as a lingering state of intense hopelessness, the latter as helplessness. (128)

"Interactive regulation" is what I am calling ideosomatic regulation; its failure in depersonalization or desomatization leads to "empathy disorders, the limited capacity to perceive the emotional states of others. An inability to read subtle facial expressions leads to a misattribution of emotional states and a misinterpretation of the intentions of others" (Schore, 134–35).

Rudnev suggests that depersonalization is the modern disorder par excellence. For example, he asks, what is it about Griboyedov's 1824 drama *Woe From Wit,* still today the second most popular play on the Russian stage (after Gogol's *The Government Inspector*), that makes us not want to consider it a "nineteenth-century Russian classic"? "Because," he says, "it is structured according to the classical canon. And there is no depersonalization in that canon. Chatsky is full of affect. The second great work of 19th-century Russian literature, Pushkin's *Eugene Onegin,* is by its very essence a novel about depersonalization" (57; see also Siebers). Onegin is so depersonalized that he cannot respond to Tat'yana's effusive love letter, and then for no obvious reason he insults and then kills his friend Lensky in a duel, following which "a more anesthetizing alienation becomes necessary for Tat'yana for her to survive the loss of Onegin and live through the hated role as the hostess of a fashionable salon" (57).

Rudnev's analysis of Tolstoy's depersonalization centers around his determination to destroy convention through estrangement: "To the extent that Tolstoy was a Rousseauist, depersonalization, the destruction of conventions (the 'social contract'), was a good thing for him. This is why in his novels a character who is too fastidious about conventions is doomed" (60). A few paragraphs earlier he argues that "the paradox of Tolstoyan depersonalization consists in the consciousness ceasing to understand and accept conventions," because "depersonalized consciousness does not accept the insincerity of small talk, which to it is somehow mechanical, meaningless" (59). In response, it seeks to lay waste to all conventionality by estranging it—by doing precisely what Carlo Ginzburg says Tolstoy learned from Marcus Aurelius and the French Enlightenment, what Viktor Shklovsky isolates as the supreme modernist gesture, laying bare the device (*obnazhenie priyoma*). For Rudnev the estranging quest of a depersonalized writer like Tolstoy is like externalizing a consciousness that has "unlearned the language of opera, and so believes that it is not an art as conventionally defined but reality, a kind of absurd, half-nonsensical reality. (It was in precisely this mode—aggressively depersonalized—that the later Tolstoy began to concern himself with art: as with something mendacious, absurd, nonsensical)" (58).[4]

Following this logic, Rudnev differs radically from Anargyros-Klinger on Tolstoy's disgust at sex, which was, he says, horrific for Tolstoy specifically "in its passage beyond the semiotic, beyond convention" (60). Rudnev says no more about it than this, but he is apparently implying here that regardless of how much Tolstoy hated the meaningless mechanisms of conventional sign systems, he was trapped in them, and even while devastating them could not imagine a moving beyond them. Estrangement thus became for him a depersonalizing strategy for making the semiotic livable, for reducing it to an "absurd, half-nonsensical reality" that he could survive in psychologically, a "lackluster world" of grotesquely twisted myth that more or less matched his depersonalized sense of the world. What Tolstoy sees beyond this depersonalized semiotic, Rudnev suggests, "is like the other side [*oborotnaya storona*] of language: the peasant muttering meaningless French words over the iron" (60). Rudnev is referring, of course, to the recurring nightmare from which Anna Karenina wakes on the morning that she hurls herself under the train, the old peasant pointing both ahead to the circumstances of her death (the couple speaking French on the train, the peasant working on the track that Anna sees just before dying) and back to her "two husbands," the two Alekseys, Karenin and Vronsky, the "something" he is indifferently doing over her with iron vaguely sexual and vaguely horrible:

> In the morning a terrible nightmare, which had come to her several times even before her union with Vronsky, repeated itself and woke her. An old man with a tangled beard was leaning over some iron and doing something, while muttering senseless words in French [*nagnuvshis' nad zhelezom, prigovarivaya bessmyslennye frantsuzskie slova*]; and as always in that nightmare (this was what made it terrible) she felt this peasant was paying no attention her but was doing something dreadful to her with the iron [*delaet eto kakoe-to strashnoe delo v zheleze nad neyu*, lit. "in iron over her"]. (Russian, 19:332, English, 680)

Rudnev's allusion to this nightmare as an exemplar of the sexual transsemiotic in Tolstoy would seem to put pressure on the reader not to read this dream psychoanalytically, certainly not to impose a single univocal pop-Freudian interpretation on it—not to explain the iron, say, as the phallus. Just as the old man's words are French but meaningless, so too is the iron horrifically sexual but ultimately inexplicable, indeterminable, mysterious. The Freudian *Traumdeutung* is specifically an attempt to push the boundary of the semiotic out far enough to encompass dreams like this, to read the oneiric as the semiotic, the iron as a sign of the phallus, or, as for Thomas Barran, as a sign of Karenin's rigidity—and all this is for Rudnev's Tolstoy impossible, because as he approaches the sexual his semiotic imagination shuts down.

Abjection

This is as far as Rudnev will take us with Tolstoy. Earlier in his essay, however, before he gets to Tolstoy, he defines depersonalization by explicit reference to Lacan's Other—"In Lacan's terms, in depersonalization the voice of the Other is extinguished" (55)—and Lacanian theory may take us a few more steps with Tolstoy's depersonalization. If we read Rudnev's diagnosis of Tolstoy's horror at the transsemiotic in terms of the Lacanian distinction between the symbolic and the real, the real as the horrific transsymbolic, we might read the iron in Anna's dream not as the phallus but as *das Ding*, the Kantian Thing as it "appears" in the real, "the beyond-of-the-signified," the "reality that commands and regulates" (*Ethics*, 54, 55): "If the Thing were not fundamentally veiled, we wouldn't be in the kind of relationship to it that obliges us, as the whole of psychic life is obliged, to encircle it or bypass it in order to conceive it" (118). Or, as Julia Kristeva theorizes this process in *Powers of Horror,* it is not so much that the voice of the Other is *extinguished* as that it is *replaced:* that the Other has created for itself an alter ego, a surrogate source of jouissance (somatic pleasure) that converts jouissance into a violent and painful and shattered passion and dislodges the Other's "grip on the three apices of the triangle where subjective heterogeneity resides," and so—here is where we return to Rudnev read through Lacan—"jettisons the object into an abominable real, inaccessible except through jouissance" (9).

The three apices of the triangle are from Lacan's Schema L, with the subject (the persona of the analysand) at top left, his or her objects (other people and things) at top right, and his or her idealized ego or ego-ideal at bottom left. This triangle is "where subjective heterogeneity resides" in the sense that it is where the subject creates a world, with a self or I or ego in heterogeneous relation to other people and things. It is the Other, the jouissant voice of the unconscious, or what I would call the channel of ideosomatic regulation, that guides and stabilizes this world-construction, gives it richness and fullness and meaningful structure. Unseated by a usurper, supplanted by a surrogate, the Other loses its power to stabilize or regulate world-construction, so that, as Kristeva says, the subjective heterogeneous world-creating triangle becomes "a 'structure' that is skewed, a topology of catastrophe" (9). The surrogate Other tries to organize world-construction, but without access to collective somatic regulation it is like the sorcerer's apprentice, setting processes in motion that are intended to bring order but instead infect order-construction with chaos, with randomness, and so tend to disrupt and disturb and undermine beyond its control. This alter ego speaks with the voice of the Law, or Morality, or Religion, of Prohibition, of Condemnation, thus occupying the place of the superego, but it sows pain and repugnance, or what Kristeva calls the "abject":

> It follows that jouissance alone causes the abject to exist as such. One does not know it, one does not desire it, one joys in it [*on en jouit*]. Violently and painfully. A passion. And, as in jouissance where the object of desire, known as object *a* [other people and things], bursts with the shattered mirror where the ego gives up its image in order to contemplate itself in the Other, there is nothing either objective or objectal in the abject. It is simply a frontier, a repulsive gift that the Other, having become *alter ego,* drops so that "I" does not disappear in it but finds, in that sublime alienation, a forfeited existence. Hence a jouissance in which the subject is swallowed up but in

which the Other, in return, keeps the subject from foundering by making it repugnant. (9)

Kristeva does not analyze Tolstoy, but her reading of "the one by whom the abject exists" (8) fits Tolstoy perfectly. In her terms, what is horrific about sex for this kind of sufferer is not just that it lies beyond the semiotic, but that it is abject, a repulsive frontier between the symbolic and the real that *structures* the self as repugnant, gives the subject a "sublime alienation" and a "forfeited existence." Hence Tolstoy's intense oscillation, all his life, across the frontier of sex, his moralistic repudiations of sex and his guilt-ridden indulgence in it, his need for both the painfully jouissant abjection of sex and the pleasurably jouissant rejection of sex. Abjection, as Kristeva writes, "takes on the form of the *exclusion* of a substance (nutritive or linked to sexuality), the execution of which coincides with the sacred since it sets it up" (17). What Tolstoy needs, in Kristeva's terms, is the abject subjectification that sex indulged-and-excluded can yield him *as frontier.* Martine de Courcel is on the right track in arguing that "Tolstoy condemns music because he is musical and sensuality because he is sensual" (205), but it is more complex than that. He is addicted neither to sensuality nor to asceticism but to the fulcrum on which sex tips in the balance, the moment of abject decision between sex and its exclusion that can torque his whole life into some kind of simulacrum of coherence.[5]

Indeed, Kristeva famously redefines the semiotic as preceding and in some sense opposing the symbolic, but also always underpinning it and charging it with maternal affect. For Kristeva the semiotic is an anarchistic emotional force arising in the infant before what Freud calls the Oedipus complex and what Lacan reformulates as the symbolic. Where the symbolic is organized around the Name-of-the-Father, Kristeva's semiotic is generated out of the Desire-of-the-Mother; a simple way of distinguishing the two would be to say that the semiotic is a feminine libidinal system and the symbolic is a masculine libidinal system. Whereas the symbolic is generated out of secondary repression, the semiotic is generated out of primary repression, that obscured event-horizon where "consciousness has not assumed its rights, and transformed into signifiers those fluid demarcations of yet unstable territories where an 'I' that is taking shape is ceaselessly straying. We are no longer within the sphere of the unconscious but at the limit of primal repression that, nevertheless, has discovered an intrinsically corporeal and already signifying brand, symptom, and sign: repugnance, disgust, abjection" (11). In the Oedipal regime that Kristeva sustains but supplements, the symbolic is thus the father's attempt to impose order on the semiotic, to structure the world coherently, but even in normals the semiotic survives this regime, saturates it with the repressed body of the mother, and leaks out through its seams in the various behavioral and verbal expressions of dream, madness, holiness, and art.

In this sense Tolstoy's campaign against "perverse" art, art that celebrates sexual pleasure, would be a campaign against the semiotic in art, the abject, the return of the (primal) repressed, and his rejection of the abject in art is so intense, so disturbingly saturated with repugnance, because its terrifying lure is so strong in him. And its lure is strong because his world is stabilized not by the Other but by its legalistic surrogate, which makes repugnance his only bastion against psychosis, his only fragile guarantor of identity. Or, as Kristeva writes of this sort of subject, in him

> abjection is elaborated through a failure to recognize its kin; nothing is familiar, not even the shadow of a memory. I imagine a child who has swallowed up his parents too soon, who frightens himself on that account, "all by himself," and, to save himself, rejects and throws up everything that is given to him—all gifts, all objects. He has, he could have, a sense of the abject. Even before things for him *are*—hence before they are signifiable—he drives them out, dominated by drive as he is, and constitutes his own territory, edged by the abject. A sacred configuration. Fear cements his compound, conjoined to another world, thrown up, driven out, forfeited. What he has swallowed up instead of maternal love is an emptiness, or rather a maternal hatred without a word for the words of the father; that is what he tries to cleanse himself of, tirelessly. (5–6)

Not only does Tolstoy want to give away all his money, all his property, the rights to all his books, his whole family—and is just barely restrained from doing so, all his adult life, by his wife, and in a sense finally succeeds in the days before his death—he also wants to give away his literary gifts, his brilliance as a novelist, because his ability to create psychologically realistic characters with their disturbing impulses and dreams opens the semiotic gates within him, channels the estranging abject (where "nothing is familiar") into the open. The battle between Chertkov and Sof'ya over his soul, the battle that ultimately drives Tolstoy out into the world and to his death at a random train station, is thus essentially a battle over whether the best way to *save* his soul is to reject everything, give up everything (Chertkov, the demanding symbolic father), or to keep everything, to learn to live with everything (Sof'ya, the demanding semiotic mother). In some sense, we might speculate that Tolstoy unconsciously seeks out an external mother and father to replace the ones he lost or "swallowed" in childhood, to help him deal with his fear, to help him maintain the fearful equilibrium he has somehow managed to construct between equally terrifying extremes—to help him "remain, discomfited, at the dump for non-objects that are always forfeited, from which, on the contrary, fortified by abjection, he tries to extricate himself. For he is not mad, he through whom the abject exists. Out of the daze that has petrified him before the untouchable, impossible, absent body of the mother, a daze that has cut off his impulses from their objects, that is, from their representations, out of such daze he causes, along with loathing, one word to crop up—fear" (6). This "daze that has cut off his impulses from their objects, that is, from their representations," is what Anargyros-Klinger and Rudnev call Tolstoy's depersonalization. Freud's Kantian theory of the ego and its objects as *representations,* as word-presentations and thing-presentations, as psychosocial constructs, will be useful again when we get to Shklovsky's theory of "the experience of the making of a thing" in chapter 3, and are faced with the vulgar-materialist (Second-International) rejection of that theory as a solipsistic rejection of "the real world," or of what Georg Lukács in *History and Class Consciousness,* coming out of Kant and Fichte and Hegel (see Rockmore), called "phantom objectivity."

So Kristeva might sum up Tolstoy's psychic regime:

> The one by whom the abject exists is thus a *deject* who places (himself), *separates* (himself), situates (himself), and therefore *strays* instead of getting his bearings, desiring, belonging, or refusing . . . A deviser of territories, languages, works, the *deject* never stops demarcating his universe whose fluid confines—for they are constituted of a non-object, the abject—constantly question his solidity and impel him to start afresh. A tireless builder, the deject is in short a *stray.* He is on a journey, during the night, the end of which keeps receding. He has a sense of the danger, of the loss that the pseudo-object attracting him represents for him, but he cannot help taking the risk at the very moment he sets himself apart. And the more he strays, the more he is saved . . . For it is out of such straying on excluded ground that he draws his jouissance. The abject from which he does not cease separating is for him, in short, a *land of oblivion* that is constantly remembered. Once upon blotted-out time, the abject must have been a magnetized pole of covetousness. But the ashes of oblivion now serve as a screen and reflect aversion, repugnance. The clean and proper (in the sense of incorporated and incorporable) becomes filthy, the sought-after turns into the banished, fascination into shame. (8)

The image of Tolstoy as a stray is particularly poignant in the story of his death, his straying from home and then, when he arrives at his sister's convent and hears that his wife knows where he is and is coming after him, his straying onto a random train, where he strays from life. But he also strays from his literary talent to the religious rigidity of his last thirty years, and from the rigidity of his ascetic ban on sex into assignations with peasant women, his wife, and his own hand: "For it is out of such straying on excluded ground that he draws his jouissance," both the painful jouissance of sex and the pleasurable jouissance of the exclusion of sex.[6]

What I find most useful in that passage for a discussion of Tolstoy, however, is the last line, in which the clean and proper becomes filthy. For what is Tolstoy's infection theory but an imaging of the cure in terms of the disease? The somatic transfer of joy and spiritual union is an impossibly *good* thing for Tolstoy, a pure and wonderful thing, the only source of hope in a filthy, shameful, disgusting world—and he earns himself a place in the history of aesthetics by imagining it as *infection,* as abscess, as pus, as decay. But then for Kristeva all art purifies the abject cathartically by repeating it, by effecting a "mimesis of passions" (28): "The abject, mimed through sound and meaning, is *repeated.* Getting rid of it is out of the question—the final Platonic lesson has been understood, one does not get rid of the impure; one can, however, bring it into being a second time, and differently from the original impurity. It is a repetition through rhythm and song, therefore through what is not yet, or no longer is 'meaning,' but arranges, defers, differentiates and organizes, harmonizes pathos, bile, warmth, and enthusiasm" (28).

This is Kristeva's summary of Aristotle's cathartic theory from the *Poetics,* of course, which on the face of it is a bad fit with Tolstoy's infection theory, founded as the latter is on Plato's idea of noncathartic mimesis, or what computer people these days call "garbage in, garbage out": if you imitate perversion, what comes out the other side of the imitation is the same perversion. If you imitate the disgusting, your readers will be disgusted. Abject in, abject out. By the same token, in order to spread joy and spiritual union, you have to imitate joy and spiritual union. Purity in, purity out. You can't expect to transform abjection into purity cathartically, through art. In an important sense, however, Tolstoy's subterranean task in *What Is Art?* is to transform his own abjection into purity cathartically through *theory,* to retheorize his own earthy disgust at what he takes to be perverted or abject art (which in fact turns out to be *all* art) as a deep spiritual belief in the existence and infectious power of pure art, to mystify his own inability to respond to the infectiousness of *real* art as a readiness to respond to the infectiousness of *ideal* art. Because Tolstoy himself can't respond with feelings of joy and spiritual union to existing art, *there must exist* a kind of art to which he would be able to respond in that idealized way; his own abject failure to date stands surety for his future success and for the emergence of a channel of artistic infection that would depend for its salvific effect on that success.

Tolstoy does not theorize artistic infection as cathartic, in other words, because his theorization itself rests on the mystified operation of catharsis, the idealized repetition of the abject that reorganizes disgust as joy, somatic isolation as spiritual union, felt impossibility as believed inevitability. In order to draw his own as well as his reader's attention away from the theoretical purification at work in his essay, Tolstoy convinces himself that the good art does actually exist and he has actually responded to it in the prescribed way: when he heard the peasant women singing and crying and banging their scythes as he returned from his lonely walk, he smiled, and felt a little better. And that must be it. That must be the infectious effect he is theorizing. He doesn't *know*, of course; he must guess, and often guesses in contradictory ways. He cannot possibly know because the true basis for his theory is the abject imagination of no more abjection, the depersonalized projection of repersonalization.

If Tolstoy's infection theory is overtly Platonic and only covertly Aristotelian, then, Shklovsky's estrangement theory is overtly Aristotelian, *repeating* or *miming* estrangement artistically in order to "purify" or rearrange it, and Brecht's ostensibly anti-Aristotelian estrangement theory is in fact Aristotelian to a higher degree, based on the use of cathartic effects to create impossible tensions in the audience that must be worked out intellectually.

Dialogical Group Regulation

It is well known that Julia Kristeva developed her early theories of the semiotic, the speaking subject-in-process, and intertextuality out of her engagement with the thought of Mikhail Bakhtin, especially his books on Rabelais and Dostoevsky. It was 1966, and Bakhtin had been "rediscovered" a few years earlier by a younger generation of Soviet scholars (and found, surprisingly, still alive), and like many others after her Kristeva found in Bakhtinian dialogism a powerful counterpressure to exert against the depersonalizing tendencies of structuralism and the structuralist version of Russian formalism.[7] For Kristeva Bakhtinian dialogism or polyphony issued into a kaleidoscopic conception of the speaking *subject,* who became multiple: if several subjects speak through every text, then the creative "subject-in-process" speaking or writing the text is a plural subject, a fragmentary collective, not an individual or an "identity" at all. By the same token, as readers or listeners of this sort of pluralized intertext, we must enter into the transsubjective plurality as well, must put ourselves into process as subjects in order to channel our own overlapping and fragmentary identities or voices into the engagement with the intertext, which in effect becomes part of us, or we of it: our voices mingle intertextually with those of the writers/speakers.

In Bakhtinian dialogism the ideological saturation of a language is the saturation of each individual's voice with the voices of everyone else who has used the language, with the *vocal* forces of collectivity: "The word is born in a dialogue as a living rejoinder within it; the word is shaped in dialogic interaction with an alien word that is already in the object. A word forms a concept of its own object in a dialogic way" (*Discourse,* 279). In other words, every word anyone ever speaks or writes is saturated not only with alien words but with the dialogues in which those alien words were uttered—the metaphor of "saturation" encouraging us to imagine other people's words as a solution in which other people's words are dissolved, "other people's words" and "one's own words" dissolved in "each word" as a new internally dialogized *mixture*— each voice as a compound solution of many voices. Ideological saturation, then, implies that voice is the liquid vehicle through which collective regulatory belief and value systems are iteratively disseminated through the bodies of individual members of a society, dialogically dissolved in the heteroglot speech of individual language users. Bakhtin's metalinguistics is normatively oriented toward the spoken word, the voiced word, the accented or tonalized word, the word as shaped by the body.

This transpersonal bodily impulse is what Kristeva maternalizes as the semiotic, the word as shaped by the dead or absent body of the mother, which resurfaces in the midst of the symbolic (which seeks to repress it) through rebellious or anarchistic accents and tonalizations and other prosodic features. Kristeva's concern, of course, was to open up in the totalizing patriarchal Oedipal system envisioned by Freud and Lacan a speaking channel for the repressed mother, or rather for the repressed pre-Oedipal and pre-symbolic mother-child bond that Lacan associated with the imaginary reflections of the mirror stage; hence the importance of imagining the semiotic as inherently rebellious or anarchistic, and most powerfully found in mystical visions, delirium, and experimental art.

Attractive as Kristeva's feminist/avant-garde version of Bakhtin is, however, it is narrow. Mothers, after all, aren't just repressed; they also wield enormous power, as and through the maternal introjects their children carry around in them—and who is not one of their children? Maternal voices aren't just rebellious or anarchistic impulses surfacing through the paternal prison bars of linguistic structure; they are also hard at work imposing on their children regulatory regimes of their own. Nor do fathers wield power through reason alone, through abstract linguistic and logical and other symbolic structures; they also channel power regimes through bodily accents and tonalizations, through the threat or pleading embodied in their voices, their facial expressions, their postures, and so on. And fathers too have their own subterranean semiotic rebellions, their own bodily/affective resistances to symbolic regimes. Nor, finally, are mothers and fathers the only authorities that regulate our behavior tonally. As children we are powerfully shaped by the tonalizations of our peers, and our peers' older brothers and sisters and parents and aunts and uncles. As adults we are powerfully shaped by the tonalizations of "public opinion" in thousands of different forms. Does it really make sense to reduce all this to a powerful father who rules through abstract law and a repressed mother whose only access to power must be underground and therefore subversive and deniable? Kristeva may be a *feminist* Freudian-Lacanian thinker, but she is still very much a Freudian-Lacanian thinker, always working either within or right around the confines of what Deleuze and Guattari call the Oedipal mommy-daddy-me—and this limits her.

The moment in Lacanian theory that transcends the mommy-daddy-me, in fact, is the Other, the jouissance of the Other, which, reading Lacan through Bakhtin, I take to be a transpersonal regulatory force functioning through and as embodied dialogue—not just as the other person's tonalized word in one's own retonalized word, but as the dialogical impulse to retonalize and thus to merge group tones and affects and bodies in speech and writing for jouissance and social regulation. Because the introjected voices of the Other come to us "intersubjectively" or dialogically, they always ground our knowing and telling in community, in relation. And because they come to us interdialogically, through a succession of iterative transportations from dialogue to dialogue—what Kenneth Burke calls "the *evolutionary* processes whereby a language is built from generation to generation by gradual accretion" (*Language,* 427)—they also ground our knowing and telling in a pleasurable social regulation, in a jouissant ideosomatics that harbors in its repressive speaking body the vestigial idiosomatic memory of peripheral or centrifugal utterances as well. This means that we are normatively regulated by the ideosomatic Other as group tonalizations, but as Kristeva reminds us, those very ideosomatic voices also coach us (sub rosa) in innovative and even emancipatory utterance, and can (and do) surreptitiously validate and perpetuate counterideosomatic resistances and rebellions.

Isolation from Group Regulation

But this *normative* regulation by the ideosomatic Other is precisely what Tolstoy either never felt at all or (more likely) experienced as so dangerous, so painful, so profoundly threatening to psychic stability that it had to be "excluded" or given up. Given his novels' deep insights into human behavior, it seems reasonable to speculate that he did have access to ideosomatic regulation—to what his big brother Nikolay taught him to call the "Brother Ants" in their childhood game (de Courcel, 14–15)—and channeled that access into and through his novels, the writing of which generated the jouissance that generated the abject and so undermined his precarious psychic regime, brought him to the brink of psychosis, so he gave it up, blocked it, blocked it at such a deep level of somatic functioning that he was not even aware that it was there. This would suggest that depersonalization for Tolstoy involved not so much a *depletion* of shared feeling as a *wall* against shared feeling—a wall that he thickened against the jouissance it occasionally let through.

If this was the case, it may explain the odd fact that, while the guiding dialogized jouissance of the Other is conspicuously missing from *A Confession, What Is Art?* a decade and a half later is grounded in the notion of somatic infection, the transfer of feelings from body to body. True, Tolstoy's infection theory has nothing of the complex dialogical-intertextual-jouissant architecture of shared feeling that Bakhtin, Lacan, and Kristeva theorize, but clearly he does imagine the *possibility* of somatic transfer. What I want to do in the remainder of this chapter is to explore the infection theory of *What Is Art?* in quest of a synthesis of the depersonalized anesthesis of affect and affective infection, but first let me quickly demonstrate the failure of collective somatic guidance in *A Confession*.

A Confession is a powerful exemplar of the proposition that in depersonalization the jouissant speaking of the Other is extinguished (Rudnev) or abjected (Kristeva). Not only is there no *shared* pleasure or pain (collective somatic regulation) in his spiritual "crisis," there is no sign of either in the entire book, before or after his conversion. To put it simply, the author of *A Confession* is not someone who feels other people's feelings, pleasurable or painful, regulatory or rebellious. The book is rife with the kinds of questions people ask when they are radically isolated from the collective regulation of value:

" 'What am I?' or 'Why do I live?' or 'What must I do?' " (27), or "Above all, my personal question, 'What am I with my desires?' remained quite unanswered" (26). Most people don't ask those questions, let alone begin to obsess about suicide when they go unanswered, because the questions are answered for them in thousands of inchoate ways, through mimetic ideosomatic guidance, by the group. What are you? You're a member of the group. Why do you live? To serve the group. What must you do? Whatever, channeling group regulation ideosomatically, you feel is right. What are you with your desires? You're a valued group member who desires what the group desires that you desire. But Tolstoy feels none of this. (Martine de Courcel aptly describes his "autistic spiritual state" [163] and "intellectual narcissism" [259].) Society as Tolstoy experiences it is governed not by shared somatic guidance, which he doesn't (let himself) feel, but, as Rudnev suggests, by empty conventions— empty because they lack felt embodiment, lack the enlivening undercurrent of somatic pressure by which all mammalian species regulate group behavior. Without mimetically reproduced somatic guidance, conventions are founded on the void, and their destruction means the destruction of all value—hence, obviously, Tolstoy's ongoing spiritual crisis, the series of spiritual crises that constituted his life.

One way of reframing Lacan's theory of the jouissant speaking of the Other and Bakhtin's theory of dialogical retonalization is that most mammals continuously give and get instantaneous somatic feedback to and from the other members of their group. We do something the group considers praiseworthy, and the group rewards us with somatic approval, warm feelings that are literally infectious, that we feel empathetically. We do something of which the group disapproves and the negative feedback is equally instantaneous, charged with anger, scorn, ridicule, disgust that we feel as emotional pain. We ourselves respond somatically to the behavior of others, working alone or collectively to put pressure on individuals to act in accordance with group norms. The continual exchange of such somatic signals in group behavior not only gives us behavioral guidance, it also reassures us that others exist and care and are connected, that actions have social consequences, and thus also that we too exist.

I never get a sense, reading *A Confession,* that Tolstoy ever felt any of this. I do sometimes get a sense that he *perceived* it—saw that other humans felt it, saw how feeling this group guidance helped them, and envied them their calm certainty. Sometimes he says he feels it, but typically in a context that makes it clear that this is wishful thinking:

And I ceased to doubt, and became fully convinced that not all was true in the religion I had joined. Formerly I should have said that it was all false, but I could not say so now. The whole of the people possessed a knowledge of the truth, for otherwise they could not have lived. Moreover, that knowledge was accessible to me, for I had felt it and had lived by it [*ya uzhe zhil im i chuvstvoval vsyu etu pravdu,* lit. "I already lived by it and felt all this truth"]. But I no longer doubted that there was also falsehood in it. And all that had previously repelled [*ottalkivalo*] me now presented itself vividly before me. And though I saw that among the peasants there was a smaller admixture of the lies that repelled me than among the representatives of the Church, I still saw that in the people's belief also falsehood was mingled with the truth. (*Ispoved'*, 59; *Confession*, 79)

What people possess that makes it possible for them to live is not in fact "knowledge of the truth" but somatic group regulation, which, if it has anything to do with truth at all, constructs and reconstructs *local* truth and then only as a regulatory fiction. If Tolstoy had felt that regulation, he would have known this and not attributed to his peasants knowledge of *the* truth. He also would not have needed to *infer* the peasants' possession of that "knowledge" logically—"for otherwise they could not have lived"—and would have realized that first inferring it logically and then professing to have felt it and lived by it exposes the latter claim as a sham. Most of what he gets out of his encounter with the peasants here is philosophical, ontological, truth or falsehood, existence or nonexistence, and, tellingly, the petty mathematics of greater or smaller "admixtures" of truth and lies. Note also that the only actual feeling he displays here is revulsion, which in a functioning social somatic might indicate Tolstoy's channeling of strong group disapproval, but here seems to be only a particularly intense form of estrangement, evidence that he is not part of the group and feels panicky at any possibility of being included in it. Indeed, the Russian word he uses is *ottalkivat'*, morphologically "push away." To the extent that it is a feeling at all, it is a feeling not of disapproval but of exclusion, of not belonging, of being estranged. He also claims that he no longer feels repelled, pushed away, estranged, but then hints in the next sentence that "the lies that repelled me" are still present in this new and improved social group he's trying to migrate to, there are just fewer of them—suggesting that he still feels pushed away, just less strongly. And note how he puts the change: "And all that had previously repelled me now presented itself vividly before me." Not "all that had previously repelled me now drew me in, made me feel at home, gave me pleasure, made me feel other people's enjoyment, gave me a strong sense of belonging": after the change, all he could do was *look* at it. It was *visibly* present to him. He didn't feel it.

Tolstoy comes closest to grasping the nature of collective somatic guidance in chapter 9, in his attempts to define faith. "What, then, is this faith? And I understood that faith is not merely 'the evidence of things not seen', etc., and is not a revelation (that defines only one of the indications of faith), is not the relation of man to God (one has first to define faith and then God, and not define faith through God); it not only agreement with what has been told one (as faith is most usually supposed to be), but faith is a knowledge of the meaning of human life in consequence of which man does not destroy himself but lives" (50–51). The rejection of the mentalist grounding of faith in evidence, revelation, and verbal instructions seems to point his emphasis on "knowledge of the meaning of human life" away from a theological—systematic, intellectual—conception of that meaning and toward a practical, perhaps even unconscious conception such as might be provided by various regulatory dialogical Others in each individual's ideosomatic guidance systems; but he is still talking about *the* meaning, which suggests that he is still thinking in terms of *the* truth. Then he adds: "Faith is the strength of life." This is a good guess: what makes any functioning social group strong is a set of shared values that are constantly being circulated through the group ideosomatically, with repeated minute adjustments for changing group perceptions of the current situation—and *faith* is a term commonly used for group values like that.

In this next passage, he comes even closer: "The conception of an infinite god, the divinity of the soul, the connexion of human affairs with God, the unity and existence of the soul, man's conception of moral goodness and evil—are conceptions formulated in the hidden infinity of human thought, they are those conceptions without which neither life nor I should exist; yet rejecting all that labour of the whole of humanity, I wished to remake it afresh myself and in my own manner" (53). "The hidden infinity of human thought" is a nice phrase, but it's hard to imagine these religious conceptions being *formulated* there; surely conceptions are formulated in the public finitude of human thought. What I think Tolstoy is getting at, though, is a notion of religious notions arising out of the hidden infinity of *feeling,* feelings of awe and fear and love and so on, which then cast up into the public realm of thought verbalized images that are subsequently processed into conceptions. After all, to the extent that gods and souls and morality and so on are *conceptions,* theological concepts, dogmas, they are not produced by the labor of the whole of humanity but by a small group of priests. But it is possible to imagine the whole of humanity working collectively on the *somatics* of religion, the processing of locally shared feelings into more easily transportable and analyzable images. His recognition of his own need to reject that collective faith and rework everything through his depersonalized isolation—"yet rejecting all that labour of the whole of humanity, I wished to remake it afresh myself and in my own manner"—is rueful and regretful, here, but it remained his approach to religious truth the remaining three decades of his life.

He cuts even closer at the end of the next paragraph. "I began to understand that in the replies given by faith is stored up the deepest human wisdom and that I had no right to deny them on the ground of reason, and that those answers are the only ones which reply to life's question" (53). The deepest human wisdom, which is to say any form of collective values, is "stored" in the words believers in those values produce when you ask them questions. Another way of putting this is that the shared values that make any community functional are stored and circulated somatically but issue into language, including literary language: this is the birth of the somatics of literature out of the somatics of language, which in turn is the birth of verbal language out of the regulatory somatics of body language. Tolstoy is using "faith" to mean faith in God, of course, a specific kind of Christian faith, but his very willingness to avoid specifying the kind of faith he means signals something like his proximity to the recognition that any "faith" is ultimately faith in the group, faith in the group's power to make collective decisions seem not only right but inevitable, and even universal.

But this is as close as he can get to it: observing but not feeling the effects of collective somatic guidance, telling himself that what he sees and hears are signs of "the deepest human wisdom," which he has no right to deny "on the ground of reason." Over and over again, after his so-called conversion, we sense the distance between him and the people to whom he would like to belong, with whom he would like to join in community, but cannot.

> I was listening to the conversation of an illiterate peasant, a pilgrim [*Slushal ya razgovor bezgramotnogo muzhika, strannika*], about God, faith, life, and salvation, when a knowledge of faith revealed itself to me [*i znanie very otkrylos' mne,* lit. "and knowledge of belief opened to me"]. I drew near to the people [*sblizhalsya ya s narodom*], listening to their opinions of life and faith, and I understood the truth more and more. So also was it when I read the Lives of Holy men, which became my favourite books. Putting aside the miracles [*Isklyuchaya chudesa*] and regarding them as fables illustrating thoughts, this reading revealed to me life's meaning. There were the lives of

> Makarius the Great, the story of Buddha, there were the words of St. John
> Chrysostom, and there were the stories of the traveller in the well, the monk
> who found some gold, and of Peter the publican. There were stories of the
> martyrs, all announcing that death does not exclude life, and there were
> the stories of ignorant, stupid men, who knew nothing of the teaching of the
> Church but who yet were saved. (*Ispoved'*, 52; *Confession*, 73–74)

As his first words in this passage make clear, what he means by "I drew near
to the people" is that he eavesdropped on them: he isn't even talking *with* the
illiterate *strannik* but *listening to his conversation.* This *strannik,* estranged from
hearth and home, is Tolstoy's ascetic ideal, what he will long to become all the
rest of his life and will only in a sense become in the last days of his life; but
even here he cannot join in the conversation. There is a kind of Zeno's paradox
to his approach to the people, an infinite fractalization of the distance between
himself and them that he can never actually cross. And the result in him is,
once again, not faith but *knowledge* of faith, not felt participation in the community of faith but visual and aural observations of the outward signs of that
faith, leading to an incremental increase ("more and more") in what he takes
to be truth. When he reads the kind of books these "ignorant, stupid" people
love, he puts aside or "excludes" (*isklyuchaet*) the miracles that they take for
the truth and regards them "as fables illustrating thoughts," as intellectual al-
legories of theological concepts. This is the best he can do.

Disinfecting the Infection Theory

If Tolstoy, then, doesn't feel other people's feelings, doesn't experience the
jouissance of the Other, doesn't feel in his voice the guiding force of other
people's tonalizations, how is it that he came to theorize the infectiousness of
art, the somatics of literature? Does his 300-page treatise on the contagion of
feeling, the somatic "brotherhood of man," written in his late sixties, suggest
that a decade and a half of Christian love has truly now begun to convert him,
to open him up to collective feeling?

I don't think so. In *What is Art?* he still writes about somatic guidance without the benefit of somatic guidance. The book is a scandal not just because he
rejects high art, including *War and Peace* and *Anna Karenina,* but because it is
mired in stupid and stubborn inconsistencies, indeed impossibilities, born, I
want to suggest, out of his depersonalization, out of his abjection—out of his
inability to be guided by the very ideosomatic forces that he is theorizing. Tolstoy writes about somatic guidance as one who has borrowed what he knows

about it from other people, has taken over their aesthetic descriptions anesthetically and imposed on them rational universalizing principles borrowed
from an idealized/depersonalized vision of human life.

Sides

For example, look back at the quotation excluding "any activity" from the
determination of true art: "If a person, without any activity on his/her side
and without any change of standpoint, while reading or having heard or seen
another person's work, experiences a state of mind that unites him with this
person and with other people who also perceive the object of art as he does,
then the object evoking that state is an art object." I noted before that for Tolstoy this distorting "activity" was fundamentally the operation of civilization
in the individual. It's also important to note, however, that the estranging root
stran- appears in this passage, in the form of *storona* "side," the etymological
boundary that splits the key words derived from it into here and there, good
and bad, strange and familiar: "if a person," Tolstoy writes, "without any activity on his/her side [*svoey storony*] and without any change of standpoint." *Svoya
storona* is grammatically the subject's side and phenomenologically *this* side,
the familiar side; etymologically in Russian whatever is on this familiar side is
strana "country," while whatever is on the other side is *stranniy* "strange." The
inostranets, someone from the other side of the line, from a different country
(*iz inoy strany*), is a foreigner. The *strannik* "pilgrim" is someone who estranges
himself from hearth and home and family, crosses the line from familiar to
strange.[8]

But to the extent that Tolstoy follows Rousseau in seeing civilization as the
regulatory ideosomatics over on the *other* side, the foreign side, the "strange"
side—and "any activity" as the disturbing and distorting leakage of that
ideosomatic regulation over into the attitudes or motivations or cognitions of
the individual on this side—he breaks with the collectivist Russian etymology
that associates this side, the familiar side, with the country, the group, one's
own culture. For Tolstoy, what is on this side is the isolated Rousseauistic
individual, the Noble Savage, shaped only by God and Truth, unaffected by
others, unconditioned by ideosomatic regulation to want or expect anything
in particular out of a work of art. Before his "conversion" he attunes himself so as to feel, or to seem to be feeling, the emotional infection from late
Beethoven that others expect him to feel; a few years later, when Masha dies,
he again attunes himself to pretend to feel what society expects him to feel.

Both emotional "attunements" to group guidance are for him equally corrupt. Tolstoy claims to desire the unification of all human beings in moral guidance through the artistic infection of feelings, but in reality any specific real-world instance of ideosomatic regulation is "strange" to him and must be condemned as either perverted or fake. This animus against the group is thematized in Tolstoy specifically as directed not against collectivity itself but against any group smaller than all humanity; as Thomas Barran writes, "Both Rousseau and Tolstoy condemn the role of partial societies within the larger socio-political organization. Tolstoy objects to them because of the pressures they can exert on an individual to pull away from the community and follow his or her own selfish interests" ("Rousseau," 11n). The apparent contradiction there is, in fact, only apparent: it is not that membership in the community can pull the individual away from the community but that membership in a *real* group can pull the individual away from "the community" defined ideally as all humanity, as the "universal brotherhood of man," an abstraction that can only exist in the imagination of the isolated Romantic individual and thus on the safe "familiar" side of the split. Real groups, shunted in Tolstoy's imagination to the other side, the strange side, are—strangely—associated with "selfishness."

These social groups for Tolstoy are the enemy; it is precisely their regulatory work that he is constantly at pains to undermine throughout his tract. "It is true," he says, "that this indication is an *internal* one and that there are people who, having forgotten what the action of real art is, expect something else from art (in our society the great majority are in this state), and that therefore such people may mistake for this aesthetic feeling the feeling of diversion and a certain excitement which they receive from counterfeits of art" (227). "There are people," he says—at first suggesting that it's only a small group, say, the upper classes—who have "forgotten" or fallen away from this pure Rousseauistic capacity to be infected by the pure feelings of joy and spiritual union, but then it turns out that *the great majority* are in this state, indeed perhaps even everyone, with the result that people almost invariably feel the wrong feelings: "the feeling of diversion and a certain excitement which they receive from counterfeits of art." This is patently a kind of infection of artistic feeling, but Tolstoy despises it and wants to distance himself from it as far as possible in order to elevate to definitive status a specific *idealized* and *universalized* somatic infection. The privileged infection is here grounded experientially, by inversion, in Tolstoy's own depersonalization; the pure infection of joy and spiritual union he theorizes in the book is precisely his own depressed isolation turned imaginatively inside out.

Tellingly, many of the examples he gives of this pure infected state are based on other people's reports: "I lately read of a theatrical performance among the savage tribe—the Voguls. A spectator describes the play . . . The audience, as the eye-witness describes them, are paralysed with suspense: deep groans and even weeping are heard among them. And, from the mere description I felt that this was a true work of art" (225–26). "From the mere description": for Tolstoy the infection theory works best in theory, through hearsay, through descriptions he can read and think about on his own. When he is personally present at this sort of artistic event, his response is almost invariably the depersonalized inverse. He comes away from a performance of *Hamlet* disgusted: "I experienced all the time that peculiar suffering which is caused by false imitations of works of art" (225)—and by "false imitation" he doesn't mean the performance alone; he means Shakespeare's play as well. It isn't real art; it's counterfeit. Reading Zola, Kipling, and others, "I was provoked with the authors all the while as one is provoked with a man who considers you so naïve that he does not even conceal the trick by which he intends to take you in. From the first lines one sees the intention with which the book is written, the details all become superfluous, and one feels dull. Above all, one knows that the author had no other feeling all the time than a desire to write a story or a novel, and so one receives no artistic impression" (224)—an estranging reading strategy typical of Tolstoy's approach to everything in life. He attends a performance of day two of Wagner's *Ring* in Moscow and is again disgusted:

> Sit in the dark for four days in company with people who are not quite normal, and through the auditory nerves subject your brain to the strongest action of the sounds best adapted to excite it, and you will no doubt be reduced to an abnormal condition and be enchanted by absurdities. But to attain this end you do not even need four days; the five hours during which one "day" is enacted, as in Moscow, are quite enough. Nor are five hours needed; even one hour is enough for people who have no clear conception of what art should be and who have concluded in advance that what they are going to see is excellent, and that indifference or dissatisfaction with this work will serve as a proof of their inferiority and lack of culture.
>
> I observed the audience present at this representation. The people who led the whole audience and gave the tone to it were those who had previously been hypnotized and who again succumbed to the hypnotic influence to which they were accustomed. These hypnotized people being in an abnormal condition were perfectly enraptured. (216)

You'll recall Michael Denner telling us in chapter 1 that in preliminary drafts of *What Is Art?* Tolstoy presented hypnotism as parallel to, and as an image or trope of, true infection. Indeed, Tolstoy's third-hand description of the Vogul audience's response, "paralyzed with suspense," sounds like what Bertolt Brecht will later derogate as a hypnotic trance or a drugged state. But when Tolstoy is physically present and observes that state with his own eyes, he is repelled. He says that Wagnerites will protest that you have to see the *Ring* in Bayreuth, in the dark, with the orchestra out of sight, and every detail of the performance brought to the highest perfection, and retorts: "Yes, naturally! Only place yourself in such conditions and you may see what you will. But this can be still more quickly attained by getting drunk or smoking opium" (216).

"So one is quite at a loss," he remarks early in the treatise, referring to the works of high art that so disgust him, "as to whom these things are done for. The man of culture is heartily sick of them, while to a real working man they are utterly incomprehensible. If any one can be pleased by these things (which is doubtful), it can only be some young footman or depraved artisan, who has contracted the spirit of the upper classes but is not yet satiated with their amusements, and wishes to show his breeding" (79). Since the whole point of his book is that "men of culture" are almost without exception "falsely" enraptured or hypnotized or drugged by high art, feeling all the wrong feelings of "diversion" and "excitement," all he can mean by "the man of culture is heartily sick of them" is that *he himself* is sick of them—that his overwhelming response to the emotional infectiousness of so-called great art is one of disgust and revulsion. Almost everyone at these performances is powerfully affected by them, but he describes their infection as an artificial, hypnotic, drugged state that is something like the demonic inverse of the ideal state he is theorizing. The only kind of viewer that he can imagine actually responding authentically to these works is an ambitious upwardly mobile footman or artist "who has contracted the spirit of the upper classes"—which is to say, again, that the perversion with which the upper classes have been infecting the lower orders *is* an infection and not mere fakery.

For the most part, then, Tolstoy builds his argument in the book around his observations of aesthetic response in the actual or virtual body language of other people—both the "bad" kind, which he tends to observe in the flesh, and which he wavers between identifying as sheer mummery and attributing to an infection of perverse pleasures, and the "good" kind, which he tends to read about in books and articles by other people, and is better able to trust because without the distorting and disgusting impact of actual body language he can *imagine* the idealized sort of body language he believes the universal effect of true aesthetic infection will provoke. But he does give us a few examples of his own actual experience of the latter kind of artistic infection, such as the famous one I alluded to in an earlier section: "A few days ago I was returning home from a walk feeling depressed, as sometimes happens. On nearing the house I heard the loud singing of a large choir of peasant women. They were welcoming my daughter, celebrating her return home after her marriage. In this singing, with its cries and clanging of scythes, such a definite feeling of joy, cheerfulness, and energy, was expressed, that without noticing how it infected me I continued my way towards the house in a better mood, and reached home smiling and quite in good spirits" (221).

It's telling, here, that as his favorite daughter Masha arrives home from her wedding, Tolstoy is off on a lonely walk, feeling depressed, and that he describes his homecoming from the walk again in solitary terms, not as "rejoining the others" but simply as "continuing my way towards the house" and "reaching home." Tolstoy spent the decades after his "conversion" almost entirely alienated from his family: "Through the window I can hear them playing tennis and laughing . . . Everyone is well, but I feel depressed and can't control myself. It's like the feeling I had when [my childhood tutor Prosper de] St. Thomas locked me in and from my dungeon I could hear everyone enjoying themselves and laughing" (Tolstoy's diary, July 31, 1896, one year before Masha's wedding; 2:430). Still, it clearly suggests that Tolstoy may have been physically capable of responding with shared feeling to some moments of artistic expression—just not very often or very strongly ("in a better mood," "quite in good spirits"). It may be, also, that the cries and clanging of scythes helped him respond; they were strange enough, alien enough from the high culture on which he had been raised, that they pierced through his depressed/depersonalized indifference.

The Temporal Dynamic: The Old and the New

This rare case of apparently authentic infection and therefore "real art"— "the song of the peasant women was real art transmitting a definite and strong feeling" (223)—does seem a bit strange in another way, though, in that it is Tolstoy's theory throughout the book that true or real art must infect the audience not just with a "definite and strong feeling" but with *new* feelings:

The first result—the impoverishment of subject-matter—followed because only that is a true work of art which transmits fresh feelings not before experienced by man. As thought-product is only then real thought-product when it transmits new conceptions and thoughts and does not merely repeat what was known before, so also an art-product is only then a genuine art-product when it brings a new feeling (however insignificant) into the current of human life . . .

The same powerful impression is made on people by feelings which are quite new, and have never before been expressed by man. And it is the source from which such feelings flow, that the art of the upper classes has deprived itself of by estimating feelings not in conformity with religious perception but according to the degree of enjoyment they afford. There is nothing older and more hackneyed than enjoyment, and there is nothing fresher than the feelings springing from the religious consciousness of each age. It could not be otherwise: man's enjoyment has limits established by his nature, but the movement forward of humanity which expresses itself in religious consciousness has no limits. At every forward step taken by humanity—and such steps are taken in consequence of a greater and greater elucidation of religious perception—men experience new and fresh feelings. And therefore only on the basis of religious perception (which shows the highest level of life-comprehension reached by the men of a certain period) can fresh emotion, never before felt by man, arise. (149–50)

Technically, then, the song of the peasant women should only have been considered true art if it infected Tolstoy not with a slightly better mood but with "fresh feelings not before experienced by man." And perhaps it did. Perhaps the "definite feeling of joy, cheerfulness, and energy" that Tolstoy felt infected by was in some way unique, so perfectly shaped by the honest feelings of these peasant women that no one had ever felt it in the world before. It is difficult to imagine just how these new feelings of the peasant women might have been shaped by "a greater and greater elucidation of religious perception," but here perhaps we can give Tolstoy the benefit of the doubt and assume (contrary to the evidence he marshals in *A Confession,* but never mind) that the Russian peasants are the Rousseauistic noble savages of his time, uncorrupted enough by upper-class civilization as to be perfectly attuned to "the highest level of life-comprehension reached by the men of a certain period."

The crippling difficulty Tolstoy faces in making this argument, of course, is epistemological. How on earth could he ever *know?* How is he in a position to know what every other person in the world has felt? Does he even know his own feelings well enough to distinguish an old one from a new one? What if these women always sing this song in exactly this same way, with exactly these same feelings, and he has simply never heard it before? What if their singing is so conventionalized that their mothers and grandmothers and great-grandmothers sang it in exactly the same way, with exactly the same feelings?

In order for his claim to have any factual basis, he would have to have the god-like power to feel every feeling any human being ever felt on earth; clearly, he doesn't.

If, on the other hand, he means that any true sincerity necessarily generates a new feeling, then he can assume that new feelings are quite common experiences, perhaps so common as to be mundane, things that every human being on earth experiences many times a day. This assumption would let him off the hook of trying to claim that he can distinguish a new feeling from an old one, but it would still leave the burden of proof on him to distinguish between sincerity and shamming. ("His" peasants aren't just pretending to love the master and his family sincerely; their love is real—he can tell.)

Really, the only way for him to avoid having to prove that he has godlike powers of discrimination would be for him to admit that all of our feelings are always new—that, as Heraclitus says, we never step into the same river twice. But, since the perverse elitist faker patently never steps into the same river of fakery twice either, this argumentative stratagem would allow high aesthetic fakery the same claim to newness that he wants to reserve for the sincerity of true art. Hard as he works to distinguish bad art from good, fake art from true, disturbing parallels between them keep surfacing:

> There is only one explanation of this fact: it is that the art of the society in which these versifiers lived is not a serious, important matter of life, but is a mere amusement; and all amusements grow wearisome by repetition. And in order to make wearisome amusement again tolerable it is necessary to find some means to freshen it up . . . The substance of the matter remains the same, only its form is changed. It is the same with this kind of art. The subject-matter of the art of the upper classes growing continually more and more limited, it has come at last to this, that to the artists of these exclusive classes it seems as if everything has already been said, and that to find anything new to say is impossible. And therefore to freshen up this art they look out for fresh forms. (166–67)

The significant difference between this self-exhausting newness of elitist art and the ever-replenished newness of true art for Tolstoy is that true art is replenished by true religion. Because "the movement forward of humanity, that which is voiced by religious perception, has no limits," the peasant women don't have to go restlessly searching for fresh forms. The "greater and greater elucidation of religious perception" does the searching for them; all they have to do is open themselves up to that perception.

One way of framing the epistemology behind Tolstoy's discriminatory argument here is that he *just knows*. He just knows the difference between true and false newness, between true and false sincerity, between true and false religious perception, and therefore also between true and false art. Judging from his rhetoric in *What is Art?*, this is how things seemed to Tolstoy himself. Another, less idealized way of putting that is that he *doesn't* know and somehow has rhetorically (and perhaps even psychologically as well) to convert his not-knowing into an ideal form of knowing, into the truest and most perfect form of knowing. As Caryl Emerson suggests, drawing on Barran's tracing of Tolstoy's thought to Rousseau, Tolstoy wants to run the utopian (Rousseauistic) temporal dynamic both ways: he wants the authentic infections of true art to be the alpha and the omega, the primeval force of innocence arising out of the unfallen past *and* the new utopian future in which the primordial innocence of Edenic shared feeling is restored.[9] What he ends up with instead, though, is the confusion arising out of his own depersonalization. Unable to respond emotionally in the present to the old or the new, determined to imagine a utopian future built out of a restored Edenic past, he has to try to sort out his many examples by depersonalized or derealized remote control, guessing anesthetically at which example might be appropriate for which phenomenon. So he theorizes true art in terms of the infection of new feelings but gives his rare examples of true art based on the infection of old feelings, the oldest of all, the pure feelings of joy and spiritual union arising out of the true primeval (precreation) meaning of Christianity and "instinctively"—with the instincts of depersonalization—associates the infection of new feelings with the perverse repetitions of exhaustion.

Viktor Shklovsky theorizes estrangement in the seam of this same problematic temporal dynamic, and it is even more of a problem for Bertolt Brecht—but neither twentieth-century Tolstoyan estranger is much more conscious of the complexity than Tolstoy himself. The problem is not just that emotional effects grow old—it is impossible for any human being to continue responding in precisely the same way to precisely the same work of art, or even the same feeling from another person, because each experience of the artwork or the feeling changes us. It is also that whatever we do to refresh an emotional effect also grows old, so that estrangement too grows old and must itself be estranged, and so on, and each time the effect grows weaker. For Shklovsky the solution to the problem of the world's effect on us growing old is estrangement, and while he recognizes that old forms cease to be "felt," cease to have any kind of somatic impact on us, and therefore cease to be "artistic," he never stops to consider the possibility that the estranging effect of a given poem on a single given reader today may have grown dull and even anesthetic by tomorrow. For Brecht the solution is to set up a kind of Hegelian reciprocal estrangement between theater group and audience, each estranging the other, each pushing the other beyond existing strategies and solutions, so that theoretically this theater-house dialectic will keep pushing estrangement into a constantly renewed future; but as Brecht is dimly aware, this dialectic too is subject to conventionalization.

Historicism and Universalism

Part of Tolstoy's problem is that, like Brecht after him, he wants to use estranging interpretive strategies to historicize and thus denaturalize high art—but unlike Brecht, once he has destroyed his rival he wants to install his own idealized/naturalized universals in its place. He wants us to historicize the current enemy and then stop historicizing when he makes his case for timeless universals. He gives us a radically relativistic history of aesthetics, beginning with the power of the dominant religion in each culture to determine what counts as great art: "Religions are the exponents of the highest comprehension of life accessible to the best and foremost men at a given time in a given society—a comprehension towards which all the rest of that society must inevitably and irresistibly advance. And therefore only religions have always served, and still serve, as bases for the valuation of human sentiments. If feelings bring men nearer the ideal their religion indicates, if they are in harmony with it and do not contradict it, they are good; if they estrange men from it and oppose it, they are bad" (127–28). His examples include the religions of the ancient Hebrews, Greeks, and Romans, the Chinese, and the Buddhists, seemingly making it clear that to Tolstoy Christianity is not the sole universal repository of religious truth but merely the latest religion to dominate culture, specifically (though he never says this), Western culture. The problem—the rival tradition—arises in the Renaissance, he says, as the educated rich begin to doubt Christianity: "If in externals they still kept to the forms of Church teaching, they could no longer believe in it, and held to it only by inertia and for the sake of influencing the masses, who continued to believe blindly in Church doctrine and whom the upper classes for their own advantage considered it necessary to encourage in those beliefs" (131). Because true Christianity negates their privileges, they reject it, but because Christianity is still a great tool for the control of the masses, they end up with only the outward forms of religion—and support art not for religious reasons but for pleasure, which is their only religion. "So that the majority of the highest classes of that age, even the popes and the ecclesiastics, really believed in nothing at all . . . So these people remained without any religious view of life; and having none, they could have no standard whereby to estimate what was good and what was bad art, except that of personal enjoyment" (134).

This is where he begins to fall down. Obviously, even if we take him at his word that the popes and the ecclesiastics were left with only the outward forms of Christianity, they did still believe in something, namely in their own traditions, in everything that sustained their power. His historicizing of religion's control of art has illustrated the importance for aesthetics of *ideosomatic regulation:* every culture has its source(s) of collective somatic guidance, of felt shared values, including the deep-seated (guided) feeling that this work of art is good and that is bad, this work should be allowed to infect us with joy and spiritual union and that should be blocked, quarantined, disinfected. Now that his history has brought us to himself, however—to the depersonalized conflict in him between his background in upper-class power culture and his postconversion idealism—Tolstoy needs for us to accept his historicized, debunked, estranged take on the former and not extend that take to the latter, so that it can represent the absolute truth. He needs for us not to ask, for example, whether his universalizing idealism isn't actually just a form of class treason—one with recognizable social and cultural motivations (rebellion against a decaying social order), but at an even deeper level, perhaps, one psychologically motivated as well, part of a larger idiosomatic rebellion against ideosomatic regulation of all kinds, in all times and places, and thus structured by his inability to feel that regulation, what Rudnev diagnoses as his depersonalization disorder.

For clearly, even in elevating a collective faith like "the true meaning of Christ's teaching" (263) to the role of aesthetic arbiter, he has to do it not in the name of the collective, not in the name of the ecclesiastical authorities— "Church" Christianity, which he despises—or even in the name of "true believers," but in the name of his own depersonalized *rebellion* against that faith. In this sense Tolstoy *is* rejecting the religion of his time—certainly of his class. He would argue, of course, that he is embracing the religion of the people, the peasants, but as we've seen, he couldn't do that either. He has created his own personal religion, based on what he thinks is right—because he doesn't *feel* what other people know is right. He is excommunicated by the Russian Orthodox Church not only because he is a celebrity rebel who publicly rejects its authority, but because his public denunciations of the Church are divisive, tend to drive wedges between people and their "faith"—which is to say, their ideosomatic guidance. Ironically, this is precisely the crime of which he accuses non-Christian art: "Art, all art, has this characteristic, that it unites people. Every art causes those to whom the artist's feeling is transmitted to unite in soul with the artist and also with all who receive the same impression. But non-Christian art while uniting some people, makes that very union a cause of separation between these united people and others; so that union of this kind is often a source not merely of division but even of enmity towards others" (238–39). How hard does he have to be working here not to notice that the aesthetic he is preaching does the exact same thing and that this is inevitable?

It is inevitable, of course, because every culture has its own ideosomatic coherence, whose borders are policed by somatomimetically disseminated binary impulses to divide theirs from ours, foreign from local, strange from familiar, alien from own. Properly historicized, Tolstoy's aim is to create a competing culture, one that will split "Church Christianity" off from the "true Christianity" that he is defining, one that will foreignize or alienate or estrange what now to hundreds of millions of people feels local, familiar, like their own. Tolstoy, in other words, incapable of being guided ideosomatically himself, seeks to become the ideosomatic authority to the rest of the world—and, since Romain Rolland, Mahatma Gandhi (see Green), Maksim Gorky, Ludwig Wittgenstein (see Thomas and Thompson), and thousands of others during his lifetime and after were inspired by him, he may even have partially gotten his wish. He is simply mystifying his own will to power by pretending that it is the next great step in the movement of history: "Above all he can no longer say that we do not know the real meaning of Christ's teaching. That meaning has not only become accessible to all men of our times, but the whole life of man to-day is permeated by the spirit of that teaching, and is, consciously or unconsciously, guided by it" (263–64). Clearly, this is a utopian rather than an empirical statement. Tolstoy does not mean that, deep down, "all men" everywhere in the world today are true Christians (an argument that he has been rejecting throughout the book); he means that they are about to become true Christians, about to have always been true Christians, in the idealized revolutionary fulfillment of his visionary dreams:

In former times when the highest religious perception united only some people (who even if they formed a large society were yet but one society surrounded by others—Jews, or Athenian or Roman citizens), the feelings transmitted by the art of that time flowed from a desire for the might, greatness, glory, and prosperity, of that society . . . But the religious perception of our times does not select any one society of men; on the contrary it demands

> the union of all—absolutely of all people without exception—and above
> every other virtue it sets brotherly love to all men . . .
>
> Christian, truly Christian, art has been so long in establishing itself, and
> has not yet established itself, just because the Christian religious perception
> was not one of those small steps by which humanity advances regularly, but
> was an enormous revolution which, if it has not already altered, must in-
> evitably alter the entire life-conception of mankind, and consequently the
> whole internal organization of that life. It is true that the life of humanity,
> like that of an individual, moves regularly; but in that regular movement
> come, as it were, turning-points which sharply divide the preceding from
> the subsequent life. Christianity was such a turning-point; such at least it
> must appear to us who live by the Christian perception of life. (236–37)

It *was* an enormous revolution, *was* a sharp turning point—but it hasn't happened yet. It is a past revolution that will occur in the future. Tolstoy's mys-
tificatory rhetoric makes this temporal dynamic seem like a simple empirical
confusion over whether it has already happened—"which, if it has not already
altered, must inevitably alter the entire life-conception of mankind"—but
clearly the underlying mythology is tied to the same theological transcendence
of mere historical time that we saw in his fudging of the old and the new.
Specifically, it is a typological theology of "already—not yet," modeled analo-
gously on (though tacitly rejecting) the Christian belief that Jesus' redemption
of the world happened in the past (in Abraham's sacrifice of the ram in place
of Isaac, say, or in the death on the cross and resurrection) and that it will not
happen until the end of the world, and that it has always existed and will always exist because it lies outside of time.[10] The same shift from the temporal
to the transcendental, from historical time to the timeless, from the "was" and
the "will be" to the "should be," also informs the disjointed argumentation in
the first paragraph of that quotation. The statement that earlier religious art
only *had* local appeal and therefore divided people is an empirical observation,
but the empirical observation that Christianity too only *has* local appeal and
therefore divides people is irrelevant and therefore not stated, because the utopian fact that Christianity is a universalizing religion that "*demands* the union
of all" takes precedence. The divisive effects of Christianity's missionary universalism throughout history are just empirical reality; the union of all people
that Christianity demands is a transcendental and timeless truth.

Hence, he concludes, "people talk about incomprehensibility; but if art is
the transmission of feelings flowing from man's religious perception, how can
a feeling be incomprehensible which is founded on religion, that is, on man's

relation to God? Such art should be, and has actually always been, comprehensible to everybody, because every man's relation to God is one and the same" (178). That last "is" refers not to empirical reality, where it would be a laughable absurdity, but to the idealized anesthetic-cum-transcendental realm in which the depersonalized Tolstoy lives.

What Tolstoy leaves for Shklovsky, then, is a series of problems. The biggest one is what to do about widespread depersonalization and specifically what kind of literature will most effectively banish it. Shklovsky offers up more of the same, in fact, more estranged modernism, more of what Tolstoy diagnosed as the disease—but as a different kind of homeopathic cure than what Tolstoy imagined. For Tolstoy, the cure enlists emotional infection to fight emotional infection; for Shklovsky, it enlists *estranged* emotional infection to fight estranged emotional infection, by belaboring the smooth forms that Tolstoy requires. Pace Rudnev, what makes this estrangement of estrangement possible as a homeopathic cure is that Shklovsky does not share Tolstoy's suspicion that there is nothing livable beyond the semiotic—and what lies beyond the semiotic or symbolic, as Bakhtin and Lacan suggest, is the somatic (or, as Kristeva would say, the semiotic *is* the somatic).

Nor can Shklovsky solve the problematic temporal dynamic Tolstoy mystifies: the fact that emotional infections, even homeopathic cures for bad emotional infections, grow old, fade, lose their power to transform and cure, leading to the deadening conventionalization of forms among conservatives and the exhaustion of forms among radical innovators. This is a problem that Bertolt Brecht raises, sort of, in Part III—but again without really solving it, possibly because there is no solution. All three of the theorists whose ideas I explore here are firm believers in the power of art to transform the social psychology of whole populations and would hate to admit that art may be ultimately powerless in the face of human alienation, but in the end they may have no choice.

PART TWO

Ostranenie
Shklovsky's Estrangement Theory

3 ▮ Shklovsky's Modernist Poetics

In a 1966 article entitled "Obnovlenie ponyatiya," "The Renewal of a Concept," the 73-year-old reformed Russian formalist Viktor Shklovsky returned in print to his most famous critical coinage, the *priyom ostraneniya* or "estrangement device" from his 1917 article "Art as Device." Specifically, he examined the cultural afterlife of that concept, in Bertolt Brecht's transformation of it into his *Verfremdungseffekt* and the official Soviet reinterpretation of the concept as dangerous and misleading (both the Brechtian and the Soviet response only implicit in the article, to be read between the lines).[1] I return to the Soviet reinterpretation below and to Brecht's possible debt to Shklovsky in chapter 5; for now let's simply let him introduce the notion:

> Estrangement [*ostranenie*] is a term signifying a specific way of perceiving or realizing an already automatized phenomenon.
>
> More than forty years ago I introduced—first, as I then thought—the concept of "estrangement" into poetics.
>
> The imagination of the ordinary as strange, as newly surprising, as it were "moved aside," seemed to me a phenomenon common to Romantic, realistic, and so-called modernist art.
>
> Now I know that the term "ostranenie" is, first of all, incorrect, and second, not original.
>
> I'll start with the second.
>
> In his *Fragments*, Novalis underscores a new quality of Romantic art, saying: "The art of making things in a pleasing way strange [*iskusstvo priyatnym obrazom delat' veschi strannymi*], making them alien [*delat' ikh chuzhimi*]

and at the same time familiar and attractive—in this consists Romantic poetics."[2]

Even if the term was new, in other words, the observations were not. (304–5, my translation)

Novalis's original German is: "Die Kunst, auf eine *angenehme* Art zu *befremden,* einen Gegenstand fremd zu machen und doch bekannt und anziehend, das ist die romantische Poetik" (685, #668; emphasis in original). But within the Shklovsky quotation I've translated the Novalis fragment indirectly, from the Russian translation that appeared in the early 1930s. Ironically, the translators of that text, Sil'man and Kopubovsky, translating Novalis nearly two decades after Shklovsky coined the noun *ostranenie* and its verb form *ostranyat'* but only a couple of years after formalism was officially banned and Shklovsky was made to recant his theory publicly, somehow could not think of a Russian verb for Novalis's *befremden* (the first verb Bertolt Brecht had used for estrangement when he began to theorize his estrangement effect in the mid-1920s), and had to render it *delat' strannymi* "to make [them] strange." Had they used Shklovsky's term from 1917—rendered that first clause "iskusstvo priyatnym obrazom *ostranyat'* veschi"—it would have been strangely awkward for Shklovsky to claim the newness even of his term! (Or perhaps Osip Brik's. Nikolay Trubetskoy says in his notes that Roman Jakobson told him that Brik actually invented the term and gave it to Shklovsky.)[3] A direct translation of Novalis's German might go: "The art of pleasing estrangement, of making an object strange and yet familiar and attractive: that is Romantic poetics"—but then Shklovsky could not read German and so was dependent for his sense of Novalis's term on the Russian translators, who were either ignorant of *ostranenie* or, more likely, avoided it for political reasons. Note also that, because they had to shift to *delat' strannymi* "make strange" to cover Novalis's *befremden,* Sil'man and Kopubovsky had to use *delat' chuzhimi* "make alien" to cover his *fremd machen,* using precisely the Russian root *chuzh-*"alien" that Brecht's Russian translators V. A. Nedelin and L. Yakovenko would use in 1960 in rendering Brecht's *Verfremdungseffekt* into Russian as *effekt otchuzhdeniya* "alienation effect."

Novalis is not the only inventor of Romantic estrangement, of course; the concept is one of the central ideas of German and English Romanticism and German Idealism, closely tied to Hegel's dialectical exfoliation of Rousseau's concept of alienation (to which we return in chapter 4) and Friedrich Schlegel's Romantic irony (to which we return in chapter 5). The basic idea is that conventionalization is psychologically alienating, anesthetizing, and that the reader therefore stands in need of some sort of aesthetic shock to break him or her out of the anesthesis. Everywhere we look in Romantic and Idealist thought, in fact, we find pronouncements on the nature of poetry that anticipate Shklovsky's formulation. In the 1798 advertisement to the *Lyrical Ballads,* Wordsworth writes that "Readers accustomed to the gaudiness and inane phraseology of many modern writers, if they persist in reading this book to its conclusion, will perhaps frequently have to struggle with feelings of strangeness and awkwardness" (i–ii); in the 1817 *Biographia Literaria,* writing of their plans for the *Lyrical Ballads,* Coleridge says that "Mr. Wordsworth, on the other hand, was to propose to himself, as his object, to give the charm of novelty to things of everyday, and to excite a feeling analogous to the supernatural by awakening the mind's attention from the lethargy of custom and directing it to the loveliness and the wonders of the world before us; an inexhaustible treasure, but for which, in consequence of the film of familiarity and selfish solicitude, we have eyes which see not, ears that hear not, and hearts which neither feel nor understand" (2:442). In the "Defence of Poetry" (written in 1821 but not published until 1840), Shelley says that "Poetry lifts the veil from the hidden beauty of the world, and makes familiar objects be as if they were not familiar" (542); and so on.[4]

Shklovsky's models or mentors for the concept, however, stood closer to him in time and space: the poetic disruptions of the Russian Futurists, especially Khlebnikov and Mayakovsky, of the Russian Symbolists, especially Andrey Bely (whose 1909 essay "Magiya slov," "The Magic of Words," was of particular significance),[5] and above all of Tolstoy, whose fiction struck Shklovsky as overwhelmingly estranging. Shklovsky does not name as *alienation* or *depersonalization* the psychosocial problem that his estrangement device is intended to combat; he doesn't even seem to recognize that "estrangement" is not only a potential cure for alienation but a typical symptom of it, rendering his theory problematic in ways that he does not address. Following Henri Bergson, and his friend and fellow formalist Lev Yakubinsky, who derived the formalist concept from Bergson,[6] he calls the problematic state *automatization* and describes it anthropologically as part of the human condition:

> If we begin to unpack the general laws of perception, we will see that as they become habitual, actions become automatic. Thus do all our practical skills retreat into the realm of the unconscious-automatic; whoever remembers the sensation [*oschuschenie*] he had holding a pen in his hand or speaking in an alien tongue for the first time, and compares that sensation with the one he experiences while doing it for the ten thousandth time, will agree

with us. The process of automatization explains the laws of our prosaic speech, its unfinished phrases and half-spoken words. This is a process, the ideal expression of which is algebra, where things are replaced by symbols. ("Iskusstvo," 11, my translation; all page references to this and other *O teorii prozy* essays are to the 1929 edition)

The Capacity to Flow

In historical context, this is perhaps a surprising time for a young Russian literary theorist to be working out a general theory of automatization and the poetic estrangement of automatization. As Shklovsky writes his article from December 1915 to December 1916, his country is at war, a war he is fighting as well, but, as he says in the opening lines of *A Sentimental Journey,* as a "privileged" soldier: "Before the revolution, I worked as an instructor in a reserve armored division, which made me one of the more privileged soldiers" (*Sentimental,* 7).[7] In fact, he is transferred to St. Petersburg/Petrograd to instruct armored-vehicle personnel in 1916, while he is writing the article; should we imagine the automatization he writes of there as having some historical, biographical referent, or as simply generalized to all repetitive action? He writes of this period in his life, "I remember running furtively down the streets after eight o'clock at night and being restricted to the barracks for three months . . . where men torn from their duties rotted on bunks with nothing to do, the dreariness of the barracks, the dull despair and resentment of the soldiers at being hunted down in the streets" (*Sentimental,* 7). Should we assimilate the "rotting on bunks" (*gnoilis' . . . na narakh*) and "dreariness" (*toska*) and "dull despair" (*tyomnoe tomlenie,* lit. "dark languor, lassitude") to the specific automatizing disorder of depersonalization, and contrast that with the deautomatizing effects of "running furtively down the streets" (*vorovskuyu pobezhku po ulitse,* lit. "running like thieves"; *Sentimental'noe,* 21)? Or is automatization simply part of the universal human process of habitualizing actions like holding a pen in one's hand? Is there any sense in which writing the article about the deautomatizing effects of literature *is* one of his own personal deautomatizing strategies, one of the ways he fights and overcomes the "dreariness" and "dark lassitude" to which he and many of his fellow Petrograd-based soldiers are subject while confined to barracks with nothing to do?

Not just writing it, in fact: once it has been passed by the censor, in late 1916 or early 1917, he and Osip Brik set about publishing it in their second volume of *Sborniki po teorii poeticheskogo yazika* ("Collections on the Theory of Poetic Language"). All around them, as the article is making its way into print, Russian civil society is collapsing. In a two-week period at the end of February and the beginning of March 1917, the February Revolution leads to the establishment of a provisional government and the abdication of the tsar, and Shklovsky, who is of the party now in power, seems like a kid in a candy shop. ("I was happy with these crowds. It was like Easter—a joyous, naïve, disorderly carnival paradise"; *Sentimental*, 16.) In April, Lenin returns to Russia, and Shklovsky is appointed by the Provisional Government as a commissar attached to the Russian army; in this capacity he ships out to the Galician (Western Polish) front, where he dashes from regiment to regiment trying to boost morale, exhausting himself ("Fatigue, hatred for the war and for ourselves kept us from thinking about self-preservation," 53), giving orders without authority, and leading troops into battle. In July, as the article is coming out, Shklovsky is wounded (shot in the stomach: "I kept crawling and felt happy," 53), and soldiers and workers stage insurrections all over Russia. While the revolt is violently suppressed, it is increasingly clear that the country is out of control.

After the October Revolution, he joins the Socialist Revolutionary Party, the so-called SRs (pronounced "essers"), which controls a majority of the Constituent Assembly (two-thirds SRs to one-third Bolsheviks) until that assembly is disbanded in January 1918 by a small group of Bolshevik soldiers. But he also ridicules the bovine stupidity of the party (indeed of any party). After fighting on the southwestern front (mostly Ukraine) and Persia he returns in the summer of 1918 to Petrograd and joins the Union for the Rebirth of Russia, an SR conspiracy attempting to restore the Constituent Assembly, which fails. He flees arrest to Kiev, which is occupied by the Germans, and works for the Germans' puppet Hetman Shoropadsky. With Gorky's help in January of 1919 he obtains a pardon for his "terrorist" activities against the Bolsheviks and again returns to Petrograd. It is bitterly cold, and the city has no infrastructure; there is no heat and little food. Some, he tells us, burn the furniture and then the floorboards and then move on to another apartment ("It wasn't so much swinishness as the use of things from a new point of view, and weakness," 177); others freeze or starve to death.

Despite these miserable conditions he marries Vasilisa Kordi and continues to pursue his theoretical interests: "There's a roaring in your ears, you're half-dead from the strain and you fall down. But your head keeps thinking by itself about 'The Connection between Plot Devices and General Stylistic Devices'" (177; see the "Deautomatization" section below). He meets weekly with his fellow formalists and others, including Maksim Gorky, Aleksandr Blok, Osip Mandel'shtam, Nikolay Gumilyov, often in locations extremely unconducive to intellectual discussion—"Once we met in a room that was flooded . . . Sometimes we met in the dark" (177). That winter and the following spring, he lectures on literary theory at the Translators' Studio that Gorky has founded in his World Literature Publishing House; his students include the writers who will eventually form the workshop or school called the Serapion Brothers, and his colleagues include Korney Chukovsky, Nikolay Gumilyov, Evgeny Zamyatin, and his fellow formalist Boris Eikhenbaum.

Traveling to Kherson, Ukraine, in 1920 to look for his wife (who has been there for a year), he forms a five-man demolition unit for the Reds, and in a careless moment ignites a German primer cylinder in his hands and tears eighteen holes in his body. Shipped back to Petrograd to recover, lying in an infirmary, the metal fragments sliding out of his wounds into his clothes, he writes his first Civil War memoir *Revolution and the Front,* which will eventually become part one of *A Sentimental Journey.* In early 1922 the Cheka begin arresting SR "terrorists," in particular those involved in the conspiracy of the summer of 1918, and gearing up for a show trial. Despite his earlier pardon for his involvement in that conspiracy, Shklovsky hears that he has been named as a coconspirator by the Soviet government's prime witness, a man who calls himself Grigoriy Semyonov, and flees across the winter ice from Petrograd to Finland, leaving his wife behind and going into a year-and-a-half exile in Berlin, already packed with 300,000 (mostly conservative monarchist but also artistic and intellectual) Russian exiles.

There the "dark lassitude" of his prerevolution confinement to barracks is repeated: bitterly unhappy, lonely, unable to speak or read the language, he holes up in his apartment and writes. In the weeks of his arrival and arrest/quarantine in Finland and the first ten days of his exile in Berlin, he finishes his memoir of the Civil War and reorganizes it into a kind of Sternian nonfiction novel,[8] riddled with ironic digressions and playful metafictional interruptions ("This whole digression is built on the device which in my 'poetics' is called retardation [*zaderzhaniem,* lit. holding back]"; *Sentimental'noe,* 185; *Sentimental,* 183), ending with his escape to Berlin ("Now I live among emigrants and am myself becoming a shadow among shadows"; *Sentimental* 276). He titles it, after Laurence Sterne's memoir, *A Sentimental Journey: Memoirs, 1917–1922.* He collects thirty-six short essays, reviews, and feuilletons (written and originally published between 1919 and 1921 in the theater journal *Zhizn' iskusstva* "The

Life of Art"), adds two prefaces and an epilogue, and titles them *Khod konya* ("Knight's Move")—comparing literary conventions to chess conventions but also in his first preface tying his title to his flight from Russia. The knight's move, he writes, is "not free . . . because it is forbidden to take the straight road," but it is nevertheless not a "coward's move": "I'm no coward" (*Knight*, 3–4). He publishes both *A Sentimental Journey* and *Knight's Move* in 1923, with Helikon-Verlag in Berlin. He writes his first book of cinema criticism, *Literatura i kinematograf* ("Literature and the Cinematographer") and publishes it too in Berlin. He falls in love with El'za Triolet, sister of Osip Brik's wife Lilya, and she rejects him; he builds his correspondence with her, including seven actual letters from her (one of the first of which requires him not to write of love), into an epistolary memoir-novel entitled *Zoo, or Letters Not About Love, or the Third Héloïse*, a series of fragmentary self-undermining Sternian/modernist reflections on everything, including love, grounded in the misery of his exile.[9] (A third volume of this fictionalized memoir or memoirized fiction is to follow upon his return to Russia, *Third Factory*, arising out of the pressure being brought to bear on him to recant his formalism.)

After several impassioned petitions to the Central Committee to pardon him, powerfully supported by Gorky and Mayakovsky, he is allowed to return in late 1923, and becomes a prolific screenwriter, sometime actor, and respected literary critic. One of the first things he does when he arrives in Moscow is to collect some of his published articles, including "Art as Device," into an essay collection entitled *O teorii prozy* ("On the Theory of Prose"), which appears in 1925. As the political pressure builds against formalism, beginning with the fifth chapter of Trotsky's *Literature and Revolution* in 1924 and culminating in an official ban on formalism in 1932, Shklovsky adapts.[10] He dons protective coloring, publishing more formalist essays under the title *Gamburgsky schyot* ("The Hamburg / Score Rankings") in 1928 and an expanded edition of *O teorii prozy* in 1929, but then a sneaky mock-retraction of his formalism in 1930 ("Pamyatnik") and a series of equally sneaky mock-denials of his own theory in later life. As he says in *A Sentimental Journey*, adaptability comes naturally to him:

> If I were to wind up on an uninhabited island, I'd become not Robinson Crusoe, but an ape. That's what my wife said about me. I never heard a truer definition. It wasn't hard for me.
>
> I have the capacity to flow, to change, even to become ice or steam. I can fit into any kind of shoes. I went along with the others. (169)

This, it should be clear, is the polar opposite of Tolstoy's depersonalized response to ideosomatic pressure from other people. Tolstoy doesn't even feel that pressure and so feels isolated, individualized, alienated, cut off from shared meaning; Shklovsky feels that pressure so strongly that he is able to surrender self to it. As a result, where Tolstoy theorizes the unbelabored infectiousness of joy and spiritual union as a utopian cure for his own estrangement, Shklovsky at least in part theorizes estrangement and belabored form as an adjustment or resistance to his own tendency to go along, to adapt, to become like everybody else. His dry irony throughout his fifty books and hundreds of articles works complexly to mobilize the shifting boundary between "own" and alien, the familiar and the strange: "It was strange to see [*stranno bylo videt*] some of the soldiers urinating right on the bunks" (*Sentimental'noe*, 173; *Sentimental*, 168). At the very simplest level, here, his estranging irony helps him *not* urinate on the bunks.[11]

It might also be argued that the automatization process Shklovsky describes in his early essays, while not necessarily anything that he has personally experienced in response to specific historical events, is sociohistorically grounded in a broader sense, in that same general turn-of-the-century depersonalization—loss of shared sensation or feeling, breakdown of ideosomatic regulation—that Tolstoy too felt and attacked twenty years before. In his 1915 review of Mayakovsky's "Cloud in Trousers," for example, he writes (while himself fighting the war as an armored-vehicle driver):

We Russians didn't know how to write about today. Art, no longer coupling [*sparivaemoe*] with life, from its continuous marriages between close relatives—old poetic images—shrank, expired. Myth expired . . . The application and simultaneously the coexistence of all artistic epochs in the soul of the passéist most fully resembles a cemetery where the dead are no longer enemies. And life was left to chronicles and cinema. Art departed that life into the crowded circle of people, where it led its spectral existence like a memory. And we lost our feeling for matter [*u nas propalo chuvstvo materiala*], began to give cement the form of stone, iron the form of wood. Thus began the century of the zinc mould, the stamped gesture, and the oleograph. Guinea pigs with severed leg nerves gnawed off their toes. Having lost together with art the sensation of life, the world [*Mir, poteryavshyi vmeste s iskusstvom oschuschenie zhizni*] is now most monstrously committing suicide. In our time of dead art the war bypasses consciousness [*soznaniya*], which explains its great cruelty, greater than that of the religious wars. ("Vyshla," 42–43, my translation)

The first thing to notice about this passage is that in it Shklovsky, often read as *celebrating* the machine age, here clearly associates mechanical reproduction ("the zinc mould, the stamped gesture, and the oleograph") with the death of art. So far from putting us in touch with the material world, this deadly downflowing of conventionalized art into science and technology is accompanied by a feeling of object-loss, a decreased sense of contact with reality.[12] Myth may have expired, but Shklovsky here promotes a myth of his own: as art-as-promiscuous-sex (a Wildean image of art ever restlessly creating and coupling with new images of life) degenerates into the incestuous marriage of conventionalization, we lose our "feeling for matter," our "sensation of life," no longer feel pain, and so leave ourselves open to the "great cruelty" of suicide-by-war. On the surface all Shklovsky is saying here is that the social world and the aesthetic world have lost the sensation of life (or, to extrapolate a little, that *we* have lost our sensation of life in our experiences of other people and of artworks)—a simultaneity of social and aesthetic sensation-loss that might be attributed, following Hegel, to the alienation produced by advanced capitalism (see chapter 4). But it is just possible that Shklovsky, like Tolstoy, blames "bad art" (Tolstoy) or "dead art" (Shklovsky) for all the evils of the present moment. The main difference between them is, of course, that for Tolstoy the quintessence of "bad art" is precisely the kind of modernist estrangement Shklovsky is calling for, and for Shklovsky "dead art" comes from endless tired imitations of Tolstoy (or any other established writer).

The second thing to notice is that this book review from Shklovsky's twenty-second year is a nascent somatics of literature, which he may even have learned from Tolstoy: a conception of literary works as able to infect readers with the sensation of life, with a feeling for matter. This conception lies at the heart of Shklovsky's formalism. The analysis of literary forms that many readers have taken to be his primary or even sole concern is merely a means to this end, the end of harnessing literature to the old liberal aim of helping people live their lives better. His somatic theory is never particularly well developed theoretically—a case in point here is his insistence that "The war bypasses *consciousness*" when what he is specifically saying is that the war bypasses *sensation*—and in general it should be relatively uncontroversial to suggest that Shklovsky was always better at poetic insights than he was at methodical argumentation. But the somatic theory saturates all his writings of the teens, when he is in his twenties, and it does take on definition and a certain degree of theoretical complexity as he moves toward the Stalin era and the end of formalism. Above all, he carefully reads Broder Christiansen's 1909 *Philosophie der Kunst* in Fedotov's 1911 Russian translation, hears a good deal about William James's 1890 *Principles of Psychology* from his fellow formalists (and may even read James a little), and begins to develop a relatively detailed sense of how readers' somatic responses to literary works give shape to and take impetus from literary form.[13]

For example, by the time he writes his 1919 essay "The Relationship Between Devices of Plot Construction and General Devices of Style," which has a long quotation from Christiansen (to which we return below), Shklovsky is able to apply the Jamesian principle that feeling is a mental mapping of sensation or emotion: if it is consciousness (feeling-becoming-mind) that makes sensation available to us as "reality," then the dulling or anesthetization of consciousness will indeed dull or anesthetize sensation as well. When he raises this notion in "Art as Device," more of the raw analytical materials are available to him than in the Mayakovsky review the year before, and he does more with them—just what he does with them forms the central focus of this chapter—but they remain still relatively inchoate. His primary example for this anesthetization in "Art as Device," of course, is the 68-year-old Tolstoy wiping up dust with a rag in his guest room in Nikol'skoe, the house on the outskirts of Moscow of his friends the Olsuf'yevs, where he has fled the schisms of Yasnaya Polyana (and where he keeps busy writing letters and the early chapters of *What Is Art?*):

> I was wiping dust [*obtiral pyl'*, "dusting with a rag"] in the room and, moving around, came up to the divan and couldn't remember whether I'd wiped it or not. Because these movements are habitual and unconscious, I couldn't—and felt that it was impossible to—remember. Thus if I had wiped it and forgotten doing so, i.e. acted unconsciously, it was the same as if it had never happened. If some conscious person saw, it could be recovered. If no one saw or did see, but unconsciously; if the whole complex life of many people passes unconsciously, then it is as if that life had never been. (quoted in Shklovsky, "Iskusstvo," 11, my translation)[14]

"So, unheeded," Shklovsky adds, "does life fade away. Automatization swallows up things, dress, furniture, one's wife, and the fear of war. 'If the whole life of many people passes unconsciously, then it is as if that life had never been'" ("Iskusstvo," 11, my translation). Then comes his key passage, which I'd like to quote in Shklovsky's Russian and my slightly foreignized translation:

И вот для того, чтобы вернуть ощущение жизни, почувствовать вещи, для того, чтобы делать камень каменным, существует то, что называется искусством. Целью искусства является дать ощущение вещи, как видение, а не как узнавание; приемом искусства является прием „остранения" вещей и прием затрудненной формы, увеличивающий трудность и долготу восприятия, так как воспринимательный процесс в искусстве самоцелен и должен быть продлен; и с к у с с т в а е с т ь с п о с о б п е р е ж и т ь д е л а н ь е в е щ и, а с д е л а н н о е в и с к у с с т в е н е в а ж н о.

And so, in order to restore the sensation of life, to feel things, to make the stone stony, there exists what we call art. Art's purpose is to give us the sensation of a thing as seeing rather than as recognizing; art's device is a device for the "estrangement" of things, a device of belabored form that increases the laboriousness and duration of perception, because in art the perceptual process is self-purposive and should be prolonged. *Art is a way of experiencing the making of a thing, but the thing made in art is not important.*

The Four Things

Let me begin to unpack this theory by comparing it with the received Soviet reinterpretation, running from Lev Vygotsky's critique in the third chapter of his 1925 dissertation on the psychology of art to Shklovsky's own near-chameleonic recapitulation of that critique in his 1966 postmortem on his theory, the article we've already begun looking at, "Obnovlenie ponyatiya" ("The Renewal of a Concept").

Ironically, both Vygotsky and the older Shklovsky fault the 1917 article for its "contradictory" argumentation, but they miss the one actual contradiction that is there and focus on points that are not contradictory at all. The actual contradiction in the key paragraph is that Shklovsky gives us at once a *purpose* for perception in art ("Art's purpose [*tsel'*] is to give us the sensation of a thing as seeing rather than as recognition") and an idealized aestheticist statement of the ultimate *purposelessness* of perception in art ("in art the perceptual process is self-purposive [*samotselen*] and should be prolonged"). Perhaps not purposelessness, exactly: *samotselen* "self-purposive," literally "self-purposed," means that it does have a purpose, just no purpose beyond itself. Still, in one sentence he is clearly saying that artistic perception does have a purpose beyond itself, to restore the sensation of life in readers, and in the other he is saying that it doesn't. It could, of course, be argued that there is no contradiction here—that the purpose of giving us the sensation of a thing *is* the self-purpose of artistic perception, that the aestheticism of "the perceptual process is self-purposive and should be prolonged" is self-identical with the aestheticism of giving the sensation of the thing as seeing. Are sensing and seeing, after all, not both perceptual operations?

But this reading would ignore the important fact about Shklovsky's essay that he is subordinating aesthetics to a specific psychological task, one that has been called "millennial" (Clark) and "traditionalist," harking back to the "socio-psychological mission of art" as imagined by nineteenth-century thinkers like Thomas Carlyle and Friedrich Hebbel (Tihanov, "Poetics," 673–74): restoring something valuable to us that we have lost, our sense that we are living our lives. This contradiction lies at the core of Shklovsky's intellectual crossroads at the time, his attempts in the mid-teens to mediate between an older conception of art as socially responsive and responsible (art's purpose is to help us live our lives more fully) and a futurist *zaum* aestheticism (art is self-purposive) that came to be associated exclusively with his and his fellow formalists' thought. The latter is the Shklovsky that has been isolated for blame by Soviet thinkers (beginning in 1924 with Trotsky) and for praise by Western and post-Soviet structuralists and poststructuralists; the former, who is just now beginning to be excavated from the rubble of the established structuralist reading, will be my focus here.

But as I say, neither Vygotsky nor the older Shklovsky mentions this actual contradiction (Vygotsky comes close a few pages later);[15] instead, they seize upon an absurdly bogus one that reflects the concerns of a normative vulgar Marxism. Here is Vygotsky:

> It turns out, subsequently, that that device from which artistic form arises does have its purpose, and in defining that purpose the formalists' theory falls into a surprising contradiction: it begins with the assertion that in art things, materials, contents are not important, and concludes by asserting that the purpose of artistic form appears to be "to feel a thing," "to make the stone stony," that is, to experience more strongly and more sharply that very material they began by rejecting. Thanks to this contradiction the true importance of the laws of estrangement and the rest found by the formalists is lost, so that the purpose of this estrangement in the final analysis turns out to be the very same perception of things. This fundamental failing of formalism—not understanding the psychological significance of material—leads it to a one-sided sensualism, just as failing to understand form did the Potebnyans to a one-sided intellectualism. The formalists suppose that in art material plays no role and that a poem about the destruction of the world and a poem about a cat and a stone are equal from the standpoint of their poetic action. (*Psikhologiya*, 75–76, my translation)

Intuitively, it does seem right, of course, to insist on the importance of the difference between a poem about the destruction of the world and a poem about a cat and a stone, and therefore to dismiss a critic who denies the existence or the importance of that difference as one-sided. But at the very least it is not clear that Shklovsky *is* denying the importance of a poem's topic or theme. The complexity that Vygotsky fudges in Shklovsky revolves around the word *vesch'* "thing," and what it means to "feel" or "make" one (more on that in a moment).

In 1966 Shklovsky is still echoing this official reinterpretation in print:

The incorrectness of the term consists in the fact that I was offering a stylistic means as the final purpose of art, thus depriving art of its true function.

Furthermore, the term *ostranenie* at its inception was contradictory. The contradiction consisted in the fact that I simultaneously asserted that art is "not an inscription, but a decorative pattern or design" [*ne nadpis', a uzor*], one can only "estrange" and restore to sensation something that exists in reality and is felt, as was clear from all my examples. But art, according to my theory of the time, was not supposed to be tied to reality, to phenomena; it was a purely linguistic and stylistic phenomenon.

The erroneous theory was self-contradictory even in a single article.

According to that theory, which I've now been recollecting, some artistic air reverberated with magnetic storms that even now could not have caused radio interference or kept anyone from sending a telegram.

The world of art in that theory was created as if once. Then the works of art just kept changing clothes and standing around being compared [*pereodevalis' i sopostavlyalis'*].

Now I know that at the foundation of art lies a striving to penetrate through to life. Seeing and feeling life, we will not believe that it does not exist, will not deny our world-awareness, leaving ourselves only the inhibition of sensation on the very verge of awareness [*tormozhenie oschuscheniya, samoyo ostanovku pered poznaniem,* lit. "the braking of sensation, the very stop before awareness/cognition"]. We will not set limits to human reason, because when we step up to such a limit, we find only the limit of our own cognition.

We will watch how humanity breaks through to awareness, how far we've come, we will understand why we reorganize the world, how by reorganizing it we become aware of it, we will set art at the forefront of human reason, attacking awareness. (305–6, my translation)

At first glance this is a mess. Shklovsky's critique of his own early essay seems not only incorrect on every point but utterly incoherent. But Shklovsky was always a devious writer, never quite the perfect chameleon as which we saw him posing in *The Sentimental Journey*, always leaving a few uncamouflaged spots to signal to the careful reader what he was really up to. And that, I suggest, is what the "mess" is here: a carefully constructed mixture of political camouflage and devious signaling. If I'm right, Shklovsky's strategy in the passage is to attack his own theory for all the wrong reasons and then surreptitiously to reiterate that theory in detailing what he says he "now knows."

The wrong reasons he gives are that he never wrote anything like "art is 'not an inscription, but a decorative pattern or design,'" and it would have made no sense in his theory if he had; it is impossible to "restore to sensation something that exists in reality" (you can only restore to sensation a *sensation* of or *feeling* about something that exists in reality, which indeed all his examples showed, and at which his phrasing here—"and is felt"—hints); art in his theory was never "a purely linguistic and stylistic phenomenon"; and "some artistic air reverberat[ing] with magnetic storms that even now could not have caused radio interference or kept anyone from sending a telegram" and the world of art being created just once and then standing around changing clothes are pleasantly absurd fantasies that had nothing to do with anything he wrote.

What he now knows is what he's always known: "that at the foundation of art lies a striving to penetrate through to life," specifically by inhibiting sensation on the verge of awareness so as to *intensify* both sensation and awareness, specifically to intensify that awareness (mental mapping) of somatic response that gives us our sense of reality, our feeling for matter, our sense of contact with the material world. When he says we *won't* leave ourselves "*only* the inhibition of sensation on the very verge of awareness," he implies on the surface that this is a new "postconversion" resolution in line with the official Soviet materialism, while implying just below the surface that this was his resolution all along: we won't, because we never did. The inhibition of sensation was never *only* that; it was an instrument in the recovery of an intensified sensation of reality.

His rhetorical deviousness reaches a kind of gloriously bathetic nadir in the two short paragraphs that follow:

> Like a beaver's tooth, it [art] is blunted gnawing on wood, but sharpened on awareness, on work [*v rabote*].
>
> But let us leave beavers in their preserves, though they live peacefully and nurse their young, having lifted them in their wet paws. Let us return to literature. (306)

The first paragraph simply restates his theory of estrangement, precisely that which he is supposedly ruefully regretting ever having penned: the blunting of the beaver's tooth is the reader's automatization, the fading of the sensation of life or the feeling for matter, and the awareness that sharpens that tooth is the product of the psychological work that estranged or belabored literary form makes us do (more on "work" later). This is the 73-year-old Shklovsky shamelessly thumbing his nose at his Soviet censors, who are apparently too stupid to notice what he's doing here.

The animal-kingdom bathos of the second paragraph, though, introduced by the absurdly digressive "though" (*puskay*), is sheer devious fun. What began as a tricky metaphor is here extended recursively into a satirical conceit, a series of subtle parodies of Soviet ideals (materialism, peace) that ends in absurd irrelevancies (nursing, wet paws). Beavers are not only creatures in the real material world, which he has now supposedly learned *really exists;* they are peace-loving and hard-working creatures, like the communist citizens of Soviet propaganda. And the wonderfully anticlimactic wet paws are redolent of the anticlimactic cattle that bring the whimsically satirical Old Testament Book of Jonah to a close: "And should not I pity Nineveh, that great city, in which there are more than a hundred and twenty thousand persons who do not know their right hand from their left, and also much cattle?" (Jonah 4:11, RSV). The Soviets are Jonah, his totalitarian rage multiplied exponentially, hegemonically, institutionally; Shklovsky, of course, is the book's amiably tolerant but allegorically tongue-in-cheek-pedantic God.

The contradiction Vygotsky claims to find in Shklovsky's argument (for I believe Vygotsky in his dissertation is thumbing his nose at the censors in precisely the same vein as the older Shklovsky)[16] is indicative of the vulgar-Marxist materialism of the Second International, Stalin, and Zinoviev, on which official discussions of Soviet socialist realism were eventually to be based. As Vygotsky presents the matter, the contradiction arises in Shklovsky because a thing is a thing, a material object pure and simple, and if Shklovsky first says that the purpose of art is to make readers feel a thing more strongly or to experience the making of a thing, then it makes no sense for him to say that the thing itself is not important. But the young Shklovsky is no Marxist, but a left-leaning Hegelian who here anticipates the Hegelian Western Marxism of Georg Lukács (the critique of "reification" and "phantom objectivity" in *History and Class Consciousness*) by six years.[17] Shklovsky is talking about very different things, indeed different *orders* of things, at least four:

Thing 1: the stone as an experienced or felt or "somatically seen" object
Thing 2: the stone as an algebraic or "recognized" reduction of Thing 1
that in fact feels like *no* thing at all
Thing 3: the poetic image of a stone as a representation of Thing 1
Thing 4: the poem itself

His theory of the estrangement device begins, then, in the insistence that as Thing 1 is increasingly habitualized, algebraically reduced to an "outline" that is merely "recognized," it becomes Thing 2, which is to say, begins to "fade away" (*propadat*), to lose experiential heft or reality. (Technically speaking, the distinction between Thing 1 and Thing 2 is not a binary but a sorites series, an infinite number of fractal gradations between the seen/felt thing and the unseen/unfelt thing, or between richly experienced thinginess and an experience of no-thinginess.) Since Thing 1 is essentially our experience—or, as Freud says, our "representation"—of the material world we live in, this progressive desomatizing of Thing 1 is quite disastrous. If we do not feel ourselves acting on the world around us, we lose all sense of our own reality as well. The experiential erosion of Thing 1 as it becomes Thing 2 is in effect a nightmarish version of Emerson's apocalypse of the mind,[18] in which the world is destroyed by neither water nor fire but habit.

Thus the importance, as the older Shklovsky says, reporting what he "now knows," of the artistic "striving to penetrate through to life." For the younger Shklovsky this penetration was the task of Thing 3, the poetic representation of Thing 1, which, by rendering perception of the thing difficult, by increasing the labor involved in coming or learning to see it somatically, kicks Thing 2 in the seat of the pants and transforms it back into Thing 1. Since Thing 2 is, of course, not a material pants-wearing object but our severely attenuated *experience* of the object, to "kick it in the pants" is actually to kick our perceptual activity in the pants, to make us somatically regenerate the living experience that is Thing 1. (An algebraic translation of the phrase *delat' kamen' kamennym* "to make the stone stony" might be "to make Thing 2 Thing 1." That translation of course protects Shklovsky's powerful poetic image against politically correct misreadings at the cost of its ability to make the stone stony.)

Finally, we have Thing 4, which is what Shklovsky says is not important: *sdelannoe* "the thing made." It requires close critical attention to Shklovsky's last sentence to figure out that *delan'ye veschi* "the making of a thing" in the previous clause refers to *artistic* making, and indeed to the very making of Thing 3 that makes Thing 2 Thing 1, so that it becomes clear that what

Shklovsky is dismissing as unimportant is not the theme or topic or "material" of a poem but the poem itself, the made thing.

Part of the problem here, of course, is that the last line in that key paragraph is one of the typically vatic pronouncements that make Shklovsky's essay at once so memorable and so easy to misread: for what *is* the "thing made"? Even if we gloss this as "the poem itself," what does that mean? In a sense Thing 3 is "the poem itself," too. Why is that thing important and Thing 4 not? The answer, of course, is that Thing 3 is the poem as psychological effect, and Thing 4 is the poem as dead literary object, the object of literary study, including so-called formalist literary study, the poem as algebraically reduced to "form" or "content" or "form plus content."[19]

We return to the four Things in connection with Hegel in chapter 4 and in connection with Brecht's spatiotemporal dynamic of estrangement in chapter 5.

Restoring Sensation to Life

As I say, Shklovsky never explicitly links automatization to alienation or depersonalization and never even notices the complexly integral relation between his own theory of the reorienting estrangement *of* the world in art and the disorienting estrangement *from* the world that is symptomatic in depersonalization. This failure to theorize the difference between literary estrangement and psychopathological estrangement leaves Shklovsky wide open to accusations like Vadim Rudnev's to the effect that there is no difference at all, that Shklovsky *is* infecting literary theory with the psychopathology of depersonalization:

> In this way we may say that "estrangement," the poetics of depersonalization, could be revealed in Tolstoy precisely by Shklovsky and precisely because Shklovsky worked out what can be called the "depersonalization of poetics." The literary work appears in Shklovsky as something alienated or estranged. No habitualized images, no scientific "lyrics." He takes pride in daring to view literature as the sum of devices, which is to say in the very thing that deprives him of that measurement that Dostoevsky's underground man ironically called "high and excellent." In essence, Shklovsky views literature precisely as Natasha Rostova views the opera. He doesn't seem to realize what is "excellent" before him. This very position of nonunderstanding was the beginning of theoretical poetics as authentic science. This was the science of depersonalization. Hence the many paths that emerged from it. First in line, of course, it is customary to name the morphologist of the

fairy tale Vladimir Propp, and likewise the formalists Yury Tynyanov, Boris Eikhenbaum, Boris Yarkho, and many other scholars of this critical orientation. But Shklovsky's position was the most radical of all; not for nothing was he the formalists' standard-bearer.

And precisely for this reason Tolstoy was the favorite object of Shklovsky's scientific manipulations, from the Tolstoyan fragments in *The Theory of Prose* of 1925, to the excellent 1928 book *Matter and Style in Lev Tolstoy's* War and Peace, to the late biography of Tolstoy in the "Life of Extraordinary People" series.

Tolstoy became the mirror of Russian Formalism. Why, for poetics to become a true science, did depersonalization become necessary?

Let's imagine a surgeon who, looking at a patient's wound that he will have to sew up, begins to sob, wring his hands, say "Oh my god that's disgusting!", "I can't stand it!" and so on. In order to perform the operation, the surgeon will have to depersonalize his human relation with the patient. That is precisely why poetics had to be depersonalized as well in order to obtain the shiny results that it obtained in the twenties, and even in the sixties and seventies. (61)

[handwritten marginal note: What about Compassion?]

Note that this is not only a much more complex misreading of Shklovsky than the official Soviet misreading proffered by Vygotsky in 1925 and Shklovsky himself in 1966 but the *exact opposite* misreading. Where the Soviets refused to recognize the existence of alienation or estrangement in Soviet life, the post-Soviet theorist Rudnev thinks Shklovsky sees or spreads nothing but alienation and estrangement in life, literature, and theory.[20] Where the older Shklovsky ridicules his theory of estrangement as poetic nonsense that pales into insignificance before scientific phenomena like radio interference or the telegraph, Rudnev assimilates it to precisely the same kind of scientific device or attitude, "the sum of devices," "authentic science," the depersonalized surgeon.

What is complex about Rudnev's misreading, though, is that it *doubly* alienates and estranges Shklovsky's theory; for Rudnev "literary work appears in Shklovsky as something alienated and estranged" ("kak nechto otchuzhdyonnoe i ostranyonnoe"), suggesting both that Shklovsky *finds* literature already alienated and estranged and that he *alienates* and *estranges* literature. But Rudnev's examples of this reading include on the one hand the absence from literature of habitualized images, which sounds like a literature that has been artificially and simplistically (idealistically) purged of all automatization, and thus empowered to serve as the estranging and dealienating force Shklovsky was theorizing, and on the other "daring to view literature as the sum of devices" and "nonunderstanding," which sound like the wandering-blind in an alienated world of a depersonalized literary critic. Thus literature becomes simultaneously an unalienated and unestranged (what Tolstoy might want to call "uninfected") device for the dealienation and deestrangement of life and an alienating and estranging device that infects life and literary theory with its scientifically depersonalized nonunderstanding.

The Homeostatic Regulation of Reality

Part of the confusion here is that both alienation/*otchuzhdenie* and estrangement/*ostranenie* have come to mean opposite things: a passive, pathological isolation from communal feeling and meaning and an active, transformative hypermimesis of that feeling of isolation for the therapeutic purpose of communal reintegration. Hence the Moebius-strip return of alienation to dealienation, of estrangement to deestrangement: the purpose of the artistic alienation or estrangement that Shklovsky and later Bertolt Brecht preach and practice is to dealienate and deestrange, to render things more alien and strange in order to push audiences to break out of their alienated and estranged state. We will see more of this confusion in chapter 5, when the American playwright John Guare, responding to John Willett's translation of Brecht's *Verfremdungseffekt* as "alienation effect," wonders why a playwright would ever want to alienate an audience.

Nor is this simply Rudnev's or Guare's failure to distinguish between two distinct uses of a term; the darker, more pathological, more isolating sense of alienation and estrangement is always vestigially present in Romantic and modernist theories as well. If your idea is to dealienate audiences by infecting them with a homeopathic or hypermimetic dose of alienation, it is crucial, obviously, to titrate your dosage just right, or you *will* just alienate them further; but given the complexity of the somatics of literary response, such precise regulation of estranging dosages is impossible. What is just right for some readers or viewers will alienate others; what is just right for those ideal readers or viewers today may alienate them tomorrow.

What makes Shklovsky's essay particularly problematic in this respect is that he not only borrows something like Tolstoy's homeopathic or hypermimetic method but cuts the (de)alienating mimetic force of Tolstoy's infectious cure even closer to the disease. Both theorists want to cure infectious depersonalization with infectious repersonalization, but where Tolstoy thematizes his cure as Christian joy and spiritual union, the idealized polar opposite to the disorder that has blighted his seventy years, Shklovsky thematizes his as estrangement, literary estrangement as—at least by semantic contagion—an estranging imitation of psychopathological estrangement. In medical terms, this strategy significantly increases the homeopathic dosage and thus also the potential for the contamination of the cure by the disease, the "like" by the "like" in "like-cures-like."

For example:

> The deautomatization of the perception of things is achieved in art in various ways; in this article I want to point out one of those ways that was used almost constantly by Lev Tolstoy—that writer who, for Merezhkovsky at least, seems to present things as he himself sees them, sees to the end, but does not alter them.
>
> Tolstoy's estrangement device consists in his not calling a thing by its name but describing it as if he were seeing it for the first time, or an event as if it were happening for the first time, in the course of which he uses for the description of things not the accepted names of their parts but the names of the corresponding parts of other things. Let me give an example. In the article "Shame" Tolstoy estranges the concept of flogging . . . "people who have broken the law are stripped, thrown to the floor, and beaten on the backside with switches," and, after a few lines, "lash about the denuded buttocks." Around here he remarks: "And why precisely this stupid, savage means of causing pain and not some other: prick the shoulder or some other body part with needles, squeeze the hands or feet in a vise, or the like?" I apologize for the disturbing [*tyazhyoliy*, lit. "heavy"] example, but it's typical of the way Tolstoy reaches through to the conscience. The habitualized act of flogging is estranged both by the description and by the proposal to change its form without changing its essence. This method of estrangement Tolstoy used constantly: in one of the cases ("Kholstomer") the story proceeds from the person of [is narrated by] a horse, and things are estranged not through our perception of them but the horse's. (13–14, my translation)

Because Tolstoy *sees* things strangely, and presents them as he sees them, his writing is estranging. While the estranging effect is intended, as Shklovsky says, to "deautomatize the perception of things," clearly other effects are also possible, as he hints in apologizing for the "disturbing example." The example needs to be "heavy" or disturbing in order to estrange us therapeutically, but too heavy a disturbance may estrange us countertherapeutically—may infect us not with Tolstoy's indignation against flogging but with his estrangement from the ordinary way of doing things. After all, his indignation emerges out of his estrangement from ideosomatic regulation, his depersonalization; there is no binary between them. If anything, there is a fuzzy logic between them, a sorites series in which the passive psychopathology of depersonalization is gradually transformed into an activist clarity about the dehumanizing and indeed depersonalizing effects of flogging. And Tolstoy's and Shklovsky's readers may find themselves responding to the example from anywhere along that sorites series: readers may already be so depersonalized as to find the example realistic and hilarious, or so habitualized to the ordinary way of doing things as to find it unrealistic and frightening, or anything in between. It may push them along that series in either direction; and the effect on them of several re-readings may be cumulative in either direction as well, tending to depersonalize or repersonalize them over time. (This would be the unpredictable temporal dynamic that we saw Tolstoy reaching toward but unable to formulate—let alone deal with—in chapter 2; Shklovsky does not even raise the problem.)

This passage also suggests the specific psychological mechanism by which the estrangement device works on readers: by dividing their entire emotional-becoming-mental perception of a thing into two parts, the familiar and the strange, and contaminating the former with the latter, perhaps also in some cases the latter with the former. In a sense this method simply transposes Paul's divided salvational geography of self and other, local and foreign, familiar and strange, near and far into the reader's perceptual apparatus and polices traffic from one side to the other, in particular letting a little strangeness in where there is too much familiarity, where excess familiarity is deadening, but also, perhaps—though Shklovsky does not explicitly theorize this here—letting a little familiarity in where there is too much strangeness. (He will later hint at the latter in *A Sentimental Journey,* in noting that in the midst of the chaos of the Civil War, there arose even in the most dedicated adventurers "a kind of fatigue or a craving for peace and quiet," so that, for example, "many men who had lived adventurously" ended up marrying older women who took care of them; 146.) As my tentative formulation in the previous paragraph hinted, while too much familiarity can be numbing/depersonalizing, too much strangeness can be disturbing/depersonalizing. Depersonalization is experienced along much the same sorites series from numb unreality to a nightmarishly distorted, disorienting surreality, all of the fractal increments on that series radically off the therapeutic (re)integrative or repersonalizing familiar-to-strange track.[21]

What this model points to, in fact, is a kind of somatic homeostatic regulation of our sense of reality. When we feel somatically integrated with the community, when we feel other people's regulatory feelings, we feel connected to reality, grounded in collectively defined reality; but that groundedness can become overfamiliar, anesthetic, numbingly conventionalized, and the resulting depletion of felt connection with collective reality can depersonalize us, flip us over into numb depersonalization. This is the state Shklovsky seeks to cure by adding strangeness to the mix: if, when life becomes overly conventionalized and we begin to feel numb, a poem can add a little strangeness to the mix, we may be able to reconnect with the sensation of life being lived and resist the pull of depersonalization. When on the other hand we feel both somatically integrated with the community and pleasantly different, with an enjoyable sense of the strange, the odd, the dissonant, the off, we feel grounded in a slightly more idiosyncratic but nevertheless collective reality; but that groundedness can become overstrange, nightmarishly surreal, and the resulting depletion of felt connection with individualized collective reality can flip us over into disturbing or disorienting depersonalization. This last is a state Shklovsky does not recognize; as a result, the obvious poetic cure for it—adding a little familiarity to the mix—is one he does not theorize.

Proprioception and the Phantom Limb

Caryl Emerson has an interesting article comparing Shklovsky's concept of estrangement with Mikhail Bakhtin's of *vnenakhodimost'* "being-outside, outsideness," which leads her to suggest something quite similar to my homeostatic model—a theoretical world in which bodies that feel too little invent theories of intensified sensation and bodies that feel too much dream of a numbing distance. "We do not know," she writes, "to what extent Shklovsky's body, with its eighteen pieces of shrapnel embedded in it from that civil war wound, also spoke up for the rest of his life. Nor can we know whether chronic pain would have prompted Shklovsky to modify the idea of ostranenie, which he had penned as a healthy young man in Petrograd and had made so dependent for its aesthetic benefits on intensified sensate perception" (649).[22] Bakhtin, on the other hand, who spent the first half of his life in intense pain from osteomyelitis and only after his infected leg was amputated practically to the hip, at age 43, was able to work more or less normally (but never without pain), envisions artistic distancing not as a making-strange but a getting-outside: "When, as the result of an illness, we lose control over one of our limbs—a leg, for example—this leg appears to us as something precisely alien, 'not mine', although in the externally visual and intuitable image of my body it is undoubtedly part of the whole of myself" (quoted in Emerson, 649). Emerson comments:

It should be noted that "experience" here does not mean—as it appears to mean for Shklovsky—friction, tension, exaggeration or exacerbation but precisely the opposite. Bakhtin is striving for connectedness and inner integration, the ideal of a body that has forgotten itself. If a body does not experience this integration, if I see the part but have "lost control" of it, then "I am quite prepared to reject a given fragment as not mine, as not part of my body" . . . In fact, I must reject this dead part. If I fail to do so, I will be unable to perform those movements through space, which require above all a sense of the seamless whole. Intriguing parallels might be drawn between this dead, "othered" leg and the Russian Formalist passion for impeding, braking, de-facilitating, and estranging objects and processes, the better to perceive them as art (and the better, the more vividly, to perceive life through its refraction in artistic form). From the perspective of Bakhtin's subject, such a desire to set up deliberate, artificial obstacles and woundings could only be the whim of a healthy and limber body. Bodies in pain, which already feel too much, partake of other fantasies. (649–50)

Of course, the perspective of Bakhtin's body-in-pain is only one extreme in the homeostatic system. From the standpoint of Shklovsky's numbed/depersonalized Tolstoyan subject, pain seems like a luxury: at least you know you're alive! The "dead, 'othered' leg" of the osteomyelitic is precisely *not* parallel to the belaboring of form and estranging of things that Shklovsky theorizes; it is (at least metaphorically) a symptom of the disease that he is trying to fight. The situation Bakhtin is describing sounds, in fact, a bit like the case of the woman David Bohm describes in *Thought as a System*

who woke in the middle of the night hitting herself. What had happened was that she'd had a stroke that damaged her sensory nerves, which would tell her what she was doing. But the stroke left the motor nerves so that she could still move her muscles. Apparently she had touched herself, but since she wasn't being informed that it was her own touch she assumed right away that it was an attack by somebody else. Then the more she defended the worse the attack got. When the light was turned on, the proprioception was reestablished because she could then see with her eyes what she was doing, so she stopped hitting herself. (121)

This is not entirely accurate: what happened when the woman turned on the light was *not* that "proprioception was reestablished" but rather that another bodily monitoring system was activated, the visual. Normally vision, the vestibular system, and the proprioceptive system work together to coordinate our sense of our own body for movement; if any one of them is damaged or disabled, the other two can compensate somewhat, but movement becomes extremely laborious. Proprioception is *only* the inner (nonvisual) sense we have of where our body parts are, what they are doing; if it is destroyed, vision alone doesn't restore it. The woman fighting herself has lost her proprioceptive sense that her arms are her own; they seem "othered," as if they were someone else's arms. There are similar stories of people waking up to find someone else's detached leg in bed with them and throwing it away in disgust, and finding to their surprise (as they fly off the bed) that they are still attached to the leg. This is the "dead, 'othered' leg" that we find in Bakhtin: the leg that has been "rejected" or "othered" or "found outside" by proprioceptive failure.

The total-body numbness that Tolstoy describes in his diary entry is actually more like the case of Christina from Oliver Sacks's *The Man Who Mistook His Wife for a Hat* (44–53), who suffered damage to her proprioceptive fibers and lost *all* sense of her own body. She had to teach herself to walk again visually, by watching each leg come forward and plant itself in front of the other, then deciding to shift weight to it, and then watching the other come forward. Unlike Bakhtin's body-in-pain or the woman fighting herself, Christina felt *nothing,* had no sense of the connectedness of any part of her body, and needed to learn how to integrate her visual and vestibular senses of body parts in order to walk, to move around in the world, to function. Bakhtin, by contrast, desperately attempting to integrate disparately sensed and numbed body parts so as not to find motion derailed by partial disembodiment, feels driven to redistribute recognition so as to build out of his own body a kind of makeshift Frankenstein's monster, selecting some parts or fragments for inclusion in the new patchwork whole, rejecting or "othering" others, "finding them outside" (the morphological sense of *vnenakhodimost*), reallocating them to the other side of the embodied dialogue with other people. "Healthy bodies, it would appear," Emerson writes, "are healthy precisely because they do not feel. Coordinated from within, spatial movements flow smoothly and unselfconsciously; the correct habits and training will always result in a certain anesthetization. Such blankness, far from being feared or deliberately provoked back to life, is the ideal for any dynamic, perfectly realized spatial art" (650).

But this is really only how things may come to look from the perspective of the body of which Bakhtin's "butler-chauffeur" Vladimir Turbin wrote: "Did that pain ever recede, even temporarily? Or did he simply live that way, carrying that pain in himself? That pain was itself a continuation of the pain from prior years, from very far back, a pain that he had hoped to rid himself of by undertaking the amputation. When did this ancient pain first begin to speak to him? Doubtless long ago. And to remove it, to muffle its voice, was impossible" (quoted in Emerson, 649). If pain is your body's unceasing, unmuf-flable voice, then it may come to seem as if the smooth and unself-conscious functioning of the normal body involves a kind of "anesthetization." In fact, smooth function is precisely what the anesthetized body is least capable of; coordinated spatial movement absolutely requires an *unconscious* propriocep-tive sense of the body's functioning. What Emerson is talking about here is the osteomyelitic's dream of *slightly less pain:* the anesthesis not of proprioception but of pain's distractions, pain's irritations; the homeostatic ratcheting back of pain to a slightly more tolerable level.

The phenomenological opposite of Bakhtin's willingness to reject a numbed or excessively painful or otherwise out-of-control body "fragment" is the phantom limb phenomenon, which Emerson mentions in passing (652; the Bakhtin passage she selects for close reading is from "Author and Hero in Aes-thetic Activity," most likely written in the early to mid-1920s, when Bakhtin was not yet 30 and still possessed both his legs), and which in fact is closer to what Shklovsky is imagining as estrangement. The phantom limb represents the other extreme of proprioception: whereas Christina felt no sensation in existing limbs (that therefore did not seem like her own), the amputee feels sensation in a limb that does not exist (but that still seems like his or her own). The body's proprioceptive system continues to generate a sense of the phe-nomenological "reality" of the amputated limb. The functioning of the prop-rioceptive system is one of the most powerful neurophysiological arguments we have against Descartes' mind-body dualism: our sense of whether the *res extensa* exists or does not exist, whether it is attached to us or separate from us, is controlled unconsciously by the nervous system, which in its unconscious-ness and its felt intensity is neither an internal rational "I" nor an external inert "it."

The proprioceptive sublation of the mind-body dualism is even more com-plex (and to a Cartesian binarist even more insidious) than this: Oliver Sacks quotes Michael Kremer to the effect that "no amputee with an artificial lower limb can walk on it satisfactorily until the body-image, in other words the phantom, is incorporated into it" (67). For an amputee trying to walk with a prosthetic leg, the "smooth functioning" that Bakhtin thinks requires anes-thesis in fact requires the incorporation of sensation from a no-longer-existing limb into the prosthesis—though of course one must immediately add that for an amputee in pain like Bakhtin, smooth functioning might require the reintegration of the phantom limb *and* the anesthetization of some or most of the pain. The proprioceptive system, in effect, polices the inside/outside, own/

alien, local/foreign, near/far border crossing far more creatively than Paul's Jesus. The phantom limb phenomenon might even be thought of as proprioception's "literary" creativity: making the amputee care as deeply about a limb that exists "only in the imagination" as about one that can be seen and poked and prodded, and indeed infusing the mechanical/scientific artificiality of the prosthetic device with the estranging/enlivening power of the "only imagined" phantom limb.

Indeed, Sacks describes one amputee waking up in the morning and finding his phantom leg still asleep, still numb or "anesthetized," still phenomenologically "outside" (*vneshno*), making walking on his prosthetic leg impossible; he begins to slap his stump vigorously until the phantom limb is, as Sacks wonderfully puts it, "fulgurated forth." This would make an excellent trope for Shklovsky's estrangement device: slapping the stump until the phantom limb is fulgurated forth out of numbness. If Thing 1 is what Georg Lukács would call the phantom objectivity of the unamputated leg, and Thing 2 is the numbing of sensation in the amputated leg, Thing 3 would be the slapped fulguration of the phantom limb.

But of course the athletic vigor of this man slapping his stump is also entirely alien to the osteomyelitic body-in-pain of an amputee like Bakhtin (who quickly gave up trying to walk on a prosthetic leg). As Emerson rightly insists, Shklovsky's estrangement does depend for its therapeutic effect on an initial deprivation of sensation. It is totally wrong for one who suffers from too much sensation.

Proprioception of the Body Politic

Note also that the fulgurative stump-slapping scene is *only* a trope for estrangement. The numbness that Tolstoy describes and Shklovsky theorizes may be *like* proprioceptive failure, but it is not the same thing. Tolstoy, moving around the room wiping up dust, is not reduced to the virtual immobility of Christina; his proprioceptive system is working fine. His failure occurs at a higher level of mental processing: his proprioceptive system generates unconscious mental maps of his body's position and movements, but he loses the ability to make those proprioceptive maps conscious, loses the ability to map the maps. If this is a kind of proprioceptive failure, it is a failure not of the proprioception of the body (the only kind neurophysiologists speak of) but, to use David Bohm's intriguing term, of the proprioception of thought. By this he means something like awareness and control of the thought process, on the model of our proprioceptive awareness and control of our bodies; Bohm argues that proprioception is just another layer of awareness, so that, as we can generate a proprioceptive map of body movements, and that map can become a mental image or thought, so too can we generate a proprioceptive map of our thoughts. Proprioception of the body prevents us mistaking the arms touching us for someone else's, thinking that we are being attacked; proprioception of thought prevents us from making the same mistake on the emotional or mental level, as in paranoia, thinking that certain persecutory thoughts or feelings or intentions are coming from other people when in fact they are being generated inwardly. Just as the woman who awoke fighting herself drew the proprioceptive boundaries of her physical body too narrowly, excluding her own arms, so too does the paranoiac draw the proprioceptive boundaries of his or her socioemotional body too narrowly, excluding his or her own desires, fears, motivations, projections, and so on. Whatever is excluded from "own" becomes by default "other." Conversely, of course, it would be equally debilitating to draw those boundaries too widely, to believe that the fist smacking you in the face is your own when in fact it belongs to someone else, or to believe that the manipulative pressures being brought to bear on you are your own when they are being directed to you by someone else.

But note that that woman, feeling touched by a hand from the other side (*s oborotnoy storony*) of the own/other line, did not experience that touch as random or neutral; she experienced it as an *attack*. The experience of being touched physically by someone else is not just a matter of not proprioceiving the touch, not just a matter of the touch lacking the inward feeling of proprioception that would tell us that the touch was coming from our own limbs; it is *actively* and *meaningfully* alien. We experience another person's touch *as* something, not just as "not ours." We experience it as the touch of a stranger, an enemy, an athletic opponent, a child, a mother, a friend, a lover. We feel impersonal indifference in it, or irritation, or open violence, or soothing reassurance, or sexual seduction. In order to be able to think proprioceptively about a perceived attack, caress, handshake, or tickle, in order to be able to distinguish "external touch" from "internal touch," we need more than just *internal* proprioception of the body or thought; we need to be able to *compare* internal and external proprioceptions. There needs to be a proprioceptive channel that enables us to scan the whole interactive body that might be touching us—the body that includes other people. We can, for example, only be tickled by another, not by ourselves, because ticklishness is collectively conditioned as an intercorporeal act, with agency proprioceptively assigned to the "other" body. This would suggest that proprioception of the body operates on a larger scale than that confined by the boundaries of our skin: that there is a kind of collective social proprioception of the body as well, which guides our somatic response when someone else touches us, assigns ideosomatic meaning to that touch. The same is true of the proprioception of thought. We may be able to distinguish quite clearly between our own emotional state and the state of someone close to us, but will not experience that other person's body state as simply "not ours"; it will have meaning for us, meaning organized and guided and explained collectively by a collective social proprioception of thought.

This collectivization of proprioception is the direction in which Bohm moves, from individual proprioceptive thought to what he calls "collective thought" or "participatory thought," or, more broadly, collective/participatory *thinkings and feelings*,[23] *thoughts and felts*—or what I would prefer to call the *proprioception of the body politic*:

> It's possible to see that there's a kind of level of contact in the group anyway. The thought process is an extension of the body process, and all the body language is showing it, and so on. People are really in a rather close contact—hate is an extremely close bond. I remember somebody saying that when people are really in close contact, talking about something which is very important to them, their whole bodies are involved—their hearts, their adrenalin, all the neurochemicals, everything. They are in far closer contact with each other than with some parts of their own bodies, such as their toes. So, in some sense there is established in that contact "one body." And also, if we can all listen to each other's opinions, and suspend them without judging them, and your opinion is on the same basis as anybody else's, then we all have "one mind" because we have the *same content*—all the opinions, all the assumptions. At that moment the difference is secondary.
>
> The point then is that you have in some sense one body, one mind. It does not overwhelm the individual. If the individual has another assumption he can have it, it's shared with the group and the group takes it up. There is no conflict in the fact that the individual does not agree. It's not all that important whether you agree or not. There is no pressure to agree or disagree. (204)

Of course, in groups there often *is* pressure to agree or disagree. What Bohm means is that groups do not impose absolute tyrannical templates on individual behavior or thought; there is wiggle room. The problem with Bohm insisting that "there is no pressure to agree or disagree," however, is that he thereby underemphasizes the importance of group pressure for social regulation. Groups do have this tendency to regulate the bodily-becoming-mental processes of all their members so as to move collectively toward unity, and ultimately to cast out any member who repeatedly or systematically refuses to conform. This is what Aristotle would call the entelechy of group behavior, the core organizing principle on which regulation is based: the *telos* of unity. To miss this is to paint the proprioception of the body politic (as, in fact, Bohm tends to do) as a kind of Rousseauistic social contract, where everyone lives in one-body-one-mind peace and harmony because each respects the others' autonomy.

The mimetic theory of somatic transfer offers an explanatory model for the sharing not only of "contact," of socialized or collectivized sensation, the "one-body-one-mind" phenomenon Bohm is talking about, but also of social regulation, which, as I say, he tends to neglect. When my as-if body loop simulates your body state, it is not just building a bridge between us but connecting both of us somatomimetically to the community, to the ideosomatic guidance of the collective. In somatic theory, the "body politic" is not simply a metaphor that allows us to *think* about collective action as if it were being performed by a single body; it is a quite literal physiological description of the collectivized body of ideosomatic guidance.

It is this larger proprioceptive system that goes numb in Tolstoy: he is like Sacks's Christina in the sense that he cannot feel his body, but the body that he cannot feel is not the one encased in his skin (which for most of his long life is healthy and athletic) but the social body of ideosomatic regulation, the body politic. He can't feel the body of other people, the body he shares with other people. Because he cannot feel what they are feeling, he doesn't know what he himself is feeling; because he doesn't share collective feelings and because the circulation of meaning and value through the ideosomatic body politic is where *reality* comes from, nothing makes sense to him. This ideosomatic proprioceptive system doesn't just coach us to act in normative ways, to apply "common sense" or "practical reason" (read: group norms) to every tiny decision we make; it coaches us to see the world through group eyes, to construct our social and natural environments as they have been constructed by the collective. This homeostatic stabilizing effect of millions of minute somatic mimeticisms, this continual collective dissemination of tiny empathetic regulatory adjustments through the population, is the proverbial glue that holds society together. Not to feel this ideosomatic proprioception is not to feel alive, not to feel real; as Tolstoy himself writes, "If no one had seen or had seen unconsciously, if the whole complex life of many people passes unconsciously, then it is as if that life had never been." "Seeing" here means being available for the somatic exchange, for mutual visual/somatic modeling, for the reciprocal mimetic observation and simulation of body language that circulates meaning and value; but even when someone is seeing you wipe the furniture, if you don't *feel* what they are feeling as they see you, they might as well not have been there at all.

Imagine someone else walking into the room as the 68-year-old Tolstoy is wiping dust off the furniture. He himself envisions this person serving purely as a kind of objective verifier of specific physical actions: "Yes, you already wiped that" or "No, you haven't touched that yet." But this observer would have had to be either another guest (which, given that on February 25 he tells us that the guests left, would most likely have meant only his daughter Tat'yana, who is there making clean copies of his drafts of *What Is Art?*) or a member of his hosts' household—and it is difficult to imagine this person's contribution to Tolstoy's wiping being restricted to an simple objective yes or no. As Mikhail Bakhtin would say, anyone who walked into the room and watched him wipe for a while would invariably inflect whatever bit of verbal or body language s/he emitted with an *evaluative accent,* and that evaluative accent would channel into the current exchange the ideosomatic proprioception of all the groups to which that person belonged. Adam Vasil'yevich Olsuf'yev and his wife Anna Mikhaylovna are his friends, and are still willing to take him in, despite the world of trouble he has been getting his disciples and friends into. (Chertkov and Pavel Ivanovich Biryukov have just been exiled, Chertkov to England, Biryukov to Latvia; his English translator Aylmer Maude has been deported back to England after ten years in Russia; Tolstoy himself is under police surveillance.) So they know not to expect "normal" aristocratic behavior from him. But no matter how tolerant they are, in their society an elderly aristocratic guest of either gender (let alone the greatest living Russian writer) wiping up dust in his room is behaving oddly, even aberrantly, and the *sense* of that aberrancy would show in the body language of anyone who happened to walk in—even in their attempts to suppress any body language of disapproval. All these people would know what is normal and what is deviant behavior because they would be guided proprioceptively by the body politic, by their membership in their various social groups (especially class and gender), by the circulation through their bodies of ideosomatic regulation; and those regulatory impulses, different for each of them, would be what they would inexorably and unconsciously express, what they would unwittingly display in their body and possibly even verbal language ("oh, please, you don't need to do that") for Count Tolstoy's somatomimetic emulation.

This *is* what I'm calling the proprioception of the body politic: this infectious channeling of group norms from one body to another, in the form of verbally or nonverbally signaled ideosomatic pressure to conform to collective expectations, in millions of encounters just like this one. The meetings of people—both in outward physical reality and in the virtual reality of memory and the imagination, including the encounters we have with characters and narrators in literature—are the body politic's macroversion of the synapses that channel microproprioception through any individual's nervous system.

It is this collective proprioception, ultimately, through which the boundaries between the self and the other, the own and the alien, the familiar and the strange are policed. Bohm gives the example of tribal xenophobia:

> But participatory thought has some aspects that are very inadequate, or even dangerous. For example, in some tribes, the word for "human being" was the same as the word for a member of that tribe. When they met another tribe, the very word suggested that the other tribe was not human. They might have known in some sense they were, but the power of such words is enormous. Therefore, that tribe may not have been able to include other tribes in their "participation"; it would break down at that point, and they would begin fragmentary thinking. (*Dialogue*, 87)

Bohm's binary between "participatory thinking" and "fragmentary thinking" here will not stand, of course; the xenophobic tribe that defined members of another tribe as alien and therefore not human were obviously still thinking participatorily. They were simply not extending the proprioceptive boundaries of "the human" as far out as Bohm's tribe does. What Bohm is calling a *breakdown* in collective proprioception is simply a *boundary imposed* by collective proprioception, part of the group cognitive structure disseminated somatically throughout the population as a guide to "correct" behavior; his inclination to thematize it as a breakdown rather than a boundary is conditioned by his own "tribal" proprioception.

The "natural" feel of this sort of universalization of collective proprioception is one of the primary regulatory effects of collective proprioception. It is just as obvious to Bohm that those members of the other tribe *are* human as it is to his hypothetical tribe that others aren't. His own tribal proprioception guides him more or less unconsciously to the assumption that he is right and they are wrong, to the proprioceptive assumption that his proprioceptive assumptions are universal and can therefore issue into large-scale descriptive binary distinctions between "participatory" and "fragmentary" thinking. The kind of "proprioception of thought" that he is attempting to theorize, an awareness of the directionalities and consequences of our thought that will help us guide thought-based behavior in new ways, is in a sense an attempt to step cognitively outside the group, to analyze ideosomatic regulation from an imaginary position above or beyond the group—a cognitive process that we will see Bertolt Brecht attempting to instigate in his audiences in chapter 5. Important as that process is for social change, it is also extraordinarily difficult, unless itself guided by the ideosomatic proprioception of some group of counterhegemonic thinkers—as Brecht's was by the ideosomatics of Marxist proprioception, and as my analysis of Bohm's binary "error" is by the ideosomatic proprioception of critical theorists.

Assuming that I'm right about this—or rather, that your and my joint membership in the group of critical theorists will incline you to agree that I'm right—indeed, that our shared group proprioception will incline you to allow me to make universal-sounding pronouncements about the inevitable non-universality of group proprioception without simply declaring my reasoning fallacious and therefore dismissible—indeed, that it will incline you further to allow me to lay bare or estrange the universalizing tendency of my anti-universalizing truth-claim without undermining your proprioceptive agreement with me, because laying bare the device (*obnazhenie priyoma*) is one of the main things Shklovsky among many others has taught our group to do—though I'm also guessing you may well be growing impatient with what you consider the self-indulgence of my series of dashes in this sentence—then we will almost certainly want to agree that Shklovsky is not nearly self-conscious enough about his own universalizing tendencies in "Art as Device."[24] His theory of the estrangement device seems to be based on the unexamined belief that whatever he feels is automatized *is* automatized, for everyone, and whatever he feels is estranging *is* estranging, again for everyone. That belief patently (at least to members of the group you and I belong to) neglects to take into consideration the facts (they seem like facts to us) that (a) every society is made up of many overlapping groups that variously impose this sort of proprioceptive cognitive structure on their members' somatic sense of familiarity and strangeness, and therefore of what will count as familiarizing and what will count as estranging, (b) our experiences are never perfectly ordered by group regulation (there is always room for the idiosomatic or counterideosomatic marking of experience), and (c) there are psychosocial disorders like Tolstoy's that block collective proprioception altogether, making *everything* seem strange to the people who suffer from them. An idealized theory like Shklovsky's depends cognitively on the assumption that everyone experiences precisely the same proprioceptive boundary between the familiar and the strange, the own and the alien, and that any given literary estrangement device will therefore have precisely the same dealienating effect on every reader; the "fact" (see above) that the incomplete and overlapping group regulation of behavior makes this assumption unrealistic is a major limitation on the theory and helps explain how Vadim Rudnev can assume that Shklovsky is deliberately *spreading* depersonalization.

Still, even if Shklovsky does not theorize the divergent/overlapping proprioception of the body politic, I don't think that in reading that theory into the interstices of his argument I am simply reversing him, as Mikhail Bakhtin—who everywhere overtly insists on the transindividual guidance I am here theorizing, under the rubric of "dialogism"—would probably want to argue. When Shklovsky writes about the disastrous consequences of automatization, his list of anesthetized phenomena includes not only inanimate objects but close human relationships and collective regulatory feelings: "Automatization swallows up things, dress, furniture, one's wife, and the fear of war." And as we'll see later in this chapter, for Shklovsky the purpose of poetic estrangement and belabored poetic form is specifically to build an empathetic (*[so] perezhivayushiy,* lit. "[with-]across-living") and somatic (*oschutimiy* "tangible, sensed, felt") bridge from the reader back to the poet. Thus while I agree that Bakhtin is more insistently cognizant than Shklovsky of the enlivening power of human relationship, I would ultimately disagree with his take (as exfoliated again by Caryl Emerson) on Shklovskyan estrangement:

> In his essay "The Problem of Content, Material, and Form in Verbal Art," written in 1924 but published only posthumously, Bakhtin expands on this crucial difference between his approach to a work of literature and that of the Formalists. Bakhtin is gentler on his opponents than is his Marxist associate Medvedev, who several years later accuses ostranenie of outright nihilism. But Bakhtin nonetheless faults the Formalist "material aesthetics" for failing to invite two consciousnesses to experience one another within a work. "There are works which indeed do not deal with the world, but only with the word 'world' in a literary context," Bakhtin . . . writes. Their content is not co-cognized or co-experienced; "rather, one work of literature comes together with another, which it imitates or which it 'makes strange,' against the background of which it is 'sensed' as something new." For art, this was the wrong sort of distancing and the wrong sort of sensation. No inter-personal obligation is created; no urgent human need is satisfied by it, nothing comparable to the clear blue sky that a compassionate outsider can offer to a suffering person. "The so-called '*ostranenie*' of the Formalists is at base nothing more than a function of isolation," Bakhtin . . . remarks

further in the same essay, " . . . and in most instances incorrectly related to the material." Such distancing cannot create value, if what is estranged is only the *word.* Bakhtin regrets that this process is so crudely psychologistic: the object, its value, the event—all are stripped of cognitive and ethical meaning. The decision to isolate acts in this scientific manner does indeed render form perceptible, Bakhtin admits, but the price is high. "The word, the utterance, ceases to expect or to want anything beyond its own borders . . . a prayer ceases to have need of a God who could hear it, a complaint ceases to have need of assistance, repentance ceases to need forgiveness . . . The author enters, as it were, the isolated event and becomes a creator in it, without becoming a participant" . . . (Emerson, 656–67)

As we'll see, this is a fundamental misreading of Shklovsky's argument in "Art as Device": the purpose of art for him *is* precisely to push the reader past language to a reworking not just of perception but of embodied participatory experience in general.[25]

Deautomatization

Shklovsky's conception of literature is often criticized as mechanical; in fact, it borders on the mystical, and bears comparison with Henri Bergson's concept of "real" or "living" time, *durée,* his quasimystical antidote to the automatizing effects of "false" or "mathematical" time:[26]

Pure Duration is the form which the succession of our conscious states assumes when our Ego lets itself *live,* when it refrains from separating its present state from its former states. For this purpose it need not be entirely absorbed in the passing sensation or idea; for then, on the contrary, it would no longer *endure.* Nor need it forget its former states: it is enough that, in recalling these states, it does not set them alongside its actual state as one point alongside another, but forms both the past and the present states into an organic whole, as happens when we recall the notes of a tune, melting, so to speak, into one another. Might it not be said that, even if these notes succeed one another, yet we perceive them in one another, and that their totality may be compared to a living being whose parts, although distinct, permeate one another just because they are so closely connected? (*Time,* 100)

An even better guide to deautomatization in Shklovsky than Bergson, however, is Arthur Deikman's much later (1966) paper "De-Automatization and the Mystical Experience." Deikman first summarizes the research on automatization and deautomatization, saying that the contemporary psychological understanding of deautomatization is born out of Heinz Hartmann's study of the automatization of motor behavior in *Ego Psychology and the Problem of Adaptation:* "In well-established achievements they [motor apparatuses] function automatically: the integration of the somatic systems involved in the action is automatized, and so is the integration of the individual mental acts involved in it. With increasing exercise of the action its intermediate steps disappear from consciousness . . . not only motor behavior but perception and thinking, too, show automatization" (quoted in Deikman, 329). This is the smooth functioning that Bakhtin speaks of, obviously, which is automatized (not anesthetized) precisely because the proprioceptive system is working well. The somatic and mental systems are so well integrated with motor behavior that it may *seem* to be anesthetized, but that is simply a phenomenological side-effect of automatization. "De-automatization," then, as Merton M. Gill and Margaret Brenman write in *Hypnosis and Related States,* "is an undoing of the old automatizations of apparatuses—both means and goal structures—directed toward the environment. De-automatization is, as it were, a shake-up which can be followed by an advance or a retreat in the level of organization . . . Some manipulation of the attention directed toward the functioning of an apparatus is necessary if it is to be de-automatized" (quoted in Deikman, 329).

The specific form automatization takes in both Shklovsky and Deikman is abstraction, or what Shklovsky follows Bergson in calling algebraization; the deautomatizing mystical discipline Deikman opposes to abstraction, the rough equivalent of the reading of poetry for Shklovsky, is contemplative meditation:

> In reflecting on the technique of contemplative meditation, one can see that it seems to constitute just such a manipulation of attention as is required to produce de-automatization. The percept receives intense attention while the use of attention for abstract categorization and thought is explicitly prohibited. Since automatization normally accomplishes the transfer of attention from a percept or action to abstract thought activity, the meditation procedure exerts a force in the reverse direction. Cognition is inhibited in favor of perception; the active intellectual style is replaced by a receptive perceptual mode. (329)

And the desired deautomatizing effects of meditation and poetry reading are uncannily similar in the two theories, inhibiting analytical cognition in favor of enhanced sensuous perception and receptivity. Or, more specifically:

> Automatization is a hierarchically organized developmental process, so one would expect de-automatization to remit in a shift toward a perceptual and cognitive organization characterized as "primitive," that is, an organization

preceding the analytic, abstract, intellectual mode typical of present-day adult thought. The perceptual and cognitive functioning of children and of people of primitive cultures have been studied by Werner, who described primitive imagery and thought as (1) relatively more vivid and sensuous, (2) syncretic, (3) physiognomic and animated, (4) de-differentiated with respect to the distinctions between self and object and between objects, and (5) characterized by a de-differentiation and fusion of sense modalities. (329–30)

This is an extraordinarily apt list of attributes for the desired effect of Shklovskyan deautomatization as well: (1) enhancing the vivid sensation (*oschuschenie*) of experience, (2) fusing disparate modes and channels of perception syncretically, so that the intensity of experience overpowers analytical or "algebraic" distinctions, (3) paying close loving attention to outward appearances and movements as expansive signs of life, (4) blurring the boundaries between self and other, so that experience flows through people and things rather than being rigidly and "aridly" compartmentalized, and (5) blurring the boundaries between sensory modes, estranging anesthesis into synesthesis.[27] The result of deautomatization is the experience of life reintensified, renewed ("I was like a new man in a new world": Billy Bray, quoted in Deikman 330), or as William Blake says, "If the doors of perception were cleansed every thing would appear to man as it is: infinite" (39).

As this parallel with Blake suggests, the theory of deautomatization is part of Shklovsky's significant inheritance from the Romantics and post-Romantic thinkers like James and Bergson.[28] It is based on the assumption that the automatization of what I've been calling the higher-level proprioception of the body politic, which is to say, alienation or depersonalization, is far more common in modern capitalist society than proprioceptive disorders like the body numbness that befell Sacks's Christina; that individualism and scientific thought and what Hegel calls the alienation of labor (the subject of chapter 4) have the baleful effect of dulling and numbing our *imaginative* proprioception, our sense of connectedness to other people and the world of things, and reducing our perception to a gray sameness.

In the rest of this chapter, then, I propose to read closely the key paragraph in "Art as Device," unpacking it in terms of the specific strategies or channels of deautomatization: work (belabored form), the making of a thing, sensate or somatic seeing, and rhythm.

Work (Belabored Form)

If the first point on which Shklovsky turns Tolstoy on his head is that he wants to fight estrangement not with the joy and spiritual union of pure deestranged infection but with hypermimetic estrangement, the (de)estranging mimesis of estrangement, the second is that he wants to ground that mimesis not in Tolstoy's smooth (automatized) form but in "difficultized" or *belabored* form (*zatrudnyonnaya forma*), which is often translated as "impeded form," and might also be rendered loosely as "deautomatized form." In his formulation of the estrangement device Shklovsky uses two words containing the *work* or *labor* root *trud-*, *zatrudnyonnaya* "made difficult," morphologically "belabored," and *trudnost'* "difficulty," literally, "laboriousness": art's device, he says, is a device of estranging things and a device of belabored form, which he paraphrases in the next clause as the enhancement of the difficulty or laboriousness and duration of perception. Shklovsky wants to make the audience *work harder and longer* to perceive things so as to enhance the intensity and therefore the sensuousness and vividness of their perception. The twist Shklovsky puts on Tolstoy, using his own diary entry, suggests that habit automatizes perception by numbing the *experience* of work, the feeling that one is working—wiping, for example. (Part of the difficulty or laboriousness of this passage is that Shklovsky comes into it talking about work but then buries the "work" keywords in abstract adjectives and nouns and builds its punch line around making, a totally new topic.) Work becomes so automatized that it does not feel like work at all and therefore does not feel like life at all; in order to restore to this sort of person the sensation of life, the artist makes him or her work harder and work longer hours to perceive things. The analogy is clearly with tedious repetitive work in a factory: if the workers are becoming numb to their work and as a result are making mistakes or skipping work, the owner should shake them out of their numbing routines by giving them new challenges, making them work harder and longer at something new. In particular, the image suggests that the kind of intensification of labor that is most dealienating and deautomatizing is work that gives workers an experience of actually *making* the thing they're manufacturing, like an artisan or skilled craftsperson in an earlier (pre-Industrial Revolution) stage of capitalism—what we will see Hegel calling the state of simple labor, in chapter 4.[29]

The Making of a Thing

The image of making is also Shklovsky's own. He represents the deautomatizing restoration of sensation as channeled through the "experiencing [of] the *making* of a thing." Life numbs us not merely to perceiving, Shklovsky's main topic so far, but to *making.* As I say, this word, *delan'ye,* from *delat'* "to make, to do," comes utterly out of the blue in Shklovsky's essay: he has been talking about Tolstoy wiping the furniture; now all of a sudden somebody's making a thing. As a result, his English translators don't quite know what to make of the making: Lemon and Reis render it "artfulness" ("*Art is a way of experiencing the artfulness of an object; the object is not important,*" 720), Robert Scholes "the process of construction" ("*In art, it is our experience of the process of construction that counts, not the finished product,*" 84), Benjamin Sher "the process of creativity" ("*Art is a means of experiencing the process of creativity. The artifact itself is quite unimportant,*" 6).[30]

Once we know the specific image Shklovsky evokes in Russian, it is not difficult to see how these translators decided on the conceptual shifts behind their renditions; and it does seem to me that "the artfulness of an object" and "the process of construction/creativity" fit the style of an academic essay in general, and even this one in particular, far better than "the making of a thing." But all three conceptual shifts take Shklovsky's image in precisely the wrong direction. The artfulness of an object is a heightened sense of its having-been-made-ness, an abstract quality, a virtual quality, something that might be suggested equally well by a sticker saying WORK OF ART, and thus in the end what Shklovsky would call a product of algebraic reduction. The process of creativity or construction is perhaps closer, in that it is something like the actual making activity performed by the artist, but these images too are algebraically reduced, rendered conceptually vague by a shift from the body movements of making a *thing* to a more general "construction," an abstract noun for making or building, or "creativity," a general readiness or skill (note the increasing abstraction in the series "process of making a thing," "process of creating a thing," "process of creation," "process of creativity"). And the schematism of "process" suggests flow charts, the reduction of an activity first to a series of discrete steps and then to symbolic notation. The phrase "the making of a thing" may jar, but Shklovsky needs that jar. "Making" is one of the passage's keywords.

Art for Shklovsky not only highlights that making but offers us a channel through which it can be "refelt," relived, by the audience. The Russian word he uses for "experience" is *perezhit',* morphologically "across-live," "trans-live," to live across some barrier or boundary into someone else's experience—a verb often used loosely for empathy.[31] What Shklovsky is arguing is that art generates in its audience the impulse and the means by which they can relive or reexperience the shaping act, project themselves empathetically into the doing of the *work* by which the artwork was made. The made thing, the artwork itself, is insignificant, except as the empathetic channel through which readers and other audience members come to feel like artists themselves, come to feel not just the characters' emotions but the deautomatizing or "fulgurating" effects of the artist's own body movements. The intensified work they do in perceiving the poetic stone's belabored form is the slapping of the stump that brings forth the collectivized phantom limb of the poet's making.[32]

What does this mean in practice? How can belabored form instigate in the reader the reexperiencing of the author's "making of the thing"? And how can that reexperiencing have a deautomatizing effect on the reader? We should recall from chapter 2 Julia Kristeva's description of depersonalization as a "daze that has cut off [the subject's] impulses from their objects, that is, from their representations"—a daze precipitated by the creation of a surrogate Other that is unable to mobilize the organizing jouissance that would cathect those objects as significant parts of a world. A depersonalized subject projects a dead and meaningless world, a posthuman nonworld scattered with isolated objects (people and things) that remain meaningless because they remain unincorporated into the social world projected somatically (through jouissance) by the Other—by that intertextual transsubject that I am calling ideosomatic regulation, the shared felt guidance of the group. To translate Deikman's deautomatizing agenda into Kristeva's terms, the artistic/mystical attempt to render perception "(1) relatively more vivid and sensuous, (2) syncretic, (3) physiognomic and animated, (4) de-differentiated with respect to the distinctions between self and object and between objects, and (5) characterized by a de-differentiation and fusion of sense modalities" is an attempt to remobilize the jouissance of the Other for the semiotic (re)organization of the symbolic subject-object-ego triad *as* Other, as the mediary enjoying of the body of the Other. This Kristevan model would suggest that Deikman's third transformation entails less a "de-differentiation" of self and object than the organization of self and object into a more animistically functioning transsubjectivity, in which the regulatory feelings of the group are circulated kinetically throughout the social and physical world that they construct and maintain. When this transsubjective system is activated and organized by the jouissance of the Other, it is organized not in the individual subject but in the whole transsubject, the somatomimetic flow of animation through all linked subjects and objects, people and things, so that the whole system (the whole ideosomatically pro-prioceived "world") comes to feel "relatively more vivid and sensuous," more "syncretic," more "physiognomic and animated."

This is the re(trans)personalized sense in which the somatic theory would take Rei Terada's depersonalized claim that "We would have no emotions if we *were subjects*" (4): emotions are conditioned by the ideosomatic transsubject. The subject "dies" in postliberal theorizations only in the sense of becoming recognized as part of a larger proprioceptive body, which assigns a fictitious but nonetheless extremely useful phenomenological subjectivity to each individual body wrapped by skin.

Through this process, then, the author and the reader participate in a trans-subjective animation or "making" of the thing, not just the poetic thing but the worldly thing, the worldly thing as modeled imaginatively on and substan-tiated somatically through the poetic thing. In this way they—we—come to experience the thingy world not just as alive but as *coming alive through us,* as partaking of the same jouissant animation that animates us, as circulating the same ideosomatic regulation channeled to it through us.

Just how this mobilization of the jouissance of the Other, this instigation in the reader of the experiencing of the author's "making of the thing," is accom-plished by the estrangement device and the device of belabored form, though, Shklovsky does not help us determine. He doesn't know. I tease a tentative but still inconclusive model of this mobilization out of Shklovsky's reliance on Broder Christiansen's *Philosophie der Kunst* below, then take another run through this problematic in chapter 4, using Shklovsky's philosophical roots in Hegel to explore a Hegelian externalization-of-self / internalization-of-other solution. Finally, we see Bertolt Brecht tackling this problem in chapter 5, working from the assumption (also loosely tied to Hegel) that the trick is not just to *belabor* form but to arouse in the spectator *conscious and critical aware-ness* of the contradictions posed by belabored form.

Somatic Seeing

The third deautomatizing effect of Shklovsky's estrangement device is the intertwining of sensation and seeing, in "Art's purpose is to give us the sensation of a thing as seeing [*oschuschenie veschi kak videnie*] rather than as recognition [*uznavanie*]." This is a distinction, seeing versus recognizing, that Shklovsky originally borrowed from Henri Bergson for his 1914 essay

"Voskreshenie slova" ("The Resurrection of the Word"): "When words are being used by our thought-processes in place of general concepts, and serve, so to speak, as algebraic symbols, and must needs be devoid of imagery, when they are used in everyday speech and are not completely enunciated or completely heard, then they have become familiar, and their internal (image) and external (sound) forms have ceased to be experienced [*perestali perezhivat'sya*]. We do not experience [*perezhivaem*] the familiar, we do not see [*vidim*] it, but recognize [*uznayom*] it" ("Resurrection," 41–42; translation modified in accordance with "Voskreshenie," 36).[33] He develops the distinction all through the "Art as Device" essay as well. A few paragraphs before the key passage, for example, he writes: "In this algebraic method of thought, things are taken as calculation and space; they are not *seen* by us, but *recognized* by their primary outlines [*oni ne vidyatsya nami, a uznayutsya po pervym chertam*]. The thing passes by us as if under wraps: we know that it's there by the place it occupies, but we see only its surface. Under the influence of this sort of perception the thing withers away, at first as perception, then this begins to take its toll on its making" (11, my translation; emphasis added). Compare Bergson's *Time and Free Will* (1889): "Mechanics necessarily operates through equations, and . . . an algebraic equation always expresses a *fait accompli*. For it is of the very essence of *durée* and of movement that they appear to our consciousness as being unceasingly in the process of formation: Thus, algebra could interpret the results taken in a certain moment of *durée* and the positions occupied by a certain body in space, but not *durée* and movement as such" (79, quoted in Curtis, 114).

Shklovsky's Russian keywords here are *videnie* "seeing," from *videt'* "to see," and *uznavanie*, from *uznavat'* "to be recognizing, to be learning, to be finding out, to be getting to know." The first important point in the distinction is repetition: *uznavanie*, derived from an imperfective verb, suggests repeated action. As he remarks a few paragraphs later, "Things perceived several times begin to be perceived through recognition [*uznavaniem*]: the thing is in front of us, we know about it, but we don't see it, so we can't say anything about it" (12, my translation). The kind of automatized perception that he calls "recognition" is what we experience when we append a silent "Oh, yeah" to the beginning of our utterance: "It's just Joe." We've seen Joe so many times before that there's nothing striking about recognizing him.

More than sheer habitualizing repetition, though, what's most typical about Shklovsky's version of Bergsonian recognition is that it is *insensate*. It's not just that recognition is conditioned by repetition to be automatic; it is that the automatism works by bypassing sensation, that visually channeled but mimetically reembodied sense of Joe's body language that tells us not just who he is but what he's feeling. "Art's purpose is to give us the *sensation* of a thing as seeing rather than as recognition": a fuller paraphrase of *videnie* there might be *oschutimoe videnie* "sensed/felt seeing," "somatic seeing," seeing with the whole body. Indeed, in *Knight's Move,* he writes that "changes in art are not the results of changes in everyday life. They are the results of unending petrifaction [*vechnogo kameneniya*], the unending passage of things from sensed/felt perception to recognition [*iz oschutimogo vospriyatiya v uznavanie*]" (*Khod,* 94, my translation), making it clear that the movement from Thing 1 to Thing 2 is specifically a desomatization of our experience of the world.

Here again, then, Shklovsky is talking about empathy, embodied empathy, somatic mimeticism: mimetically simulating the body states of the thing or the person we're seeing. True seeing, bodily seeing, somatic seeing, gives us the *sensation* of a thing: it isn't a mere algebraic registering of the simplified facts, "calculation and space," perceived as if "under wraps."

Just how that somatic seeing works, though, Shklovsky doesn't say. He uses two feeling-words in this key paragraph, *oschuschenie* "feeling, sensation" and *pochuvstvovat'* "to feel," *vernut' oschuschenie zhizni, pochuvstvovat' veschi,* literally "to return the sensation of life, to feel things," but nowhere in the article does he stop to theorize either—a failure that has perhaps contributed to the depersonalizing structuralist misreading of him. Another factor contributing to the established misreading of Shklovsky, however, is that the bulk of his formalist writing is devoted to a series of examples of formal devices in specific narrative texts, making it seem to the casual reader that this is all he is interested in. Indeed as Peter Steiner (56) has shown, there seems to be a movement in his work of the early twenties away from the author psychology of the earliest articles from the mid-teens (especially the 1916 essay "O poezii i zaumnom yazyke" [On poetry and trans-rational language]) and the reader psychology of the late teens ("Art as Device," "The Relationship Between Devices of Plot Construction and General Devices of Style," and "The Structure of Fiction") in the direction of "pure" form, of the *abstract* structure of fictional devices— in fact, as Rudnev suggests, in the direction of machinic depersonalization.

Thus in the 1921 essay on *Tristram Shandy* (reprinted in the 1925 and 1929 editions of *O teorii prozy*), his discussion from two years earlier (in the plot construction and style essay, also collected in those two editions) of the *reader's* differential sense of artistic novelty (of which more below) is abstracted out as "a definite stylistic device based on differential qualities [*differentsial'nikh kachestvakh*]" ("Parodiyniy," 148; "Parody," 156). The idea is still grounded in reader psychology, but the reader's actual somatic response has been "idealized" as textual qualities or properties. The importance of emotion in reader response from that earlier essay is also severely attenuated: Shklovsky now writes "By its very essence, art is without emotion [*vneemotsional'no*, lit. 'outside-emotionally']" ("Parodiyniy," 151; "Parody," 159), implying, in the context of the book as a whole—that is, taking the Sterne chapter as built upon the theoretical foundation of the plot construction and style chapter—that the emotion we associate with art is not "in" the art itself but in the reader's response to it. Perhaps because that theoretical foundation is already established, he does not recur to it but moves on to a machinic analogy:

> In art, blood is not bloody. No, it just rhymes with "flood." [*Krov' v iskusstve ne krovava, ona rifmuetsya c "lyubov'*," lit. "rhymes with love."] It is material either for a structure of sounds or for a structure of images. For this reason, art is pitiless or rather without pity, apart from whose cases where the feeling of sympathy forms the material for the artistic structure [*kogda chuvstvo sostradaniya vzyato, kak material dlya postroeniya*]. But even in that case, we must consider it from the point of view of the composition. Similarly, if we want to understand how a certain machine works, we examine its drive belt first. That is, we consider this detail from the standpoint of a machinist and not, for instance, from the standpoint of a vegetarian. ("Parodiyny," 151; "Parody," 159)

This is precisely the kind of analogy that has led Shklovsky's critics to depersonalize him and to assume that he depersonalized literary theory: we should examine not the *operator* of the machine but its drive belt. It could be argued that by "cases where the feeling of sympathy forms the material for the artistic structure" Shklovsky means specifically the *reader's* sympathy, which the author is attempting to manipulate through form; but even here he insists that "we must consider it from the point of view of the composition," not reader psychology.

There are, however, any number of things wrong with the assumption that this focus on abstract form, exclusive of any psychosocial considerations outside the text, is the *true core* of Russian formalism in general or Viktor Shklovsky's formalist theorizing in particular—that, for example, the somatic aspect of his theory either doesn't exist or is an early conservative atavism that is purged by the essays of the early twenties. First, as we saw above, he is still talking about the slide from felt perception to recognition in the *Knight's Move* essays, written between 1919 and 1921 and published in 1923. Second, he publishes two editions of *Theory of Prose* in the twenties, in 1925 and 1929, and does not edit those somatic "atavisms" out of the first three essays (all written in the teens) in either edition. Third, the emphasis on readerly *oschuschenie* "sensation" as the driving force behind formal innovation is still in evidence in his 1926 book *Third Factory*. And fourth, in his ostensible recantation of formalism in the 1930 "Monument to a Scientific Error," he does not present the abstraction of literary form out of its social contexts (the "scientific error" of his title) as the formalist method that he is *now* abjuring; he presents it as an early scientific hypothesis that he and the other OPOYaZ members began with and subjected to systematic scrutiny, which proved it wrong by about 1924. In other words, he is not so much recanting formalism as he is declaring that the attempt to study pure abstract form never really worked in the first place and that there is therefore nothing to recant.[34]

Let me briefly review, then, the foundation Shklovsky lays for formalism in the reader's somatic response in those first three essays of the 1925 and 1929 editions of *Theory of Prose* and in the 1926 *Third Factory*. In each *Theory of Prose* essay he is interested in a specific formal device or collection of such devices—estrangement in "Art as Device," motifs and decelerations in "The Relationship Between Devices of Plot Construction and General Devices of Style," framing and threading devices in "The Structure of Fiction"—but in addition to copious literary examples, he provides for each specific formal device he is exploring a *psychological* motivation, an effect the author is attempting to have on the reader, or a sense of how the formal device is shaped by the way human beings read. In all three essays this motivation is grounded in the two somatic terms I mentioned above, *oschuschenie* "sensation" and *chuvstvo* "feeling"; in *Third Factory* "feeling" has dropped out, leaving only "sensation."

In the 1919 "Relationship" essay, that somatic theorization takes the form of a lengthy (two-page) quote from the German aesthetician Broder Christiansen's 1909 book *Die Philosophie der Kunst* (the philosophy of art), translated into Russian in 1911 by G. P. Fedotov as *Filosofiya iskusstva*. This book was an extremely important source of aesthetic thinking for the formalists; it was used extensively not only by Shklovsky but also by Tynyanov, Eikhenbaum, and Jakobson. Combined with and influenced by William James's *Principles of Psychology* from 1890—which Shklovsky may or may not have read but referred to and relied on in some form,[35] possibly through word of mouth from his better-read formalist colleagues—Christiansen formulated what we might call the somatic theoretical foundation on which the "abstract forms" of Russian formalism rested.

In "The Relationship Between Devices of Plot Construction and General Devices of Style," Shklovsky first mentions some Maupassant stories that are clearly structured around a certain expected kind of reader response, then offers a "general rule: a work of art is perceived against a background of and by association with other works of art." This means not only that "the form of a work of art is determined by its relationship with other pre-existing forms" but that *the content of a work of art is invariably manipulated, it is isolated, 'silenced'.*"[36] The artist's creation of a new form is motivated by the desire "*to replace an old form that has already outlived its artistic usefulness*" ("Relationship," 20). Then Shklovsky breaks off his own text and inserts the long block quotation from Christiansen, excursus-style, without his own commentary, setting up this idea of "artistic usefulness" in terms of art's use for the *reader*, its power to disrupt the reader's somatic response through form (I translate Christiansen directly from Fedotov's Russian translation but provide key terms in square brackets from both Christiansen's original German and Fedotov):

> I single out only one group of unfelt forms [*nicht-sinnlichen Formen*, lit. "non-sensuous forms"; *nechuvstvennykh form*]—the one that to my mind is the most important: differential sensations or sensations of differences [*Differenzempfindungen; differentsial'nye oschuscheniya ili oschuscheniya razlichiy*]. When we experience [*empfunden*, lit. "sensed/felt"; *ispytaem*] anything as a deviation from the usual, from the normal, from some active/effective [*geltend*, lit. "in force/effect"; *deystvuyushego*] canon, in us is born an emotional impression [*eine Stimmungsimpression*, lit. "a mood impression"; *emotsional'noe vpechatlenie*] of a particular quality, which differs from the emotional elements of felt forms [*sinnlicher Formen; chuvstvennykh form*] not in kind, but only in that its antecedent would appear to be a sensation of dissimilarity [*eine Differenz; oschuschenie neskhodstva*], that is, something unavailable to felt perception [*etwas nicht sinnlich Wahrnehmbares*, lit. "something not sensuously perceptible"; *nechto nedostupnoe chuvstvennomu vospriyatiyu*]. (Christiansen, *Philosophie*, 118, and *Filosofiya*, 104, quoted in "Svyaz," 27)[37]

This is, after all, where form "exists": in the reader's constitutive sensations, in his or her mapping of those sensations in feelings. The conceptual framework Christiansen and his Russian translator are working with here is clearly William James's between emotion and feeling: for Christiansen (especially in Russian translation) it is possible to experience (*ispytat'*) or sense (*empfinden/oschutat'*) a difference or deviation or dissimilarity at the level of "emotional impression" or "emotional element" without actually feeling (*chuvstvovat'*) it, which is to say, without mapping it mentally. As James writes in the *Principles of Psychology:*

> Our natural way of thinking about these coarser emotions is that the mental perception of some fact excites the mental affection called the emotion, and that this latter state of mind gives rise to the bodily expression. My theory, on the contrary, is that *the bodily changes follow directly the perception of the exciting fact, and that our feeling of the same changes as they occur* is *the emotion.* Common-sense says, we lose our fortune, are sorry and weep; we meet a bear, are frightened and run; we are insulted by a rival, are angry and strike. The hypothesis here to be defended says that this order of sequence is incorrect, that the one mental state is not immediately induced by the other, that the bodily manifestations must first be interposed between, and that the more rational statement is that we feel sorry because we cry, angry because we strike, afraid because we tremble, and not that we cry, strike, or tremble, because we are sorry, angry, or fearful, as the case may be. Without the bodily states following on the perception, the latter would be purely cognitive in form, pale, colorless, destitute of emotional warmth. We might then see the bear, and judge it best to run, receive the insult and deem it right to strike, but we should not actually *feel* afraid or angry.[38] (2:449–50)

It is possible to read here one psychological prototype for the somatics of Shklovskyan estrangement: "Without the bodily states following on the perception, the latter would be purely cognitive in form, pale, colorless, destitute of emotional warmth. We might then see the bear, and judge it best to run, receive the insult and deem it right to strike, but we should not actually *feel* afraid or angry." Perception without bodily states, without somatics, without "sensate seeing," would be "purely cognitive," "destitute of emotional warmth," algebraic, alienated from interactive somaticity—indeed depersonalized, "a foreign body within an impersonal consciousness." The artist's task is to restore sensation and thus somatic connectivity—an idea that James seems to anticipate a few pages earlier: "As emotions are described in novels, they interest us, for we are made to share them. We have grown acquainted with the concrete objects and emergencies which call them forth, and any knowing touch of introspection which may grace the page meets with a quick and feeling response" (448). (Bertolt Brecht was also influenced by James, and we return to this distinction between emotion and feeling in chapter 5.)

The distinction borrowed from Christiansen's Russian translator between "felt form" and "unfelt form," therefore, is that the former is available to *consciousness* and the latter is not—but specifically to a Jamesian somatic consciousness or awareness, a physical-becoming-mental awareness that emerges out of somatic guidance. In this case the guidance is negative: the "canon" (in Christiansen *geltender Kanon* "canon in force/effect," which Fedotov translates into Russian as *deystvuyushiy kanon* "active/effective canon," which Sher in turn translates into English as "guiding canon," 20) is the ideosomatic regulation of linguistic form, the collectivized sense of normal usage that helps us organize communication meaningfully, and the reader here experiences or senses a deviation from that, a newness of some sort, an idiosomaticity. Shklovsky riffs on the ecclesiastical metaphor of the "canon" in his "Collective Creativity" piece from *Knight's Move:* "Creativity—even the revolutionary-artistic type— is traditional creativity. Violating the canon is possible only when a canon exists, and blasphemy presupposes a religion that hasn't yet perished. There exists a "church" of art in the sense of a gathering of those who feel it [*v smysle sobraniya ego chuvstvuyushikh*]. This church has its canons, created by the accumulation of heresies" (*Khod,* 89; *Knight,* 45). Only those who *feel* ideosomatic regulation can sense or feel the creative movement of "blasphemy," of deviation from the canon.[39]

Following Christiansen, Shklovsky is especially interested in the unfelt sensation or experience the reader gets of *becoming-deregulated* form, of form breaking or sliding away from ideosomatic regulation, which is to say, in the *slippage* between ideosomatic regulation and idiosomatic novelty. This is artistic estrangement, this is the *belaboring* or impeding of form: the artist's attempt to manipulate this slippage in the reader's unfelt sensation or experience so as to frictionalize the smooth functioning of ideosomatic regulation, to deautomatize what has become automatic. Shklovsky returns to his long quotation from Christiansen for an example (now in Sher's translation back from Fedotov's Russian translation):

> Why is the lyrical poetry of a foreign country never revealed to us in its fullness even when we have learned its language?
>
> We hear the play of its harmonics. We apprehend the succession of rhymes and feel the rhythm. We understand the meaning of the words and are in command of the imagery, the figures of speech and the content. We may have a grasp of all the felt forms, of all the objects. So what's missing? The answer is: differential experience [*Differenzimpressionen; differentsial'nykh vpechatleniy*]. The slightest aberrations from the norm in the choice of expressions, in the combinations of words, in the subtle shifts of syntax—all this can be mastered only by someone who lives among the natural elements of his language, by someone who, thanks to his conscious awareness of the norm [*ein lebendiges Bewußtsein des Sprachnormalen,* lit. "a living consciousness of the language-normal"; *zhivomu soznaniyu normal'nogo,* lit. "a liv-

ing consciousness of the normal"], is immediately struck, or rather irritated [*wie einer sinnlichen Erregung,* lit. "like a sensuous excitement/arousal/thrill; *podobno chuvstvennomu razdrazheniyu,* lit. "like a felt irritation"] by any deviation from it.

Yet, the domain of the norm in a language extends far beyond this. Every language possesses its own characteristic degree of abstraction and imagery. The repetition of certain sound combinations and certain forms of comparison belong to the realm of the norm, and any deviation from it is felt fully only by a person who is thoroughly at home in the language [*empfindet nur in voller Stärke, wem die Sprache als Muttersprache vertraut ist,* lit. "is sensed/felt only in full strength (by one) to whom the language is familiar/intimate as mother tongue"; *oschuschaet lish' tot, komu yazik blizok, kak radnoy,* lit. "senses only that (person), to whom the language is close, as 'one's own'"]. Every change of expression, of imagery, of a verbal combination, strikes him as a felt experience . . .

Moreover, there is the possibility of dual and inverse differentials. A given deviation from the norm may, in its turn, become the point of departure and yardstick for other deviations. In that case every return to the norm is experienced as a deviation . . . ("Relationship," 21, translation modified in accordance with "Svyaz," 27, and Christiansen, *Philosophie,* 118–19; *Filosofiya,* 104)[40]

Here, clearly, literature only comes into existence as literature to the extent that its forms are sensed by a reader—and sensed specifically as deviance from the prosaic regulatory norms that make ordinary verbal communication possible. Those prosaic norms too are sensed or felt by speakers of the language—they are *ideosomatic* norms, collective guidance stored somatically in the bodies of everyone who speaks the language well, everyone who is "thoroughly at home in the language." Literary form for Shklovsky exists as precisely this sort of felt or sensed deviance from the "active" or "effective" canon, which is to say that for him the *idiosomatics* of literary form exists as a deviation from the *ideosomatics* of ordinary discourse: as estrangement, as belabored form, as impedance, as foreignization. "Aristotle says that poetic language should have the character of the foreign . . . Poetic language is therefore a laborious, belabored, impeded [*trudny, zatrudnyonny, zatormozhenny*] language" ("Iskusstvo," 18, my translation).

Poetic language, obviously, can only be those things *to a person* and, specifically, can only be *sensed* or *felt* by a person. Theorizing them, as Shklovsky does for the first decade or so of his professional life, tends to reduce them to abstract structures, to devices, to machines, but in these early essays from the teens he lays the Jamesian theoretical foundation for the proper understanding of his own theoretical abstractions as constructs based on somatic reader response. They take their power from the reader's somatics, obviously: the reader's ability to sense or feel the slightest deviations from the ideosomatic norm gives literature's impact on us the intensity Shklovsky says we need in order to deautomatize our perceptions, to restore sensation to life, to make the stone stony. But it's not just therapeutic power or impact or intensity that literary devices take from somatic response; they take their form from it as well. Authors reshape the traditional forms of literature precisely in order to manipulate the reader's somatic response as powerfully as they can. In the formalist essays of the early twenties, just before and just after his exile to Berlin, he may even have forgotten the grounding of his theory of literary form in somatic response and begun to treat literary devices like impersonal machines, but he could only afford to do so because he had already laid the somatic groundwork for that mechanization of form in his own earlier essays.

You'll recall that in my preface I mentioned Gerald L. Bruns's summary of Shklovsky's aim as to "turn signs back into things"; that summary, interestingly enough, is based on Shklovsky's third important statement of his somatic theory in *Theory of Prose*, from the third essay in the 1925 and 1929 editions, "The Structure of Fiction." He tells a story from Chekhov's notebooks of a man who walks past a store sign for fifteen or thirty years, and every time reads it as saying "Bol'shoy vybor sigov" (large selection of white fish), and wonders "who needs a large selection of white fish?" Then one day he walks by and, seeing the sign taken down and leaned up against the wall, reads it correctly as "Bol'shoy vybor sigar" (large selection of cigars ["Stroenie," 79]).[41] Here is Shklovsky's theorization of that shift in literature:

> A poet removes all signs from their places. An artist always incites insurrections among things.
>
> Things are always in a state of revolt with poets, casting off their old names and adopting new names and new faces. A poet employs images as figures of speech by comparing them with each other. For instance, he may call fire a red flower or he may attach a new epithet to an old word, or else, like Baudelaire, he may say that a carcass lifts its legs like a woman with lascivious intent. In this way he brings about a semantic shift. He wrests the concept from the semantic cluster [*ot togo smyslovogo ryada*] in which it is embedded and reassigns it with the help of the word (figure of speech) to another semantic cluster. We, the readers, sense [*oschuschaem*] the presence of something new, the presence of an object in a new cluster. The new word

envelops the object, as new clothes envelop a man. The sign has been taken down. This is one of the ways in which an object can be transformed into something felt [*nechto oschutimoe*], into something capable of becoming the material of an artistic work. ("Structure," 62, slightly edited in accordance with "Stroenie," 79–80)

Here are the signs and the things that Bruns discusses, and true enough, the signs are undergoing radical change, but the change is not from sign to thing. The signs are transformed not into things but into *new* signs, signs that "we the readers" feel more powerfully and that therefore come to seem to us more like "artifacts." If this renewed artifactual construct *seems* like a thing to us, that is because its sensuous or somatic signification has been not eradicated (as for Bruns) but (re)intensified. Bruns is right that Shklovsky sees the artist as "disrupting the signifying function," but for Shklovsky the artist does so not in order to destroy that function, to slough it off as no longer necessary, but rather to transform it, to bring it to new life, to make us *feel* things by "casting off their old names and adopting new names and new faces." "Things are always in a state of revolt with poets" (*veschi buntuyut u poetov*) for Shklovsky, not because they are being freed from the symbolic order and so revealed as pure posthuman objects but because the poet incites insurrections in the symbolic order that *projects* things, that makes things meaningful. Clearly, here, Bruns depersonalizes Shklovsky, projects his own modernist depersonalization onto Shklovsky's "signs"—but note that, in Shklovsky's terms, even this patent misreading is simply another resomatization of his signs, a strategy for ripping them from Shklovsky's context and inserting them into a new one, one that bears the label "depersonalization" but only makes sense to us because we feel, we sense, the modernist ideosomaticity of Bruns's artifactualization.

Finally, in *Third Factory* Shklovsky returns briefly to Broder Christiansen's somatic reader psychology in the course of admitting that the evolution of literary form is influenced by social factors:

In brief, I see the matter in this way: change can and does take place in works of art for non-esthetic reasons—for example, when one language influences another, or when a new "social demand" appears. Thus a new form appears in a work of art imperceptibly, without registering its presence esthetically [*neosoznanno i esteticheski ne uchityvaemo*]; only afterward is that new form esthetically evaluated [*otsenivaetsya*], at which time it loses its original meaning, its pre-esthetic significance.

At the same time, the previously existing esthetic construction ceases to be sensed [*perestayot oschuschat'sya*], losing, so to speak, its joints [*teryaya, tak skazat', svoi sustavy*], and fuses into a single mass [*odin kusok*]. (*Third*, 58, translation modified in accordance with *Tret'ya*, 373)

Shklovsky here claims that a new form is first sensed (*oschuschaetsya*) and then gradually, as the somatic impact of its newness wears off, as it ceases to be sensed as form and "loses its joints"—the reader's sensation of moving parts— and thereby seems to "fuse into a single mass," only gradually comes to be recognized (*osoznayotsya*), registered or inventoried (*uchityvaetsya*), and evaluated (*otsenivaetsya*). It is clear that "recognition" here—*osoznavanie*—is not exactly the same thing as his older term for Bergsonian automatized "recognition," *uznavanie,* which was so automatized as to be invisible ("we don't see it, so we can't say anything about it"), and therefore unavailable for the conscious (*soznatel'ny*) aesthetic inventory (*uchyot*) and evaluation (*otsenka*) performed by the formalist critic; but the root (*zna-*) of both words is in knowledge, and certainly they are both in the same conceptual ballpark.

It should be obvious, though, that even this expanded somatic theoretical framework has not answered the question of how the estrangement device and the device of belabored form restore sensation to life. With the help of Broder Christiansen, Shklovsky has now clarified how it is possible for us to feel literary form so intensely: because we are guided so complexly by the ideosomatics of our own everyday prosaic language, we feel every tiny poetic deviation from the "active canon" of that language strongly. But if this "differential sensation" sends powerful ripples through our ideosomatic transsubjectivity, how exactly do those ripples mobilize the jouissance of the body of the Other?

Rhythm

Shklovsky's last chance to answer this problem in "Art as Device" comes at the end of his article, in his discussion of *rhythm.* After pages and pages of examples of estrangement, he returns to Herbert Spencer's book *The Philosophy of Style,* citing a passage on rhythm that he claims is from Spencer but is actually from Veselovsky's paraphrase of Spencer (see Tihanov, "Politics," 682–83); here is the original passage that Shklovsky never saw, restored by his English translator Benjamin Sher:

> Just as the body in receiving a series of varying concussions, must keep the muscles ready to meet the most violent of them, as not knowing when such may come: so, the mind in receiving unarranged articulations, must keep its perspectives active enough to recognize the least easily caught sounds.

> And as, if the concussions recur in definite order, the body may husband
> its forces by adjusting the resistance needful for each concussion; so, if the
> syllables be rhythmically arranged, the mind may economize its energies by
> anticipating the attention required for each syllable. (14)

The impact of verbal rhythms on the body would appear to be an excellent
place to look for an explanation of the somatic power of literature to restore
sensation to life, especially, here, as Spencer seems to be talking about the same
kind of nuanced bodily economy of accommodation and resistance to an "active canon" as the one Shklovsky borrowed from Christiansen—but Shklovsky
isn't up to it. Indeed, Jurij Striedter argues that this is the theoretical potential of Russian formalism that Viktor Shklovsky was not able to develop and
Bertolt Brecht was because Shklovsky worked with written texts and Brecht
worked with the bodies of actors (xxv–xxvi). (We return to this topic in chapter 5.)

"This seemingly persuasive observation," Shklovsky remarks in response to
Spencer, "suffers from the common sin of confusing the laws of poetic and prosaic language" ("Iskusstvo," 19, my translation). As his own further comments
make clear, he agrees with Spencer here—there is patently no "sin"—but only
in the case of a limited group of rhythmic texts, which he associates with prose
or "the working song, of the 'Dubinushki,' [which] on the one hand replaces
the crew's need to 'yell in unison,' [and] on the other hand makes the work
easier by automatizing it" ("Iskusstvo," 19–20, my translation), and the march,
which allows the marchers to march unconsciously. He concludes:

> In this sense, prosaic rhythm is important as an *automatizing* factor. But
> poetic rhythm is not. In art there is "order," but not one column of a
> Greek temple precisely executes its order, and artistic rhythm consists in
> the rhythm of prose *disrupted;* attempts have already been undertaken to
> systematize these disruptions. These attempts represent today's task in the
> theory of rhythm. It may be, however, that these systematizations will not
> succeed; for in fact what is at issue here is not a complicated rhythm but
> the disruption of rhythm itself, a disruption that cannot be predicted; if
> this disruption enters the canon, it loses its power as a belaboring device.
> ("Iskusstvo," 20, my translation)

The first thing to note here is that Shklovsky is juggling too many binaries: prose versus poetry, ordinary life versus art, and, ultimately, speech
versus the artistically enhanced language of literature, including prose *and* poetry. Hence his confusions in associating the automatizing power of "prosaic

rhythm" with conventional poetic forms like work songs and marches and the disruptive power of "poetic rhythm" with great literary fiction like Tolstoy's. The real problem with his truncated argumentation here, however—he leaves the working out of this issue for a later "book," which he never gets around to writing—is that he doesn't actually deal with the artistic pole of his rhythm binaries. The only binary that should really count for him is that between automatizing and deautomatizing rhythm, the rhythmic automatizations of conventional art (marches, work songs, or, in our day, advertising jingles and Hallmark greeting cards) and the rhythmic deautomatizations of estranging art. Yet he doesn't know how to map deautomatization onto the poetic *disruption* of rhythm, so he breaks off and promises to return to the topic later. Estranging literary rhythms are disruptive and therefore potentially deautomatizing, but because these rhythms are unpredictable and unsystematizable and therefore work on the ideosomatic canon from the outside, he intimates that they can't be theorized as disruptive or deautomatizing *rhythms* but must simply be negated as "the disruption of rhythm itself." The strong argument for him to make here is that great verbal art *also* (re)organizes the body rhythmically, also (de/re)structures perception through sensate or somatic or kinesthetic "seeing"—just more complexly than work songs and marches, indeed, precisely through disruption, through the reorganizing and reinvigorating power of interruption, complication, fragmentation, broken repetition, syncopation, and so on. Just as an automatizing rhythm helps organize behavior into an ideosomatic "canon," a deautomatizing rhythm might help revivify overautomatized behavior by inciting insurrections—or even just what Spencer calls resistances—throughout the regulatory system.

In "The Relationship Between Devices of Plot Construction and General Devices of Style," Shklovsky returns briefly to the question of rhythm, again arguing that art is not mere instrumental rhythm, not merely a steam hammer that helps work crews do a job more effectively. This time he is subtler. "Art," he says, "is not a march set to music, but rather a walking dance to be sensed/felt [*oschuschaetsya*] or, more accurately, a movement constructed only in order that it might be sensed/felt [*dvizhenie, postroennoe tol'ko dlya togo, chtoby ono oschuschalos*]" ("Relationship," 22, slightly edited in accordance with "Svyaz," 28).

In other words, art *is* connected in some complex way with the body—literature specifically with the somatics of language—but not robotically. Like Tolstoy, Shklovsky shies away from the notion that poetry or music might simply take over our bodies, but he doesn't know how to analyze the complex somatic mediation by which we do experience art as an estranging bodily movement, and by which that movement changes us, deautomatizes us, restores sensation to life. He draws heavily on the somatic theories of William James, Broder Christiansen, Herbert Spencer, and others in order to chart a new path for modernist estrangement through literature's somatic impact on the reader's body—an impact intended to play off against what Christiansen calls "differential sensations," the divergence of aesthetically stimulated idiosomatic responses from the regulatory ideosomatics of the effective linguistic canon—but he doesn't get very far. What *does* the verbal artist do to the reader's body that makes possible the therapeutic transformation of that body's habitualized numbness into full-bodied living? How does the reader of a poem come to feel its making, and why is this a transformative feeling? These are questions that Shklovsky raises and does not answer. They are answered more fully by Bertolt Brecht. Brecht, after all, as a theater director, is far more qualified to theorize about art as a body movement than either Tolstoy or Shklovsky.

Before we move on to Brecht, however, we need to take a detour through Hegel.

4 | *Shklovsky's Hegelianism*

I noted in connection with my tabulation of the "four Things" in chapter 3 that Shklovsky was a left-leaning Hegelian thinker who anticipated the Hegelian Marxism of Georg Lukács by several years—and that the Soviet ban on formalism came out of the Second International Marxist tradition pioneered by Plekhanov, Kautsky, and Bernstein and institutionalized in the Soviet Union by Lenin and Stalin, a tradition that Lukács associated with the "phantom objectivity" of bourgeois reification. According to the orthodox Soviet Marxists, you were either a materialist objectivist or an idealist subjectivist: either you accepted that a thing was a thing and that human thought was passively shaped by the economic base and class position, or you were a "Kantian" who believed in superstitions and fairy tales. There was no middle ground. (Ironically enough, as we've seen, the structuralists simply assimilated Shklovsky to the "positive" or positivistic side of this vulgar-Marxist binary, clearing him of "subjectivism" by depersonalizing him, by pretending that he had no interest in the phenomenological construction of things.)

The middle ground that Shklovsky maps out between objectivism and subjectivism is, I suggest, specifically Hegelian. We've already seen exhibit A of this case, namely, the degree to which the four Things are reminiscent of the Hegelian dialectic: Thing 1, the stone as a sensually experienced object, is sense-certainty (*sinnliche Gewißheit*) or unmediated consciousness (*unmittelbares Selbstbewußtsein*) as thesis; Thing 2, the stone as algebraically "recognized" or reduced object, is perception (*Wahrnehmung*) as antithesis; and Thing 3, the poetic representation of Thing 1, which incorporates the algebraic reduction into a higher (resensualized) experience, is understanding (*Verstande*) as synthesis. Or, as Hegel writes in the *Phenomenology:*

> The object is therefore part unmediated being, or a thing in general, which corresponds to unmediated consciousness [Thing 1]; part a becoming-otherwise [*Anderswerden*] of itself, its relationality, or *being-for-another* and *being-for-itself*, determinateness, which corresponds to *perception* [Thing 2]; part essence or in the capacity of the universal, which corresponds to the understanding [Thing 3]. The object as a whole is the conclusion/closure/syllogism [*Schluß*] or the movement of the universal through determination to the individual, as also the inverse, from the individual through the sublated [*aufgehobne*] individual or determination to the universal. (*Phänomenologie*, VIII.I.789, 603; my translation)

The stone we step on with a bare foot (Thing 1) is an "unmediated" being or thing because we experience it directly, through our senses, which convey to the brain the overwhelming certainty (sense-certainty as unmediated consciousness) that there is something hard jabbing at us from underneath our foot. (That our nervous system mediates this experience for us mitigates Hegel's notion that this is *unmediated* being, of course.)

This sensual experience of the stone begins to dissipate or "become-otherwise" after we walk away and perhaps begin to talk with others about stepping on the stone, or even, as the sensual experience grows dimmer in our memories, about the general and vague "experience of stepping on a stone": here is the dulled or perceptually determined relationality of "being-for-another" that Shklovsky describes as the algebraic reduction of mere repeat "recognition" (Thing 2). The abstract concept or "determination" (*Bestimmung*) of "stone" is the same for everyone because it has been perceptually reduced to its quality of otherness, to being-for-another. The fading or blurring of the stone's "unmediated" or sensual thinginess in algebraic conceptualization is for Hegel a "becoming-otherwise of itself."

When the stone is now represented poetically, in Thing 3, Shklovsky says that it is rendered once again *stony*, turned back into a stone, which I noted was basically the same thing as making Thing 2 Thing 1, but of course Thing 3 is not *just* Thing 1. It is Thing 1 *and* Thing 2 sublated as Thing 3, which contains not only an artistically heightened or transcended version of Thing 1 but also the negated or emptied-out externalization of Thing 2—what Hegel calls the movement of the universal through determination (*that* stone that I just stepped on) to the individual, which is also, dialectically, the inverse movement from the individual stepped-on stone through sublation to the universal.

Thing 4, obviously, the "algebraically" reduced or objectified image of the literary text, would be a new "becoming-otherwise" perception as second-tier antithesis—and in chapter 5, I push Bertolt Brecht's theory of the *Verfremdungseffekt* on a round of something like this higher-level dialectic, arising out of Brecht's refusal of Thing 4 as the new antithesis.

The first critic to notice Shklovsky's Hegelianism in Russia was Boris Paramonov in 1996. Insisting that he is not drawing a genetic connection between Hegel's thought and Russian formalism but merely drawing structural parallels, Paramonov also notes that Shklovsky is the only formalist ever to mention Hegel, and not just in his late works, such as *The Bow-String* (*Tetiva*, 1970), where his frequent quotations from Hegel are usually cited from Lenin's thoroughly Hegelian *Philosophical Notebooks* and thus might be thought of as "a mere sham, camouflage, a demonstration of ideological loyalty" (Paramonov, 35; all translations from Paramonov are my own). Shklovsky began to build bridges from formalism back to Hegel in 1922, back when, as Paramonov says, "no one was forcing him to ground his theory in Marxism" (35); more Hegel references and Hegelian puns appear in *The Theory of Prose* (1925),[1] one year after Trotsky's critique but still five years before the "recantation" of "Pamyatnik nauchnoy oshibke." As Paramonov writes, "Among Marxists, in precise accordance with Shklovsky's descriptions, dialectic, once canonized, became a stamp, a stereotype, no longer perceived in its true existence. No longer 'experienced,' it was merely 'recognized.' The trick was to see it 'estranged'" (36).

Paramonov's article ranges widely, covering the Hegelian elements in Shklovsky's entire literary and critical production, as well as the German Romantic elements—specifically ideas from the Schlegel brothers and Novalis—in formalism in general. He compares Shklovsky's emphasis on the prolongation of artistic perception with Hegel's idea of the dialectical coming-into-being of the world. He finds a "seed" of estrangement in the second volume of Hegel's *Realphilosophie* lecture notes, which Shklovsky discovered and cited in a late essay: "Hegel," Paramonov writes, "was talking about fashion: its significance, Hegel thought, lay in the fact that clothing, a dress, constantly being renewed, should point to what is hidden; a woman should renew her clothing so as to renew herself. Otherwise perception becomes automatized, and the woman disappears, her 'matter' is dematerialized, disembodied" (39).

Paramonov fudges to a large extent the question of how deeply and widely the young Shklovsky was reading Hegel—say, in the teens and twenties. The general perception of Shklovsky is that he was not a great reader, that he mostly picked up odds and ends of other thinkers' ideas from his friends. Certainly, conditions in the late teens and early twenties were not particularly conducive to extensive library research, but it may well be that Shklovsky's brilliantly impatient personality would not have lent itself to such research even had conditions been better. We do know that Shklovsky quoted Hegel in this period, but then he quoted other scholars as well, such as William James, that he almost certainly had not read. My claim in this chapter is not, therefore, that Shklovsky was a Hegel scholar or even that he knew much about Hegel; it is rather that, for whatever reason, by whatever channel of ideosomatic contagion, Shklovsky was a Hegelian thinker, and that it can therefore shed considerable light on his thought to read Hegel through him.

Alienation

In the rest of this chapter I explore in detail a specific parallel between the two writers that Paramonov does not mention: their dialectical conceptions of alienation and dealienation, estrangement and deestrangement. Hegel is generally regarded as the inventor of the modern understanding of alienation, based on his radical rethinking of Rousseau, but in fact he went through several stages in his rethinking of alienation, from his early writings, in which alienation was a negative characteristic of the "positivism" of Christianity, to more complex and specifically dialectical understandings in his later writings. I want to devote this section to a comparison of Shklovsky's theory of estrangement with Hegel's dialectic of alienation in the *Phenomenology*, but first let me quote Alvin W. Gouldner's description of the early conception and Georg Lukács's analysis of the transition:

> Hegel here indicates a foundation for the *materialist* critique of religion subsequently developed by Feuerbach, Strauss, and Marx, which views deity as a projection formulated by people; and specifically by persons living in a world "alien" to them, i.e., by alienated men. Hegel objects to Christianity because its deity can be reached only by supplication, pleas, and prayers but remains "a divinity beyond the reach of our power and our will." Men are thus impotent, "reduced to the level of passive onlookers . . . content to wait for a revolution at the end of the world." What men now seek is a response to their supplications or a voluntary gift, but is not the result of their own potency: "we wait to receive it without our own intervention." Here Hegel's critical platform appears to be a version of the "gospel of labor," a this-worldly activism that overlays and sublimates a passive millenarianism.
>
> In viewing the "objectivity" of Christian deity as the projection of an alienated people, Hegel's concept of alienation is not only a psychological

estrangement, not simply a *feeling* of distance from the object, but entails a practical, everyday absence of *control* in a world where persons have become spectators, "passive onlookers," incapable of themselves achieving their own values by their own efforts—in effect, waiting for the revolution. In this critique of Christianity, Hegel is grounding himself in some tacit alternative conception of what is appropriate to humanity; or of what kind of persons are "normal" proper "subjects"; or, what "subject-hood" means to him. To be a subject, for Hegel, means to have power and control, not simply psychological union or closeness; it means the capacity to achieve one's goals against resistance and without supplication. (178–79)

Georg Lukács traces the development of Hegel's later thinking on alienation in *The Young Hegel*, suggesting that Hegel initially identifies the process of "externalization" (*Entäußerung*) or "objectification" (*Gegenständlichkeit*) by which objects are brought into "positive" being, and then splits off from that process the social institutions generated by it, which themselves assume a kind of alienated (*entfremdete*) objectivity or thinghood (*Dingheit*). As Lukács writes, Hegel gradually comes to believe that "work not only makes men human . . . it not only causes the vast and complex array of social processes to come into being, it also makes the world of man into an 'alienated,' 'externalized' world . . . In the concept of 'externalization' . . . we find enshrined Hegel's conviction that the world of economics which dominates man and which utterly controls the life of the individual is nevertheless the product of man himself" (333; see also Gouldner, 179). This alienated world is unavoidable, an integral part of and continual production by and through our life in the body, a repeated physical(ized) projection of spirit; Hegel's idealism inclines him to reconnect the alienated or externalized object world with spirit, and thus to bring about the discovery and acceptance of the reality and unity of Absolute Spirit, but ultimately alienation is essential to his dialectic and is never completely sublated.

Hegel's fullest exploration of the process of externalization comes in chapter 8 of the *Phenomenology*, where the self begins by being conscious of an object and objectifying its image of the object as *its* object, and thus as the contents of self-consciousness; then empties those contents out into the world, externalizes them, negates or sublates their existence, alienates them, relinquishes them. This negating or alienating or self-sublation (*Sich-selbst-aufheben*) of the objectified contents of self-consciousness is, in fact, a positive for self-consciousness because the externalization of the object that alienates/sublates it also establishes the self as object and the object as (externalized) self, and both ultimately as being-by/with-yourself (*Bei-sich-sein*) or being-otherwise (*Anderssein*). The process also entails the sublation and reintegration into the self of self-relinquishment and objectification, so that what is sublated/reintegrated is the object-becoming-nothing, the self-becoming-empty, and the self-becoming-external-object. The soul is another such externalization of the self, or of the "Ich," the "I," which Freud's English translators would eventually call the ego, another "thing" that is represented specifically, Hegel says, "as an invisible, intangible (and so on) thing, in fact not actually as unmediated being, and not as what one means by thing" (VIII.1.790, 604; my translation). Most things that we call things, however, are physical objects, apparently external to ourselves and therefore subject to "objective" knowing; but the positivistic science that splits the knower from the known, the I from the it, the self from the thing, is a product and producer of alienation, of the alienated world. For, as Hegel insists,

> *The thing is I;* in fact the thing in this unending judgment [*Urteil,* meaning the sentence or judgment pronounced by the judge, who in this case for Hegel is reason] is sublated [*aufgehoben*]; it is nothing in itself; it has meaning only in relationships, only *through I* and *in reference/pull [Beziehung] to I.* This moment arose for consciousness in pure insight and enlightenment. Things just are *useful,* and are only to be considered according to their usefulness. The trained/educated [*gebildete*] self-consciousness, which has run through the world of self-alienated [*sich entfremdeten*] spirit, has through its externalization [*Entäußerung*] created the thing as itself, and therefore still keeps itself in the thing, and knows its unself-sufficiency [*Unselbstständigkeit*], knows that the thing *essentially* is only being-for-another [*Sein für Anderes*]; or, to express fully the relationship, i.e. what here alone constitutes the nature of the object, so for it the thing counts as a *being-for-itself [fürsichseiendes],* it proclaims sense-certainty as absolute truth, but this being-for-itself itself as a moment that vanishes and passes over into its opposite, into a relinquished being for another. (VIII.1.791, 604–5; my translation)

What this Hegelian model gives us is a strategy for reconciling the formalist focus on form with the objectivist focus on content—the focus on form as psychology, as the shapes of internal emotional-becoming-mental representations of external things (including not only stones but loved ones, and war, and God, and the soul), and the focus on content as dead matter. The Kantian/Hegelian idealism of formalist theory does posit the absolute inaccessibility of the *Ding-an-sich,* the thing as perfectly isolated from the constructive/poetic activity of human knowing, and therefore seems to the objectivist to be a form of solipsism; but the idealist tradition insists on placing human consciousness and (especially for Hegel, and Shklovsky as well) dialectical self-consciousness at the center of the human universe, and seeing form and content, the I and the it, the self and the thing as intensely and integrally interrelated there. Self-consciousness created the thing as itself, externalized itself as the thing, and therefore knows that the thing is being-for-another, cannot exist without the other, which for the thing is the creative I of self-consciousness; but the externalized or alienated thing is also the other for the I, and thus an externalizing and alienating impulse *within* the I. The transitional "moments" of the Hegelian dialectic are never merely serial, extended in time; they are also multiply embedded, so that every thing and every I contains its opposite, being-for-itself and being-for-another, and contains the relinquishment of that opposite as well—and contains them as sublated physical moments of force, lever or torque points through which the dialectic is spiritually leveraged onward.

In that sense Shklovsky's stone as Thing 1 exists not as a piece of objective dead matter but as the "unmediated" sense-certainty of the dialectical interaction or interrelation between the hardness of the thing and the pain in the foot (which itself exists only in the interaction or interrelation between the nerve endings in the foot and the pain centers in the brain), and consciousness's awareness of that interaction and interrelation itself exists in the dialectical stone-foot-brain interactions and interrelations of *self*-consciousness.

What is increasingly lost in Thing 2, then, is no purely alienated object but relationality, the dialectic: as awareness of the otherness of the stone gradually fades from consciousness, consciousness also gradually fades from the self-consciousness of the (imaged) stone, so that everything comes to seem less real, less alive. Ironically, in fact—but in terms of the dialectic inescapably—it is precisely the enhanced objectification (externalization, alienation, or what Shklovsky calls algebraization) of the stone that causes a loss of object, a self-canceling sensation or somatic anesthesis of consciousness of the object, and indeed the self-conscious sense of a loss of sensation. "For this reason," Hegel says, "it must be said that nothing is known that is not *experience,* or as the same thing is also expressed, that is not available as *felt truth,* as *inwardly revealed* eternity, as *believed* sacrality, or whatever other expression we want to use" (VIII.3.802, 613; my translation). The kind of radical empiricism that would isolate the object from relation, from experience as dialectical interaction (as "the human factor"), decreases the availability of felt truth and thus the possibility of knowing anything.

The move from Thing 2 to Thing 3 begins, for Hegel, at the transitional moment when self-consciousness gives up hope of escaping—canceling, transcending, superseding, sublating—alienation:

> The movement by which the form of spirit's knowing-itself is driven forth is the work [*Arbeit*] that it brings to fullness [*vollbringt,* lit. "full-brings"] as *actual history* [*wirkliche Geschichte*]. The religious community, insofar as it is at first the substance of absolute spirit, is the raw consciousness whose existence is all the more barbaric and harsh the deeper its inner spirit is, and its lumpish self has a labor all the flintier in dealing with its essence, with what to it are the strange/foreign/alien [*fremden*] contents of its consciousness. Not until it has given up all hope of sublating [*aufzuheben*] that being-strange/-foreign/-alien [*Fremdsein*] in an external (i.e. strange/foreign/alien) way does it turn, because the sublated strange/foreign/alien way [*aufgehobne fremde Weise*] is the return into self-consciousness, to its own self, to its own world and present time, reveals that way as its property [*Eigentum,* lit. "ownness"] and has thus taken the first step in climbing down from the ideal intelligible world [*Intellektualwelt*], or rather in animating [*begeisten,* lit. "spiritizing"] that world's abstract element with actual self. (VIII.3.803, 614; my translation)

The alienated world or automatized thing that seems external, because it is the product of externalization, cannot be banished or transcended because it is found inside the externalizing and alienating/alienated consciousness, and any attempt to banish it, to alienate it, is itself always already saturated with the same alienation, the same externality. Once self-consciousness ceases to attempt to separate itself from an alienation that is part not only of its self but of its attempts to police the boundaries of the self, those alien(ating) attempts are revealed as the sublated "return into self-consciousness, to its own self, to its own world and present time . . . as its property," which is to say, the alien is its own, alienation is its ownness.

Work

For Hegel, as the first sentence of that last quotation makes clear, this dialectical-historical process is characterized by *work,* labor, *Arbeit.* It is the spirit's work that drives its self-knowing forth and cranks the levers and torque wrenches that leverage the dialectical movement forward, transforming self-knowing into actual history, history that is "actual" (*wirklich*) because it is grounded in the "acting on (things and people)" (*Wirken*) of work. And since by "spirit" or *Geist* Hegel means not God or a ghost or an abstract mental phenomenon but human being, real people thinking and saying and doing things, and since, as Sean Sayers says, "material labour is a 'spiritual' activity in that it leads to human development" (118), the actual work that is done that becomes actual history includes things like sitting at a computer terminal and writing or clicking, washing dishes, standing in a train yard dispatching trains, turning a torque wrench at Joe's Garage, sentencing people to death, and so on. Work. Human beings, acting in the working world, working interactively with other people and things, interactively, dialectically, rework the past as the future and the future as the past, the self as other and other as self, alien as own and own as alien.

But Hegel's references to work in the *Phenomenology* are sketchy at best and not particularly appropriate to Shklovsky's discussion of working and making in "Art as Device." He is more forthcoming in the *System of Ethical Life* (*System der Sittlichkeit*) and the *Jenaer Realphilosophie* lecture notes, and, on the topic of artistic creation as the highest and freest form of work, in the *Aesthetics* lectures as well. He wrote the *System of Ethical Life* around 1802–3, but it was not published in German until 1913, too late for Shklovsky (who was one-quarter German but could not read the language) to have read it before writing "Art as Device" in 1916. The *Realphilosophie* lectures were delivered at Jena University in 1803–4 and 1805–6 but were not published in German until 1931; the *Aesthetics* lectures were published in 1835–38, shortly after Hegel's death—early enough for Marx to have learned greatly from them—but did not appear in Russian translation until 1938. In reading Shklovsky on work through Hegel I am, then, still arguing from ideological or methodological kinship rather than direct influence.

Shklovsky does not theorize the prealienation state, but in his assumption that belabored artistic form and the reexperiencing through poetry of the making of a thing will overcome automatization or alienation, he is clearly imagining some such state—dialectically, I would argue, as both a nostalgic return to a simpler form of life and a more complex transformative sublation of that return through art. Hegel tracks just such a dialectical movement, in fact, in his writings on work. In his conception, human history moves through three stages, from a state of nature through a state of simple labor to a state of rationalized labor, and we find, in the third state—the one that he and we live in—that we wish to flee its alienations back into the second, the state of simple labor. That flight is impossible in economic reality but quite possible in the artistic imagination, which is not mere escapism but may actually have a transformative effect on the way we feel we live our lives. Sean Sayers's description

of the state of simple labor roughly encapsulates the kind of therapeutic state
the artist attempts to sublate for the alienated victim of surplus labor:

> Through work, says Hegel, the human being impregnates the external world
> with his will. Thereby he humanises his environment, by showing how it
> is capable of satisfying him and how it cannot preserve any power of in-
> dependence against him. Only by means of this effectual activity is he no
> longer merely in general, but also in particular and in detail, actually aware
> of himself and at home in his environment . . . In the language Marx uses in
> the *Economic and Philosophical Manuscripts,* this is the process of "objectifi-
> cation" [*Vergegenständlichung*] ("The product of labour is labour embodied
> and made material in an object, it is the objectification of labour. The reali-
> sation of labour is its objectification" . . .). There are two aspects to this pro-
> cess. In the first place, by objectifying ourselves in our products, we come to
> recognise our powers and capacities as real and objective. Thus we develop
> a consciousness of ourselves. Second, by humanising the world, we cease to
> feel that we are confronted by a foreign and hostile world. We overcome our
> alienation from the natural world and gradually, through a long process of
> social and economic development, come to feel at home in the world and
> in harmony with it. Hegel makes these points as follows.
>
> Man brings himself before himself by practical activity, since he has the
> impulse, in whatever is directly given to him, in what is present to him exter-
> nally, to produce himself and therein equally to recognise himself. This aim
> he achieves by altering external things whereon he impresses the seal of his
> inner being and in which he now finds again his own characteristics. Man
> does this in order, as a free subject, to strip the external world of its inflexible
> foreignness and to enjoy in the shape of things only an external realisation
> of himself. (111)

But this is idealized: freedom is never this easy for Hegel. He defines the
idea of freedom, in fact, as a quasi-illusionary byproduct of, or reaction to, the
state of rationalized labor, a negative rejection or "non-recognition of property, in its cancellation," or, more fully, a heroic attempt to reconstitute that
negative as a serenely non-repressive positive, a difference from universalized
property that no longer recognizes itself as "the lack and concealment of difference" (*Ethical,* 119). Sayers is setting up work in the state of simple labor as a
form of unalienated freedom, or perhaps, since for Hegel alienation is endemic
to human social reality, and certainly to work, of re-dealienated freedom, the
restoration of some now-lost self-recognition and self-realization. It is true
that Hegel imagines simple labor as dialectical in its effects, both alienating
humans from the natural world they work on and relationally transforming

the world and themselves, and so bringing about some degree of dealienation; it is also true that he imagines art as having the power to dealienate us, or seem to dealienate us, or to give us the sense that we are overcoming alienation, on a higher, more complex level. Ultimately, however, for Hegel dealienation is impossible.

What I propose to do here is to follow Hegel's three levels as he develops them in the *System of Ethical Life,* and then to jump over to the *Aesthetics* lectures for a discussion of the higher-level dealienating power of art. Hegel theorizes the emergence of ethics out of what is essentially a somatics of desiring that is dialectically complicated from simple appetite (a, the state of nature), through the relationality of serial love for the product, the tool, and the work (b, the state of simple labor), to the economics of surplus labor, product, and need (c, the state of rationalized labor), which generates legality and ethics. Hegel characterizes this and all his other thesis-antithesis-synthesis subtriads in terms of the same general oppositions: on the first level, concept is subsumed to feeling or intuition; on the second level, the collectivized and therefore "objective" and "universal" concept subsumes feeling or intuition and thus collectivizes or socializes the relation between subject and object; and on the third level, the relation between feeling and concept is synthesized.

The State of Nature

The first general level, then, the state of prealienation nature, is defined in terms of the separation between subject (the desirer) and object (the desired). In that state the subject's consumption—what Hegel calls the "negation" or "annihilation"—of the desired object sublates the separation between subject and object. Simply put, separation here is need, and enjoyment is separation sublated: you're hungry, so you eat an apple, and the apple becomes part of you. Before you eat it, it's separate from you, an external object; once you've eaten it, it has been assimilated to your subjectivity. As Hegel puts it, the separation has been sublated in a perfectly singular and identical-without-difference way, because this level does not yet involve the alienated consciousness of human desiring; there is no alienation yet for the subject to (fail to) sublate.

Feeling on the first level is purely appetitive; the transitional movement to the second level involves the emergence of a *conscious* feeling (in this case, enjoyment) out of the consumption of the object and thus the elimination of separation, the creation of unity and thus ideality out of difference. This "ideal determination of the object" requires a more complex sublation of unconscious separation-as-need, namely, what Hegel calls "absolute self-feeling." Antonio Damasio would call this the generation of mentalized body maps of appetite, consisting of desiring images of both the desired object and its consumption or negation, which idealize it differentially as something inner: inner as desired, inner as consumed. This becoming-conscious involves effort and labor, the labor of concept-formation or form-conceptualization, becoming-conscious as the laborious creation of form but also physical labor as the *channel* of the becoming-conscious. Specifically, self-feeling-as-form-as-difference generates labor as "negative practical intuition," intuition directed interactively with objects, the product and possession as difference, and tools. Because it's a conscious differentiated feeling, a social feeling, it is not only regulated by the concept but it channels regulation through work, product, possession, and tool as well, circulating regulatory feeling through the entire working-system.

The State of Simple Labor

This second level thus becomes the level of simple labor, which Shlomo Avineri describes as a move from annihilation to construction:

> Labour appears then as the transformation of the appetites from their initial annihilative character to a constructive one: whereas primitive man, like the animals, consumes nature and destroys the object, labour holds up to man an object to be desired not through negation but through re-creation. While the goal of production is thus explained as recognition through the other, its motive is still need. Consciousness, by desiring an object, moves man to create it, to transform need from a subjective craving and appetite into an external, objective force. Labour is therefore always intentional, not instinctual for it represents man's power to create his own world. Production is a vehicle of reason's actualization of itself in the world. (89–90)

Again, this is nostalgic, an idealized imaginary return to a simpler mode of labor and of life, but the nostalgia is in large part Hegel's as well. As Sean Sayers shows, while Hegel considered alienation to be endemic to all social life and all labor, he did consider certain societies to be less alienated than the one he himself lived in:

> The ideal, unalienated condition for him is a middle way [the state of simple labor or second level] between the extremes of simple idyllic circumstances [the state of nature or first level] and excessive modern development [the state of rationalized labor or third level]. As regards work, at least, he looks

back to an earlier "golden age" when production was still on a domestic and local scale; and when producers could relate to their products and feel at home in a world which they could still comprehend as their own creation.

In such a mode of life man has the feeling, in everything he uses and everything he surrounds himself with, that he has produced it from his own resources, and therefore in external things has to do with what is his own and not with alienated objects lying outside his own sphere wherein he is master. In that event of course the activity of collecting and forming his material must not appear as painful drudgery but as easy, satisfying work which puts no hindrance and no failure in his way . . . (124)

The two primary examples he gives of this sort of golden age in the *Aesthetics* lectures are ancient Greece and seventeenth-century Holland:

Agamemnon's sceptre is a family staff, hewn by his ancestor himself, and inherited by his descendants. Odysseus carpentered himself his huge marriage bed . . . [E]verything is domestic, in everything man has present before his eyes the power of his arm, the skill of his hand, the cleverness of his own spirit, or a result of his courage and bravery. In this way alone have the means of satisfaction not been degraded to a purely external matter; we see their living origin itself and the living consciousness of the value which man puts on them because in them he has things not dead or killed by custom, but his own closest productions. (quoted in Sayers, 124)

These disclose a people who, as a result of their industry and history, are at home in their world. The Dutch themselves have made the greatest part of the land on which they dwell and live; it has continually to be defended against the storms of the sea, and it has to be maintained. By resolution, endurance, and courage, townsmen and countrymen alike threw off the Spanish dominion . . . and by fighting won for themselves freedom in political life and in religious life too . . . This citizenship, this love of enterprise, in small things as in great . . . this joy and exuberance in their own sense that for all this they have their own activity to thank, all this is what constitutes the general content of their pictures. (quoted in Sayers, 125)

"This," as Sayers says, "is Hegel's vision of unalienated society, and it provides the standard by which he criticises modern industrial conditions. For Hegel, that ideal is now irretrievably past and gone: large-scale industry is an inescapable part of modern life. Ultimately, Hegel has no wish to renounce the modernity which has seen the development of individuality and freedom, despite the alienation and other problems it brings with it. These problems are insoluble, he believes: the best that can be hoped is that the state will ameliorate some of their harsher effects" (125).

What Sayers fails to point out, however, is that Hegel's "vision of unalienated society" is based on art—on his reading of Homer and his viewing of
the paintings of the Dutch Masters, especially perhaps Vermeer. In this sense
the Hegelian imagination of dealienation is a therapeutic *effect* of art, what
Shklovsky would call a poetic estrangement of or from modern estrangement.
Whether that effect has any transformative power over the alienated world of
surplus labor—the desomatization of humans living in it, the derealization of
that world in their imaginations—remains to be seen.

In the *System of Ethical Life*, Hegel imagines a series of embedded triads on
the second level, each subtriad arising theoretically out of the synthesis above
it but embedded within it, so as to constitute not so much a new dialectic
or an advancement of the dialectical movement as a retardation and inward
expansion of the state of simple labor. Thus Hegel unfolds simple labor (b)
in terms of the triads of (ba) serial internalization of the object as desire, (bb)
externalization of desire as object, and (bc) mediation between the two by reason, which last again takes triadic form in (bca) the child, (bcb) the tool, and
(bcc) speech, which last yet again takes triadic form in (bcca) body language,
(bccb) the corporeal sign, and (bccc) the spoken word.

Hegel describes the serial internalization of the object as desire (ba) as the
sublation through labor of each individual object (in series) by replacing it
with another, and the investing of the same desire as obstructed/deferred enjoyment in each internalized object. Hegel does not mention the term here,
but this sounds very much like addiction:

> The nullification of the object or of the intuition, but, *qua* moment, in
> such a way that this annihilation is replaced by another intuition or object;
> or pure identity, the activity of nullifying, is fixed; in this activity there is
> abstraction from enjoyment [*Genuß*], i.e., it is not achieved, for here every
> abstraction is a reality, something that *is*. The object is not nullified as object
> altogether but rather in such a way that another object is put in its place,
> for in this nullification, *qua* abstraction, there is no object or there is no en-
> joyment. But this nullification is labour whereby the object determined by
> desire [*Begierde*] is superseded [*aufgehoben*] in so far as it is real on its own
> account, an object not determined by desire, and determination by desire
> *qua* intuition is posited objectively. (*Sittlichkeit*, 12–13; *Ethical*, 106)

"In labour," Hegel concludes,

> the difference between desire and enjoyment is posited; the enjoyment is
> obstructed and deferred [*gehemmt, und aufgeschoben*]; it becomes ideal or a

relation, and on this relation, as a result of labour, there is posited as now immediately emerging[:] . . . [baa] the ideal determining of the object by desire: this is *taking possession* [*Besitzergreifung*] of the object . . . [bab] the real annihilation of the object's form, for objectivity or difference remains—the *activity* of labour itself . . . [and bac] the *possession* of the product . . . which consists in annihilating its form and in its being given a new form by the subject [*der Vernichtung seiner Form unter der Formgebung*]—i.e., the possibility of a transition to enjoyment which, however, remains wholly ideal. (*Sittlichkeit*, 13; *Ethical*, 106)

In this process "pure identity, the activity of nullifying, is fixed" as an addiction is fixed, one that begins in this case as a consumption addiction but, through sublation, becomes an addiction to producing *and* consuming *and* still possessing the object, which must thus somehow remain available for addictive enjoyment despite its consumption. Clearly, here, the failed or attenuated (but ideal and therefore perpetually renewed potential for) enjoyment lies not in consuming the object but in making-and-consuming-and-having the object, making your cake and having it and eating it too, so that, in practical terms, as you finish one cake you have to make another to start in on. The focus in this thetic moment is on the subjective experience of consumption and/or labor, which Hegel describes as the *Hemmung und Aufschiebung,* the inhibition/retardation/restraint/obstruction and postponement/deferral/delay (what Shklovsky calls the *zatrudnenie* "belaboring" and *zatormozhenie* "impedance, retardation," lit. "braking"), of enjoyment and the incorporation of that *Hemmung* and that *Aufschiebung* into desire (*Begierde*) and possession (*Besitz*) or occupancy (*Besitzergreifung*), or the "ideal determining of the object by desire"—the dialectical internalization of the object as addictive object within the subject's internal desiring system. The subject thus becomes addicted to the idealized image of the object, and secondarily to the desiring/laboring processes that provide for the satisfaction of desire.

Hegel next describes the externalization of desire (bb) as a shifting of the dominant focus in the subject-object relation from the subject to the object, so that the object comes to be seen in its aspect of the outer rather than the inner, and of the real rather than the ideal. Here again enjoyment is obstructed or impeded or "belabored," but now the impeded desire is externalized, through the labor of *creating* the desired object, and invested in the object itself, which thus becomes what Marx will call a fetish object. Marx's late theory of commodity fetishism is in fact deeply indebted to Hegel's analysis on this point, the "double forgetting" of the dialectic by which the subject first forgets that it has invested desire in the object (rendering it special) and then forgets that the object ever was especially important (rendering it familiar). In Hegel's analysis the subject *misses* the consumed object and decides to *possess* it, in the sense of preserving it: the subject "considers the relation of the inhibited feeling [*das Verhältnis des gehemmten Gefühls*] to the object inhibited by its nullification [i.e., by the labour expended to change it (Harris and Knox's note)], or the difference present even in labour, namely, the difference between the reality and proper nature of the object and the way it is to be, and is, ideally determined by labour" (*Sittlichkeit*, 13–14; *Ethical*, 107). This is the origin of the tool, the use-object, and (though Hegel does not stop to theorize this here) the art-object: you whittle a tool or a figurine and destroy it, discard it, "nullify" it in some way, and only then, only when it's gone, find retroactively or reconstructively that you enjoyed the making so much and so strongly feel the pinch of the obstruction or impedance of that body state (*Gefühl* or feeling) that you start another.

This notion that through labor enjoyment is obstructed or impeded and that this impeded feeling is then (ba) internalized as a more complex form of desire, as a kind of partial or parceled consumption/transformation of the subject (the attenuation of enjoyment), and (bb) externalized as the ideal or imaginary enjoyment of the labor that produces the object, obviously stands in some sort of significant relation to Shklovsky's conception of belabored form. If what defers or obstructs or impedes or belabors enjoyment is the labor expended to rework the object from its "proper nature" to "the way it is to be," desire is the inward form of enjoyment impeded by labor, and labor is the outward form of impeding consumption/transformation (sublation) launched by desire. In this desiring system, clearly, impedance is essential to subjective desire and the feeling of production and possession; decreased impedance or obstruction diminishes the impeded or roughened or belabored *feeling* of desiring, making, and consuming, so that the entire process comes to seem less real, yet without becoming ideal. Since subjective feeling for Hegel grounds experience in the real, subtracting or draining feeling does not elevate experience to the ideal; it simply drains *consciousness* of the real.

In (bc), then—the third movement of the second level—reason "enters as mediator; it shares the nature of both subject and object or is the reconciliation of the two" (111). As I say, Hegel traces this third movement through three sub-triads, starting with the state of nature within the state of simple labor (bca), where the mediating term is "a real absolute identity, a real absolute feeling, the absolute middle term, explicit in this entire aspect of reality, existing as an individual," that is, "the *child,* the highest individual natural feeling, a feeling of a totality of the living sexes such that they are entirely in the child, so that he is absolutely real and is individual and real in his own eyes" (112), and proceeding thereafter to the state of simple labor *within* the state of simple labor (bcb), where the mediating term is the tool:

> Because in the tool the form or the concept is dominant, it is torn away from the nature to which the middle term of sexual love [the child (Harris and Knox's note)] belongs, and lies in the ideality, as belonging to the concept, or is the absolute reality present in accordance with the essence of the concept. In the concept, identity is unfilled and empty; annihilating itself, it exhibits only the extremes. Here annihilation is obstructed [*Hier ist die Vernichtung gehemmt*]; emptiness is real and, moreover, the extremes are fixed. In one aspect the tool is subjective, in the power of the subject who is working; by him it is entirely determined, manufactured, and fashioned; from the other point of view it is objectively directed on the object worked [*objektiv gegen den Gegenstand der Arbeit gerichtet*]. By means of this middle term [between subject and object (Harris and Knox's note)] the subject cancels [*hebt . . . auf,* sublates] the immediacy of annihilation; for labour, as annihilation of intuition [the particular object (Harris and Knox's note)], is at the same time annihilation of the subject, positing in him a negation of the merely quantitative; hand and spirit are blunted by it, i.e., they themselves assume the nature of negativity and formlessness, just as, on the other side (since the negative, difference, is double), labour is something downright single and subjective. In the tool the subject makes a middle term between himself and the object, and this middle term is the real rationality of labour; for the fact that work as such, and the object worked upon, are themselves means, is only a formal mediation, since that for which they exist is outside them, and so the bearing of the subject on the object is a complete separation, remaining entirely in the subject within the thinking of intelligence. In the tool the subject severs objectivity and its own blunting from itself, it sacrifices an other to annihilation and casts the subjective side of that on to the other. At the same time its labour ceases to be directed on something singular. In the tool the subjectivity of labour is raised to something universal. Anyone can make a similar tool and work with it. To this extent the tool is the persistent norm [*Regel,* rule] of labour. (*Sittlichkeit,* 20; *Ethical,* 112–13)

Note here that subsumption of feeling under the concept grounds mediating rationality in dead matter: this is an important first step toward alienation, which for Hegel is a largely positive state, against which we nevertheless struggle. The subject uses the tool to rework the world into object, a process that has the effect of "blunting" (*stumpf machen*) the subject as well; in severing the resulting objectivity and blunting from itself, the subject enlists the object and the work as means to the thinking of the subject's own intelligence. The "other" that the subject sacrifices to annihilation is the singular aspect of the world that the subject is working on; the subject sacrifices it to annihilation in the sense of universalizing it through labor, through the rational mediation of the tool, which is infinitely repeatable and therefore universal, which makes labor itself universal.

The highest (synthetic) form reason takes in the state of simple labor is *speech* (bcc), which combines the living intuitive feeling of the child and the ideality at the core of the dead inner being of the tool (middle term in labor) into a new intelligent totality. In terms of Shklovsky's notion of the dealienating poetic return to the state of simple labor, this synthesis of living intuitive feeling with dead inner being in speech is crucial: in the alienated state of rationalized labor all three of these movements will have gone dead, the child, the tool, and speech, and all will therefore need to be revivified on a higher level—not just a *return* to the state of simple labor but an artistic *sublation* of that state—in the estranging poem. If this Hegelian narrative works at all for Shklovsky's theory, the estranging poem might itself be thought of as the higher-level version of speech, the mediating moment that dialectically unites within itself the opposites of living intuitive feeling (the somatic "sensation" restored by the poem, or "belabored content") and the dead inner being of the tool ("belabored form").

Just as Shklovsky imagines the poem in terms of whole-body seeing, somatic seeing, so too does Hegel imagine speech in terms of the body. Speech for him is subjective in the sense that it is "in intelligent individuals," produced by them for their own purposes, but it is also "objectively universal in its corporeality," as intuition is—he seems to mean by this corporeal objective universality something like the ideosomatics of speech, the collective somatic regulation of speech. Speech is immediate, malleable, and transparent, capable of assuming every form, and also instantly passes away as soon as it is created—"its appearance is this immediate conjunction of appearance and passing away." It is "a subject aware of itself," and therefore a channel and tool and child of self-consciousness. Also important for the somaticity of Hegel's conception of speech is that he insists that it must be distinguished from the "formal concept" of speech, something like the linguistic code, what Saussure will call *la langue,* abstract logical system as an objectified form of subjectivity, a subjectivity with the abstraction that is characteristic of the object.

Again Hegel takes speech up through the three levels: subsumption under feeling, where speech is body language (bcca: "Die Gebärde, die Miene und die Totalität derselben, die Affektion des Auges," *Sittlichkeit,* 22; "*Gesture,* mien, and their totality in the glance of the eye," *Ethical* 114); subsumption under the concept, where speech is the "corporeal sign" (bccb: an Other's smile or frown or body alignment as a sign of approval or disapproval), and the synthetic totality of the two, where speech is the spoken word (bccc). Body language is subjective, Hegel says, while the corporeal sign is objective, expresses the concept, and therefore is bound up with what is formal and universal. Subjective body language is "not torn loose from the subject and is not free," and the corporeal sign is not torn loose from the object and does not carry knowledge (its subjective element) in itself directly but tacks it onto the object, "accosts" it and remains accidental to it. The corporeal sign is objective in the sense of being collective, shared, therefore outside the subjectivity of the individual speaking body; it is the Other side of the somatic exchange, the moment of Otherness in the somatic exchange, the sign of somatized cultural regulation coming back to the speaker from an Other, to which the speaker then attaches (through what Althusser calls interpellation) a subjective moment of knowledge. The spoken word, then, unites the objective corporeal sign of the other with the subjective body language of the self and gives it an independent individual intelligent single fixed body that exists under the sign of the concept, which articulates and establishes all indefiniteness, and immediately destroys itself. This moves recognition past the dumb recognition of the objective corporeal sign to the absolute recognition of speech. "The animal does not produce its voice out of the totality contained in this solitude; its voice is empty, formal, void of totality. But the corporeality of speech displays totality resumed into individuality, the absolute entry into the absolute monadic point of the individual whose ideality is inwardly dispersed into a system" (116).

The State of Rationalized Labor

Things begin to go bad on the third level, the state of rationalized labor, at first because *making*—the labor involved in producing a whole product—is partitioned into subtasks that are apportioned to different workers, reducing the process for each worker to a mechanical repetitiveness that feels alien or foreign or strange (*fremd*) to what Hegel calls "the living whole."

The particular, into which the universal is transferred, therefore becomes ideal and the ideality is a partition of it. The entire object in its determinate character is not annihilated altogether, but this labour, applied to the object as an entirety, is partitioned in itself and becomes a single labouring; and this single labouring becomes for this very reason more mechanical, because variety is excluded from it and so it becomes itself something more universal, more foreign to whole [*der Ganzheit fremderes wird*]. This sort of labouring, thus divided, presupposes at the same time that the remaining needs are provided for in another way, for this way too has to be laboured on, i.e., by the labour of other men. But this deadening [characteristic] [*Abstumpfung*] of mechanical labour directly implies the possibility of cutting oneself off from it altogether; for the labour here is wholly quantitative without variety, and since its subsumption in intelligence is self-cancelling [*sich aufhebt,* sublates itself], something absolutely external, a thing, can then be used owing to its self-sameness both in respect of its labour and its movement. It is only a question of finding for it an equally dead principle of movement, a self-differentiating power of nature like the movement of water, wind, steam, etc., and the tool passes over into the *machine,* since the restlessness of the subject, the concept, is itself posited outside the subject [in the energy source]. (*Sittlichkeit,* 25–26; *Ethical,* 117; all English insertions added by Harris and Knox)

Here, obviously, in Hegel's description of the "rationalization" of work in the Industrial Revolution, is one theory of the source of Shklovsky's automatization: as work becomes mechanical and repetitive, as it comes to exclude variety and thus to be assimilated to the alienated externalized universality and quantitativity of objectivity, its subsumption in intelligence cancels itself out, and it has a deadening effect on both the subject (depersonalization) and the object (the machine, mechanization). What is left over in this process is the subject's restlessness and the object's energy source, suggesting that the leftover needs are important to the working of the whole, but they need to be reworked, "labored on, by the labor of other men." "Thus this possession has lost its meaning for the practical feeling of the subject and is no longer a need of his, but a surplus," so that its use is universalized and becomes the use of others, the need for the product is abstracted into "need in general": "the bearing of the surplus on use is a general possibility of use, not just of the specific use that it expresses, since the latter is divorced from the subject" (*Ethical,* 118).

In Hegel, things keep getting worse; in Shklovsky, this is the point where poetry intervenes and deautomatizes or repersonalizes human life. I want to return to Hegel's analysis of the spread of alienation in the state of rationalized labor later, but first let us follow the sequence of Shklovsky's argumentation and look at Hegel's conception of Romantic form from the *Aesthetics* lectures.

Romantic Form

There is a certain rough isomorphism between the triad we've just been tracking in *The System of Ethical Life* and Hegel's main triad in the *Aesthetics* lectures, from Symbolic form through Classical form to Romantic form: namely, Symbolic form for Hegel stands closest to the state of nature, Classical form comes representationally closest to the kind of social utopia he envisions in the state of simple labor, and Romantic form seems to embody something like the estrangement born out of the state of rationalized labor. Obviously, any closer scrutiny of this isomorphism must take into account the manifest differences between *consumption* (the unself-conscious annihilation of the object) in the state of nature and *artistic creation* (the inadequate embodiment of ideas in artistic form) in the state of nature, and so on, but there is something suitably haphazard, stumbling, ad hoc, and therefore not quite dialectical about the ancient Indian artists whose work Hegel calls Symbolic:

> The Indian poets and sages also have material there for them as their starting-point; natural elements, sky, animals, rivers, etc., or the pure abstraction of the formless and empty Brahma; but their inspiration is a destruction of the inward life of subjectivity; the subject [i.e. the artist (Knox's note)] is given the hard task of working on what is external to himself and, owing to the intemperance [*Maaßlosigkeit,* lit. "measurelessness"] of his imagination which lacks any firm and absolute direction, he cannot create really freely [i.e., Romantically] and beautifully [i.e., Classically], but must continue to produce in an unruly way and range around in his material. He is like a builder who has no clear ground; ancient debris of half-ruined walls, mounds, projecting rocks obstruct him, quite apart from the particular ends which are to dictate the construction of his building, and he can achieve nothing but a wild, unharmonious, fantastic structure. What he produces is not the work of his own imagination freely creating out of his own spiritual resources. (*Aesthetik,* 2:69; *Aesthetics,* 1:478)

The "measure" and "firm and absolute direction" (cf. Shklovsky's "calculation and space") that Hegel says these artists lack are the products of reason at work, reason in a state of labor; the prerational or irrational artist or architect forced to adapt willy-nilly to an alien environment is like the human or animal in

the state of nature who is not yet capable of transforming his or her environment through labor or of directing his or her own activities through reason,
but must simply consume.

Again, his account of Classical art is far more idealized than his analysis of
the state of simple labor, is in fact so utterly lacking in dialectical opposition
or complexity as to constitute almost a caricature of traditional idealizations
of the ancient Greeks—no whiff of addiction or fetishization here—but in
that very idealizing tendency it seems to reflect Hegel's own nostalgia for the
simpler and more harmonious world he read about in Homer and saw in
the paintings of the Dutch Masters: "What impresses us about these [Greek
(Knox's insertion)] gods is in the first place the spiritual *substantial* individuality which, withdrawn into itself out of the motley show of the particularity of
need and the unrest of the finite with its variety of purposes, rests secure on its
own universality as on an eternal and clear foundation" (1:481–82). Indeed, as
I suggested earlier, his nostalgia for the state of simple labor is obviously conditioned by his experience of this idealized Classical art. Where Symbolic artists
simply fail to deal with the foreignness of the foreign, fail even to recognize
the alienness of the materials they incompetently assimilate, Classical artists
assimilate all foreign or alien elements so perfectly and so harmoniously as to
create what Tolstoy calls smooth form, unbelabored form:

> Accordingly the Greek artists evince themselves as genuinely creative po-
> ets. All the varied foreign ingredients [*vielfachen fremden Ingredienzien*] they
> have brought into the melting-pot, yet they have not made a brew out of
> them like what comes from a witches' cauldron; on the contrary, in the pure
> fire of the deeper spirit they have consumed everything murky, natural,
> impure, foreign, and extravagant [*alles Trübe, Natürliche, Unreine, Fremde,
> Maaßlose*]; they have burnt all this together and made the shape appear puri-
> fied, with only faint traces of the material out of which it has been formed.
> Their business in this connection consisted partly in stripping away the
> formless, symbolic, ugly, and misshapen things which confronted them in
> the material of the tradition, partly in emphasizing the properly spiritual
> which they had to individualize and for which they had to seek or invent the
> corresponding external appearance. (*Aesthetik,* 3:70; *Aesthetics,* 1:479)

Such nostalgic idylls, however, overwhelmingly attractive as they are, exist only in a certain kind of art and so for Hegel cannot serve us as a social
model of reality. Living as we are in the midst of the complex estrangements
of the state of rationalized labor, we cannot merely wish ourselves back to a

simpler time, much as Classical art may make us long for that escape. Rather, an alienated era generates an alienated art, a Romantic art; form is foreignized, estranged, alienated:

> But, thirdly, when the Idea of the beautiful is comprehended as the *absolute* and therefore as spirit, as the spirit which is free in its own eyes, it is no longer completely realized in externality [*in der Äußerlichkeit*], since its true determinate being it has only in itself as spirit. It therefore dissolves that classical unification of inwardness and external manifestation and takes flight out of externality back into itself. This provides the basic type of the *Romantic* art-form, for which, in that its content due to its free spirituality demands more than what representation in the external and the bodily can supply [*als die Darstellung im Äußerlichen und Leiblichen zu bieten vermag*], the shape becomes an *indifferent* externality [*die Gestalt zu einer gleichgültigen Äußerlichkeit wird*], so that Romantic art brings in anew the separation of content and form from the opposite side of the Symbolic. (*Aesthetics*, 1:302, translation modified slightly in accordance with *Aesthetik*, 2:406)

Äußerlichkeit is literally externality, outsideness, *vnenakhodimost'*, but here in the specifically Hegelian sense of that which has been alienated from the self, it means externalized inwardness; Hegel is defining the forms of Romantic art in terms of a reinternalization not just of the external world, including one's own and the other's body, and indeed not just of the externalized or alienated I either, but of the entire erstwhile externalized in-out or self-other or own-alien dialectic. This is Shklovsky's conception of estrangement or estranging form as well: what makes the stone stony is a reinternalization of the stone as inward sensation; what makes the poem poemy is a reinternalization of the alienated experience of making it oneself.

The interesting modifier in that passage, though, is *gleichgültig:* the Romantic art-form becomes a *gleichgültige Äußerlichkeit*, which I've translated literally above as an "indifferent externality." What is *gültig* is valid, in force; what is *gleichgültig* is so equally in force on different sides that you can't decide between two or more options and don't really need or care to decide; they're all the same. Hence *Gleichgültigkeit* is indifference, in the dual sense of an objective lack of a difference and subjective indifference, a spatial nongap and an emotional neutrality, or even (as the word is also used in German) a lack of curiosity, nonchalance, lackadaisicality, casualness. Indeed, it seems reasonable to suggest that the gap between the objective and the subjective, between outside gaps and inside attitudes toward those gaps, is precisely what Hegel sees collapsing in Romantic form: the opposite sides on which the externality of Romantic form is equally or indifferently in force are the inside and the outside, the self and the other, the own and the alien.

In the Symbolic, the I or Idea or Self is "abstract and indeterminate and therefore does not have its adequate manifestation on and in itself, but finds itself confronted by what is external to itself, external things in nature and human affairs" (1:300); in the Classical, "spirit, as free subject, is determined through and by itself, and in this self-determination, and also in its own nature, has that external shape, adequate to itself, with which it can close as with its absolutely due reality" (1:301). This latter shift allows Classical artists to create art in which idea and representation, subject and object, content and form are in perfect harmony, but a harmony based on abstraction: "the free subject, which classical art configurates outwardly, appears indeed as essentially universal and therefore freed from all the accident and mere particularity of the inner life and the outer world, but at the same time as filled solely with a universality particularized within itself" (1:301). Romantic art breaks up this harmony, separates form and content again, but does so by passing through the wall of Classical unity to the "opposite side" (*die entgegengesetzte Seite*) from the Symbolic disunity—to a dialectical disunity attained through a reparticularization of self and other, "the inner life and the outer world," as an indifferent externality, which is to say, as absolute spirit.

What this means in artistic practice, Hegel does not tell us. But it seems suggestively close to Shklovsky's *priyom ostraneniya*, entering into alienation in order to engineer dealienation, estranging itself from itself in order to find its way to deestrangement:

> But however far this identification is grounded in the essence of the Absolute itself, still, as spiritual freedom and infinity, it is no immediate reconciliation present from the beginning in mundane, natural, and spiritual reality; on the contrary, it is brought about only by the elevation of the spirit out of the finitude of its immediate existence into its truth. This implies that the spirit, in order to win its totality and freedom, detaches itself from itself and opposes itself [*sich von sich abtrenne*], as the finitude of nature and spirit, to itself as the inherently infinite. With this self-diremption [*Zerreissung*] there is bound up, conversely, the necessity of rising out of this state of scission [*Abgeschiedenheit*] (within which the finite and the natural, the immediacy of existence, the natural heart, are determined as the negative, the evil, and the bad) and of entering the realm of truth and satisfaction only through the overcoming of this negative sphere. Therefore the spiritual reconciliation is only to be apprehended and represented as an activity, a movement of the

spirit, as a process in the course of which a struggle and a battle arises, and grief, death, the mournful sense of nullity, the torment of spirit and body enter as an essential feature. (*Aesthetik,* 2:126–27; *Aesthetics,* 1:522)

Hegel has just been talking about "the diffusion of this self-contemplation of spirit, of its inwardness and self-possession," which he calls "peace, the reconciliation of spirit with itself in its objectivity—a divine world, a Kingdom of God, in which the Divine (which from the beginning had reconciliation with its reality as its essence) is consummated in virtue of this reconciliation and thereby has true consciousness of itself" (1:521–22). But this peace and this reconciliation begin to sound too much like the collapse of the dialectic back into the calm unified *repose* of the Classical, with everything balanced and harmonious. In the long extract above, therefore, he breaks the reconciliation, converts it from static immediacy to slow dialectical mediation, reframes estrangement from self as "the necessity of rising out of this state of scission," "as an activity, a movement of the spirit, as a process in the course of which a struggle and a battle arises, and grief, death, the mournful sense of nullity, the torment of spirit and body enter as an essential feature." Thus Rousseau's alienation from nature becomes at once a problem to be solved and a goad to further growth, a limitation on totality and freedom and the ground of possibility that make the achievement of totality and freedom possible.

What is conspicuously missing in Hegel, however, is a dialectical bridge from work to art, or from art to work—in particular, a dialectical social psychology of the relationship between artist and audience as mediated by the *work* of art itself. In his discussion of the emergence of ethical life, he discusses the social psychology of *working;* in his discussion of art, he reduces the artwork to a static mural or tableau in which spirit's struggles and conflicts are merely immanent. If a married couple's relationship is changed by the mediation of the child; if the subject's relationship with the object, as mediated by the tool in labor, changes both the subject and the object; if the speaker's relationship with the hearer is changed by the mediation of speech (itself a mediation between outgoing and incoming body language)—surely there is something interesting to say in a series of lectures on aesthetics about the transformative impact of Symbolic, Classical, and Romantic art on their artists and their audiences?

Shklovsky's suggestion that rhythm is a poetic tool with which the poet works on the reader, for example, is one tentative step in this direction. In what ways is literature a *material* tool, wielded on the reader as a material being?

How does wielding that tool shape the reader, and, as Hegel would have asked in his discussion of the emergence of the ethical life, how does wielding that tool shape the "worker" or poet as well? What is the material infectiousness of poetic rhythm? How does it organize the reader's breathing, heartbeat, and body movements, including not just footsteps but gestures and even posture? How does it condition somatic guidance in both the poet and the reader? Lev Vygotsky will take a few more tentative steps in that direction in an article published in 1926, coming out of his Revolution-inspired excitement with the new materialist sciences of human behavior: "That emotional background of poetic experience is the same or at least similar to the one that the author has at the moment of creating, since in the writing of his speech his breathing rhythm becomes fixed. From here—the 'infectious nature' of poetry. *The reader feels like the poet since he breathes in the same way*" (quoted in Van Der Veer and Valsinger, 30; emphasis in original). Bertolt Brecht attacks this sort of behaviorist thinking as typical of American advertising: "Hollywood's and Broadway's methods of manufacturing certain excitements and emotions may possibly be artistic, but their only use is to offset the fearful boredom induced in any audience by the endless repetition of falsehoods and stupidities. This technique was developed and is used in order to stimulate interest in things and ideas that are not in the interest of the audience" (Willett, *Brecht*, 160). Indeed, most of the twentieth-century work done on the impact that rhythm (or what is now called "progressive stimulation") has on body movements and somatic guidance has been done by companies marketing audio and video Muzak to retail businesses, to regulate their customers' moods and movements through stores. But Brecht does not simply reject behaviorism, which in fact fascinated him as a young man; he incorporates it into a more complex theory and practice of gestic transformation (see chapter 5).

Even without this materialism, however, there is implicit in Hegel's own argument what is explicit in Shklovsky's, that poetic estrangement is an essential tool in an era of psychosocial estrangement—that, as Hegel says, "spirit" splits or estranges itself from itself in order to escape that estrangement. Since "spirit" means the human spirit, human thought and feeling, human speech and behavior, human writing and reading, it should be clear that spirit's estrangement of its own estrangement in Hegel needs to be unpacked as something like the writer's estrangement of the reader's estrangement, rationalized labor as the process by which the reader is estranged and the estranging poem as the tool by which the writer works on that estrangement, reworks it, deestranges it.

But how? What is that working? These are questions to which Bertolt Brecht returns us in chapter 5.

Also missing in the *Aesthetics* lectures, especially given Hegel's attention to social and economic change elsewhere in his thought—his discussion of the state of nature, artisan culture, and the Industrial Revolution in *The System of Ethical Life,* for example—is a discussion of the connections between social and economic change and art. He associates Symbolic art with ancient Persia, India, and Egypt, and those cultures with the childhood of humanity; he associates Classical art with the ancient Greeks, without assigning them a metaphorical age in the lifespan of the human race; Romantic art is associated with nobody. Presumably we are to assume that he means the art of Goethe and Lenz and Schiller, of Haydn and Mozart, possibly the English Romantics as well; but without examples and socioeconomic analyses he could equally well mean some other period entirely, or some Romantic essence in every period in history or every national art in the world. If he does mean the art of his own time and place, surely some mention of the French Revolution would be in order? He does associate Romantic art with freedom—where Symbolic artists left disunity from sheer incompetence and Classical artists created a perfected unity out of spirit's quest for harmony, Romantic artists created a broken unity out of spirit's quest for freedom—but what freedom? Freedom from what, and, as Nietzsche would later ask, freedom for what?

Alienated Labor

If Hegel fails to theorize the relationship between socioeconomic change and the impact of art on its audience, so *a fortiori* does Shklovsky; indeed Shklovsky's failure to historicize automatization renders Hegel's analysis of the state of rationalized labor largely irrelevant to a discussion of Shklovsky's theory. What I propose to do in this last section, therefore, is to trace Hegel's thought on the state of rationalized labor quickly, as a kind of stripped-down guide to the questions Shklovsky *doesn't* ask and so can't possibly answer, and that he therefore leaves for later thinkers to worry about—especially Brecht.

Most important in Hegel's analysis for a study of Shklovsky is the notion of alienated labor, which Marx will pick up after him—and which will, due to the vagaries of the posthumous storage and publishing of manuscripts, not become conceptually available in either its Hegelian or its Marxian mode until the early twentieth century, when Hegel's *Der System der Sittlichkeit* is published for the first time in German in 1913 and the *Realphilosophie* lecture notes are published for the first time in 1931, and Marx's *Ökonomisch-philosophische Manuskripte aus dem Jahre 1844* are published for the first time in 1932. We return to Marx on alienated labor in chapter 5 in connection with Brecht's theory of *Verfremdung*. For now, though, let us note that Hegel analyzes the alienation of labor dialectically as a byproduct of the surplus, the subject's production of more than s/he needs, or, as Hegel puts it, the making of a thing that "has lost its meaning for the practical feeling of the subject and is no longer a need of his, but a *surplus*" (*System*, 118).

The alienation of labor begins, in other words, as a surplus of *product,* which alienates from the producer (worker or maker) that part of "practical feeling" or *need* that is associated with the surplus product. As soon as a line is drawn between "needed product" and "unneeded product," then, that line is relocated between subjects, between needers or users, becoming a line between "own need" and "other's need," between "own product" and "other's product," and between "own use" and "other's use." The use of the surplus product is thus universalized as "the use of others"; the need for it is similarly abstracted into "need in general," which effectively generates the universalized concept of *property.* Possession, Hegel says, is property, but this does not mean that the subject simply possesses property; rather, the subject is collectively *recognized* as possessor of property by others, recognized through a universal repetition of abstracting/idealizing/othering perceptions, perceptions collectivized by a mechanical stamping process that produces a series of such othered recognitions, not-me, not-me, "the abstraction of ideality, not ideality in the others" (118). The abstract/universal/infinite ideality of property and possession and the alienable surplus is made real through the sublation of the subject's enjoyment of possession through consumption, "the real connection with use and need" (120). This is the beginning of "thoroughgoing ideality," as "with surplus labour this intelligence ceases even in need and labour to belong to need and labour. The relation to an object which this intelligence acquires for need and use, and which is posited here, namely, the fact that intelligence has not worked up the object for its own use since it has not consumed its own labour on it, is the beginning of legal, and formally ethical, enjoyment and possession" (120).

In other words, ethics begins with the surplus—that product which the subject's intelligence has produced but does not consume. Needing and using the product you have produced grounds possession in reality; the surplus, because it is not needed or used by the subject that labored to produce it, generates the ideality of property and law and ethics. This means that the abstract ideal universality of recognition makes all things equal, and the abstraction of that equality is *value,* equality as abstraction. This alienated process of abstract/mechanical/repetitive recognition that generates universality also generates an abstract system of rights that it allocates to individuals. In this way the individual's "inalienable rights" to life, liberty, and property posited by the French Enlightenment are actually originally generated through the alienation of individual need, individual use, and individual labor to the collective (this is the core of what Hegel takes from Rousseau, of course), so that "a right to property is a right to right; property right is the aspect, the abstraction in property, according to which property is a right remaining for its other, the particular, as possession" (118). Freedom becomes a quaternary concept, based on the (4) negation of the (3) universal concept of property, which emerges out of the (2) alienation of the (1) individual, "or the negative in so far as it constitutes itself positively and sets itself up in difference against the universal, so that it bears on it and is not the lack and concealment of difference" (118–19).

The core situation in the state of rationalized labor is thus that needy intelligences face at once a surplus and an unsatisfied need; to resolve this situation they transform the objective product/possession "into something that is subjectively linked with need" (121) but specifically with generalized/universalized/alienated need, the need of the community, which is to say that the objective product is transformed into the ideality of property. When this ideal relation is then once again made real, it becomes exchange: "Property enters reality through the plurality of persons involved in exchange and mutually recognising one another" (121). Both the surplus and the need are forms that repeat the same universal object, but the core of exchange is the transformation of the one into the other, each into its opposite.

This is an extremely efficient system of production, which tends both to generate increased need and to satisfy those new needs with increased production. The only problem with the system is that it achieves efficiency through alienation, through the idealization of difference between the individual and his or her needs. The line between "own need" and "other's need" is dialectically at once moved closer to the individual, so that all need is eventually "other's need," alienated or idealized need, and farther from the individual, so that this alienated or idealized "other's need" becomes the totality of the individual's "own need." This process entails a collective cooptation and transformation of feeling, so that work is no longer able to satisfy it; work is fed into the alienated ideosomatic regulatory system, which generates alienated needs and alienated satisfactions of those needs. Work becomes, as Hegel says, "an alien power [*eine fremde Macht*], over which [the worker] has no control and on which it depends whether the surplus, which he possesses, constitutes for him the totality of his satisfactions" (*Schriften zur Politik,* quoted in Avineri, 92). As he writes of this state in the *Realphilosophie* lecture notes:

> The particularisation of labour multiplies the mass of production; in an English manufacture, 18 people work at the production of a needle; each has a particular and exclusive side of the work to perform; a single person could probably not produce 120 needles, even not one . . . But the value of labour decreases in the same proportion as the productivity of labour increases. Work becomes thus absolutely more and more dead, it becomes machine-labour, the individual's own skill becomes infinitely limited, and the consciousness of the factory worker is degraded to the utmost level of dullness. The connection between the particular sort of labour and the infinite mass of needs becomes wholly imperceptible, turns into a blind dependence. It thus happens that a far-away operation often affects a whole class of people who have hitherto satisfied their needs through it; all of a sudden it limits [their work], makes it redundant and useless. (quoted in Avineri, 93)

And again:

> In the same way, [the worker] becomes through the work of the machine more and more machine-like, dull, spiritless. The spiritual element, the self-conscious plenitude of life, becomes an empty activity. The power of the self resides in rich comprehension: this is being lost. He can leave some work to the machine; his own doing thus becomes even more formal. His dull work limits him to one point, and labour is the more perfect, the more one-sided it is . . . In the machine man abolishes his own formal activity and makes it work for him. But this deception, which he perpetrates upon nature . . . takes vengeance on him. (quoted in Avineri, 93)

Needless to say, we find none of this in Shklovsky's essay. Automatization in his theory of estrangement involves neither surplus production nor exchange, neither factories nor machines; it is purely and universally a function of repetitive action. We have no sense, reading Shklovsky on automatization, whether Russian peasants would be as susceptible to object-loss and reality-loss as an elderly male aristocrat wiping up dust in a guest room in a large country manor house; whether automatization would plague urban factory workers more or less than rural farmers and landowners; whether it has anything at all to do with the economic system governing production in the society at large.[2] That his only example of automatization is Tolstoy wiping dust off the furniture in a friend's guest room suggests that it probably has nothing to do with the economic system. When Tolstoy writes his diary entry in the late 1890s, nearly a century after Hegel's lecture notes on the European Industrial Revolution, this sort of factory automatization is still in its infancy in Russia. While it does make striking headway in the two decades that elapse between Tolstoy's diary entry and Shklovsky's article, it is still quite new. And certainly the sort of industrial automatization that Hegel analyzes would not have the slightest relevance at Nikol'skoe, or Yasnaya Polyana, or even Tolstoy's (quasi-rural) Moscow house. But educated Russians in this period are *aware* of the Industrial Revolution. Tolstoy comments on it in his work, and as we've seen, Shklovsky (the armored-car driver and mechanic) is generally fascinated with the machine and modernity—just not in "Art as Device," despite the article's machinic title. Shklovsky does not even stop to ask what a late-nineteenth-century Russian male aristocrat in his late sixties was doing wiping dust, let alone what connection this activity might have with culture, technology, industry, or social psychology in the world outside Tolstoy's guest room at the Olsuf'yevs'. He does not ask whether the fact that Tolstoy was also a world-famous novelist who began to write fiction out of his diaries might have made him more likely than peasants or factory workers or other late-nineteenth-century elderly aristocratic males to *notice* himself experiencing those losses—to write them down in his diary and so make literature out of them, fodder for literary theory—and in so doing not to lose them. For Shklovsky, that Tolstoy is a late-nineteenth-century Russian, that he's an adult male in a patriarchal society that designates house-cleaning as "women's work," that he's an aristocrat in a feudal society that designates manual labor as "peasants' work," that he's pushing seventy, that he's a realistic novelist who has become world-famous noticing such moments as not remembering whether you've wiped the divan and turning them into literature—all this is perfectly irrelevant. All that matters to Shklovsky is that "this happens." This is the human condition: "Automatization swallows up things, clothes, furniture, one's wife, and the fear of war." (The human condition has a wife, which is interesting, but not to Shklovsky; to him it's the most natural thing in the world.)[3]

Cynically, and reductively, we might note that Shklovsky's solution to alienation is poetry. For Hegel there is no solution; for Marx the only thing that can repair or redress the loss of reality and objects is the revolution that occurred a few months after Shklovsky's article was published. For the Left Hegelian Shklovsky, though, even in the midst of the war that led to the revolution, the solution is poetry as estranged labor. Even more cynically and simplistically, we might suggest that Shklovsky is taking from Tolstoy more than just the diary entry—for doesn't poetry as estranged labor as salvation from alienation sound just a tiny bit like Tolstoy's religious conversion? If life feels empty, go, give all you have to the poor, and *work,* wipe the dust off the furniture; if emptiness still plagues you, go into your study and write about it.

The unfairness of this reduction should be clear from my argument here in Part II: in a Kantian/Hegelian idealist approach to the world, it is far from escapist to attribute an enlivening power to the imagination. The structure and significance of the world are generated imaginatively; if the collective, what I called in chapter 3 the proprioception of the body politic, begins imaginatively to generate an alienated world, the poetic imagination is one of the most powerful tools (perhaps even the *only* powerful tool) we have against that alienation. If through the power of art to infect whole populations with new visions, new understandings, the poet can alter the course of the collective imagination and so save us from our alienation, then it is the poet's responsibility as a human being to attempt to bring about that salvation. This is the idea behind the Romantic apocalypse, the central task assigned the poet by the German and English Romantics, and much the same Romantic conception survives in Shklovsky's theory of poetic estrangement as well.

But Kantian/Hegelian idealism is rejected, canceled, Hegel would say sublated, by Marx as materialism, as the idea that material conditions shape consciousness far more than consciousness shapes material conditions—and the thinker whose application of Shklovsky will engage us in Part III, Bertolt Brecht, was a Marxist. That he was a Hegelian and in some sense a Shklovskyan and Tolstoyan Marxist complicates things but not terribly, as Marx himself remains heavily grounded in the Hegel whose idealism he overturns. Brecht expands Shklovsky's estrangement device into an anti-Aristotelian theory of drama and envisions art thus conceived as working through Tolstoy's artistic infection to transform the human race Romantically, apocalyptically, along Marxist lines.

PART THREE

Verfremdung

Brecht's Estrangement Theory

5 ∎ Brecht's Modernist Marxism

There are, roughly speaking, four explanatory models of how Bertolt Brecht developed the idea of the *Verfremdungseffekt.*

1. He based it on (or even translated it from) Viktor Shklovsky's *priyom ostraneniya.* Stories vary on how he encountered Shklovsky's theory but most involve Sergey Tret'yakov. This etiology was first adumbrated in 1959 by John Willett and since has been championed by a wide variety of scholars, including Paul Böckmann, Reinhold Grimm, Stanley Mitchell, Katherine Bliss Eaton, Hans Günther, and Fredric Jameson.
2. Brecht was simply the latest in a long line of German theorists of es-trangement, beginning with Novalis on Romantic *Befremdung* and proceeding through Hegel and Marx on capitalist *Entfremdung.* The groundbreaking work on Brecht's Hegelianism was done in 1957 by Heinz Schäfer in his University of Stuttgart dissertation *Der Hegelianis-mus der Bert Brecht'schen Verfremdungstechnik in Anhängigigkeit von ihren marxistischen Grundlagen,* and has been continued by Ernst Bloch, Ernst Schumacher, Ilya Fradkin, Tamás Ungvári, and others. Reinhold Grimm argues that the *Verfremdungseffekt* is born out of Brecht's reading of *The German Ideology;* Ungvári, mostly agreeing with Grimm, argues that the influence of the *Theses on Feuerbach* is even stronger (198–99). Pe-ter Demetz stresses the Shelley connection, and Walter Muschg points to the connection with Shelley, Novalis, and Kleist; more recently,

J. E. Elliott aligns Brecht with the Hegel of the *Phenomenology* at the sublatory midpoint between the liberating Romantic irony of Friedrich Schlegel and the capitalist alienation of labor of Karl Marx.

3. Brecht learned the *Verfremdungseffekt* from Mei Lanfang's impromptu performance in Moscow of the Chinese acting styles popularly known as Beijing Opera, and his major influences are therefore Chinese or generally Asiatic. This explanatory avenue has been pursued in books by Antony Tatlow and Eric Hayot; articles by Ronnie Bai, Carol Martin, Yan Hai-Ping, and Sun Huizhu; and Ph.D. dissertations by Lane Eaton Jennings, Renata Berg-Pan, and Becky B. Prophet.

4. Brecht developed all of the key concepts and strategies of his epic theater, including the *Verfremdungseffekt,* in his practical work in the theater in Munich and Berlin in the 1920s, especially through his collaboration with Erwin Piscator, and merely found confirmation and above all *names* for some of the key strategies in other traditions. Brecht's long-time musical collaborator Hanns Eisler, for example, said that "the fairground show had a stronger influence on Brecht than any theory" (paraphrased by Ungvári, 220); Ilya Fradkin insists that Brecht learned most from Meyerhold's, Eisenstein's, and Pudovkin's films. We might explore under this head the argument made by several scholars (Rainer Friedrich; Marc Silberman, 9) that Brecht responded to disastrous social and economic conditions in postwar Germany, even before he became a Marxist, by imagining a utopian surrender of self. I, however, focus exclusively on yet another strand of the "practical work" etiology, Juliet Koss's suggestion that Brecht's undialectical rejection of empathy in his early theorizing of the epic theater came out of his reaction against the popularity of Georg Fuchs's right-wing empathy theory at the Munich Artists' Theater beginning a decade or more before he began working in theater.

I put the Shklovsky etiology first for obvious methodological reasons—a book on estrangement in Shklovsky and Brecht could hardly do otherwise—but I do not intend this methodological priority to indicate historical preference or precedence. I don't believe Shklovsky's indirect influence on Brecht to be weightier or more decisive than any other; in fact, I assume that Brecht developed his concept out of his "own" sense (to some fairly large extent conditioned ideologically by the German tradition) of the importance of making things strange in art, which was reinforced and complicated by his work with Erwin Piscator and others in Munich and Berlin in the twenties, and then that he named his concept first out of his reading in the German tradition, then out of his interactions with people close to Shklovsky, especially in Moscow in the spring of 1935, especially in connection with Mei Lanfang's impromptu performance.

Shklovskyan Ostranenie and the Politicization of Formalism

As Stanley Mitchell noted in 1974, the split between scholars who trace the etiology of Brecht's *Verfremdungseffekt* back to Shklovsky and those who trace it back to the German tradition (especially Hegel and Marx) tends to run along ideological fault lines: Marxists in the former German Democratic Republic (GDR) and Soviet Union (both of which, of course, were still existing political entities when Mitchell wrote) tend to deny any connection between Shklovsky and Brecht; the idea that Brecht learned or borrowed or even translated Shklovsky's *priyom ostraneniya* as the basis for his *Verfremdungseffekt* tends to be the exclusive provenance of Western scholars on both the right and the left. "For the right," as Mitchell sees it, "it is a way of deMarxising Brecht; for the left largely a means of distancing him from a 'realistic' aesthetic."[1] Mitchell himself argues that "the left has another and more profitable choice, Brecht's own: that of 'refunctioning', to use his word, the insights and discoveries of the 'avant-garde' " (80, n. 2).

The Story

John Willett is generally considered the first to assert Brecht's borrowing of the concept of estrangement from Shklovsky (see, e.g., Ungvári, 218, and Günther, 144, n. 2). In his 1959 book *The Theatre of Bertolt Brecht,* Willett argues rather cautiously (post hoc, but not quite propter hoc) for a methodological parallel between Brecht's *Verfremdung* and Shklovsky's *ostranenie* ("For the purpose of 'Verfremdung', which Brecht launched immediately after his Moscow visit of 1935, . . . is just that which Shklovskij had given for his 'Priem Ostrannenija' [*sic*] or 'device of making it strange,' " 207). In 1964, in his edition/translation *Brecht on Theatre,* he throws caution to the wind and tells us flat out that "the formula itself is a translation of the Russian critic Viktor Shklovskij's phrase 'Priem Ostrannenija', or 'device for making strange', and it can hardly be a coincidence that it should have entered Brecht's vocabulary after his Moscow visit" (99) in the spring of 1935. Similar arguments were made by Paul Böckmann in 1961 and Reinhold Grimm in 1963.[2] In 1974

Stanley Mitchell, drawing on a memoir by the East German theater director Bernhard Reich published in 1970, confirmed this guess. Reich, who lived for many years in the Soviet Union, was present in Sergey Tret'yakov's apartment for the discussion with Brecht of an estranging theater experience they'd had. Tret'yakov was himself a playwright and screenwriter who had begun his career working (along with Sergey Eisenstein) with Vsevolod Meyerhold, the radical Russian theater director who had broken with his great mentor Konstantin Stanislavsky and founded his own theater. In the 1920s, on frequent visits to Berlin, he and Eisenstein had collaborated with Erwin Piscator and Brecht in their radical theatrical experiments, which had led to the formulation of the "epic theater." Tret'yakov was a coeditor of Mayakovsky's international journal *LEF* (*LEviy Front* "LEft Front"), and later the editor-in-chief of *Noviy lef* (The new LEF)—both of which Shklovsky also worked on—and one of Brecht's Russian translators. Piscator had moved to Moscow in 1931 and was the prime instigator of Brecht's visit. He had invited Brecht in a letter of January 7, 1935, to come confer with friends, "collecting a few good people for a constructive discussion" (quoted in Willett, *Brecht,* 76)—especially Eisenstein and Tret'yakov.

Reich writes of that discussion in Tret'yakov's apartment:

Recollections are developed impressions. They often lie about unusable for a long time, then unexpectedly surface, become tangibly alive. So do I see myself transported back into the dark room Tret'yakov had on the Spiridonovka. I sat there together with Tret'yakov and Brecht, who was lodging there. We were speaking of an extraordinary theater performance—but whether it was of Mei Fan-Lan [*sic*] or a staging of Okhlopov, I can no longer say today. I was mentioning a production detail when Tret'yakov corrected me: "Yes, that is an estrangement" [*Ja, das ist eine Verfremdung*], and cast Brecht a conspiratorial glance. Brecht nodded. That was the first time I learned the expression *Verfremdung.* I must therefore assume that Tret'yakov brought [*zutrug*] Brecht this terminology: I think that Tret'yakov had reshaped [*umbildete*] the terminology formulated by Shklovsky, отчуждение [*otchuzhdenie*] "to distance, to repel/reject [*abstoßen*, lit. 'to push away']."

Brecht's *Verfremdung* aims at "making-conspicuous" [*Auffälligmachen*], but Shklovsky and his adepts were recommending this "making-conspicuous" mainly for the cinema; they saw in it the opportunity to call up in viewers an intense impression, and that through an utterly formal juxtaposition. From this Brecht's conception differed quite substantially, despite the word's semantic similarity, both in terms of its point of departure (in Brecht the "making-conspicuous" is a logical necessity, insofar as habit and familiarity make it difficult to recognize phenomena) and of its result (Brechtian estrangement helps one see the content/purpose/mission of life [*Lebensinhalt*] more clearly). (371–72, my translation)

There are two significant problems with this memory. The first is the obvious fact that Reich only *assumes* Tret'yakov translated and reshaped Shklovsky's term as *Verfremdung* and presented it ready-made to Brecht; certainly, his hearing it here for the first time does not mean that this is the moment of Russian-to-German terminological transfer. Brecht and Tret'yakov could have had any number of *Verfremdung*-related conversations prior to this moment; indeed, Tret'yakov's conspiratorial look at Brecht would seem to suggest some such history. Given the rare usage of the word in German—as Ernst Bloch tells us, the first mention of it in Grimm's dictionary is from 1842, and it only appears one more time after that—it is unlikely that Tret'yakov himself invented it as a translation of *ostranenie*. It is far more likely that Brecht himself found it in Grimm and tried it out on Tret'yakov—perhaps in the course of a conversation on estrangement, Novalis's *Befremdung* and Hegel and Marx's *Entfremdung* for Brecht, Shklovsky's *ostranenie* for Tret'yakov—and that Tret'yakov is therefore "citing" Brecht's own near-coinage back at him, "conspiratorially," in the conversation Reich witnesses.

Second, Reich clearly does not know Shklovsky's original article from nearly twenty years before; he has heard people talking about Shklovsky's central concept in cinema circles in Moscow, where Shklovsky has been working as a screenwriter since his return from exile in Berlin in 1923. He does not know the original term *ostranenie;* he thinks the term is *otchuzhdenie* "alienation," which is probably the politically correct circumlocution "Shklovsky and his adepts" use for the banned *ostranenie*. Reich does not even know that *otchuzhdenie* is the established Russian translation of Hegel's and Marx's *Entfremdung* "alienation"; he translates it "to distance, to reject." He is, therefore, really in no position to provide reliable information about the transfer of Shklovsky's term to Brecht; he doesn't know the term, and he wasn't present at the transfer (if it actually occurred).

Shklovsky himself seems to have "confirmed" this transfer of his term to Brecht through Tret'yakov, in a comment he made in a 1964 interview in Paris with Vladimir Pozner, one of the former Serapion Brothers who by then had become a well-known French novelist.[3] Pozner published the reminiscence in two issues of *Les Lettres Francaises*. As Ungvári reports, "Sklovsky [*sic*] himself claimed, that Sergei Tretiakov, 'a great man', was instrumental in conveying his discovery to Brecht, who christened it *Verfremdung*" (218). But, of course, Shklovsky was not present at the transfer either. And twelve years later, as Galin Tihanov reports, "in an interview conducted in the German Democratic Republic, Shklovsky . . . flatly denied Reich's conclusion: 'Hier muß es sich bei Reich um einen Irrtum handeln' [Here Reich must have made a mistake]. Was Shklovsky simply a tactful guest who did not want to erode Brecht's reputation in the country that had turned him into a classic and a hero? Was he, perhaps for ideological reasons, reluctant to claim precedence and originality? He may have been afraid of exposing himself to charges of attempting to undermine a pillar of the socialist literary canon (which by then Brecht no doubt was). Or was he telling the truth? What is, then, the status of his statement in the Paris interview?" ("Politics," 688, n. 42). The real question is: How could Shklovsky know one way or the other?

Still, there are moments in Brecht's piece on Chinese acting that could very well have been written by Shklovsky: "Der Artist wünscht, dem Zuschauer fremd, ja befremdlich zu erscheinen. Er erreicht das dadurch, daß er sich selbst und seine Darbietungen mit Fremdheit betrachtet. So bekommen die Dinge, die er vorführt, etwas Erstaunliches. Alltägliche Dinge werden durch diese Kunst aus dem Bereich des Selbstverständlichen gehoben" (202). Or, in my slightly foreignized translation: "The artist wishes to appear to the spectator strange [*fremd*], indeed disconcerting/disturbing [*befremdlich,* from Novalis's term]. He achieves this by viewing himself and his performances with strangeness [*Fremdheit*]. Thus do the things that he brings forth take on some aspect of the astonishing [lit. 'receive something astonishing']. Everyday things through this art are raised out of the realm of the self-evident." The "realm of the self-evident" is something like Shklovsky's realm of automatization; indeed, Willett translates it "the level of the obvious and the automatic" (92). The quasi-Hegelian "raising" (*Heben*) of the *Dinge* or "things" of this realm up out of it into the artistically enhanced realm of strangeness and astonishment is precisely what Shklovsky calls the estranging task of the artist in Thing 3. (But then, it is also what is identified as the estranging task of the Romantic poet by Novalis, in German, without any need for Brecht to have learned this from Shklovsky.) "In both theories," as Stanley Mitchell writes of Shklovsky's *priyom ostraneniya* and Brecht's *Verfremdungseffekt,* "the (proper) role of art is seen as one of de-routinisation, de-automatisation: art is the enemy of habit; it renews, refreshes our perceptions; by 'making-strange', it defamiliarises" (74).

Translation Problems

The problematic nature of this moment of transfer or translation from Shklovsky's *ostranenie* (or *otchuzhdenie*) to Brecht's *Verfremdung* anticipates, in fact, a whole history of problematic translations of the various terms. In 1960, V. Nedelin and L. Yakovenko translate Brecht into Russian, using for *Verfremdungseffekt* the "Shklovskyan" term Bernhard Reich heard being batted about in Moscow in the mid-1930s, *effekt otchuzhdeniya* "alienation effect."[4] In fact, as we saw at the beginning of chapter 3, back in 1934, right around the time Reich says Shklovsky and his followers were using the term *otchuzhdenie* in the Soviet film studios, T. I. Sil'man and I. Ya. Kopubovsky had translated Novalis into Russian using *delat' strannymi* "make strange" for *befremden* and *delat' chuzhimi* "make alien" for *fremdmachen*. Presumably, there was some sort of ideological mandate in the Soviet Union to shift from Shklovsky's *ostranenie* "estrangement" to *otchuzhdenie* "alienation." Thus the first sentence of Brecht's article on Chinese acting, "Im Nachfolgenden soll kurz auf die Anwendeung des Verfremdungseffekts in der alten chinesischen Schauspielkunst hingewiesen werden" (200)—the first mention in print of the *Verfremdungseffekt*—is rendered into Russian by Nedelin and Yakovenko as "Nizhe ya ostanovlyus' kratko na primenenii 'effekta otchuzhdeniya' v drevnem kitayskom iskusstve aktyorskoy igry."

Four years later, in 1964, in his translation/compilation *Brecht on Theatre*, John Willett translates that same line as "The following is intended to refer briefly to the use of the alienation effect in traditional Chinese acting" (91). As I mentioned above, in a note Willett calls Brecht's term a translation of Shklovsky's, which he renders explicatively as "device for making strange." Rather than choosing an English term for Brecht's effect that reflects his belief in Brecht's debt to Shklovsky, however—like "making-strange effect," or the translation that Shklovsky and Brecht scholars now almost universally prefer, "estrangement effect"—Willett renders it "alienation effect" or "A-effect" for short. Since he has just told us that Hegel's and Marx's term for alienation, *Entfremdung*, is Brecht's previous and now discarded term for the effect, this is a somewhat odd choice. Could it be that Willett's rendition was somehow influenced by the Soviet shift from *estrangement* to *alienation*? As is clear from his book *Art and Politics in the Weimar Period*, Willett was extraordinarily well plugged into the Berlin-Moscow axis in avant-garde art and art theory, so some sort of carryover effect from Soviet usage to his own is conceivable, but he says nothing to indicate that such is the case. (Shklovsky's *ostranenie* rendered in German, incidentally, beginning with Gisela Drohla's 1966 translation, is always *Verfremdung*.)

In 1965, then, in *Russian Formalist Criticism: Four Essays,* Lee T. Lemon and Marion Reis published the first English translation of Shklovsky's essay, translating the *priyom ostraneniya* as "defamiliarization device"—taking us out of the semantic realms of estrangement and alienation altogether, obviously, but interestingly (and almost certainly coincidentally), into the semantic realm of the first English translation of Brecht's term, from the same year as the original Chinese acting article, 1936, where the *Verfremdungseffekt* is rendered as "the effect of disillusion" (see Günther 145, n. 4). In both translations the emphasis is off the strange *and* the alien and on the undoing of the undesirable psychological state, familiarity or illusion, instead—not a bad solution to the problem we saw in chapter 3, where because both estrangement and alienation have come to be used as terms for the disease and the cure, the one is often mistaken for the other. Disillusion and defamiliarization make it quite clear that what the artist is attempting to do is to break through the anesthetizing or illusory effects of familiarization, conventionalization, automatization. Had that early translation of Brecht's effect caught on, the American playwright John Guare would have been much less likely to dismiss Brechtian theater, in a lecture I once heard him give, by wondering what playwright in his right mind would ever want to *alienate* the audience. Guare himself is a powerfully disillusioning or defamiliarizing playwright; had the early translation caught on, Brechtian theater might have seemed intuitively obvious and right to him. Puncturing the audience's illusions, of course—every playwright should do that! But alienate the audience? Since Willett believed Brecht's term was a translation of Shklovsky's, it is tempting to speculate that had he undertaken his translation even four or five years later, after Lemon and Reis's translation of Shklovsky had had time to take hold, he might have rendered it "defamiliarization effect," and the common mistake Guare made would have been avoided.

As should be clear from my discussion of Shklovsky in chapter 3, however, the disorienting semantic overlap between estrangement/alienation as disease and estrangement/alienation as cure is crucial to the theory's dialectic. Familiarization/defamiliarization and illusion/disillusion are binaries; the estrangement of estrangement and the alienation of alienation are steeped—mired, some would say—in dialectical strange/familiar and alien/own complication, in the border crossing that Paul tries to binarize by setting Jesus at the checkpoint, but that inevitably exceeds any tidy either/or one attempts to impose on it. Whether we translate Brecht's key term as "alienation effect" or "estrangement effect," we have resonances with Hegel and Marx, with depersonalization. If we gravitate to "estrangement effect" we have additional resonances with "foreigner/stranger" words: French *étranger* and Spanish *estranjero,* from Latin *extra* "out," so that foreigners are etymologically "outsiders," which takes us to German *Ausländer* "foreigner," literally "outlander" (which also contains the *aus* "out" of *Entäußerung* "alienation/externalization," and, of course, in English *outlandish* is a synonym for *strange*). The foreigner linkage also directs our attention to the morphological connections between Shklovsky's *ostranenie* and *inostranets* "foreigner," from *inaya strana* "different country," a person from across the dividing *storona* "side" from which *stranniy* "strange" and *strana* "country" etymologically derive. As Svetlana Boym notes, "Ostranenie means more than distancing and making strange; it is also dislocation, *depaysement. Stran* is the root of the Russian word for country—*strana.* Shklovsky claims that according to Aristotle, 'poetic language' has to have the character of a foreign language (*chuzhezemnyi*)" ("Estrangement," 245).

Historical Context

Brecht is, of course, a foreigner in Moscow, watching the performance of a foreigner from China before an impromptu audience that for him is filled with foreigners as well, Russians and Germans. When he goes "home" from Moscow he returns not to Germany, which has been rendered foreign and alien to him by Hitler, but to Denmark, where he is also a foreigner. As Hitler conquers more and more of Europe, Brecht keeps moving further and further north, until he arrives in Finland, which, impoverished by the Winter War with the Soviet Union in 1939–40 and denied Western aid, joins a military alliance with Hitler in 1941 to provide food for the Finnish people and easy access to Leningrad for Hitler. So Brecht and his family take the trans-Siberian railroad to Vladivostok and a ship from there to San Pedro, California, where he lives as a foreigner in Santa Monica until 1947, when he is summoned to testify before the House Un-American Activities Committee. After testifying, he flees the country to Switzerland, where he is again a foreigner. When, the next year, in 1948, he finally "returns" to Germany, it is to a country that he has never visited before, the Marxist German Democratic Republic, where he is, in a sense, even living in his old city Berlin, still a foreigner.

Stanley Mitchell admirably captures the historical specificity of estrangement or alienation in Shklovsky and Brecht, writing in terms borrowed loosely from *The Communist Manifesto* of the late-nineteenth-century imperialist phase of European capitalism,[5] which "posed anew the problem of boredom, captured in Baudelaire's images of *ennui*," leading in turn to a massive capital investment in novelty, which "proved profitable because novelty is quickly exhausted." As capitalist alienation spread and intensified, "society became more 'subjective': the class which had distinguished itself historically by its constant need to revolutionise its instruments of production now, in its parasitic phase, turned more and more neurotically to 'revolutionising' its means of consumption. 'Serious' art reflected this development, passing through the most rapid succession of schools and styles ever known." This is essentially the disease of which Tolstoy writes, without the Marxist descriptors. "Philosopher and novelist discovered an 'anti-mechanical' time (Bergson's *durée,* Proust's memory). Futurists fetishised dynamics and speed. Painters and poets plundered the colonies for 'direct' emotions or timeless conditions (Gauguin, Picasso, Baudelaire, Rimbaud). Each innovation was assimilated and mass-reproduced." In Marx's analysis of these developments (to which we return below), "the market economy is experienced as something naturally-unnatural, familiarly-alien until class struggle can lay bare the social relations of capital and labour which underly [*sic*] its mystifying 'objectivity'" (74–75). And, Mitchell adds:

> It is only within this broad context that one can begin to make use of the coincidence between Shklovsky's and Brecht's terms, *ostranenie* and *Verfremdung.* These terms capture the theoretical imagination because they strike at their objective homonym, *ie* the alienation of consciousness which is the reflex of capitalism. Capitalist dialectics "domesticate" this alienation. The resisting theoretical and artistic consciousness seeks to unmask, make alien the alienation. But the intellectual and artistic consciousness does not revolt merely out of wounded dignity. Russian Formalism came into being during the first world war and on the eve of the Bolshevik Revolution; some of its personalities, though not the main ones, were Bolsheviks. Brecht developed his theory of alienation on the eve of the fascist counter-revolution as a means to shock people out of a passive-fatalistic acceptance of authoritarian and manipulative politics. If, in the general European context, we draw a line back from Brecht and forward from Shklovsky, we shall find a meeting-point. In the 1920s the Russian Formalists joined forces with the left Futurists to produce the magazine and forum of *LEF* and *Novy Lef,* edited by Mayakovsky. Brecht's 'epic theatre' drew inspiration from Piscator, Meyerhold and Eisenstein. The various theories and practices of montage, functional theatre, documentary may all be brought under the head of *making-strange.* Russian Formalism was politicized. The theorems of 'making strange', 'exposing the device' were applied sociologically and politically to the writer's craft (or rather production) and his place in society.

The formalist-sociologists (known as *forsotsi*) argued that the writer should engage with his 'material' no differently from a worker in a factory, for he was no more than a literary producer. So down with inspiration, creativity, illusion: these were the manifestations of bourgeois and class culture which used artists as a special elite to satisfy the needs of a ruling class which had no wish to see itself in reality, ie [*sic*] as an exploiting class. To this end, went the argument, art mystified reality into *established* reality, reality as seen and desired by the ruling class. Positivism and realism were the intellectual and artistic props of the bourgeois order. (76–77)

The historical "meeting-point" between Shklovsky and Brecht is, roughly speaking, the Weimar period, during which of course both men spend time in Berlin (Brecht far more than Shklovsky) and Moscow (Shklovsky far more than Brecht), but more importantly during which the entire European avant-garde seems stretched between Berlin and Moscow. It is the period between the Russian Revolution (and the publication of Shklovsky's signature essay) and the swearing-in of Hitler as Chancellor of Germany (and the beginning of Brecht's fourteen-year exile). It is an extraordinarily productive and divisive period in the history of avant-garde art, most of it saturated with Baudelaire's summons to shock the bourgeoisie: dada, surrealism, constructivism, epic the-ater, functionalism, atonality, reportage, montage, and on and on. All of this is effectively quelled in Nazi Germany and the Soviet Union at around the same time, the mid-thirties, banned as "Bolshevik" in Hitler's Germany and as "cosmopolitan" and "formalist" in Stalin's Russia. While it lasts, though, it is effectively the era of artistic estrangement, or what Stanley Mitchell calls the politicization of formalism by leftist artists and theorists. As Mitchell writes, "The Formalists had formalized contradiction. The point was to give life to their formalisations. This Mayakovsky did in his poetry and Brecht in his plays. The techniques of neologistic rhyme, montage, *Verfremdung* were means of 'bombarding' reality to discover its possibilities, to specify its contradic-tions, to make it go 'your way'" (80, n. 1). Gone (or perhaps only sublated) were the days of quasi-mystical and essentially conservative assaults on the boredom of bourgeois consumerism, and even the days of the radical demysti-fication of art, the "laying bare" of art's devices, which had been so important to Shklovsky in the teens: for Brecht, Mitchell says, "More important than puncturing the 'illusions' of the theatre and the other arts was to use every formal means discovered by the avant-garde to reveal the workings of capital-ist society, to demonstrate the mechanisms of social conditioning so that these appeared no longer fixed, but changeable in a rational way" (77–78).

Verfremdung: *Brecht's Estrangement Theory*

The German Tradition and the Alienation of Alienation

I noted at the beginning of this chapter that, as of 1974, anyway, when Stanley Mitchell made the point, Brechtians seemed to be divided between those in the capitalist West who traced *Verfremdung* back to Shklovskyan *ostranenie* and those in the socialist East who traced it back to Hegelian and Marxist *Entfremdung*—specifically, back to Hegel's dialectic of alienation as read by Marx. The sensible thing for me to do now that I've explored Brecht's Shklovskyan roots, therefore, would be to go back through the Hegelian material from chapter 4 and show the specific new Marxist spins Brecht puts on each of those points.

But I think not. For one thing, it would be tedious: the differences between Shklovsky and Brecht in their reliance on Hegel are not significant enough to wring much estrangement out of a second pass through. Moreover, the Hegelian Brecht is in many ways an idealized Brecht, Brecht as his followers would have liked him to be, Brecht perhaps as he himself (in some moods) would have liked to be. Steeped in Hegel as he was, Brecht was never much of a Hegelian thinker. His mind didn't work that way. Hegel's systematicity was alien to Brecht's imagination, in two related senses: not only is there no way he can manage that sort of philosophical control, but the synthetic closure that Hegel kept (temporarily) bringing to his antitheses felt like a trap or a prison cell to Brecht. In some sense—the sense, obviously, in which he thinks of himself as a Hegelian thinker—the ponderously and unstoppably brilliant movement of the Hegelian dialectic toward a new synthesis is an ideal toward which Brecht strives, but he doesn't try very hard or successfully. In later sections on Chinese acting and Brecht's practical work in the theater, I construct complete Hegelian dialectics out of Brecht's thought, but I do so specifically out of his failures to complete them—out of an unresolved confusion in the Chinese acting essay, and then, in the practical work section, out of his lifelong binarization of empathy and estrangement, his almost total inability to think of those impulses dialectically.

Temperamentally, Brecht is more like a Schlegelian (Romantic/modernist) ironist, expert at creating complex images and characters that are impossible to resolve to a single univocal theme, than he is like a Hegelian dialectician. One of his contradictory impulses, however, is a Marxist inclination toward didacticism and dogmatism, toward the inculcation of simple and easily accessible lessons. His dramatic and theoretical work has numerous examples of both extremes, the ironist and the dogmatist, but the work that we remember and admire him for is not so much a Hegelian synthesis of the two as it is an awkward but strangely effective juxtaposition, an attempt to hold both opposed impulses (Schlegelian irony as thesis, Marxist activism as antithesis) at once not just in his own mind but in the reader's and spectator's as well. Specifically, what he hopes most to accomplish is the liberation through Schlegelian irony of the worker-spectator-producer's intelligence from the "self-evident" thinking of capitalist alienation, so that the worker-etc. him/herself will go off and do the important Marxist work of rethinking and reshaping the "established" or "given" reality of capitalism.

In one sense this means that Marx serves Brecht as an anchor in material reality: as much fun as it would be to indulge the modernist irony and estrangement of the avant-garde for its own sake—as humor, as the new, for its shock value—he always feels the tug of oppression, of exploitation, of alienated labor, and ties his avant-garde strategies to the revolution. As J. E. Elliott writes, for example:

> Small wonder, then, that in the appendix [to the "Little Organon"] following the "joke of contradiction" above, Brecht shifts its implication by mounting a quick attack on bourgeois theatre, whose performances "always aim at smoothing over contradictions, at creating false harmony, at idealization" . . . The joke that threatens independence from the political, even as a utopian finality, is the joke that goes too far, turning not only the past but also the future into a subject for ceaseless dialectic. Where the Schlegelian ironist experiences the furthest reach of paradoxy, the cultural materialist is compelled to reintroduce the eminently serious residue of dogma without which Marxism itself becomes, well, a farce. And yet to reintroduce such dogma only brings home how much of an extemporizing make-believe this investigation into the "liveliness of men, things, and processes" ultimately is; in the vicinity of the absolute, such frivolity is embarrassingly *de trop*. A new contradiction arises, therefore, one that cannot be farmed out to the inherent illogic of the bourgeois state: cultural materialism is fed by the same dialectical energies that must ultimately be shut down to preserve its dialectical integrity. In such a state, the blame is always placed elsewhere— here upon the mediocrities of the realist stage (the "harmonisch Platten?"), which is asked to bear the burden of an expropriated contradiction it is then accused of having no feel for. (1076–77)

But ultimately this image of Brecht invoking Marx as dogmatic synthesis to shut down the movement of the dialectic simplifies his thinking by simplifying Marx, whose theory is typically summarized in plain deironized prose ("The decisive form of alienation is now not that of man but the worker's alienation from objects he produces and from the means of production with which he produces" [Gouldner, 181]). But despite the famous hostility toward Romanticism in Marx and later Marxists—not only the Stalinists but the Weimar Left and later German Communist refugees, including Brecht—there is an irreducible element of Schlegelian Romantic irony to Marx's writing as well that Brecht found dramatically and theoretically useful. ("Nebenbei es spricht für sie (Marx und Engels) dass sie Humor haben. Ich habe nämlich noch keinen Menschen ohne Humor getroffen, der die Dialektik des Hegel verstanden hat" [*Flüchtlingsgespräche, Prosa* II.235, quoted in Ungvári, 231]—"By the way, it speaks for them (Marx and Engels) that they had a sense of humor. The thing is, I've never met a humorless person who understood Hegel's dialectic.") It's not just that Marx brings Brecht back down to earth, *away* from the modernist pleasures of irony; it's also that Marx teaches him to convert estranging irony into a revolutionary tool—or, as Fredric Jameson says, method: "Indeed, it is tempting to suggest that it is precisely Brecht's well-known slyness that is his method, and even his dialectic: the inversion of the hierarchies of a problem, major premises passing to minor, absolute to relative, form to content, and vice versa—these are all operations whereby the dilemma in question is turned inside out, and an unexpected unforeseeable line of attack opens up that leads neither into the dead end of the unresolvable nor into the banality of stereotypical doxa on logical non-contradiction" (*Brecht*, 25).[6]

Schlegel on Romantic Irony

I want to focus my Brechtian inquiry into Schlegel and Marx by selecting a single passage from each, passages that are generally considered to be among their key statements, but that, obviously, will not allow me to cover the surrounding territory with much specificity. The passage from Schlegel is *Lyceum* fragment 108, on Socratic irony; the passage from Marx is a two-paragraph stretch of *The Economic and Philosophical Manuscripts of 1844*. Here is the Schlegel, in the original German and my own translation:

> Die Sokratische Ironie ist die einzige durchaus unwillkürliche, und doch durchaus besonnene Verstellung. Es ist gleich unmöglich sie zu erkünsteln, und sie zu verraten . . . In Ihr soll alles Scherz und alles Ernst sein, alles treuherzig offen, und alles tief verstellt . . . Sie enthält und erregt ein Gefühl von dem unauflöslichen Widerstreit des Unbedingten und des Bedingten, der Unmöglichkeit und Notwendigkeit einer vollständigen Mitteilung. Sie ist die freieste aller Lizenzen, denn durch sie setzt man sich über sich selbst hinweg; und doch auch die gesetzlichste, denn sie ist unbedingt notwendig.

Es ist ein sehr gutes Zeichen, wenn die harmonisch Platten gar nicht wissen, wie sie diese stete Selbstparodie zu nehmen haben, immer wieder von neuem glauben und mißglauben, bis sie schwindlicht werden, den Scherz grade für Ernst, und den Ernst für Scherz halten. (86–87)

Socratic irony is the only thoroughly nonarbitrary/untyrannical [*unwillkürliche*], indeed thoroughly well-thought-out disguise [*Verstellung*]. It is equally impossible to fake it [*erkünsteln*] and to unmask it [*verraten*] . . . In it everything must be at once a joke and serious, at once guilelessly [*treuherzlich*, lit. "faithful-heartedly"] open and deeply disguised [*tief verstellt*] . . . It contains and arouses a feeling of the irresolvable antagonism between the unconditioned and the conditioned [*des Unbedingten und des Bedingten*], the impossibility and necessity of total communication [*einer vollständigen Mitteilung*]. It is the freest of all licenses, for through it one sets oneself way over oneself [*setzt man sich über sich selbst hinweg*]; and indeed also the most lawful/legitimate, for it is absolutely necessary. It is a very good sign when the happy booboisie [*die harmonisch Platten*] have no idea how to take this continuous self-parody, when over and over again they first believe and then disbelieve, until they become dizzy and take the joke seriously and seriousness as a joke.

First, a close look at those keywords:

Unwillkürlich: to the powerless, a tyrant's wielding of force (*Willkür*) seems arbitrary (*willkürlich*); Schlegel is arguing that Socratic irony is thoroughly *lacking* in that kind of tyrannical arbitrary force, that there is nothing either arbitrary or coercive about it. This seems to suggest that it is grounded in free, ethical, and egalitarian choice, indeed (as he says in the next sentence), that it is guilelessly or ingenuously or "faithful-heartedly" open; but of course it is the only thoroughly nonarbitrary and untyrannical *disguise,* which sets up that following sentence's ironic antithesis between openness and disguise. Note also that he describes Socratic irony in terms of an absence, a negated presence, in terms of the lack of *Willkür,* which implicitly sets arbitrary coercion up as the primary term that is then (ironically?) denied or negated.

Verstellung is disguise, dissimulation, dissemblance. Schlegel's friend Friedrich von Schiller has Octavio say unantithetically in *Die Piccolomini* that "Verstellung ist der offnen Seele fremd" (327)—disguise or dissimulation is alien to the open soul. Schlegel says that irony must be *both* open and disguised and, by extension perhaps, a two-way channel of alienation as well. The ideally open "faithful heart" is alienated in and through ironic dissimulation; from this ironized point of view it becomes clear that what seemed like the "faithful heart" was only an alienated conformity or boobish harmony idealized by an alienated society as openness and faithful-heartedness, which is actually in need of the kind of dizzying dealienation that only the disguises of irony can administer. In the throes of dealienation it once again becomes clear that irony never disguised itself or anything else but was always entirely open, frank, guileless.

Erkünsteln has *Kunst* "art" and *Künstler* "artist" in it; it is to fake, to feign, to contrive, to make by means of a tricky art or sleight-of-hand, to prestidigitate, so that the phrase *es ist unmöglich sie zu erkünsteln* might be translated as "it can't be arted up." If Socratic irony *can't* be created by these tricky artistic means, does that mean it can only be made seriously, honestly, authentically, by an unalienated craftsman, a pre–Industrial Revolution worker, such as a village blacksmith, cobbler, cooper, or tailor? Schlegel seems to be implying that the ironist has to *feel* it—that the irony has to proceed from some authentically and spontaneously felt and therefore artless (pre- or extra-artistic) source of ironic awareness. But what would that authentic source or authentic feeling be? Both Shklovsky and Brecht seem to suggest that Romantic irony or modernist estrangement must be an "arting up" of psychosocial estrangement, a feigned alienation designed to alienate alienation—and Schlegel's partial association of irony with *Verstellung* suggests that he would partially agree.

Verraten is to betray in the sense of reveal, disclose, let slip, lay bare, unmask. It is also to betray in the sense of "rat on" or "rat out," but that false cognate (German *Rat* is council or counsel/advice) is perhaps less relevant to our purposes here. If, for Shklovsky and Brecht, to estrange is to lay bare the device, this definition suggests that Socratic irony can't be estranged—because irony is not the kind of secret device that can be laid bare, or because it *is* the kind of secret device that *can't* be laid bare, or, most likely, both possibilities at once, as either of them alone would collapse the antithesis. The ironic disguise suggests a mask that can be torn off, a trick that can be revealed. The "faithful-hearted openness" suggests that there is no secret, no trick, nothing to be unmasked; the antithesis between the two suggests various higher-level explanations, such as that irony is itself already a laying-bare and is not subject to its own operation, and that it *is* subject to its own operation, is continually laying itself bare, and thus always a step ahead of any would-be unmasker—and, once again, both at once.

Das (Un)bedingte: the (un)conditioned. Peter Firchow translates *Widerstreit des Unbedingten und des Bedingten* as "antagonism between the absolute and the relative" (13), and obviously that which is unconditioned is absolute, and that which is conditioned is relative to its conditioning. But the root of *bedin-*

gen is *Ding* "thing": originally the verb means (transitively) "to thing," to make something a thing; *bedingt* would thus be "thinged," *unbedingt* "unthinged." The German etymology by which the verb moves from "thinging" to "conditioning" is mercantile, passing through three stages: (1) in a barter economy, *bedingen* means "to make things equal or comparable," thus "to agree, arrange, haggle, negotiate"; (2) in an expanding and increasingly abstract/alienated money economy, it comes to mean "to set or stipulate terms or conditions" (for a contract); and (3) in the philosophical idealization (abstraction or alienation) of economic processes, it comes to mean "to condition," so that *bedingt* is "conditioned, contingent, relative," and the *conditio sine qua non* is *die absolute unerläßliche Bedingung* (and, I should add, "thinging" proper, reification, becomes *Verdingung*). We might analyze *Mother Courage* along the same three-step path: (1) first, Mother Courage haggles with a cook over the value of a capon; (2) then she haggles with Yvette and the one-eyed colonel over the terms by which she will pawn her wagon to buy her son Swiss Cheese off charges that he stole the regimental cash box (if Yvette will get the colonel to give her two hundred guilders for two weeks, Mother Courage will buy off the officers holding Swiss Cheese, go with him to find the cash box he hid, and use the money in it to redeem her wagon); and (3) finally Brecht "conditions" the Thirty Years' War (and by extension war in general) in his play, sets its conditions in the business world, on three levels: small business (Mother Courage's wagon), big business (the business of war, who is exploited and who is killed in order to guarantee whose profits), and idealized business (the mystification of business as religion, deals with and redemptions by God). Theoretically, of course, for Brecht the Marxist materialist this Schlegelian antithesis between the conditioned and the unconditioned ultimately breaks down—*das Unbedingte* "the unconditioned" would inevitably be just this sort of mystification of *das materialistisch Bedingte* "the materialistically conditioned"—but dramatically he always works to strand his characters antithetically between mystification and demystification, theory and practice, idealism and cynicism, illusion and disillusionment. Indeed, Schlegel seems to be describing just this sort of dramatic *creation* of antagonism between the two: "It contains and arouses a feeling of the irresolvable antagonism between the unconditioned and the conditioned." It's not that the antagonism (let alone the antithesis) *exists;* it's that irony contains and arouses a *feeling* of that antagonism.

Eine vollständige Mitteilung, morphologically "a full-standing with-sharing," is translated by Firchow as "a complete communication" (13). *Mitteilen* is "to share with," specifically to share information or truth with someone else, thus "to communicate." Since *Teil* is "part," and *teilen* is "to divide" *and* "to share," the morphological implication is that the truth that is shared with someone else is divided into two parts, the first kept by the self, the second given to the other. If the possession of truth is the thesis, then, the dividing or splitting of truth would be the antithesis, and the elimination of division in the perfect or complete sharing of truth in communication would be the synthesis that Schlegel calls necessary but impossible. What is not only possible but inevitable is the splintering or fragmentation of truth, the ironic breakdown of communicational sharing even, perhaps, within the self, within the individual consciousness: you divide the truth up in preparation for sharing, but the sharing fails, leaving you with fragmented and compromised truth. Something like this post-Romantic assumption about the necessary failure of communication fuels Brecht's modernist Marxism, what hard-line Marxists from the late 1920s until his final years in the GDR deplore as his "formalism": you can't just cut off a piece of Marxist "truth" and pour it into the proletariat's collective head. That won't work. You have to take into consideration the inescapable communicational gaps between people, try to develop strategies for putting those gaps to work. As we see later in the chapter, in his forties Brecht begins to move past a depersonalized focus on rationalist isolation to a sense of a shared feeling of "interests," or what I'm calling ideosomatic guidance; but even this ideosomatic collectivization of communication does not make it possible in Brecht's world to "deposit" an unbroken truth in someone else's head. There are always gaps to be crossed, divides to be negotiated.

Setzt man sich über sich selbst hinweg is usually translated "one transcends oneself" (thus Firchow, 13) but also can be "one disregards himself" (Feger, 128, n. 32). Schlegel's phrase might be read as a kinesthetically detailed depiction of what Hegel would later call *Aufhebung* (though, of course, Hegel's term is kinesthetic too, meaning "heaving onto," as what one might do to a sack of flour by way of loading it onto a flatbed), a physical *setting* oneself way over oneself. (*Hinweg* is morphologically "toward-away" and is typically used to mean "from here to there"; but in *über etwas hinweg* constructions, lit. "over something toward-away," it means something like "completely, totally," and would normally be translated "way over": *über alle Köpfe hinweg* is "way over everybody's head.") Schlegel's formulation here suggests the ironic splintering of the self, of one *sich* (the German reflexive particle) or self-splinter from another, so that it becomes possible to set one way over another, and thus also implicitly to leave one way below the other. Schlegel's phrase suggests the Heideggerian hypostatization not only of *das Man* but of *das Sich* as well, both as internal splinters of *das Selbst* "the self," with *das Man* as the collectivized or ideosomatized self, moving from outside to inside and from many to one, and *das Sich* as the individualized self, moving from one to many and from inside to outside (way above, way below). Grammatically, too, it should be noted that *das Sich* is the direct object of *das Man*. The internalized collective self wields the externalized individual selves as its objects, and indeed externalizes and individualizes them as its objects, splits them and sets them in various outside positions relative to each other in order to achieve specific ironic purposes.

Die harmonisch Platten are literally "the harmoniously flat." *Platt* is platitudinous, trite, flat, dull; the *harmonisch Platten* are those who think and speak in platitudes, which are "harmonious" in the sense of containing no irony, no estrangement, and therefore no edge—they are perfectly harmonized by the regulatory effects of ideosomaticity, what Broder Christiansen calls the *geltender Kanon* "canon in force." In translating the phrase "the happy booboisie," I'm tacitly shifting Schlegel (and by extension Brecht as well) to the American 1930s, to H. L. Mencken's ridicule of the great majority of happily stupid conservative Americans, who supported their president and feared socialism like the plague. (Mencken is often thought of these days as a libertarian conservative, and may have been, but he also ridiculed religion, deplored the domination of American culture by business, and supported Sacco and Vanzetti.)

"Booboisie" also uneasily strands the audience on which post-Romantic irony or estrangement is intended to have its "dizzying" or disorienting effect between the bourgeoisie and the proletariat—a kind of third-class category outside those two and containing at least those parts of both that Mencken thematizes as the boobs content with the status quo. As a Marxist, again, Brecht would be unwilling to write off that all-important class distinction: for while the bourgeoisie and the proletariat have both been artificially rendered more or less content with the status quo through the ideological manipulation of their self-interests, Brecht would want to insist on the redeemability of the proletariat and the irredeemability of the bourgeoisie, and thus the importance of bringing the dizzying disorientations of estrangement to bear on the former but not on the latter. This Marxist binarization of the two classes is alien to Schlegel, who lumps into the same category not only the happy boobs but, as Georgia Albert argues at some length (831–33), himself as well. The boobs, Schlegel says, "become dizzy and take the joke seriously and seriousness as a joke," implying that *he* for one knows the difference, and can recognize when a joke is being mistakenly read as a serious statement and vice versa. But this belief in one's ability to tell the difference is itself the defining characteristic of the *harmonisch Platten,* implicating Schlegel too in the boobishness he ridicules: "The sentence says: there is a right and a wrong way to read irony: the wrong way is to think that there is a right and a wrong way. But by making this distinction, it makes the very mistake it warns against; more importantly, it puts itself into a double bind from which it cannot be freed" (832).

The Double Bind

That "it" in "from which it cannot be freed" is a bit misleading, though: its antecedent in Albert's sentence is "the sentence," of course, which is not a human subject capable of being trapped in or freed from the double bind. There are two idealized *persons* who can be trapped in or freed from the double bind, the ironist and the boob, which is to say, for Schlegel, the writer and the reader, or, for Brecht, the theatrical troupe and the theater audience. And as Brecht takes over Schlegelian irony in his dramatic theory and practice, his strategy is to use the dramatic double bind against its older cousin in the audience's ideological being, ironically or estrangingly double binding his doubly-bound audience, so as to precipitate in them a thought process that begins in awareness of the ideological and economic double binds from which (it seems) they cannot be freed and ends in freedom from those double binds.

Here it might be useful to take a look at the classical formulation of the double bind developed by Gregory Bateson back in the mid-1950s, as an articulation of the emotionally pressurized mixed messages from parents to children that he suggested were involved in schizophrenogenesis. His model showed the double bind working dialectically but in a negative or nightmarish or "demonic" dialectic that traps and binds rather than liberating for progress or growth. In this demonic dialectic, the thesis is a "primary negative injunction," such as "don't do X or I'll punish you"; the antithesis is a "secondary injunction conflicting with the first at a more abstract level, and like the first enforced by punishments or signals which threaten survival," usually channeled nonverbally, but sometimes verbalized in paralyzing ways as "Do not see this as punishment," "Do not see me as the punishing agent," "Do not submit to my prohibitions," "Do not think of what you must not do," and "Do not question my love of which the primary prohibition is (or is not) an example." The synthesis is "A tertiary negative injunction prohibiting the victim from escaping from the field," but I would add that for some (the happy booboisie) this synthesis is an *anesthesis,* for others (notably the schizophrenics Bateson is analyzing) a *dysthesis.* As he notes about the latter, "the complete set of ingredients is no longer necessary when the victim has learned to perceive his universe in double bind patterns. Almost any part of a double bind sequence may then be sufficient to precipitate panic or rage" (206–8). His classic example of the dysthetic double bind is an encounter he witnessed in an institution:

> A young man who had fairly well recovered from an acute schizophrenic episode was visited in the hospital by his mother. He was glad to see her and impulsively put his arm around her shoulders, whereupon she stiffened. He withdrew his arm and she asked, "Don't you love me anymore?" He then blushed, and she said, "Dear, you must not be so easily embarrassed and afraid of your feelings." The patient was able to stay with her only a few minutes more and following her departure he assaulted an aide and was put in the tubs. (217)

The anesthetic and dysthetic double binds are, obviously, more or less the same two extremes on the homeostatic scale I theorized in chapter 3, in connection with Shklovsky's theory of estrangement—what I called there numbing depersonalization and disturbing/disorienting depersonalization. And again, as Caryl Emerson points out, it should be clear that estrangement—this time as hypermimetic double bind, as artistically intensified double bind—is only going to work with the anesthetized: the dysthetized will need a different kind of therapy, involving a lot fewer stimuli and zero double-binding ones.

The anesthetized are those trapped by the third stage of the double bind in *acceptance* of the double-binding status quo, trapped specifically in a not-seeing/not-feeling of the double bind, trapped in the anesthesis prescribed by the double bind. For them, the double bind is just the way things are, the human condition; whether they are content or discontent in it, they know they have to put up with it. Because there's no changing it, short of suicide there's no escaping it. Where the dysthetized feel the double bind too strongly, indeed overwhelmingly, and so can't live in society (and can't live alone), the anesthetized have so successfully stifled their somatic response to the double bind that they feel nothing—or feel only a vague anomie that they are mostly able to suppress without too much difficulty, and paper over with the manufactured positive feelings ("happiness," "contentment," "gratitude") mandated by the anesthetizing double bind. Where the dysthetic double bind tends to make its victims intelligent and edgy (and endlessly tormented), the anesthetic double bind tends to make its victims stupid and boring and harmoniously boobish.

Double-binding society provides a different anesthesis for every group: for men and women, for gays and straights, for families, for different ethnic groups, for different workplaces, for every social class. The upper and middle classes are just as anesthetized as the working classes and the underclass, but the anesthetic double bind takes different forms for each. Brecht, coming out of Marx, is mainly interested in using the double bind dramatically to instigate a liberatory *Durcharbeitung* in his working-class audience, anesthetized by double binds like these:

THESIS: Get a job, any job (a paycheck is a paycheck, and any kind of work beats sitting around at home watching TV), or risk being thought of as a slacker.

ANTITHESIS: Don't enjoy your work (work is work, play is play; don't confuse the two); don't get sick of doing mindless repetitive work; don't dream of doing something more interesting for a living (what's the point? it'll never happen anyway, and what if there *is* no work that you'd really enjoy doing?); pay no attention to the things you enjoy doing (that's just play).

ANESTHESIS: Be grateful that you live in a free capitalist country where you can choose where you want to work, and aren't just randomly assigned a job like some kind of communist flunky.

THESIS: Don't be lazy at work or you will get laid off.

ANTITHESIS: Despite working hard you may get laid off anyway.

ANESTHESIS: If that happens, don't blame management; be grateful for what you have (it's tough all over; it's the economy; everybody's suffering, many worse than you); feel guiltily selfish if you are tempted to complain.

THESIS: Even if things aren't going so well for you financially, don't begrudge your church a tithe.

ANTITHESIS: If the church offers you material help, think of it as charity (and charity as a form of pity and contempt, a condemnation of your failure as a human being), and refuse it.

ANESTHESIS: Be grateful that you live in a country that allows you to worship your God as you choose. Be grateful to that God for all the abundant blessings He's given you. Anticipate bliss someday in heaven. Suppress any temptation you might feel to complain; that's from the devil.

The traditional "consciousness-raising" approach to this sort of double binding is to explain to people just how they're being screwed. Brecht takes a different approach: he wants to *tighten* the screws, to intensify the feeling of being trapped in the double bind, to reproduce the alienating/anesthetizing double bind hypermimetically until he breaks through the anesthesis and the working-class spectator/producer begins to *feel* the pain that the double bind has suppressed, and hence to feel the need to work through it intellectually, to figure out what is being done to him or her—not just to spectate but to *produce* the transformative aesthetic/ideological effect in his or her own life. Adam Carter's discussion of Schlegel's *Lyceum* fragment 103 is germane here:

> The fragment is directly concerned with the aesthetic artifact and critiques "the powerful . . . instinct for unity in mankind" which when confronting the work of art covers over "the *motley heap* [*bunter Haufen*] of ideas" provided by "solid, really existent fragments." Schlegel critiques the instinct for unity for "deceiving even the exceptional reader" and, in parallel to Rorty's outline of a liberal ironist's utopia, praises the "motley heap of ideas" as being analogous to "that free and equal fellowship in which . . . the citizens of the perfect state will live at some future date." The "motley heap" is a configuration in which each individual has its own autonomy and direction and yet loosely connects with the whole through an "unqualifiedly sociable spirit." The supposedly unified work, on the other hand, only achieves its coherence through *unnatural* manipulation. Extending the political analogy Schlegel applies to the fragmentary text to the falsely unified work[,] the latter [*sic*] appears analogous to a highly coercive normalizing authority. (28)

The "coercive normalizing authority" that unifies the work of art through false or unnatural manipulation also creates "the powerful . . . instinct for unity in mankind"—an "instinct," my reading of the anesthetic double bind would suggest, that is generated through the collective anesthesis of contradiction. As Carter goes on to explain, Schlegel's political analogy for his ironic or skeptical revolt against this normalizing/unifying authority is what he calls *insurgente Regierung* "insurgent government": "As a temporary condition skepticism is logical insurrection; as a system it is anarchy. Skeptical method would therefore more or less resemble an insurgent government" (quoted in Carter, 28). This should remind us of Shklovsky saying that the poet incites insurrection among *things*, which is to say, in the symbolic/ideosomatic order that organizes things meaningfully. Carter adds:

> Schlegel's fragments constitute an attempt to negotiate between, on the one hand, a tradition of enlightenment liberalism with its attendant faith in universality, reason, and progress, a tradition which was widely believed to have precipitated the French Revolution, and on the other hand, a more conservative response to the violence, rapid change and disempowerment the Revolution produced. Schlegel (at this stage in this [*sic*] career at least) supported many of the democratic and republican ideals of the Revolution[,] proving himself to be an insightful critic of the Prussian Absolute State of which he was a subject. However, along with the others in his circle of the Jena Romantics, he remained critical of the violence instigated by the

French Revolution—a suspicion that is manifested forcefully in Schlegel's philosophical and aesthetic critique of the violence of abstract conceptuality and universality exercised upon particularity and individuality. (Carter, 28)

Marx on Alienated Labor

For Brecht, of course, revolution meant not the bourgeois French Revolution but the proletarian Russian or German one, based not on Montesquieu but on Marx. Brecht began studying Marx in earnest in 1926–27, and thereafter began historicizing not just current events but his own theater strategies and drama theories in Marxist terms as well. Tamás Ungvári speculates that Brecht began to theorize the epic theater in terms of *Entfremdung* and *Verfremdung* in the early to mid-1930s partly because Marx's book *Economic and Philosophical Manuscripts of 1844,* which had been lost, was published for the first time in German in the Soviet Union in 1932 (176). If Brecht did read this book, though, he never did remark on the odd lexical, ideological, and economic parallels between the estrangement effect and Marx's remarks on "the estrangement of labor":

> Der Gegenstand, den die Arbeit produziert, ihr Produkt, tritt ihn als ein *fremdes Wesen,* als eine von dem Produzenten *unabhängige Macht* gegenüber. Das Produkt der Arbeit ist die Arbeit, die sich in einem Gegenstand fixiert, sachlich gemacht hat, es ist die *Vergegenständlichung* der Arbeit. Die Verwirklichung der Arbeit ist ihre Vergegenständlichung. Diese Verwirklichung der Arbeit erscheint in dem nationalökonomischen Zustand als *Entwirklichung* des Arbeiters, die Vergegenständlichung als *Verlust und Knechtschaft des Gegenstandes,* die Aneignung als *Entfremdung,* als *Entäußerung.* (511–12)

> The object that labor produces, its product, confronts the laborer as a *strange being,* as a *force detached* from the producer. The product of labor is labor fixated in an object, labor that has been made thing-like, that is, the *objectification* of labor. The making-real of labor is labor's objectification. This making-real of labor appears macroeconomically as the *making-unreal* of the laborer, objectification as the *loss of and thralldom to the object,* appropriation as *estrangement,* as *alienation.* (my translation)

Note first of all, here, Marx's antithetical (rather than Hegelian/synthetic) argumentation: "this *making-real of labor* appears macroeconomically as the *making-unreal of the laborer,* objectification as the *loss of and thralldom to the object,* appropriation as *estrangement,* as *alienation.*" There is no movement toward a synthesis here; the clash of antitheses is precisely what drives the class struggle, which does move history forward, but not through a series of synthetic triads, rather as constant struggle. Labor *is* made real, and the laborer *is* made unreal; labor *is* objectified, and the object *is* lost, and the laborer *is* enthralled to the lost object. Each antithetical event happens, each is the antithetical product of the other(s), each seems or seeks to negate the other(s) but cannot.

Note also Marx's gleefully antithetical word play: "[der] Produkt . . . als eine von dem Produzenten *unabhängige Macht,*" the product as a force detached from its producer, "[die] Verwirklichung der Arbeit . . . als *Entwirklichung des Arbeiters,*" the making-real of labor as the making-unreal of the laborer, "die Vergegenständlichung als *Verlust . . . des Gegenstandes,*" objectification as object-loss. He is not *merely* having fun with words, of course—this is no display of sheer Romantic verbal virtuosity, certainly not just Schlegelian Romantic irony. For Marx each side of each antithesis represents a material event for a different social group, specifically, for owners on one side and workers on the other: the making-real of labor *for the owners* entails the making-unreal of the laborer *for the laborers;* the objectification of labor *for the owners* entails the loss of and thralldom to the object *for the laborers.* To the extent that there is a Schlegelian Romantic-ironic impulse at work in Marx's rhetoric here, it is Romantic irony in the service of the demystification of the class struggle. But it should be clear that that Schlegelian impulse *is* at work creating a logical insurgency in Marx's analysis, laying the rhetorical groundwork for an insurgent government. Marx is not just preaching revolution; he is putting antithetical reasoning to demystificatory and ultimately revolutionary work. Revolution, to put that differently, is not mere content in Marx's writing; it is form as well. Brecht's "formalist" or modernist (ironic/estranging) Marxism is not the oxymoron that his hardline Marxist detractors took it to be.

If we look at the roots of Marx's key words in German, they all have to do with standing apart, acting on, and ownness versus otherness:

standing apart:
Vergegenständlichung (objectification) < Gegenstand (object) < stehen (to stand) + gegen (against or opposite)
gegenübertreten (encounter, confront) < treten (to step) + gegenüber (over across [from])
unabhängig (detached, autonomous, independent) < un (negation) + ab (off, from) hängen (depend, hang)
Entäußerung (alienation) < ent-(away from, de-/dis-) + Äußerung (externalization, expression) < aus (out)

the ability to act, effective power:
Macht (power or force) < Gothic magan, German mögen (to be able)
Verwirklichung (making-real) / Entwirklichung (making-unreal) < ver (for)
  / ent (away from) + wirklich (real) < wirken (to act on, to effect, to have
  an effect on)

ownness and otherness:
Aneignung (appropriation) < an (at, to) + eigen (one's own)
Entfremdung (estrangement) < ent (away from) + fremd (strange)

To paraphrase, then: the object or article or commodity that labor produces
is itself already, morphologically, something that stands against (*Gegenstand*).
That it has been detached from its producer, made autonomous or independent (*unabhängig*) of its producer, cut loose from its "hanging off" the producer, should not therefore be taken as some kind of tragic or ironic fall from
a Golden Age (Hegel's state of simple labor) in which laborers still owned and
took pride in the fruits of their labor. That laborers look up and see the product "standing against" them, stepping away or apart or across (*gegenübertreten*)
from them as a strange or alien being (*ein fremdes Wesen*), as an autonomous
force with the power (*Macht*) or the ability (*magan/mögen*) to produce things
on its own, is not the result of some degenerative process in capitalism that
deprives workers of their human rights; it is precisely this that makes them
laborers. These are the disciplinary conditions under which laborers become
laborers. This alienation of their labor is the very essence of their being (*Wesen*)
under capitalism. As Brecht writes in a 1929 notebook entry, "*Mann = Mann /
counterpart: the technician / . . .* for the worker is no prince. he comes into being not by birth, but insofar as he is violently remade. therefore all human beings can be turned into workers" (quoted in Doherty, 451). Labor is made real
(*verwirklicht*) in and by and through the very fact that laborers are made unreal
(*entwirklicht*)—which is to say, etymologically, that labor is constituted as having the power or the ability to act or wield influence (*wirken*) by or through the
constitution of laborers as lacking the power to act. "Producing" and "acting"
under capitalism are always already alienated from the laborer and invested in
labor itself, so that the laborer is by definition one whose producing produces
nothing and whose acting or influencing or effecting has no active effects,
whose influence is disabled and can therefore produce no power. Because the
product is by definition that which has been detached from the laborer and
attached to labor, and because labor belongs to the owner (*Eigentümer*), who
has appropriated (*angeeignet*) it or made it his "own" (*seine eigene*), the laborer
has no "own," can own nothing of his or her own; what might ideally have

been his or her own is by law and in fact other, strange, alien, *fremd*—has been *entfremdet,* estranged, or *entäußert,* alienated. But again, this is not a process of deprivation, not an act that strips laborers of their right to own, to make, to act; it is not even, Brecht to the contrary, a *violent* remaking. Rather, it is the simple working out of a disciplinary system that defines and creates laborers in terms of these estrangements and alienations, that creates the subjectivity of laborers in terms of the objectification of their labor as other, as alien.

The result of this disciplinary system for laborers is not only physical starvation but, en route to starvation, the physical-becoming-mental state of alienation, depersonalization, estrangement, the state of "not feeling alive," indeed of being anesthetized to working and producing:

> Die Verwirklichung der Arbeit erscheint so sehr als Entwirklichung, daß der Arbeiter bis zum Hungertod entwirklicht wird. Die Vergegenständlichung erscheint so sehr als Verlust des Gegenstandes, daß der Arbeiter der notwendigsten Gegenstände, nicht nur des Lebens, sondern auch der Arbeitsgegenstände, beraubt ist. Ja, die Arbeit selbst wird zu einem Gegenstand, dessen er nur mit der größten Anstrengung und mit den unregelmäßigsten Unterbrechungen sich bemächtigen kann. Die Aneignung des Gegenstandes erscheint so sehr als Entfremdung, daß, je mehr Gegenstände der Arbeiter produziert, er um so weniger besitzen kann und um so mehr unter die Herrschaft seines Produkts, des Kapitals, gerät. (512)

> The making-real of labor is so much a making-unreal of the laborer that the laborer starves to death. Objectification is so much an object-loss that the laborer is robbed of the objects most necessary not only for life but for labor itself. Indeed labor too becomes an object, which he can seize only with the greatest effort and the most irregular interruptions. The appropriation of objects is so much an estrangement/alienation that the more the laborer produces, the fewer he can possess, and the more he comes under the mastery of his product, capital. (my translation)

As I've been saying, the established analysis of Brecht's response to this anesthetic alienation of workers under capitalism is that he seeks to deanesthetize them through a (de)alienating theater, a hypermimetic dramatization of double-binding/doubly bound alienation that will alienate his audience's alienation (Ewen, 220), push his anesthetized audience to recognize and re-think and rework their alienated state. And I think that analysis is almost entirely valid. But the situation is slightly more complicated than that. There is, first of all, the fact that classically trained (empathetic) actors often complained, especially at first, in the 1920s, that Brecht was doing to them what capitalism does to laborers, alienating them from their labor. Before Brecht had established himself well enough in the theater to be able to cast his plays and train his actors himself, the actors who performed in his plays typically resented and resisted him, fighting with him over the way he kept pushing them to act. In 1922, for example, he and his friend Arnolt Bronnen decided to stage Bronnen's play *Vatermord* (Patricide) in Berlin, with Brecht directing and producing; it was not long, however, before the "estranger"-producer had so thoroughly alienated the actors that rehearsals came to a halt and Brecht had to be replaced by Bertold Viertel (Ewen, 102).

And again, John Guare asks, in regard to Brechtian theater, perhaps prophetically: "Why would anyone want to alienate the audience?" As I say, this understanding of what Brecht is trying to do is conditioned in large part by John Willett's English translation of the *Verfremdungseffekt* as "alienation effect," which does make it sound as if Brecht is interested in doing to the audience as well what capitalism does to laborers, but there is more to this reaction against Brecht than just a misleading translation. Many of his audiences found his productions cold, uninviting, like a slap in the face. And he was often hostile to those audiences, as in the 1926 "Conversation with Bert Brecht":

> A. I don't let my feelings intrude in my dramatic work. It'd give a false view of the world. I aim at an extremely classical, cold, highly intellectual style of performance. I'm not writing for the scum who want to have the cockles of their hearts warmed [*Ich schreibe nicht für jene Abschaum, der Wert darauf legt, daß ihm das Herz aufgeht*].
> Q. Who do you write for?
> A. For the sort of people who just come for fun and don't hesitate to keep their hats on in the theatre.
> Q. But most spectators want their hearts to flow over . . .
> A. The one tribute we can pay the audience is to treat it as thoroughly intelligent. It is utterly wrong to treat people as simpletons when they are grown up at seventeen. I appeal to the reason. ("Was," 282–83; "Conversation," 14)

He tries to make it clear, there, that epic theater is based on respect for the audience, on a willingness to treat the audience as intelligent, but he does also want to alienate "the scum who want to have the cockles of their hearts warmed." Anyone who has come to the theater to feel and not to think, to merge empathetically with the characters and cry and laugh and not to learn, should simply not be there, should be turned away at the door. If they make it into the house, they do need to be slapped in the face with a performance style that refuses to give them what they want.

In part, of course, this experience of a Brechtian performance as a slap in the face emerges out of the well-known phenomenology of treatment—that the "patient" has typically grown accustomed or accommodated to his or her "disorder" and therefore resists treatment, experiencing treatment as more painful than the problem it is intended to heal. The (then-Marxist) psycho-analyst Wilhelm Reich, building in 1933 on the work of Anna Freud, coined the term *Charakterpanzerung* "character armoring" for precisely the kind of anesthetic accommodation (the Freuds would say "defense") that in this case the Brechtian dramatic treatment has to penetrate. Reich conceptualized this character armoring in strikingly Brechtian terms, as a kind of defensive *Gestus*: not so much what people say as what they do, how they move their bodies and voices through time and space, how they signal their defenses through body language (posture, gait, gestures, facial expression, tonalizations, and vo-calizations).[7] Social groups, too, have their gestic *Charakterpanzerung,* their counterideosomatic protection against alien forms of ideosomatic regulation, which they vigorously repel as invaders. Reading Marx in the era of Freud and Reich, Brecht would have to assume that the anesthetized worker would have learned to love his or her alienation, would cherish even the dull aches of the functioning of the double bind as one of many "gifts" of life or "blessings" from God.

Nor should we draw hasty conclusions from the word *Abschaum* "dregs, scum," which may not have been Brecht's own word: Willett tells us that "Ber-nard Guillemin, the interviewer, prefaced [the interview] with a note saying that he had 'deliberately translated into normal language all that Brecht told me in his own manner, in Brecht-style slang'" (*Brecht,* 16; see "Was," 282). The idea here is that Brecht's term of contempt for his "resistant" (anesthetized or armor-plated) audiences was originally even stronger than *Abschaum* and that *Abschaum* therefore represents Guillemin's "normalization" of Brecht's baiting, but of course it is also easy to imagine that Guillemin *thought* he heard a con-temptuous tone in Brecht's voice and "translated" that tone into *Abschaum.*

Still, at the brash age of 28, Brecht is perfectly capable of venting his frus-tration in this manner—and the frustration must be great indeed, since any social group by default plates itself with thick ideosomatic armor against pre-cisely the kind of assault he is launching against the complacency, indifference, and anesthesis of the German proletariat: "amongst my opponents I am not the least interested in the bourgeoisie, despite all their efforts. On the other hand, I am interested in the proletariat, despite their indifference" (Kuhn and Giles, 35).

Another uncomfortable fact for Brecht is that, as a theater director and producer, he occupies the socioeconomic role in Marx's scheme of the manufacturer or the merchant, the capitalist producer who hires labor to make and sell a product to a market that is by default either openly hostile or casually indifferent to his efforts. He tries to fight this role by reconceiving the market, by reimagining the theater as a market occupied by two reciprocal producers, the theater troupe and the audience. To his mind each group, from its own side of the house, produces the play, produces the meaning of the play, produces as meaningful experience the *making* of the play. This means that the collective nature of the enterprise, one group of people having an estranging impact on another group of people, is also responsive, flexible, able to change from one night to the next, because the group of people having an estranging impact on another group of people is always bilateral or reciprocal, troupe on audience, audience on troupe. Because the audience is physically and emotionally different each night, so is the troupe.

And in a sense this reciprocal collectivity gives Brecht an enormous advantage over Shklovsky, whose theory is grounded in the image of an isolated reader reading a single static text. Something that Shklovsky tends to downplay about his theory is that the estranged labor that revitalizes our automatized perception of things is itself subject to automatization: say there is a poem you love because it estranges something powerfully, so you read it over and over; surely a time will come when you know the poem so well that it no longer makes the stone stony? There are no more surprises, so that every line that once had an estranging impact on you is totally familiar and expected and thus routine, maybe even "automatic"? Since it's just you and the poem alone in the room, there isn't much you can do except, of course, move on to a new poem. Brechtian theater by contrast is a microcosm of society that keeps circulating norms *and* novelties, familiarities and strangenesses, through an emotional and ideological economy that is never individualized enough to succumb to habit.

Chinese Acting and the Spatiotemporal Dialectic of Estrangement

But that's just the theory. The temporal dynamic of the estrangement effect can be problematic in the theater as well—indeed, as Brecht discovers at Mei

Lanfang's impromptu performance in Moscow, in the spring of 1935, what is problematic about the familiar/strange or own/alien dialectic of the estrangement effect is that it "moves" in both space (across the borders between the local and the foreign) and time (across the borders between the old and the new).

Brecht describes what he takes to be the theatrical designs of the Chinese actor:

> He expresses his awareness of being watched. This immediately removes one of the European stage's characteristic illusions. The audience can no longer have the illusion of being the unseen spectator at an event which is really taking place. A whole elaborate European stage technique, which helps to conceal the fact that the scenes are so arranged that the audience can view them in the easiest way, is thereby made unnecessary. The actors openly choose those positions which will best show them off to the audience, just as if they were *acrobats*. A further means is that the artist observes himself. Thus if he is representing a cloud, perhaps, showing its unexpected appearance, its soft and strong growth, its rapid yet gradual transformation, he will occasionally look at the audience as if to say: isn't it just like that? At the same time he also observes his own arms and legs, adducing them, testing them and perhaps finally approving them. An obvious glance at the floor, so as to judge the space available to him for his act, does not strike him as liable to break the illusion. In this way the artist separates mime (showing observation) from gesture (showing a cloud), but without detracting from the latter, since the body's attitude is reflected in the face and is wholly responsible for its expression. At one moment the expression is of well-managed restraint; at another, of utter triumph. The artist has been using his countenance as a blank sheet, to be inscribed by the gest of the body.
> The artist's object is to appear strange and even surprising to the audience. He achieves this by looking strangely at himself and his work. As a result everything put forward by him has a touch of the amazing. Everyday things are thereby raised above the level of the obvious and automatic. (92)

Watching Mei perform in Moscow, Brecht seems to have found his own experiments with epic theater in Berlin confirmed in an entire tradition of Chinese acting, and thematizes his own foreigner's surprise and amazement as the Chinese actors' *attempts* to "appear strange and even surprising to the audience." The Chinese actor, a foreigner in Moscow, performs for the small select Russian audience, which includes Brecht, another foreigner. Is he trying to appear strange? It's not an entirely outlandish thought; as a performer he must feel the different response he gets from an outlander audience, must play to it at least a little. It's also true, of course, as Yan Hai-Ping has noted, that "the Chinese artist's objective is *not* to appear 'strange' or 'surprising' to the Chinese audience, and the feeling of estrangement produced in Brecht *as a European* cannot be shared by a Chinese audience."[8] But Mei is not performing for a Chinese audience; he's performing for a European audience. Can generalizations about how Chinese actors perform in China really be extended this blithely to their performances in general, in the abstract, regardless of their audience? Chinese actors do maintain "a very subtle detachment as a sort of 'observer,'" Yan adds; "yet such 'detachment' is based not on the individual consciousness of the performer but rather on highly conventional formulas of acting." Yes, of course. But are such conventions rigid enough to resist the impact of travel, of performances before foreign audiences?

Sich freimachen

Brecht himself has fleeting senses of the spatiotemporal dialectic of estrangement, the problem of the familiar and the strange in psychological time (conventionalization, deconventionalization) and geographical or cultural space (localization, foreignization), as when he writes in the piece on Chinese acting that "es ist zunächst schon schwierig, sich, wenn man Chinesen spielen sieht, freizumachen von dem Gefühl der Befremdung, das sie in uns, als in Europäern, erregen. Man muß sich also vorstellen können, daß sie den V-Effekt auch erzielen bei ihren chinesischen Zuschauern" (206), or, in my translation (which I give because there is a problem here and Willett's translation imposes a single narrow solution on it): "it's hard, at first, when one sees the Chinese acting, to free oneself from the feeling of disturbance/estrangement (*Gefühl der Befremdung*) they awaken in us as Europeans. One must therefore be able to imagine them achieving the V-effect among their Chinese spectators as well."[9] The conceptual problem in the passage is the reflexive verb *sich freimachen* "to make oneself free," for it implies that the disturbing feeling of estrangement is a kind of bondage or slavery from which the European spectator faced with cultural difference must struggle, over time, to be free. The feeling of estrangement captures or binds or enslaves the European spectator by its disturbing newness (time) and cultural strangeness (space), neither of which Chinese spectators presumably feel because what Brecht is calling the V-effect is conventional for them, which is to say both local and current. This means that the Chinese are by definition free of the feeling of estrangement or *Befremdung* that disturbingly binds "one" as a European spectator.

What makes this a conceptual problem, of course, is that Brecht has also been presenting that very feeling as a liberating force, an effect that frees us from the mind-numbing bondage of conventionality; now conventionality suddenly seems to be the true freedom and the erstwhile liberating force a form of bondage from which one finds it hard (at first) to free oneself. Which is the true bondage, the conventionality or the feeling of estrangement? Which is the true liberator? That Brecht does not truly see the V-effect as bondage is relatively clear from his very next line—"One must therefore be able to imagine them achieving the V-effect among their Chinese spectators as well"—but does he see that achievement as a liberation? Is it possible that he is requiring "one" to imagine the achievement of the V-effect as a return to bondage in the midst of the freedom of conventionality? Almost certainly not. The V-effect is presumably still the liberator, and Brecht, the German visitor in Russia, watching a Chinese actor perform, has to force himself to imagine its liberating effect on Chinese spectators even in the midst of what he imagines as thought-binding convention. But then why this talk of self-liberation from the V-effect?

If we take a few steps back from the conceptual tangle Brecht has gotten himself into, it becomes evident that the problem in the phrase "sich freizumachen von dem Gefühl der Befremdung" is that either (1) the noun phrase after the preposition is wrong, and Brecht means self-liberation from something other than the feeling of estrangement, or (2) the verb is wrong, and Brecht means something other than self-liberation.

1. If we take the former route, we might suggest that Brecht is actually trying to talk about freeing oneself not from the disturbing feeling of estrangement itself but from the ethnocentric assumptions generated in us by that feeling. Because we as Europeans feel estranged, we assume that the estrangement effects we experience must be intended by the performers, but in fact these are conventionalized effects in China, not designed to awaken a *feeling* of estrangement in Chinese spectators at all. This is essentially the view we saw Yan Hai-Ping offering as a *corrective* to Brecht: "The Chinese artist's objective is *not* to appear 'strange' or 'surprising' to the Chinese audience, and the feeling of estrangement produced in Brecht *as a European* cannot be shared by a Chinese audience."

But if this is the idea Brecht is trying to articulate, that it's mere ethnocentrism for a European to assume that Mei Lanfang seeks to have an estranging effect on Chinese spectators, why does he then immediately go on to say that one still has to be able to imagine (*vorstellen*) Chinese actors having an estranging effect on Chinese spectators? Should one in fact be able to imagine a nonestranging estrangement effect—to imagine that in China Chinese acting achieves the estrangement effect without achieving the estrangement effect? Should one be able to imagine, for example, a *conventionalized* estrangement effect that does not actually effect a *feeling* of estrangement?

The German verb *vorstellen,* usually translated as "imagine" or "envision" or "visualize" or "represent," is morphologically a "putting before"; it is translated with vision words because traditionally it means putting something before the inner *eye* of the imagination, so that we think we "see" something that is not physically there. Nothing in these two sentences we're trying to understand here, however, indicates that when Brecht writes *vorstellen* he means the visual imagination. What exactly, then, is he saying we have to put before ourselves, and what imaginative sense organ is he requiring us to put it before? If the imaginative faculty at question in the passage is, in fact, feeling, the effect of the Chinese acting on the spectator's feeling of estrangement, then we might provisionally take him to be saying that we must be able to put the hypothetical estranging effect of Chinese acting on Chinese spectators before our own imaginative *feeling,* which is to say, before our own somatic response. But then if this requirement is born out of his sense that "one's" feeling is ethnocentric, that the guidance one's European somatic response gives one is shaped by one's experience as a European and therefore historically and culturally unreliable as a guide to the somatics of Chinese estrangement, what he must be trying to say is that one must be able to impose some sort of check or restriction on the somatics of one's European feeling of strangeness in order to put before that feeling a projected Chinese somatics of estrangement—in a sense, to *transexperience (gegenüberleben, perezhi(va)t')* or *transfeel (gegenüberfühlen, perechuvstvovat')* an imagined Chinese somatics of estrangement.

2. It's hard to tell, but this "check" or "restriction" may in fact be the direction John Willett goes with the passage. Clearly, in any case, he takes the latter route: he sees the problem to be fixed in the sentence as the verb *sich freimachen,* the implication that the feeling of estrangement for Brecht is something from which one must seek to *free oneself.* His translation reads: "when one sees the Chinese acting it is at first very hard to *discount* the feeling of estrangement which they produce in us as Europeans" (95–96, emphasis added). If we take *discount* there to be a synonym for the check or the restriction in my speculations above—one can't just trust one's own European somatic response but must disqualify or discredit or disregard or discount one's initial feeling of

estrangement in order to leave room for an imagined Chinese feeling—then Willett is indeed interpreting Brecht's phrase along the lines I was suggesting.

Of course, *discount* is also a mercantile metaphor, one that is perhaps somewhat inappropriate for Brecht the Marxist (not entirely inappropriate for Brecht the theater producer) but nevertheless interesting in its implications for the temporal dynamic of estrangement. The metaphor invokes images of shifting vendor reactions to market fluctuations: it is hard to discount a popular new product at first, when it is selling well, but as sales drop off, with market saturation or consumer product fatigue, discounting becomes increasingly attractive as a possible goad to waning consumer interest. If the "feeling of estrangement" is the epic theater's main product or commodity, this translation would suggest, it's easy to see how it will sell well at first, when it's a radical new paradigm-busting item. But what happens when it becomes the industry standard, as it apparently has in China? What happens when the theaters of an entire culture conventionalize the theatrical strategies that initially produced the feeling of estrangement and do not radically renew their conventions for four hundred years? How then do we imagine consumers continuing to want to buy the feeling *as* a novelty? The idea in the estrangement effect is that what is being sold as a product is newness itself, the newness of the new, the effect of the effect of the strange. This is already a capitalist marketing strategy for existing products—advertise them *in terms of* their newness—but through Willett's term *discount* we can imagine Brecht talking about the feeling or effect of newness or strangeness *as the only product,* a virtual product that can only be experienced subjectively, and in that sense can only be bought if you *think* you've bought it. How do you sustain *that* in the face of success and its attendant conventionalization?

As long as the operative question concerns what Chinese spectators feel at performances of the so-called Beijing Opera, of course, this is all speculation, fueled by imagined or "transfelt" Chinese somatics, which Brecht must know are for a European just as unreliable as (and indeed merely an imaginary extension of) the initial ethnocentric European somatics. But it seems to me that the really important question for Brecht must concern the possible conventionalization of his own theater in Europe. Then, instead of *trans*feeling the guidance imparted by Chinese somatics, he's *pre*feeling the guidance imparted by his own: how would it feel to him if in the future the epic theater turned into the European industry standard? How would it feel to him in 1936 if, say, some Marxist angel of the future were to tell him that twenty years hence he would die in a socialist Germany, where for the handful of years before his death his epic theater would have been simultaneously lionized as "Marxist" and (to use Herbert Marcuse's term for American liberalism) *repressively tolerated* as "formalist," and that after his death his dialectical strategies for the theater would be de-dialecticized, fossilized as rigid dogmatic blueprints?

The Four Feelings

Coming out of Brecht's possible Shklovskyanism and Hegelianism, in fact, we might exfoliate Brecht's vague sense of the problem by adapting the model of the four Things from chapter 3—rendering the four Things this time as the four Feelings, but four Feelings specifically as the next round of dialectic above or beyond the four Things, Feeling 1 as Shklovsky's Thing 3, the estranging effect of art. In Brecht we do not start on the ground floor, with inchoate objectivist notions of "reality." Almost twenty years on from Shklovsky's article, the experiential primacy of Thing 3 is taken for granted.

Brecht's Feeling 1, then, obviously, would be the feeling of estrangement he gets watching Mei Lanfang perform in Moscow, a small impromptu command performance without costume or set. This is what we might call the ground zero of the estrangement effect, Shklovsky's Thing 3, an artistically enhanced version of Thing 1.

Feeling 2 would be the feeling Brecht transfeels Chinese spectators getting while watching Mei Lanfang in China (spatiocultural difference), or that he prefeels possible European spectators getting while watching an epic theater performance in a possible future Europe (temporal difference) where Brechtian epic theater is utterly normative and conventionalized and therefore precisely what everyone expects to see when they go to the theater. This is roughly parallel to Shklovsky's Thing 2, the loss of Thing 1 brought about by depersonalization, but it is again an artistically enhanced form of *Vergegenständlichung* or object-loss, the fading of the estranging artistic effect (Thing 3) into nothingness as a result of conventionalization.

Since Feeling 2 is not something Brecht is experiencing in the here and now, but something he's preexperiencing (time) or transexperiencing (space), there are two questions for Feeling 3. First, how do we turn the depersonalized or conventionalized Feeling 2 back into a deconventionalized or repersonalized Feeling 1, which was the task of Thing 3 for Shklovsky, and which might be thought of as Feeling 3t (t for time) for Brecht? And second, how do we avoid reading Feeling 2 in terms of the ethnocentric Feeling 1, which would be achieved by Feeling 3s (s for space), the feeling of "freeing oneself from" or "discounting" Feeling 1 by recognizing its spatio-cultural difference from Feeling 2? Feeling 3t would thus be a temporally recursive/redressive enhancement of Shklovsky's Thing 3, the feeling that is required when art loses its estranging power to the temporal dynamic (conventionalization) and must be refreshed or resharpened in order once again to have its estranging effect and return Feeling 2 to Feeling 1. Feeling 3s would be something new, something that Shklovsky did not theorize but that is arguably present in his article's unconscious: the necessity of *imagining* automatization (Thing 2) as a justification for theorizing estrangement (Thing 3). In the Brechtian schema, Feeling 3s would specifically justify enhanced estrangement (Feeling 3) through a reminder of the necessity of transfeeling cultural difference—the transfeeling that the Chinese spectator's emotional response to Chinese acting (Feeling 2) will not necessarily coincide with "one's own" (Feeling 1).

The fact that Feelings 3t and 3s push in opposite directions, 3t pushing Feeling 2 back toward Feeling 1 and 3s pushing Feeling 1 up in the direction of Feeling 2, suggests that the spatiotemporal dialectic of Brecht's estrangement effect is more complex, more caught up in the pushes and pulls of internal contradiction, than Shklovsky's estrangement device. I imagine this internal contradiction, again, on the model of the double bind: it only works if it channels both a primary somatic tendency toward the strange (Feeling 1) and a secondary somatic tendency toward the familiar (Feeling 2) as well as a tertiary (now deanesthetizing) somatic blockage that prevents the spectator from escaping the dialectic (Feeling 3). As the abbreviations after the two Feelings 3 suggest, the dialectic is both temporal (the estrangement effect tending over time to become familiar and thus in need of enhanced estrangement) and spatial (what is estranging in Moscow is conventional in Beijing and vice versa, the only higher-level estranging solution to which is the short-term dislocation of travel or the long-term dislocation of exile, being a foreigner/*étranger/ Ausländer/inostranets*).

Feeling 4—something Brecht does not mention explicitly but is arguably implied in his cautionary remarks—would be the felt temptation or inclination to dogmatize the estrangement effect as an abstract universal, which is to say, the estrangement effect without the actual effect of estrangement, or, more generally, the Brechtian dialectic without dialectic, the dialectic idealized or museumized, turned into a static showcase representation of dialectic.[10] Feeling 4 is the siren call Brecht is responding against in his own formulation of the estrangement effects in Chinese acting. As he outlines the theory of the estrangement effect, he gradually begins to sense a problem, the ethnocentricity of his own feeling of estrangement in the theater in Moscow, which tends to undermine anything abstractly universalizing he might want to say about the "effect"—the theorized effect-without-effect—of estrangement. Feeling 4 might also be associated with the fossilization or de-dialecticization of epic theater in the GDR after Brecht's death, or, more recently, with the universalization of the *Verfremdungseffekt* as self-referentiality in what Marc Silberman has called the postmodernization of Brecht.

Man and *Sich*

In addition to the spatial and temporal displacements in Brecht's formulation, there is a third displacement, from the singular to the plural, from the personal to the impersonal, from the individual to the collective. I mean the pronominal shift that I've been tacitly highlighting in my discussion of the spatiotemporal dialectic thus far, from "I" to "one": "es ist zunächst schon schwierig, *sich,* wenn *man* Chinesen spielen sieht, freizumachen von dem Gefühl der Befremdung, das sie in uns, als in Europäern, erregen. *Man* muß sich also vorstellen können, daß sie den V-Effekt auch erzielen bei ihren chinesischen Zuschauern" (206)—"it's hard, at first, when *one* sees the Chinese acting, to free *oneself* from the feeling of estrangement they awaken in us as Europeans. *One* must therefore be able to imagine them achieving the V-effect among their Chinese spectators as well" (my translation and italics). It's not, in other words, that I, Bertolt Brecht, sitting in a specific place in Moscow on a specific night in the spring of 1935, find it difficult to free myself from the feeling of estrangement Mei Lanfang awakens in me; it just *is* difficult to free that externalized and objectified *sich*-self. It's not that I feel it necessary to be able to imagine Mei and his fellow actors back home achieving the V-effect in China as well: one must (*man muß*) be able to imagine this. Brecht's personal somatic experiences are generalized to incorporate or be incorporated into the somatic experiences of a larger unnamed collective, people in general.

This is an extremely important displacement for Brecht the Marxist, of course, who in many ways, in his drama theory and his theatrical practice, celebrated the death of the individual in the crowd. But it is also a problematic one, as this example clearly demonstrates: collectivizing his own experience under the rubric of "one" or *man/sich* tends to blunt the very point he is making about the local and the foreign, cultural familiarity and cultural strangeness. It seems pretty clear in context that by "*man/*one" he means himself and other Europeans—"wenn man Chinesen spielen sieht," "when one sees the Chinese acting"—but the very vagueness of that collectivization of self seems nevertheless to universalize personal experience in ways that undermine his own argument here. And if *man*/one is the European prosubject, the pronominalized European as seer and thinker and doer, *sich*/one is the European pro-object, *das Sich-Selbst,* the pronominalized European inner self that is acted upon (liberated) by the European *man*/one.

The other pronominal opposition he inserts into the passage, "us" versus "they/their," is problematic as well, not just because the binary seems not to admit slippage (and some must exist) but because it sets up a unidirectional effect-flow from what "they" do as Chinese actors to "us" as European specta-tors, and shunts the active construction or interpretation of what's happen-ing not back to a named "we" but laterally to the impersonal "one." In fact, the "one" in the passage seems to function in Brecht's thinking like a kind of metasomatic fifth estate, which does all the thinking and writes the event up for print. "They" awaken a feeling of estrangement in "us," but "we" don't try to free our *sich*-selves from that feeling: "one" does. (There is no "we.") "One" (*man*) catches the *sich*-self in ethnocentricity, too, and puts pressure on the *sich*-self to imagine that "they" (Chinese actors) have a V-effect on "their" spec-tators back home as well. Clearly, here, "they" as actors act and in so doing have a somatic effect on "us" as spectators; but the important cognitive work with the whole process, submitting somatic guidance to critical reflection and stray ethnocentric *sich*-selves to ideosomatic regulation, is done by the universalized European "one."

Practical Work in the Theater: Empathy and Estrangement

As I say, dialectical theory and practice were ideals that Brecht himself of-ten failed to achieve. This for Brecht is the intellectual's most pressing and at the same time most difficult task: the unmasking of rigidified or fossilized dialectics in the "repressive tolerance" of any given regime and setting them in motion, restarting the dialectic. Or, as Herbert Marcuse himself puts this task: "The author is fully aware that, at present, no power, no authority, no govern-ment exists which would translate liberating tolerance into practice, but he believes that it is the task and duty of the intellectual to recall and preserve his-torical possibilities which seem to have become utopian possibilities—that it is his task to break the concreteness of oppression in order to open the mental space in which this society can be recognized as what it is and does" ("Repressive," 81–82).[11] Something like this *utopian* possibility or mental space is what Brecht kept trying, all his life, in Weimar Germany and exile and the GDR, to open up in his audiences—dramatic, literary, and theoretical—but, inevitably, was many times unable to open in himself.

The Empathy-Estrangement Binary

Such was the situation with the dialectic between empathy and estrangement, which Brecht insisted on treating as a binary—for reasons that Juliet Koss suggests arose out of his practical work with the theater in Munich in the early 1920s. Specifically, she suggests, the idea of empathetic audience response to a play was anathema to Brecht for many years because it had been introduced into German dramatic theory and practice by the hard-line rightwinger Georg Fuchs, at the Munich Artists' Theater a few years before Brecht began working in the theater. As a result, she argues, Brecht came to equate empathy with repressive right-wing politics, the politics of identificatory acceptance of the status quo, and estrangement with the liberatory left-wing politics of collective self-realization and self-transformation. This is, obviously, a significantly different application of the concept of estrangement from what we found in Shklovsky, whose politics at the time of writing "Art as Device" were socialist-revolutionary but whose theory of estrangement was strangely and even conservatively apolitical. Since Brecht's initial (and long-standing) rejection of empathy as a channel of collective self-transformation is potentially a significant stumbling block for a somatics of literature based on the somatic mimeticism of empathy, I'd like to take a few pages to look closely at this problem.

As Koss reminds us, empathy or *Einfühlung* was first theorized by a German philosophy student named Robert Vischer in 1873, in order to explain the reception of art as an active psychological projection of feelings (*Fühlung* or *Gefühle*) into an object or another person. The scholarly tradition emerging out of this idea is thoroughly Hegelian in orientation, based on the intertwined assumption that empathy involves not only the subjective construction of the object as a process of emotionally charged internalization (the object as internal image) but also objectification of the self as a process of projective externalization. As Wilhelm Worringer writes in *Abstraction and Empathy* (1908), "in dieser Selbstobjektivierung liegt eine Selbstentäußerung," "in this self-objectification lies a self-alienation/externalization" (quoted in Koss 813 and 819, n. 14). As is often the case with such Hegelian dialectics, however, as this aesthetic doctrine began to assume prescriptive and ultimately political forms, one side of the dialectic atrophied and the tension between opposites went slack. Internalization as constructivist activity (the intellectual/critical/ aesthetic side that Brecht would favor) was set aside and forgotten, and empathy increasingly came to be seen as sheer externalization, sheer surrender of self to the fetishized external object. Worringer stresses the importance of this surrender, saying, "We are delivered from our individual being as long as we are absorbed into an external object," and noting that "popular usage speaks with striking accuracy of 'losing oneself' in the contemplation of a work of art" (quoted in Koss, 813).

As Georg Fuchs formulates this idea in *Revolution in the Theatre: Conclusions Concerning the Munich Artists' Theatre* (1909), the social utility of this aesthetic loss of self is largely political: through empathetic self-alienation into a militaristic or nationalistic play, the theater audience can be transported body and soul into a patriotic right-wing ideology. This is, of course, essentially the "perverted" use of artistic infection that Tolstoy castigated, the use of art to indoctrinate the lower classes with militaristic, nationalistic, racist, and other such values; but of course from Brecht's point of view Tolstoy's Christian counterinfection is equally conservative, not only because it is religious and therefore politically quietistic but especially because it bypasses critical thought.

And it is roughly along these lines that Brecht initially binarizes empathy and estrangement: empathy shuts down thought and transports the spectator into a receptive, malleable body state in which s/he is ideally susceptible to right-wing ideological indoctrination; estrangement awakens critical thought and so provokes the spectator to rethink and resist dominant capitalist ideologies. Dramatic or "Aristotelian" theater, therefore, is intrinsically conservative; epic theater is intrinsically radicalizing. As Koss writes:

> In a 1930 essay, Brecht opposed traditional, or "dramatic theater," to the "epic theater" he had developed for the modern age. While dramatic theater emphasized "suggestion" and "feeling," Brecht explained, epic theater relied more on "argument" and "reason"; whereas the former, encouraging complacency and passivity, "implicates the spectator in a stage situation [but] wears down his capacity for action," the latter "turns the spectator into an observer, but arouses his capacity for action" . . . Empathy, which defined the traditional relationship between spectator and performance, was likewise opposed to estrangement, the central concept of epic theater: "If empathy makes something ordinary of a special event," Brecht wrote elsewhere, "estrangement makes something special of an ordinary one." The

intermittent use of estrangement denaturalized the spectator's experience by making sustained absorption impossible and in this way constructed a spectator whose intellect was actively engaged. Estrangement was "necessary to avoid the intoxicating effects of illusion" . . . which it countered by calling attention to the distance between the work of art and the viewer, thus facilitating a certain criticality and thoughtfulness. Linked conceptually by many theorists besides Brecht to the use of fragments and montage—to the attempt to call attention to art's artificiality—estrangement is generally associated with progressive politics. The questioning of authority, including the authority of the artwork and the artist, is usually assumed to be a leftist approach, whereas the enforcement of the aesthetic status quo, lulling the spectator or entertaining the audience with a seamless work, is identified with conservative aesthetics. (810–11)

Dialecticization

So far, then, all is binary; there is no dialectical tension between empathy and estrangement. In dialogue with his critics and his audiences, however, Brecht gradually modulates this extreme position—identifying the evocation of empathetic audience response with a reactionary politics and first seeking to define himself against the use of it at all, then against the exclusive use of it, then against a heavy reliance on it. Generally speaking, the trend in his writing is from a rigid dogmatic rejection of empathetic appeals to the audience's emotional identification with the characters (indeed, the presence of any emotion on stage at all) to a series of more eclectic positions in which it's good to have some emotion but no empathy, or all emotion is good except empathetic emotion, or even empathy is good in small doses.

In the early 1920s, then, he is arguing that plays "ought to be presented quite coldly, classically and objectively. For they are not matter for empathy; they are there to be understood. Feelings are private and limited. Against that the reason is fairly comprehensive and to be relied on" (Willett, *Brecht*, 15). He repeatedly likens the body state into which "infectious" or empathy-based acting puts the audience to various forms of depersonalization, but depersonalization in Heidegger's sense as ideosomatic deindividualization: a trance (26), an "obstinate clinging to the pleasure element" and "addiction to drugs" (40–41), an appeal to "the mental immaturity and the high emotional suggestibility of a mob" (79), "stock narcotic attractions" (85), "a machine for simulating the effects of dope" (88), "one of the most blooming branches of the international narcotics traffic" (90), a "rape" of the spectator (93), "a view to achieving more or less primitive shock effects or hazily defined sentimental moods which in fact are to be consumed as substitutes for the missing spiritual experiences of a crippled and cataleptic audience" (160), and what he calls the behaviorism of American-style advertising and salesmanship (and note the Tolstoyan metaphor of infection): "a man goes into a showroom, mildly infected, and comes out, severely ill, in possession of a car" (67). Drama whose primary appeal is empathetic and emotional, designed to create a pleasurable identificatory transfer of emotion from the actors to the audience, he repeatedly castigates as merely "culinary," like the purely gustatory satisfactions of a good meal. Over and over, Brecht waxes hot in his condemnation of this inherently reactionary kind of artistic appeal, this bourgeois strategy for anesthetizing citizens into all-accepting placidity so that they will not begin to question just how miserable things truly are. Here, for example, is a longer attack on the same emotional appeal in symphonic music, which makes Brecht's association of the "desired" state of empathetic infections with what he takes to be the psychopathology of depersonalization (ideosomatic deindividualization) particularly clear (and which clearly echoes Tolstoy's condemnations of the infectiousness of "perverse" art):

> Most "advanced" music nowadays is still written for the concert hall. A single glance at the audiences who attend concerts is enough to show how impossible it is to make any political or philosophical use of music that produces such effects. We see entire rows of human beings transported into a peculiar doped state, wholly passive, sunk without trace, seemingly in the grip of a severe poisoning attack. Their tense, congealed gaze shows that these people are the helpless and involuntary victims of the unchecked lurchings of their emotions. Trickles of sweat prove how such excesses exhaust them. The worst gangster film treats its audience more like thinking beings. Music is cast in the role of Fate. As the exceedingly complex, wholly unanalysable fate of this period of the grisliest, most deliberate exploitation of man by man. Such music has nothing but culinary ambitions left. It seduces the listener into an enervating, because unproductive, act of enjoyment. (89)

In the early years of his career, this "enervating, because unproductive, act of enjoyment" is anathema to him because the spectator who is not actively "producing" a critical image of and critical practice for a better life is overwhelmingly vulnerable to ideosomatic manipulation by the Right. From the early 1930s to the mid-1940s, obviously, his worst fears are borne out in the news, as these "helpless and involuntary victims of the unchecked lurchings of their emotions" have become the millions of Hitler's eager followers, listening to his impassioned speeches with the same enjoyable empathetic response that Brecht attempted to block in the theater. Living in exile, probably in Sweden, around 1940 he writes: "The audience was not 'worked up' by a display of temperament or 'swept away' by acting with tautened muscles; in short, no attempt was made to put it in a trance and give it the illusion of watching an ordinary unrehearsed event. As will be seen presently, the audience's tendency to plunge into such illusions has to be checked by specific artistic means" (136). Clearly, here, "the audience's tendency to plunge into such illusions" has a topical relevance or resonance that extends beyond theater walls to the theaters of politics and war, and the (trans)aesthetic quest for a "specific artistic means" that will check that tendency has become particularly pressing.

Indeed, later in that same piece, the "Short Description of a New Technique of Acting which Produces an Estrangement Effect," Brecht explicitly contextualizes his own early rigid rejection of emotion on stage as an overreaction to the rise of National Socialism:

> The rejection of empathy is not the result of a rejection of the emotions, nor does it lead to such. The crude aesthetic thesis that emotions can only be stimulated by means of empathy is wrong. None the less a non-aristotelian dramaturgy has to apply a cautious criticism to the emotions which it aims at and incorporates. Certain artistic tendencies like the provocative behaviour of Futurists and Dadaists and the icing-up of music point to a crisis of the emotions. Already in the closing years of the Weimar Republic the postwar German drama took a decisively rationalistic turn. Fascism's grotesque emphasizing of the emotions, together perhaps with the no less important threat to the rational element in Marxist aesthetics, led us to lay particular stress on the rational. (145)

This is not entirely accurate; while it's true that the Nazis were everywhere in Munich when he moved there in 1920, at the age of 22, they were probably not the main reason he overemphasized the dangers of emotion as a young man. From early on he fancied himself "cold as a dog . . . and without a bit of human feeling" (Ewen, 83), a cynical intellectual, and all through his life he presented himself in more or less the same unemotional mold, as someone who didn't gush, who wasn't sentimental, who couldn't or wouldn't turn off his mind even for a second. Plays and movies and concerts that expected him to, that put pressure on him to let himself be "transported into a peculiar doped state, wholly passive, sunk without trace, seemingly in the grip of a severe poisoning attack," to him were assaults on his intellectual autonomy, his critical detachment. That this (anti)emotional profile fit the prevailing masculine stereotype of Brecht's day, and that his drama theory and theatrical practice might therefore with some justification be reduced, using his own method of Marxist historicization, to the simple working-out of a normative ideological role with which his society has infected him, may or may not have won his consent, had someone argued it to him. It seems reasonable to hypothesize, in any case, that his suspicion of emotional infection might well have been generated collectively in him through emotional infection, through the mimetically reembodied somatic guidance of a specific shared patriarchal normativity.

Still, as this quotation shows, by his early forties Brecht is also beginning to rethink dialectically his youthful resistance to emotion and even empathy. "The crude aesthetic thesis that emotions can only be stimulated by means of empathy is wrong." This statement is steeped in the dialectical somaticity of Feeling 3, the simultaneous inclination to accept and reject emotion and its empathetic stimulation, which is to say, the inclination to *sublate* empathy estrangingly. And indeed Brecht's many attempts to develop radically new methods for the stimulation of an audience's emotions—especially as his term for his own approach changes from the "epic theater" to the "dialectical theater"—all arise out of that same dialectical impulse. A horrific or touching or funny enough subject matter, related or played in a deadpan or other somatostylistically inappropriate or jarring manner, can still evoke emotion, despite the storyteller's or actor's utter refusal to "push" the audience with simulated emotion designed for empathetic mimicry. Teaching the serious through the silly was crucial for Brecht, using the strategies of the *commedia dell'arte,* slapstick and farce, wacky songs, signs, film clips, what Erwin Piscator called "total theater," so that the audience is like a child at the circus—or, Brecht's favorite image for the ideal audience, like a fan at a sporting event, smoking a cigar and drinking a beer—but specifically in order to push the audience into emotionally and ideologically uncomfortable confrontations with their own deepest assumptions. Or, of course, specifically the estrangement effect:

> In this case, however, there is not the same automatic transfer of emotions to the spectator, the same emotional infection. The estrangement effect intervenes, not in the form of absence of emotion, but in the form of emotions which need not correspond to those of the character portrayed. On seeing worry the spectator may feel a sensation of joy; on seeing anger, one of disgust. When we speak of exhibiting the outer signs of emotion we do not mean such an exhibition and such a choice of signs that the emotional transference does in fact take place because the actor has managed to infect himself with the emotions portrayed, by exhibiting the outer signs; thus, by

letting his voice rise, holding his breath and tightening his neck muscles so that the blood shoots to his head, the actor can easily conjure up a rage. In such a case of course the effect does not occur. But it does occur if the actor at a particular point unexpectedly shows a completely white face, which he has produced mechanically by holding his face in his hands with some white make-up on them. If the actor at the same time displays an apparently composed character, then his terror at this point (as a result of his message, or that discovery) will give rise to an estrangement effect. Acting like this is healthier and in our view less unworthy of a thinking being; it demands a considerable knowledge of humanity and worldly wisdom, and a keen eye for what is socially important. In this case too there is of course a creative process at work; but it is a higher one, because it is raised to the conscious level. (94–95)

What Brecht seems at face value to be setting up here is a *nonmimetic* somatics of drama or literature—one not based on somatic mimeticism, as I said in chapter 1 a somatics typically is, but on alternative channels of somatic transfer. For clearly some kind of somatic guidance *is* being transferred from actors to audience here: "there is not the same *automatic* transfer of emotions to the spectator, the same emotional infection," but there is *some* transfer of emotions, different emotions. "The estrangement effect intervenes, not in the form of absence of emotion, but in the form of emotions which need not correspond to those of the character portrayed. On seeing worry the spectator may feel a sensation of joy; on seeing anger, one of disgust."[12] The idea is still, as in empathetic theater, to transfer somatic guidance to the audience, but since Brecht is convinced that the somatic mimeticism of empathy was (to put it mildly) unhealthy, a form of trance, drug high, or insanity, he finds a different channel, a different—healthier and more conscious—transfer strategy. "Acting like this is healthier and in our view less unworthy of a thinking being; it demands a considerable knowledge of humanity and worldly wisdom, and a keen eye for what is socially important. In this case too there is of course a creative process at work; but it is a higher one, because it is raised to the conscious level."

The Empathy-Estrangement Dialectic

But in fact this mimetic/nonmimetic binary can itself be sublated along the dialectical lines I set up earlier in the chapter, by recognizing the tension between the internalizing and the externalizing impulses involved in a Hegelian (Vischerian/Worringerian) conception of empathy. If empathy is both the constructive/critical internalization of the object and the projective/iden-tificatory externalization of the self, then what is dangerous and reactionary in empathy is not empathy itself but its dedialecticization, its reduction to a single directional impulse, self-objectification as self-alienation/externaliza-tion. Then Brecht's increasingly dialectical sense of the interaction between empathy and estrangement or (in my terms) between mimetic and nonmi-metic somatic transfer can be translated as the contradictory working of the dialectic of empathy itself.

This reformulation of Brecht's central binary would take us well beyond Koss's suggestion that "Brecht's *Verfremdungseffekt*, in other words, is yielded by the *oscillation* between an audience's empathetic experience and its estrange-ment" (810, emphasis added), and even beyond the parallel she sets up with Bakhtin's more dialectical back-and-forth movement, in the early "Author and Hero in Aesthetic Activity" (the same long essay Caryl Emerson set up in op-position to Shklovskyan estrangement in chapter 3)—between the outward movement of "aesthetic activity as 'empathizing' or 'co-experiencing' (61) and the inward movement of the "return into myself." " 'The first step in aesthetic activity,' " Koss quotes Bakhtin from that essay, " 'is my projecting myself into him and experiencing his life from within him' . . . , he allowed, but such empathy 'must be followed by a *return* into myself, a *return* to my own place outside' . . . for 'in living experience projection and consummation are inti-mately intertwined' . . . Bakhtin argued (as Brecht would) that the theory of empathy, with its attendant loss of self, hypothesizes a passive, unimaginative spectator, whereas 'the aesthetic *whole* is not something co-experienced, but something actively produced, both by the author and by the contemplator' . . . " (817). Bakhtin is here close to the Hegelian dialectic of the first theorists of empathy:

> The principles of giving a form to the soul are the principles of giving a form to inner life *from outside,* from *another* consciousness; the artist's work proceeds here, once again, *on the* boundaries—the boundaries of *in-ner life,* i.e., at the point where the soul is inwardly turned ("adverted") *to the outside* of itself. The other human being is situated outside me and over against me not only outwardly, but also inwardly. By using an oxymoron, we could speak here of the other's *inward* outsideness and over-againstness. The other's inner experiences (his joy, anguish, desire, striving, and, finally, his directedness to meaning), even if they are not manifested in anything external (are not uttered, are not reflected in his face or in the expression

of his eyes, but are only surmised or guessed by me from the context of his life)—all these experiences are found by me *outside* my own inner world, outside my *I-for-myself* (even where I experience them in some way, they do not relate—axiologically—to me, they are not imputed to me as mine), *for me,* they are located in *being*—they are constituents of the *other's* axiological existence. (101–2)

Bakhtin's "oxymoron," of course, "the other's *inward* outsideness and over-againstness," is not oxymoronic at all but dialectical. As in Hegel, my consciousness finds you outside me and across from me, even finds your internal experience, your feelings, with or without external signs of them—but finds all that inwardly, inside me, inside an outside part of me, "outside my *I-for-myself*," or rather, perhaps, on those boundaries of internal life where the artist's work flows, on the boundary where my me-for-myself is becoming a me-for-another, or another-for-me. To some extent I am projecting my own feelings, desires, aspirations, purposes onto you, across that internal boundary from the me-for-myself to the me-for-another to the other-for-me; but because that boundary is constituted as much by my interactions with others as it is by my own consciousness, and thus by others as much as by the self, and because my crossings of that boundary in my own internal experience shape others as well, that internalized externality is also an externalized internality, and both reconstitute the boundary crossing in each person as a dialogized place. In the term I have been using in this book, this is the somatic exchange, the reciprocal transfer of somatized selfhood and otherness that constitutes us as social beings, and our being-together as society.

In his surreptitiously Shklovskyan dissertation from 1925, *The Psychology of Art,*[13] Lev Vygotsky develops a similar model. In his concluding chapter, in particular, which begins with a detailed and not particularly sympathetic reading of Tolstoy's infection theory—for Vygotsky true, but only a trivial part of the truth—he argues that "between the human being and the world stands the social environment, which in its own way refracts and directs both every irritation (*vsyakoe razdrazhenie*) acting on a person from the outside and every reaction proceeding from the person to the outside" (*Psikhologiya,* 319, my translation). Here the "human being" or the "person" (*chelovek*) seems on the face of it to be conceived as a kind of container with a wall separating it from the "outside," with "irritations" going in and "reactions" coming out, more or less the behaviorist model Vygotsky claims to be applying throughout.[14] Indeed, the Scripta Technica group that translated the book into English in the early 1970s rendered *vsyakoe razdrazhenie* "every irritation" as "the stimuli"

(*Psychology,* 252). But Vygotsky doesn't mean stimuli; he means irritation. He has just been discussing Tolstoy's remark in *The Kreutzer Sonata* that by itself music only irritates, remains an irritation unless it drives you to act: "if Mass is sung and I take communion, well, here too the music has achieved its purpose; otherwise, it is only irritation, and no one knows what to do with this irritation" (*Psychology,* 251). While an irritation might be classified as a stimulus, the image here is important: a stimulus provokes a mechanical response; an irritation exasperates, annoys, stirs up complicated and unpleasant feelings. A stimulus is an experimental procedure, a stage or a step in a scientific test; an irritation, as Tolstoy's example makes clear, is a socioemotional problem to be solved. If religious music is an irritation acting on the container that is the human individual, and that irritation creates a problem, a social problem manifested as an emotional problem, and the action of going to Mass that "solves" that problem is a reaction proceeding from within that container, then the image of the social environment that mediates between the individual human container and the "world" is particularly strange. Is there a place or a realm for a mediating social environment to "stand" between the human and the "world"? The Russian word for "environment" here is *sreda,* which also means "medium" and is related to "middle" and "means." The social environment is the medium that mediates between human and world, the refractive/directive means through or by which irritations go in and reactions come out. But what kind of medium? If music is the irritation and the social environment is the medium through which that irritation is refractively and directively mediated to the individual human being, how exactly is that environment performing its mediating task?

Since we have been reading Bakhtin's essay from a year or two or three earlier, we might suspect that the mediating social environment that stands between the person and the world is this dialogized inside-outside or outside-inside that Bakhtin writes of, the outside place inside us that is populated by our images of other people and theirs of us. Even though Vygotsky had almost certainly not been reading Bakhtin's unpublished essay, he is heading in the same direction: "Art is the social in us, and even if its action is completed in a separate individual, that does not at all mean that its roots and essence are individual. It is extremely naïve to understand the social to mean the collective, the presence of a large number of people. The social is also to be found where there is only one human being and his personal experiences [*lichnye perezhivaniya*]" (*Psikhologiya,* 314, my translation). Art is the social *in* us, our socialized selves, inside the container; the social is also a medium outside the container, or on the border between inside and outside, that mediates our interactions with the "world." Music is an irritating art form whose experiential effects on us are mediated by our social environment, which is not "the presence of a large number of people" but our own socialized or socially organized experiences. But are our artistic (and other) experiences "inside" us or "outside" us?

As Vygotsky's use of the Russian "across" word for experiences, *perezhivaniya,* literally "across-livings," suggests, his theory (like Bakhtin's, which also relies heavily on that word) seems to require that they be both: that art not be solely "the social in us" but the social outside of us as well, and indeed that art be the social as the experiential crossing itself. The social nature of the cathartic action of art, Vygotsky says later in that same paragraph, does not mean that "a feeling born in one person infects and contaminates everybody and becomes social," but rather that "the melting of feelings outside us is performed by the strength of social feeling, which is objectivized, materialized, and projected outside of us, then fixed in external objects of art which have become the tools of society" (*Psychology,* 249). Art, in other words, is the social that mediates between the inside and the outside, the irritating medium that refractively and directly channels the irritating outside (i.e., *itself*) into the inside and our actional or behavioral response from the inside back out into the outside. From the point of view of art and the sociality it mediates, therefore, there *is* no inside or outside, no container, no walls, and thus also no crossing—only mediation. Thus when, a few lines down in that same paragraph, he calls art "a social technology of feeling, society's instrument, by which it involves [*vovlekaet*] in the circle of social life the most intimate and most personal sides [*storony*] of our being" (*Psikhologiya,* 314, my translation), we should not take him to be saying that those "sides" of our being are first outside the circle and then, through art, dragged in (*vo* "in" + *vlekat'* "drag, draw"); rather, the involvement (*vovlekanie*) of our being's "sides" (*storony*) in the "circle of social life" is a precondition of our being, our social(ized) being. In some sense, the "circle" has "sides" because they are our sides. While Vygotsky does not write of estrangement in his dissertation, this passage could be taken as positing the Hegelian sublation of the "sidedness" (*storonnost*) of the local/familiar/inside/ native country (*strana*) and the outside/alien/strange (*strannost*). Art is a social technology for the involvement of the individual's feelings in the feelings of the group.

In his theories of empathy and estrangement, Brecht himself never achieved this level of dialectical complexity; the closest he came to dialecticizing empathy and estrangement was to suggest that they might uneasily coexist. As Koss writes:

> Brecht occasionally indicated a more nuanced relationship between empathy and estrangement: "In [the] new method of practicing art empathy would lose its dominant role . . . Against that the alienation effect will need to be introduced, which is an artistic effect too and also leads to a theatrical experience. This type of art *also* generates emotions; such performances facilitate the mastering of reality, and it is *this* that moves the spectator" . . . Empathy could be "a rehearsal measure" . . . During the performance, however, "two different methods are used: the technique of empathy and the technique of alienation [*die einfühlungstechnik und die verfremdungstechnik*]" . . . Each of these techniques addressed the distance between spectator and work of art. Whereas empathy, the 'feeling-in' to an object or performance, overcomes distance by means of emotional transport, estrangement maintains the audience's awareness of its distance from the artwork. But a consciousness of distance is impossible without the experience of its absence; estrangement relies on the intermittent experience of empathy. (A fully estranged spectator would get up and walk out during the performance.) If the estrangement effect entails an oscillation between distance and closeness, then empathy must play a role in Brecht's *Verfremdungseffekt*. (816–17)

What I am suggesting, though, is that the Hegelian synthesis of all three antithesis-based theories—Brecht's rather inchoate opposition of empathy and estrangement, Bakhtin's more detailed opposition of insideness and outsideness, and Vygotsky's complex exfoliation of Shklovsky's belabored form as the cathartic evocation of contradictory aesthetic response—is the notion that estrangement (Brecht) or outsideness (Bakhtin) or cathartic belabored form (Vygotsky) is *one antithetical movement* of empathy. If, in fact, the critical questioning or altering internalizations of empathy were at some point "forgotten" or split off from empathy for political reasons—to make aesthetic empathetic response a more powerful tool for the right-wing infection of pleasurably unthinking audiences—then the dialectical sublation of empathy would require that it *also* be estranged as moving through the self-undermining of otherness, the dealienation of alienation, the return of othered self for renewed scrutiny. Then it might become possible to argue that empathy only works if the empathetic consciousness retains a moment of self-consciousness, a mediating awareness of empathy going out and coming back, an estranging or alienating critical reevaluation of the alienated otherness that is coming to feel so familiar, so internal, so "own." At the simplest level, after all, the totalizing subsumption of self into other is not empathy; it is psychosis. Empathy requires both the pleasurable identificatory attachment of self to otherness and the critical or estranging detachment of self from otherness, both immersion in the other and an awareness of being different, being separate, being alienated or estranged from the other.

Brecht's Infection Theory

This expanded Hegelian/Brechtian model of the empathetic somatic exchange, then, posits two antithetical self-estrangements as essential components of collective self-regulation: the self-estrangement going out (the estrangement of self from itself in identification with the other) and the self-estrangement coming back in (the estrangement of self from the other in critical self-reflection on the nature and consequences of that identification). That ideosomatic self-regulation mostly works unconsciously, *without* this return self-estrangement of critical reflection, makes it clear that the model is specifically utopian, an idealized image of the "true" "full" form of collective regulatory empathy—precisely the form Brecht is attempting to (re)activate in his audiences through the dialectical interaction of comfort and discomfort, the familiar and the strange, the emotional and the intellectual, identification and disidentification, cigar-smoking and critical thinking. His audiences, for example, should be brought to the point of identifying empathetically with alienated antiheroes like Galy Gay in order that the estranging discomfort that this identification causes them might begin to separate them from one (capitalist) channel of ideosomatic regulation and help them reconstruct their personalities and belief systems and social and economic practices in and around and through another (Marxist).

What this empathy-estrangement dialectic means for a Brechtian literary and transliterary Marxism might be explored through the theories of two later Marxist literary theorists, Fredric Jameson and Raymond Williams. Jameson and Williams, despite their grounding in the same Marxist and structuralist/semiotic thinkers, may be taken to mark off the structuralist/depersonalized and somatic/repersonalized—or what some might want to thematize as the "tough-minded" and the "weak-minded," the rigorous and the limp, or the detached/intellectual and the liberal/sentimental—extremes of late-twentieth-century Marxist thought. What I want to argue is that Brecht moves dialectically throughout his life from something like the depersonalized former (plays "ought to be presented quite coldly, classically and objectively. For they are not matter for empathy; they are there to be understood. Feelings are private and limited. Against that the reason is fairly comprehensive and to be relied on") to something like the repersonalized latter, which I identify as Brecht's "infection theory" and theorize through Williams' social "structures of feeling."

The Depersonalization of Empathy

Look first, then, at how Jameson attempts to "neutralize" Brecht's empathy-estrangement binary by collapsing it into a more depersonalized binary between illusion and reality, absence and presence:

> In fact, I think that Brecht's positions [on empathy] are better read not as a refusal of identification but, rather, as the consequences to be drawn from the fact that such a thing never existed in the first place. In that case, "third-person acting," the quoting of a character's expressions of feeling and emotion, is the result of a radical absence of the self, or at least the coming to terms with a realization that what we call our "self" is itself an object for consciousness, not our consciousness itself: it is a foreign body within an impersonal consciousness, which we try to manipulate in such a way as to lend some warmth and personalization to the matter. (53–54)

The idea that the "outward" identificatory movement of empathy "never existed in the first place" because there is no coherent and autonomous rationalist self to will it would appear to be an expression of negative nostalgia, nostalgia without identificatory feeling, depersonalized nostalgia, a rejection of the central concept of pre-Hegelian liberal philosophy (the autonomy of the rationalist self) that remains negatively dependent on that concept. At the least the Hegelian history of the late-nineteenth-century and early-twentieth-century theorization of empathy as a *loss* or *surrender* of self to the other should preclude this sort of existential binarization of estrangement as existing and empathy as not existing: the traditional (Vischerian/Worringerian) conception of "first-person acting" is not the identification of one autonomous self (the "I") with another autonomous self (say, Martin Buber's "thou"), as Jameson seems to imply, but the externalization or alienation of the actor's "I" as the character's "I," the creation of an alien or othered self through the surrender of the own self. The audience too is inspired to surrender self to these imaginary characters on stage or on the page, letting not only self but *consciousness* of self flow outwards into identificatory objects. Jameson's insistence on the "realization that what we call our 'self' is itself an object for consciousness, not our consciousness itself" is thus doubly irrelevant to the theory, making empathetic identification dependent on both the autonomous self and consciousness, on precisely the two psychological entities that are definitively lost or surrendered in the outward movement of the original conception of empathy. Even in its most idealized form, in other words, the theory of empathy exceeds the scope of Jameson's rather puzzling beside-the-point remarks.

In fact Jameson's analysis here seems to point us back to the depersonalization of Tolstoy: "it is a foreign body within an impersonal consciousness, which we try to manipulate in such a way as to lend some warmth and personalization to the matter." An *impersonal* consciousness is not the *transpersonal* consciousness that I've been calling ideosomatic regulation or the proprioception of the body politic; it is the deadness that Tolstoy feels in relation to other people, which he too attempted to manipulate or "attune" in order to "lend some warmth" to the matter and thus give the impression of repersonalization. If the self is a *foreign* body within this deadness—not even, dialectically, an externalized projection of consciousness, which is itself an introjection of the other's regard, but *foreign* full stop—then alienation is all. There is no dialectic between the I and the you, the self and the other, the own and the alien, the familiar and the strange; there is only foreignness/estrangement/alienation in the midst of depersonalization.

You'll recall Vadim Rudnev suggesting that structuralism is born out of the formalist depersonalization of literary theory. While I argued that theoretical depersonalization is *not* at work in Shklovsky's "Art as Device," Rudnev's reading of the twentieth-century theoretical tradition emerging out of formalism is unquestionably germane to Jameson's Brecht book, which seems conceptually grounded in a depersonalized structuralist Marxism, in Marx read through the methodological transition from Vladimir Propp's formalist *Morphology of the Folk Tale* through Algirdas Julius Greimas's actantial structuralism to Jacques Derrida's 1966 deconstruction of Claude Levi-Strauss.

Structures of Feeling

This structuralist Marxism may well be useful for the early Brecht, who denied the value not only of empathy but of emotion and person altogether. It is less productive as a tool for understanding the Brecht of the 1940s, the Brecht of the Swedish speeches and especially the "Little Organon" of 1948: "For the smallest social unit is not the single person but two people. In life too we develop one another" (par. 58, Willett, *Brecht,* 197). This radically (inter)personalized conception of the social unit is far from the product of "a radical absence of the self," or the "realization" that the self is "a foreign body within an impersonal consciousness, which we try to manipulate in such a way as to lend some warmth and personalization to the matter." Late Brecht, as Juliet Koss and Hans Günther suggest, is closer to the dialogism of Bakhtin, who is also, as Craig Brandist argues, philosophically akin to Antonio Gramsci, whose thought, like Bakhtin's, comes out of a radicalization of Croce and Vossler.

It is this Gramscian tradition that Raymond Williams mines in his 1977 book *Marxism and Literature,* in setting up his conceptualization of "the socialized personal" as "structures of feeling." If the social and the personal are binarized, he notes, as they almost always are, typically the social gets studied and the personal gets ignored: "if the social is the fixed and explicit—the known relationships, institutions, formations, positions—all that is present and moving, all that escapes or seems to escape from the fixed and the explicit and the known, is grasped and defined as the personal: this, here, now, alive, active, 'subjective'" (128). This approach may even deny the very existence of the "personal" or "subjective" or "this, here, now, alive, active" realm, and so produce depersonalized theory like the (post)structuralist Marxism of Louis Althusser, Jameson, and Terry Eagleton. Whenever the phenomenological power of the personal is asserted, this hierarchy is typically flipped on its head and the personal is formalized in newly ascendant ways, including, Williams notes, the emerging eighteenth-and nineteenth-century disciplines of "aesthetics" and "psychology":

> At different moments in history, and in significantly different ways, the reality and even the primacy of such presences and such processes, such diverse and yet specific actualities, have been powerfully asserted and reclaimed, as in practice of course they are all the time lived. But they are then often asserted as forms themselves, in contention with other known forms: the subjective as distinct from the objective; experience from belief; feeling from thought; the immediate from the general; the personal from the social. The undeniable power of two great modern ideological systems—the "aesthetic" and the "psychological"—is, ironically, systematically derived from these senses of instance and process, where experience, immediate feeling, and then subjectivity and personality are newly generalized and assembled. Against these "personal" forms, the ideological systems of fixed social generality, of categorical products, of absolute formations, are relatively powerless, within their specific dimension. (129)

"Yet," Williams argues, "it is the reduction of the social to fixed forms that remains the basic error. Marx often said this, and some Marxists quote him, in fixed ways, before returning to fixed forms. The mistake, as so often, is in taking terms of analysis as terms of substance" (129). It is the binary that misleads: social versus personal, fixed versus fluid, objective versus subjective, sociological versus psychological, scientific versus aesthetic, rational versus emotional, and so on.

To combat the binarization of social experience into these radically different realms, then, Williams develops the concept of structures of feeling. Noting that there are important social changes that are neither reductively institutional nor formal but that "do not have to await definition, classification, or rationalization before they exert palpable pressures and set effective limits on experience and on action" (132), he writes:

> Such changes can be defined as changes in *structures of feeling*. The term is difficult, but "feeling" is chosen to emphasize a distinction from more formal concepts of "world-view" or "ideology." It is not only that we must go beyond formally held and systematic beliefs, though of course we have always to include them. It is that we are concerned with meanings and values as they are actively lived and felt, and the relations between these and formal or systematic beliefs are in practice variable (including historically variable), over a range from formal assent with private dissent to the more nuanced interaction between selected and interpreted beliefs and acted and justified experiences. (132)

We are concerned here, clearly, with somatics, though Williams does not know the term:

> We are talking about characteristic elements of impulse, restraint, and tone; specifically affective elements of consciousness and relationships: not feeling against thought, but thought as felt and feeling as thought: practical consciousness of a present kind, in a living and interrelating continuity. We are then defining these elements as a "structure": as a set, with specific internal relations, at once interlocking and in tension. Yet we are also defining a social experience which is still in process, often indeed not yet recognized as social but taken to be private, idiosyncratic, and even isolating, but which in analysis (though rarely otherwise) has its emergent, connecting, and dominant characteristics, indeed its specific hierarchies. These are often more recognizable at a later stage, when they have been (as often happens) formalized, classified, and in many cases built into institutions and formations. By that time the case is different; a new structure of feeling will usually already have begun to form, in the true social present. (132)

What Williams lacks here—what his gropings toward a somatic theory fail to give him—is a channel of transmission that could account for both structure and change. He says that the structures of feeling are "interlocking and in tension" and constitute a social experience with "its emergent, connecting, and dominant characteristics," but he has no idea how the structures might interlock or connect, how the tensions and pressures might emerge out of and be disseminated through social interaction. Since his theory of the structures of feeling is born out of Gramscian hegemony theory, he has the regulatory effects of social feeling, but he lacks both the *storage* of those effects in bodies (of learned somatic markers in individual limbic systems) and the *altering* of those effects as they pass through individual bodies. This means that he cannot account for either the stability or the changing reactivity of his structures of feeling; they are more or less stable (therefore a "structure," a "set, with specific internal relations"), and they are also emergent, responding to and precipitating social change, but he cannot explain how they emerge or what they emerge out of, how they adjust to and disseminate social change, how they infect the hegemonic feelings they transmit with destabilizing and resistant (counterhegemonic) impulses. This lack has an impoverishing effect on Williams's application of the structures of feeling to literature as well:

> The hypothesis has a special relevance to art and literature, where the true social content is in a significant number of cases of this present and affective kind, which cannot without loss be reduced to belief-systems, institutions, or explicit general relationships, though it may include all these as lived and experienced, with or without tension, as it also evidently includes elements of social and material physical or natural) experience which may lie beyond, or be uncovered or imperfectly covered by, the elsewhere recognizable systematic elements. The unmistakable presence of certain elements in art which are not covered by (though in one mode they may be reduced to) other formal systems is the true source of the specializing categories of "the aesthetic," "the arts," and "imaginative literature." We need, on the one hand, to acknowledge (and welcome) the specificity of these elements—specific feelings, specific rhythms—and yet to find ways of recognizing their specific kinds of sociality, thus preventing that extraction from social experience which is conceivable only when social experience itself has been categorically (and at root historically) reduced. (133)

Yes, we do need to acknowledge and welcome specific feelings and rhythms in literature, while also recognizing their sociality; but what? How?

In the 1940 "Kurze Beschreibung einer neuen Technik der Schauspielkunst, die einen Verfremdungseffekt hervorbringt" (Short description of a new technique of acting which produces an estrangement effect), in fact, Brecht has some suggestions, which begin to point us toward his infection theory:

> It is less easy to explain the effect that such poems have on ourselves, as Marx already noticed. Apparently emotions accompanying social progress will long survive in the human mind as emotions linked with interests, and in the case of works of art will do so more strongly than might have been expected, given that in the meantime contrary interests will have made themselves felt. Every step forward means the end of the previous step forward, because that is where it starts and goes on from. At the same time it makes use of this previous step, which in a sense survives in men's consciousness as a step forward, just as it survives in its effects in real life. This involves a most interesting type of generalization, a continual process of abstraction. Whenever the works of art handed down to us allow us to share the emotions of other men, of men of a bygone period, different social classes, etc., we have to conclude that we are partaking in interests which really were universally human. (146)

This is Brecht's clearest statement of the somatics of literature—a passage specifically about the storage and participatory transmission of somatic "structures of feeling" in and through literary classics:

1. "emotions accompanying social progress" are linked with "interests," or what Tolstoy might call values, and I have been calling social regulation or guidance;

2. these interest-linked emotions are stored in us (Brecht's original phrase behind Willett's "in the human mind" is *in den Menschen* "in the human") as emotional, or perhaps collective-proprioceptive, memories of the "step forward" (*Fortschritt,* lit. "forth-step," meaning advance(ment), improvement, stride [as in "great strides"], and, noncountably, progress), even for a long time (*lange Zeit,* in fact, often centuries, sometimes millennia) after the original material step forward has started getting clobbered (*erledigt* "finished off, dispatched, taken care of, dealt with, walloped") by the next step forward;

3. these emotions or ideosomatic markers stored in "consciousness" (*Bewußtsein*) continue to have material effects "in real/concrete/material/actual life" (*im realen Leben*), again for centuries or even millennia, even as they are being pounded, jabbed, kicked, punched, etc. onto contrary interests (*auf Gegeninteressen gestoßen sind*)—more collective proprioceptive memories;

4. when these interest-linked emotions (regulatory ideosomatic markers) are stored in a work of art, their participatory or infectious impact on later generations is surprisingly strong, and cause later readers or viewers to *take part* (*teilnehmen*) in interests of a different era or different social class, which cannot possibly be universal ("The emotions always have a quite definite class basis," Brecht tells us on the previous page; "the form they take at any time is historical, restricted and limited in specific ways. The emotions are in no sense universally human and timeless," 145), but seem to us as if they *must* have been, back then ("so müßen wir annehmen, dass wir hierbei an Interessen *teilnehmen, die tatsächlich allgemein menschlich waren*": "we have to conclude that we *are* partaking in interests which really *were* universally human" [emphasis added]);[15]

5. "This involves a most interesting type of generalization, a continual process of abstraction" ("Es findet da eine Verallgemeinerung interessantester Art statt, ein laufender Prozeß der Abstraktion"). ("Kurze," 658–59)

In other words, (1) progress-related ideosomatic markers learned in one regulatory context (2) survive (*fortleben*) the death of that context into the next, and the next, and so on, despite every effort made by the regulators in the next context(s) to demolish the old ideosomatic markers, and (3) continue to shape collective life in material ways, often for centuries. So far this is simply a social somatic. But Brecht is responding specifically to Marx's wrestling in "Introduction to the Critique of Political Economy" and *The German Ideology* with the surprising power of literary works from a long-ago period to infect us with their values, their "interests," despite the utter immateriality of those interests to us today. "The difficulty we are confronted with," Marx writes in the "Introduction," "is not that of understanding how Greek art and epic poetry are associated with certain forms of social development," so that, for example, you can't have the myth of Achilles in an era of powder and lead, or the *Iliad* in an era with a printing press. "The greater difficulty is that they still give us aesthetic pleasure and are in certain respects regarded as a standard and unattainable ideal" (150). Material conditions determine consciousness:

In direct contrast to German philosophy which descends from heaven to earth, here we ascend from earth to heaven. That is to say, we do not set out from what men say, imagine, conceive, nor from men as narrated, thought of, imagined, conceived, in order to arrive at men in the flesh. We set out from real, active men, and on the basis of their real life-process we demonstrate the development of the ideological reflexes and echoes of this life-process. The phantoms formed in the human brain are also, necessarily, sublimates of their material life-process, which is empirically verifiable and bound to material premises. Morality, religion, metaphysics, all the rest of ideology and their corresponding forms of consciousness, thus no longer retain the semblance of independence. They have no history, no development; but men, developing their material production and their material intercourse, alter, along with this their real existence, their thinking and the products of their thinking. Life is not determined by consciousness, but consciousness by life. (*German,* 47)

The "phantoms formed in the human brain" that are necessarily "sublimates of their material life-process" include not just morality, religion, metaphysics, all the rest of ideology, clearly, but literature as well: "men as narrated." But if this is the case, how is it possible for the *Iliad* to infect us with its values, its interests, its interest-linked emotions, across the gulf of three millennia and countless intervening "forms of social development"? It seems that these phantoms have more power over us than the materialist model can explain. Marx's answer is that these stories represent the "childhood of man," and we all love reliving our childhoods—a flimsy guess that is basically a way of saying, "I have no idea what's going on here."[16]

Brecht's answer is cleverer: he suggests that no form of ideosomatic regulation that once brought about a true step forward in human evolution, no transitional "moment" in a Hegelian dialectic, is ever lost. It merely goes underground, into deep layers of our collective emotional/proprioceptive memory, and can be reactivated by the somatics of literature even millennia later, so that (4) through literature we participate in a channel of regulatory somatic pressure that is utterly irrelevant to our current material interests but *feels* pressing. His insistence on associating this process with (5) generalization and abstraction seems odd, unless we take him to be signaling with these terms the somatokinesthetic *spread* of emotions from one context to many: "abstraction" (*Abstraktion*) in the root sense of pulling the emotions away from their original context and into another; "generalization" or "commonalization" (*Verallgemeinerung*) in the sense of generalizing the common or communal contexts in which the regulatory ideosomatic pressures are felt, thus making us assume (*annehmen*) that those pressures were once truly "universally/generally/commonly human" (*allgemein menschlich*).

What for Brecht may in fact be *allgemein menschlich* is this hunger for progress, this instinct for the transitional moments in the dialectic, this shared kinesthetic memory of collective steps forward—this tendency, if I may generalize, to store in our collective regulatory knowing and deciding (our ideosomatics) the most important events in the long history of our learning. We store these events not as inert historical facts—what Shklovsky would call Thing 4—but as feelings, as proprioceptive "muscle memories," as a dim sense of what it felt like collectively to take that step, to turn that corner, to leap that gap, to break those shackles, and so on. Our retention of a somatized memory of each collective problem being solved, our storage of an ideosomatic marker that has guided us through such problematic situations before and will do so again, gives us collective confidence in the face of new obstacles, new oppressions, new naturalized "universal human conditions"—gives us an inkling that there *is* a way out.

There are, of course, more purely intellectual ways of retaining that information, notably the various texts of political, social, and literary history, or of structuralist sociology, psychology, or literary criticism, as a depersonalized Thing 4. The model we've found now in Shklovsky and Brecht would seem to suggest, however, that without collectivized somatic response to those textual records, their reader is left, like Tolstoy, gasping for meaning: "At first I experienced moments of perplexity and arrest of life, and though I did not know what to do or how to live; and I felt lost and became dejected. But this passed and I went on living as before."

Infectious Living Together

We might, then, sum up Brecht's somatics of literature by paraphrasing Jameson: for Brecht "third-person acting" is the demonstration of the radical collectivization of the self, or at least an interactive or interexpressive display of the coming to terms with a realization that what we call our "self" is constructed out of the flow of shared feelings through us, our feelings about others, theirs about us. These feelings police the boundaries between self and other, own and alien—condition us to construct the self as living inside our own skin, for example, other selves as living inside alien skins—but because the regulatory feelings that condition this construction are not so bound, because they are collectively disseminated through or across those boundaries, they implicitly define individuality as a slice cut out of collectivity, the self as a provisionally "own" but potentially alienable body within a transpersonal consciousness (the proprioception of the body politic). The estrangement effect in the form of third-person acting stages both the groundedness of the self in community (in *Zusammenleben* or "living together") and the communalization of each individual self: by "reporting on" the first-person voice or stance, by almost-but-not-quite occupying that voice or *Gestus,* it dramatizes the becoming-other of the self and the becoming-self of the other. Because it is thus inserted into the mediatory seam between dialectical extremes, the overlap or offset through or by which each is repeatedly and shiftingly converted into the other, the estrangement effect is the ideal (utopian) dramatic device for the altering or "refunctioning" (*Umfunktionisierung*) of both the self's empathetic identifications with the other and (self-)critical estrangements from the other.

In the early decades of his career, as we've seen, still binaristically depersonalizing his theater as pure ratiocination, Brecht uses Tolstoy's term *infection* negatively, as one of the "culinary" effects of empathetic theater; in the early fifties, after at long last getting his own theater in the GDR, in the *Katzgraben* notes of 1953, we find him describing this redirection of audiences' empathetic-cum-estranged identifications in terms so congruent with Tolstoyan infection that John Willett gravitates to the term in rendering him into English: "So müssen wir auch das Stück aufführen, wir müssen einem proletarischen Publikum Lust machen, die Welt zu verändern (und ihm einiges, dafür nötiges, Wissen vermitteln" ("*Katzgraben,*" 424)—"We must infect a working-class audience with the urge to alter the world (and supply it with some of the relevant knowledge)" ("Notes," 247). First infect them with the *desire* (*Lust*) to change the world; only then, once the emotional inclination to act is in place, provide them with some intellectual content as well.

Clearly, his accommodation of a near-Tolstoyan rhetoric of infection does not mean that he has gone over to the other side, the purely externalizing "pleasurable identification" side of empathy. He is simply now recognizing that the strategies of the epic theater themselves channel or constitute a form of emotional infection, a somatic transfer. We would not need to push very hard on this formulation—"infect a working-class audience with the urge to alter the world"—to make the claim that Brecht himself ultimately understood the dialectical interaction of pleasurable identification and uncomfortable estrangement in empathy. The desire to alter the world is specifically a dialectical desire (a) to recognize (through identificatory empathy) one's membership and unconscious emotional and intellectual investment in that world, one's circulatory ideosomatic regulation by and of that world, and therefore the familiarity and "ownness" of that world, and (b) to feel (through estranging empathy) the discomfort of alienation from that world, the strangeness or alienness of that world from one's own best interests, and yet at the same time the anxiety caused by any thought of separating oneself from it, precipitating (c) the discovery of another (Marxist) channel of ideosomatic regulation, which offers models for the *Umfunktionierung* of the world from a (de)alienated standpoint, a standpoint incorporating both the belonging of (a) and the alienation of (b).

Brecht begins to grope his way toward this sort of formulation fairly early. In 1927 he talks about the radical transformation of the theater, which "can't be the result of some artistic whim" but must "correspond to the whole transformation of the mentality of our time," so that "theatre, art and literature . . . have to form the 'ideological superstructure' for a solid, practical rearrangement of our age's way of life," which would entail "the operation of really new mental influences on our culture's aged body" (Willett, *Brecht*, 23). What he wants to change is first a "mentality," then a "way of life," and finally an "aged body," which suggests that it is neither mind nor body but the body-becoming-mind of an entire population, the way everybody lives in their bodies-becoming-minds. The Marxist vocabulary of "ideological superstructure," in scare quotes, reflects Brecht's recently commenced study of Marx and resulting emerging awareness that as a theater director he does not have access to the economic base and so in then-established Marxist terms must be content piddling around with the superstructural illusions or superstitions of ideology and other "ideas." Note, though, that he functionalizes "ideological superstructure" in that sentence as if he were writing of the economic base or some other foundation or springboard: "theatre, art and literature . . . have to form the 'ideological superstructure' for a solid, practical rearrangement of our age's way of life."

He writes this a year or so before he meets Karl Korsch, two years before he (probably) begins attending Korsch's lectures at the Marxistische Arbeiterschule, four or five years before the period of Korsch's greatest influence over his thought. But this apparent rethinking of ideology in relation to superstructure and base is deeply congruent with Korsch's radical rereading of Marx in *Marxismus und Philosophie* (published in 1923, but not available to Brecht until after this writing), and generally with the so-called "Western Marxism" being forged in this period by Georg Lukács in *History and Class Consciousness* and, a few years later, Antonio Gramsci in his prison notebooks.[17] As Steve Giles puts it, Korsch there reads the *Theses on Feuerbach*, *The German Ideology*, and *The Eighteenth Brumaire* so as to conclude that "Marx and Engels *always* construed ideology as a real material component of social and historical life, rather than as a mere epiphenomenonon " (89). Further confirmation for this reading comes with the 1932 publication of *The Economic and Philosophical Manuscripts of 1844*. For Korsch in 1923, the Second International "historical materialism" of Georgy Valentinovich Plekhanov and Karl Kautsky which relegated ideology to the realm of mere fantasy—and which formed the intellectual foundation for Lenin and Stalin and their ideologues, including the later socialist-realist Lukács—was a radical distortion of Marx's thought. Brecht in 1927 knows none of this, but he senses that art—for him, drama—*must* have a real transformative effect on how people live, what they do, what they feel, what they think, so he fudges the theoretical issue with carefully evasive quotation marks and a suggestive but plausibly deniable sentence structure.

He is considerably clearer around 1940, in Stockholm, where his plays are being performed by amateur workers' theaters. In a talk entitled "Is It Worth Speaking About the Amateur Theatre?" he speaks about how caught up he was emotionally in George Stevens's 1939 movie *Gunga Din*—how even though he knew it was an imperialist piece of propaganda for the British, it was professionally so well made that he couldn't help himself: "I felt like applauding, and laughed in all the right places" (151). Then he comments, in a vein once again strikingly reminiscent of Tolstoy on the power of immoral art to pervert its audience:

> Obviously artistic appreciation of this sort is not without effects. It weakens the good instincts and strengthens the bad, it contradicts true experience and spreads misconceptions, in short it perverts [*verfälscht*] our picture of the world. There is no play and no theatrical performance which does not in some way or another affect the dispositions and conceptions [*Vorstellungen und Gemütsbewegungen*] of the audience. Art is never without consequences, and indeed that says something for it.
>
> A good deal of attention has been paid to the theatre's—even the supposedly unpolitical theatre's—political influence: its effect on the formation of political judgments, on political moods and emotions [*die gefühlsmäßigen politischen Stimmungen*]. Neither the socialist thinker nor the parson in his pulpit would deny that our morals are affected by it. It matters how love, marriage, work and death are treated on the stage, what kind of ideals are set up and propagated for lovers, for men struggling for their existence and so on. In this exceedingly serious sphere the stage is virtually functioning as a fashion show, parading not only the latest dresses but the latest ways of behaving: not only what is being worn but what is being done. ("Lohnt," 592; "Is," 151)

That last is a bad analogy, of course, a trivializing analogy, because the theater (like any artistic or other social encounter) does not merely *parade* what is being done but puts somatic pressure on the audience to internalize it or otherwise learn from it. Brecht is talking specifically about the mimetic somatic transfer this time and even more explicitly than in 1927 about the transformative impact drama has through that transfer on the audience's hegemonic structure of feeling, the behavioral structure of "dispositions and conceptions of the audience" that includes not merely morals and "political moods and emotions" but "instincts" as well, inclinations not just to do this or that but to feel this or that way about a wide range of actions, from the trivial to the really big things like "love, marriage, work and death."

He goes on, even more explicitly:

> So political, moral and aesthetic education influences all radiate from the theatre: good when it is good, bad when it is bad.
>
> One easily forgets that human education proceeds along highly theatrical lines. In a quite theatrical manner the child is taught how to behave; logical arguments only come later. When such-and-such occurs, it is told (or sees), one must laugh [*man muß lachen*]. It joins in when there is laughter [*Es lacht mit, wenn gelacht wird*], without knowing why; if asked why it is laughing it is wholly confused. In the same way it joins in shedding tears, not only weeping because the grown-ups do so but also feeling genuine sorrow. This can be seen at funerals, whose meaning escapes children entirely. These are theatrical events which form the character. The human being copies gestures, miming, tones of voice. And weeping arises from sorrow, but sorrow also arises from weeping.
>
> It is no different with grown-ups. Their education never finishes. Only the dead are beyond being altered by their fellow-men. Think this over, and you will realize how important the theatre is for the forming of character. You will see what it means that thousands should act to hundreds of thousands. One can't just shrug off so many people's concern with art. ("Lohnt," 593; "Is," 152)

This is a brilliant description of what Raymond Williams calls hegemonic "structures of feeling," specifically childhood socialization to those structures, again through somatic mimeticism, the empathetic mimicry of laughter or tears, which teaches the child not only genuine amusement and sorrow but the dispositional structures of laughter and tears in her society, what people consider funny and what they consider sad, when is an appropriate time to laugh and when to cry. Brecht takes the idea from William James, apparently through the mediation of Sergey Eisenstein—the same passage from the *Principles of Psychology* that we saw Broder Christiansen invoking in chapter 3, where "we feel sorry because we cry, angry because we strike, afraid because we tremble, and not that we cry, strike, or tremble, because we are sorry, angry, or fearful, as the case may be." As we saw in that first Shklovsky chapter, James's formulation is focused on the response of the individual to feeling displayed as body language. What Williams does with the idea is more radically collectivistic, sociologistic: the sharing of felt representations of emotions enables us to organize our social lives collectively, at a very minute level of moment-to-moment interreceptivity. What Brecht is doing with the idea is more radical still: setting bodies in motion gestically in order to instigate in audience members a change first in emotion, then feeling, then thought. (More on the transformative power of the *Gestus* later.)

Eight years later in the "Kleines Organon," written outside Zurich in 1948, Brecht begins to tie these threads together:

> But this makes it simpler for the theatre to edge as close as possible to the apparatus of education and mass communication. For although we cannot bother it with the raw material of knowledge in all its variety, which would stop it from being enjoyable [*vergnüglich*], it is still free to find enjoyment [*sich . . . vergnügen*] in teaching and inquiring. It constructs its workable representations of society, which are then in a position to influence society, wholly and entirely as a game: for those who are constructing society it sets out society's experiences, past and present alike, in such a manner that the audience can "enjoy" the sensations, insights and impulses [*daß die Empfindungen, Einsichten und Impulse "genossen" werden können*] which are distilled by the wisest, most active and most passionate among us from the events of the day or the century. They must be entertained with the wisdom that comes from the solution of problems, with the anger that is a practical expression of sympathy [*Mitleid*] with the underdog, with the respect due to those who respect humanity, or rather whatever is kind to humanity; in short, with whatever delights those who are producing something. (par. 24; "Short," 186, translation modified slightly in accordance with "Kleines," 74–75)

The theater approaches education in its construction of "workable representations of society" that are presented so as "to influence society, wholly and entirely as a game." I'm not entirely happy with the weakness of Brecht's verbs for "enjoy" (both *sich vergnügen,* which also means "to take pleasure or delight in, to have fun with," and *genießen,* which also means "to relish" or "to savor," suggesting what Brecht would earlier have derided as a "culinary" experience) for the somatic transfer of "the sensations, insights and impulses which are distilled by the wisest, most active and most passionate among us." But that somatic transfer is patently what Brecht is writing about: not just *entertained* "with the wisdom that comes from the solution of problems, with the anger that is a practical expression of sympathy with the underdog, with the respect due to those who respect humanity," but *entertainingly infected* with that wisdom, that anger, and that respect. The "Kleines Organon" is the most concentrated of his theoretical writings, but it is also the calmest, the least given to baiting hyperbole, and is therefore in many ways the least explicit. That he is still talking about the use of emotional infection or somatic transfer in the transformation of the audience's structures of feeling is made clear a few paragraphs later, in paragraph 35: "We need a type of theatre which not only facilitates the sensations, insights and impulses possible within the particular field of human relations in which the action takes place, but employs and encourages those thoughts and feelings which help transform the field itself" ("Short," 190; translation modified in accordance with "Kleines," 79).

In paragraph 45, we get Brecht's most telling anticipation of Wittgenstein's *Lebensform* or "life form"—a concept that Wittgenstein has been fashioning around the same time, across the channel in Cambridge, and that will not be published until after his death in 1952: "Dies gilt auch für die Gefühle, Meinungen und Haltungen der Menschen, in denen die jeweilige Art ihres gesellschaftlichen Zusammenlebens sich ausdrückt" (82)—"This also goes for those human feelings, opinions and attitudes through which at any time the form of men's life together finds its expression" (193). The semantic parallel between Brecht's "form of men's life together" and Wittgenstein's "life form" is partly John Willett's doing, obviously—Brecht has "die jeweilige *Art* ihres gesellschaftlichen Zusammenlebens," the particular type or kind or form of their social life together. But Brecht is clearly writing about the same general conception of life as Wittgenstein, who writes in the *Investigations,* for example, that "It is easy to imagine a language consisting only of orders and reports in battle . . . And to imagine a language means to imagine a life-form [*Lebensform*]" (#19); "Here the term 'language-game' is meant to bring into prominence the fact that the speaking of a language is part of an activity, or of a life-form [*Lebensform*]" (#23); and "'So are you saying that human agreement decides what is true and what is false?'—It is what human beings say that is true and false; and they agree in the language they use. That is not agreement in opinions but in form of life [*Form des Lebens*]" (#241). Or, in *On Certainty:*

"One might say: ' "I know" expresses comfortable certainty, not the certainty that is still struggling.' Now I would like to regard this certainty, not as something akin to hastiness or superficiality, but as a form of life [*Lebensform*]" (#357–58). In other words, the life form consists of such contextualized practices as teaching a child to laugh or cry through theatrical modeling: "It joins in when there is laughter, without knowing why; if asked why it is laughing it is wholly confused . . . In a quite theatrical manner the child is taught how to behave"; "logical arguments only come later." But it also consists of all the million variations on those practices, such as laughing sarcastically, laughing with relief, laughing through tears, and so on, in specific social situations. It is those variations insofar as they are repeatedly recognizable or recognizably repeated. The life form is not only the occasion and the action, in other words, it is the iterative pattern of occasionality and actionality that gives form to life—that is constantly forming the life that is being lived here and now.

Those human feelings, opinions, and attitudes through which the *Lebensform* finds its expression are what Heidegger calls *das Man,* which seems so utterly and comprehensively natural and fixed that "one" thinks it must be the human condition.[18] "For it seems impossible to alter what has long not been altered. We are always coming on things that are too obvious for us to bother to understand them. What men experience among themselves they think of as 'the' human experience" (par. 44, 192). They are also Williams's structures of feeling, grounded in Gramsci's notion of hegemony, which thematizes "relations of domination and subordination, in their forms as practical consciousness, as in effect a saturation of the whole process of living . . . the whole substance of lived identities and relationships" (Williams, 110); like "die jeweilige Art [unsres] gesellschaftlichen Zusammenlebens," hegemony "is a whole body of practices and expectations, over the whole of living: our senses and assignments of energy, our shaping perceptions of ourselves and our world. It is a lived system of meanings and values—constitutive and constituting—which as they are experienced as practices appear as reciprocally confirming. It thus constitutes a sense of reality for most people in the society, a sense of absolute because experienced reality beyond which it is very difficult for most members of the society to move, in most areas of their lives" (110). And again: "A lived hegemony is always a process. It is not, except analytically, a system or a structure. It is a realized complex of experiences, relationships, and activities, with specific and changing pressures and limits. In practice, that is, hegemony can never be singular. Its internal structures are highly complex, as can readily be seen in any concrete analysis. Moreover (and this is crucial, reminding us of the necessary thrust of the concept), it does not just passively exist as a form of dominance. It has continually to be renewed, recreated, defended, and modified. It is also continually resisted, limited, altered, challenged by pressures not at all its own" (112).

But then these feelings are distilled into art, into literature, into drama, put into a form that can be presented to an audience, and the millions of tiny somatic transfers by which "what one does" or a *Lebensform* or a hegemonic "structure of feeling" is constructed and regulated and maintained become more easily malleable, organizable into what Brecht calls a "game" that can be used for various transformative purposes, to make the "form of men's life" visible, historical, temporary, to historicize it and so show that it was created through change and can theoretically be uncreated through change as well; or to instill new forms, new dispositions, new behavioral structures in audiences, to begin to bring about the imagined change. "For the smallest social unit," to quote again the passage from the "Kleines Organon" with which I began this section, "is not the single person but two people. In life too we develop one another" (197).

Gestic Transformation

As we saw in chapters 1 and 3, Lev Tolstoy and Viktor Shklovsky both worried about the robotizing impact of rhythmic music—specifically, in patriotic marches and religious hymns—on the body, and through the body on the feelings, and through the feelings on morality (Tolstoy) or perception (Shklovsky). This was a pressing issue for the psychologists of art around the turn of the century: to what extent is art designed to take control of the body? To what extent is it capable of doing so, and to what extent is that capacity desirable?

These were questions that Tolstoy and Shklovsky were unable to answer— perhaps, as Jurij Striedter argues of Shklovsky, because they were not involved in the theater, were not concerned with the impact of the playwright's and the director's words on the actors' bodies, and of the actors' bodies on the audience. Bertolt Brecht, of course, was, and his theory of *Gestus*, of the gestic or kines(thet)ic transformation of the actor and the audience, is our topic in this concluding section.

Specifically, the question Brecht raises regards the extent to which the body can be transformed gestically into a vehicle of antithesis, of antithetical estrangement. Tolstoy and Shklovsky seemed to sense the importance of bodily transformation while also mistrusting the body's capacity for robotization, for what Ivan Pavlov in 1906 called reflex conditioning. It since has been studied under a variety of terms—J. B. Watson's classical conditioning (late teens), B. F. Skinner's respondent, operant, and instrumental conditioning (late 1930s), Donald O. Hebb's afferent conditioning (mid-1940s). Brecht was fascinated by behaviorism in the early 1930s (see Giles, 71–76), largely because he was interested in the transformation of bodies, the bodies of his actors and audience members. As we've seen, though, he distinguished sharply between the mindless behaviorism that made people do things unconsciously, a behaviorism he associated with empathy and the Aristotelian theater, and the kind of mindful transformation of bodies through estrangement and antithesis that he sought. As he writes in Santa Monica in 1944: "Hollywood's and Broadway's methods of manufacturing certain excitements and emotions may possibly be artistic, but their only use is to offset the fearful boredom induced in any audience by the endless repetition of falsehoods and stupidities. This technique was developed and is used in order to stimulate interest in things and ideas that are not in the interest of the audience" (Willett, *Brecht,* 160).[19] This is precisely the kind of manipulative conditioning of bodies that Tolstoy and Shklovsky deplored in patriotic marches and religious hymns. But Brecht, unlike Tolstoy and Shklovsky, spends his adult life trying to find kinesthetic strategies to teach his actors that will have the desired effect on audiences. He is professionally driven to think about the manipulative effects of bodies on other bodies. He cannot simply dismiss bodily manipulations as perverse or evil, as Tolstoy did; he cannot set the question aside for a book that will never get written, as Shklovsky did. He needs to find a channel of complex antithetical bodily manipulation that awakens passionate critical thinking and so preserves and affirms human dignity.

This for him was the *Gestus,* defined here in the "Kleines Organon":

> The realm of attitudes [*Haltungen,* also "stances, poses, approaches, postures," lit. "haltings," as in the stopping or suspending or interrupting of smooth motion] adopted by the characters towards one another is what we call the realm of gest [*den gestischen Bereich*]. Physical attitude [*Körperhaltung,* lit. "bodily stance/pose/posture"], tone of voice and facial expression, are all determined by a social gest [*von einem gesellschaftlichen 'Gestus' bestimmt*]: the characters are cursing, flattering, instructing one another, and so on. The attitudes which people adopt towards one another include even those attitudes which would appear to be quite private, such as the utterances [*Äußerungen*] of physical pain in an illness, or of religious faith. These

expressions [*Äußerungen*] of a gest are usually highly complicated and contradictory [*meist recht kompliziert und widerspruchsvoll*], so that they cannot
be rendered by any single word and the actor must take care that in giving
his image the necessary emphasis he does not lose anything, but emphasizes
the entire complex. (par. 61; "Kleines," 89; "Short," 198)

What Brecht gives us here is the outward movement of the somatic exchange: people feel something on the inside and "out" it, display or utter or
express it outwardly (*äußern*), in the form of socially conditioned body language or the *Gestus*. The inward movement of the somatic exchange, whereby
through somatic mimeticism we internalize other people's body language as
feeling or sensation, Brecht does not analyze here, but we have seen that, at
least by the 1940s, he believed that inward feelings and sensations were also
socially conditioned. In my terms, he took the entire circulatory economy of
the somatic exchange to be a social phenomenon.

What he adds to the theory of the somatic exchange is the notion that the
outward movement of gestic expression is *mostly very contradictory,* "meist recht kompliziert und widerspruchsvoll": when people express their inner sensations and feelings on the outside of their bodies, he insists, they most often
express them antithetically, through, say, expressions of pain *and* pleasure, or
pain mixed with a slight undertone of pleasure. It is very important, therefore,
that actors reproducing those *Gestes* on stage emphasize "the entire complex,"
the pain and the pleasure, the antithetical movements of muscles and their antagonists. Brecht implies here that this is imperative for realistic purposes, but
realism is typically a rhetorical screen for him, semantic camouflage for more
complicated designs—in this case, the fact that he is most interested in the
antithetical effects of the inward movement of the theatrical somatic exchange,
the impact of gestic acting on the audience. Specifically, Brecht believes that
the audience must be offered up antithetical *Haltungen*—actorial body language as the "halting" or interrupting of smooth movement—in order to complicate and thwart and redirect into critical thinking their mimetic response to
what they watch the actors do, to turn the "gestic realm" on stage into a kind
of antithetical Trojan Horse that will be taken into their hegemonized feelings
and sensations and there wreak heuristic havoc.

The Dedialecticizing of Brecht

The desired result of this havoc, as we've seen, is that spectators begin to
(re)think their status in capitalism, their unthinking (doubly bound, anesthe-

tized, armor-plated) complicity with an economic system and a culture that alienates and exploits them. Brecht typically describes this end result as the transformation of spectators from the passive recipients of external stimuli into *producers,* coproducers with him of the epic or dialectical theater, coproducers of the transformative effects of estrangement and the *Gestus.* After all, in my terms, the somatic exchange is produced by every member of the group circulating feelings through it. Even the behaviorist somatic exchange requires that the desubjectified test "subject" produce the external signals of successful conditioning, and Brecht is looking to transform the somatic exchange in his theater into something much more reciprocal and egalitarian and liberating than this.

When we read in the 1930 notes to *Der Flug der Lindberghs* ("An Example of Paedagogics"), for example, that "the increasing concentration of mechanical means and the increasing specialization of training . . . call for a kind of *resistance [Aufstand]* by the listener, and for his mobilization and reengagement as a producer [*Produzent*]" ("Example," 32; "Zu," 88), it's important to remember that "resistance" or *Aufstand* (uprising, lit. up-standing) implies antithetical impulses: both a willingness and an unwillingness to go along, both a desire for conformity and a rejection of conformity. It is, in fact, this kinesthetic tension between opposites that for Brecht channeled the freedom that arises out of critical thinking: in the Baden-Baden music festival of 1929, for example, the actor playing the Flier "read the sections to be spoken without identifying his own feelings with those contained in the text, pausing at the end of each line; in other words, in the spirit of an *exercise . . .* This exercise is an aid to discipline, which is the basis of freedom" (32). And he adds, two decades later, in the "Couragemodell" of 1949: "Freedom comes with the principle of contradiction, which is continually active and vocal in us all" (218).

But "continually" there may be a bit utopian: it turns out that it is extremely difficult, not only for Brecht's critics but for Brecht himself, to keep channeling that "active and vocal" principle in word and deed, to avoid letting his antitheses collapse into simple monadic essences. If in the *Umbau* of radio technology that the Brecht of the early 1930s imagines (and models dramatically), the radio listener is to be mobilized and reengaged as a *producer,* for example, it is all too tempting to think of a producer as one thing, as a job, a role, a capacity, indeed a discipline, and therefore as a fairly stable result of transformative exercises. What the ideal Brechtian producer produces, of course, is more antitheses, more dialectical tensions between irresolvable opposites, but it still seems reasonable to think of this production role as a stopping point, or at least a resting point, as the word is at the end of its sentence. Once again grammar lets us down.

A good double example of this temptation to dedialecticize Brecht's *Gestus* theory is Brigid Doherty's important article on Walter Benjamin's reading of Brecht and application of Brecht in his articles, journal entries, and radio broadcasts of the early 1930s:

> *Mann ist Mann* was a touchstone for Benjamin's meditations on Brecht and epic theater, which were first made public in the form of a radio broadcast called "Bert Brecht" in June 1930. "Bit by bit," says Benjamin of the play's protagonist, Galy Gay, "he assumes possessions, thoughts, posture, and habits of the kind needed by a soldier in a war; he is completely reassembled" [*Zug um Zug nimmt er Stücke, Gedanken, Haltung, Gewohnheiten, wie ein Mann im Krieg sie haben muss; er wird vollständig ummontiert*] . . .
> The vocabulary of Benjamin's account of the *Ummontierung* of Galy Gay anticipates that of "Karussell der Berufe," where the assumption of postures and habits is understood to play a primary role in a person's adaptation to a particular occupation: "In what realm of life are habits [*Gewohnheiten*] more easily formed, where are they more vigorous, where do they more fully encompass entire groups of people, than at work?" If habits are best developed and expressed on the job, then an occupation must influence a person by fostering or requiring the acquisition of habits. It thus makes sense, as Benjamin explains, that the experiments of occupational science should assess and test the *Haltung* [posture, stance, disposition] of specific occupations entirely apart from the content of the work itself, and focusing instead on *Gebärde* [gesture], *Neigung* [aptitude, proclivity], *Fähigkeit* [capability]. "Because they assess the disposition or posture of occupations in terms of the gestures and aptitudes of their subjects, psychotechnical experiments "represent human types who would have to invent certain occupations for themselves if those occupations did not already exist" . . . They represent persons composed of bodily gestures in which a set of habits and a particular occupational posture can be recognized and tested. Hence an occupation would not necessarily have to exist in order for it to be defined experimentally; it could simply be invented after the fact, in order to give the test subject an appropriate job to do. *Mann ist Mann* proceeds from the same understanding of persons, occupations, experiments, tests, habits, posture, and gestures, and it reveals that understanding through a kind of crude reverse-engineering of Galy Gay: a human being is made insofar as he is made to demonstrate, through a series of experiments and tests, the posture and gestures of the occupation he is made to take up. (449–50)

Galy Gay "assumes possessions, thoughts, posture, and habits of the kind needed by a soldier in a war; he is completely reassembled"—reassembled into a *soldier,* a specific occupational role or discipline or set of habits, including posture and gestures. For Benjamin, as Doherty explains, occupations "represent persons composed of bodily gestures in which a set of habits and a particular occupational posture can be recognized and tested." And while it is difficult to know just where Doherty stands on this point, it does seem that in that last sentence she is not merely paraphrasing Benjamin but restating his interpretation as an accurate representation of Brecht: "*Mann ist Mann* proceeds from the same understanding of persons, occupations, experiments, tests, habits, posture, and gestures, and it reveals that understanding through a kind of crude reverse-engineering of Galy Gay: a human being is made insofar as he is made to demonstrate, through a series of experiments and tests, the posture and gestures of the occupation he is made to take up." The "human being" that is here "made" is clearly a single undialectical thing, an instantiation of the "occupation he is made to take up."

Brecht himself seems disposed to validate this undialectical conception of Galy Gay's reassembly in the 1929 notebook passage I quoted in connection with Marx: "Mann = Mann / gegenspieler: der techniker . . . denn der arbeiter ist kein fürst. er entsteht nicht durch geburt, sondern indem der mit gewalt umgebaut wird. darum kann man auch alle menschen in arbeiter verwandeln" (quoted in Doherty, 451). Here, clearly, "gegenspieler" (lit. "against-player") has nothing to do with dialectical antitheses: the violent *Umbau* of Galy Gay into a soldier is congruent with, synonymous with, perhaps even an allegorical dramatic representation of, the violent *Umbau* of any ordinary man or woman into a technician or other worker, which is, like "producer" in the quotation from the *Flug der Lindberghs* notes, the stopping place at the substantive end of the sentence. Much the same stopping place seems to figure in the 1927 "Rede im Rundfunk" or introductory speech Brecht gave before the radio broadcast of the play:

> I imagine also that you are used to treating a man as a weakling if he can't say no, but this Galy Gay is by no means a weakling; on the contrary he is the strongest of all. That is to say he becomes the strongest once he has ceased to be a private person; he only becomes strong in the mass . . . No doubt you will go on to say that it's a pity that a man should be tricked like this and simply forced to surrender his precious ego, all he possesses (as it were); but it isn't. It's a jolly business [*eine lustige Sache*]. For this Galy Gay comes

to no harm; he wins. And a man who adopts such an attitude is bound to win. ("Introductory," 264; "Rede," 42)

Note the telltale series of undialectical antitheses Brecht gives us here: Galy Gay isn't a weakling, he's strong; he becomes strong not as a private person but in the mass; it isn't a pity that he is tricked like this, it's a jolly business; Galy Gay doesn't come to harm, he wins. Galy Gay in the end is a single stable entity, a strong collective winner, who for Brecht represents "an ancestor of just that new human type I spoke of" (264)—presumably to be distinguished antithetically but still undialectically from the "old human type" that Brecht assumes the radio listener will be expecting.

That this is roughly the same undialectical antithesis that we saw in Brecht's binarization of empathy and estrangement above becomes clear in Doherty's further tracing of Brecht and Benjamin on *Gestus,* or the ideosomatic expressivity of body language: "The formulation *Mann = Mann* can also be read as a sign of the epic theater's intention to foreclose spectatorial empathy and with it the audience's mimetic identification with a play's protagonist. In *Mann ist Mann,* the transformation of Galy Gay is emphatically external, with changes, to repeat, represented in posture and gesture. For Brecht, the externality of the epic theater and its protagonist stand in opposition to the Aristotelian drama, in which 'the plot leads the hero into situations where he reveals his innermost being'" (Doherty, 451–52). Internal versus external: the opposition is stably binary. Doherty discusses at some length the neologism Benjamin remembers Brecht using in conversation in 1931, *mitahmen,* a portmanteau of *mitfühlen* "sympathize" and *nachahmen* "imitate," for the Aristotelian theater, "where sympathy does not so much engender as amount to imitation, or, more precisely, mimetic spectatorial empathy, according to which 'every spectator' as it were adopts the identity of the character on stage, not because he or she is in a position genuinely to empathize with that character, but because plot and performance effect a collapse of sympathy and imitation" (452) and builds more undialectical antitheses:

> Practicing the words outside the context of the military drill, Galy Gay learns to speak the name Jeraiah Jip as if acquiring habit: "all that counts in this world is . . . to say 'Jeraiah Jip' the way another man would say good evening" . . . At this point, Galy Gay has adopted the *Haltung* of the soldier at roll-call by demonstrating an "ephemeral habit" [*kurze Gewohnheit*]. While he has learned automatically to exclaim "Jeraiah Jip! Jeraiah Jip!," he has not yet lost track of his own name and occupation. As Benjamin in-

vokes them in recounting his conversation about *das Wohnen* with Brecht, ephemeral habits belong to a mode of living Brecht described as antithetical to *mitahmendes Wohnen,* namely *"das Gastwohnen"* [living as a guest]. Once again we might take the language of the 1931 Brecht-Benjamin conversation as a point of departure: if, in its first manifestation, Galy Gay's adoption of the soldier's *Haltung* is a matter of acquiring *kurze Gewohnheiten,* then he in effect occupies the machine-gunner's position as a guest, hence in a manner opposed to that of sympathetic imitation, or what we might call *Mitahmung,* which Brecht and Benjamin associate with the theater audience as "a mass of hypnotized test subjects." Though unmotivated by sympathy, Galy Gay's behavior is nonetheless imitative, and it represents both a response and a resistance to suggestion, a resistance he will soon relinquish. In *Mann ist Mann* the conditions of possibility for unsympathetic imitation are best represented by the situation of the test, in this instance the military drill. (457–58)

Mitahmendes Wohnen "sympathetic/imitative living" or (presumably) *lange/bleibende Gewohnheit* "long/lasting habit" versus *Gastwohnen* "living as a guest" or *kurze Gewohnheit* "short/ephemeral habit": these constitute a new binary.

But note that the binaries here do not quite overlap with their earlier equivalents. If *mitahmendes Wohnen/lange Gewohnheit* is a new thematization of the internality of empathetic Aristotelian theater, and *Gastwohnen/kurze Gewohnheit* is a restatement of the externality of the gestic epic theater, as Doherty seems to suggest, the ephemeral habits of "guest living" should not lead to Galy Gay *becoming* a soldier. They should, as the term suggests, be "short," ephemeral. Galy Gay should only *play* at being a soldier. He should not *become* strong, collective, or a winner; he should adopt the external habits of victorious strength in the mass temporarily. Doherty seems to sense the problem Brecht has created for himself in her careful hedge: "Though unmotivated by sympathy, Galy Gay's behavior is nonetheless imitative, and it represents both a response and a resistance to suggestion, a resistance he will soon relinquish." If *mitahmendes Wohnen* is sympathetic *and* imitative, and Galy Gay "occupy[ing] the machine-gunner's position as a guest" is "unmotivated by sympathy" but "nonetheless imitative," that role-occupation is not quite "a manner *opposed* to that of sympathetic imitation"; and if his imitation of a soldier's *Grundgestus* is "both a response and a resistance to suggestion," and, as it seems from Doherty's presentation, his resistance guarantees its ephemerality, then his relinquishment of that resistance in the end signals a collapse of *Gastwohnen* back into *mitahmendes Wohnen,* back into the illusion of permanent "sympathetic" dwelling in the soldier role on which the Aristotelian theater is based.

The Redialecticizing of Brecht

The first obvious solution to the conceptual problem raised here is to separate the character not merely from the actor but from the words on the page. Benjamin and Doherty, and to some extent Brecht himself as well, muddy the waters of *Mann ist Mann* by reading the play as text rather than as performance. It is only if the transformative power of the Brechtian *Gestus* is mapped onto Galy Gay as he is written into the play—or, to run that the other way, if the transformation into a soldier of Galy Gay the literary character is taken as the *locus classicus* of gestic acting—that the ephemerality of gestic *Gastwohnen* becomes a problem. At the very simplest level, Galy Gay in (say) the 1931 Berlin Staatstheater production can *become* a soldier without undermining the ephemerality of the play's soldierly *Grundgestus* because he is two: Galy Gay and Peter Lorre. Galy Gay, to put that otherwise, becomes a soldier but Peter Lorre does not—because Peter Lorre never even becomes Galy Gay, never even pretends to become Galy Gay, and therefore gestically ("quotingly") stands aloof from Galy Gay becoming a soldier. Brecht's concept of gestic acting depends, obviously, at a bare minimum on the dramatized separation between actor and character; that separation is further compounded in the performative separation between character and spectator, a separation mediated by the gestic actor. No character in a play script, no matter how complex or multilayered his or her assumption of a role in the play's action is, can stand as a theoretical emblem of gestic acting, not just because no written character has a body (and therefore body language or *Gestus*), but because no written character is capable of dramatizing the overlapping separateness of character and actor or the effect of that dramatization on an audience.

It's clear from Brecht's own writing on *Mann ist Mann* that this distinction wasn't always clear to him either. For example, in "On Looking Through My First Plays" (1954), he writes:

> I turned to the comedy *Man equals Man* with particular apprehension. Here again I had a socially negative hero who was by no means unsympathetically treated. The play's theme is the false, bad collectivity (the "gang") and its powers of attraction, the same collectivity that Hitler and his backers were even then in the process of recruiting by an exploitation of the petty-bourgeoisie's vague longing for the historically timely, genuinely social collectivity of the workers. Before me were two versions, the one performed at the Berlin Volksbühne in 1928 and the other at the Berlin Staatstheater in 1931. I decided to restore the earlier version, where Galy Gay captures the

mountain fortress of Sir El-Djower. In 1931 I had allowed the play to end with the great dismantling operation, having been unable to see any way of giving a negative character to the hero's growth within the collectivity. I decided instead to leave that growth undescribed.

But this growth into crime can certainly be shown, if only the performance is sufficiently estranging [*Bei einer gut verfremdenden Darstellung ist aber dieses Wachstum ins Verbrecherische durchaus zeigbar*]. I tried to further this by one or two insertions in the last scene. ("On," 272; translation modified slightly in accordance with "Bei," 244–45)

The problem Brecht keeps trying to solve with this play, clearly, is that Galy Gay's transformation into a soldier is morally and ideologically ambiguous, and he can't help feeling that that ambiguity must somehow be parsed into binary clarity, good or bad, admirable or reprehensible. In the 1927 radio broadcast, as we've seen, Galy Gay was a socially positive hero, a winner, strong in the crowd, an allegorical Marxist; now, nearly three decades later, he is a socially negative hero, a gang member, a criminal, an allegorical Nazi. Brecht realizes here, late in life, that the solution to his problem lies not in the writing (the play as literary text) but in the acting (the play as performance), and specifically in the estranging gestic acting styles of the epic or dialectical theater that he has been developing for roughly the nearly three decades that he's been worrying about this particular play. Of course, he also tries to *further* this performative shift by rewriting the ending (see Brecht, *Man,* 301)—but the very word *further* indicates the ancillary status of the writing, its secondary role as background support for the acting.

Note, however, that even as he reminds himself and us of the importance of estranging acting styles in order for the play to have the desired effect on the audience, his conception of the play is still not dialectical: "ist aber dieses Wachstum ins Verbrecherische," he writes, "durchaus zeigbar." Not only is Galy Gay's ideologically ambiguous transformation into a soldier named Jeraiah Jip binarily thematized here as "growth into crime"; it is represented as an objective reality that need only be "shown" (*gezeigt werden*), as what Georg Lukács derided in *History and Class Consciousness* as the survival of a bourgeois "phantom objectivity." "Its basis," as Lukács wrote about reification or alienation, "is that a relation between people takes on the character of a thing and thus acquires a 'phantom-objectivity,' an autonomy that seems so strictly rational and all-embracing as to conceal every trace of its fundamental nature—the relation between people" (*History,* 83). Brecht's 1954 GDR take on the play's ending is redolent of the undialectical vulgar-materialist Soviet Marxism attacked by Korsch and Lukács in the early twenties: Marxism good, Nazism bad; objectivity good, subjectivity bad. If Galy Gay's transformation into a representative of the new postindividual "human type" is thematized as Marxist, it is undialectically good; if it is thematized as Nazi, it is undialectically bad. And in either case, it is an ideological stance that must simply be shown, presented objectively to the audience for its internalization as reified fact.

It is easy enough to argue that Brecht, the GDR's pet celebrity theater director in the last years of his life, is simply pretending to go along with this vulgar materialism, this undialectical binarism, this phantom-objectivist Marxism, as did anyone who enjoyed any measure of success within the Soviet Union and its East European satellites. The opposite critique is just as easy to make, especially given the central event of the play under discussion: that Brecht was assimilated to vulgar Marxism just as Galy Gay was assimilated to Jeraiah Jipism; that, just as gestically pretending to be Jeraiah Jip in the end converted the packer Galy Gay into the soldier Jeraiah Jip, so too did gestically pretending to be a vulgar Marxist in the end convert Brecht into one in reified behavioral and ideological "reality."

But Brecht, annoyingly simple-minded as he can be in the interstices of his astonishing brilliance, always seems to slip out of such easy categorizations. He does, after all, briefly mention estrangement in that passage—the estranging quality of a performance of *Mann ist Mann.* He doesn't do anything with that mention, except to say that he tried to support it textually by tweaking the writing here and there, but estrangement still remains the fly in the vulgar-Marxist ointment, the counterideosomatic audience effect that evades the heavy hammer of phantom objectivity. Estrangement there works to estrange the vulgar-Marxist machinery that seems to dominate the passage, works like a hand puppet stuck up insouciantly out of the reification to remind us that the true interactive reality of the theater is not so easily numbed into objectivism.

Or maybe just a finger puppet, or the top of a finger puppet's head—for estrangement is overwhelmingly buried in the passage. Even syntactically, for example, Brecht sets up estrangement as another objective quality of the vulgar-Marxist performance: in "Bei einer gut verfremdenden Darstellung" (lit. "in a good [sufficiently] estranging performance") the adjectival phrase "gut verfremdende" is simply a static attribute of "die Darstellung." Some performances just *are* sufficiently estranging, in an abstract ontological sense. There is no mention of an audience, or actors, or a relationship between actors and audience, or anyone's body or bodies, or the temporal/somatic shift required by estrangement, the sensation audience members have to have of being pushed across some temporal/somatic boundary into a heightened experience of strangeness (and ideally, from there into critical thinking, and enhanced awareness of the contradictions with and in which they have been living, and so on) by the estranging effects of specific things actors do with their bodies. There is none of this. There is no mention of the estranging effect on an audience that the author himself might have if, say, he were to go on the air just before a radio broadcast of the play and tell the home audience that their assumptions about the "harm" or "violence" done to Galy Gay will be just in their imaginations, that it's actually a "jolly affair" or "lustige Sache" (one way of reading that *Rundfunk* speech that salvages the dialectic from what appears to be Brecht's binary conception of the play). There is just the condition that the performance be sufficiently "estranging"—as one might require that the soil in a flower pot be sufficiently moist, or that a pancake batter be sufficiently runny, or that the air be sufficiently dry. In all these conditional clauses, the relationships among living and/or otherwise changing things—between the gardener holding the watering can and the plant requiring water to grow, between the cook holding the milk bottle and the cook's later self flipping the cooking pancake, between the painter and the paint that will not dry properly in humid weather, between the actors and the audience members at a theater performance—are mystified as objective quantities of objective qualities taken as abstract measures in an objective substance.

Still, we have the entire history of Brecht's theorizing of the estrangement effect, the *Gestus,* and the other techniques of the epic/dialectical theater to refer back to, to wield as a corrective to this sort of mystification:

> All right; that's what they need to know. But how are they to demonstrate it?
> Consciously, suggestively, descriptively.
> How do they do it at present?
> By means of hypnosis. They go into a trance and take the audience with them.
> Give an example.
> Suppose they have to act a leave-taking. They put themselves in a leave-taking mood. They want to induce a leave-taking mood in the audience. If the séance is successful it ends up with nobody seeing anything further, nobody learning any lessons, at best everyone recollecting. In short, everybody feels.
> That sounds almost like some erotic process. What ought it to be like, then?
> Witty. Ceremonious. Ritual. Spectator and actor ought not to approach one another but to move apart [*entfernen sollten sie sich voneinander*]. Each ought to move away from himself [*von sich selber entfernen*]. Otherwise the

246

element of terror necessary to all recognition is lacking. ("Dialog," 280; "Dialogue," 26)

If we apply this analysis from the 1929 "Dialogue About Acting" to the problem of Galy Gay's transformation, the key becomes not the mystifications about "showing" the "growth into crime" through a performance that is "sufficiently estranging," but the actors moving their bodies (including their mouths and faces in speech, their socially organized postures and gestures and tonalizations in *Gestus*) in such a way as to set up an estranging dialectical relationship with the spectators, actors moving away from spectators and spectators from actors, each actor and each spectator moving away from him/herself. The key rather becomes the "terror" (*der Schrecken*) that the spectators experience in the moment(s) of recognition, that counterideosomatic sensation of crossing a proprioceptive boundary between the familiar and the strange, the own and the alien, that panicky disorientation that Brecht sought all his professional life to generate in his audiences, the dialectical estrangement that would instigate in them a process of ideological transformation.

This Brechtian notion of gestic antithesis might be unpacked with another digression through Lev Vygotsky's 1925 dissertation *The Psychology of Art.* In the final stages of establishing his Shklovskyan (belabored-form/antithetical) theory of the cathartic effects of art (*Psychology,* 212–13), Vygotsky invokes Darwin's treatment of habitual action from the first two chapters of *The Expression of Emotion in Man and Animals,* noting that according to Darwin humans and animals all develop habitual actions that are of service to the specific body state they are in at the moment, whether emotional or actional. Some of Darwin's examples of what Brecht will call *Gesten*:

Everyone protects himself when falling to the ground by extending his arms, and as Professor Alison has remarked, few can resist acting thus, when voluntarily falling on a soft bed. A man when going out of doors puts on his gloves quite unconsciously; and this may seem an extremely simple operation, but he who has taught a child to put on gloves, knows that this is by no means the case . . . A vulgar man often scratches his head when perplexed in mind; and I believe that he acts thus from habit, as if he experienced a slightly uncomfortable bodily sensation, namely, the itching of his head, to which he is particularly liable, and which he thus relieves. Another man rubs his eyes when perplexed, or gives a little cough when embarrassed, acting in either case as if he felt a slightly uncomfortable sensation in his eyes or windpipe. (31–32)

The first interesting observational spin Darwin puts on this initial principle is that these habitual actions, initially developed to serve specific body states, may be reperformed when those body states are not present, so that the actions themselves no longer serve any obvious purpose:

> whenever the same state of mind is induced, however feebly, there is a tendency through the force of habit and association for the same movements to be performed, though they may not then be of the least use. Some actions ordinarily associated through habit with certain states of the mind may be partially repressed through the will, and in such cases the muscles which are least under the separate control of the will are the most liable still to act, causing movements which we recognize as expressive. In certain other cases the checking of one habitual movement requires other slight movements; and these are likewise expressive. (28)

What Vygotsky wants from Darwin here, though, is the second observational spin he puts on his original principle, which he calls the "principle of antithesis" and develops in his second chapter: "we shall find that when a directly opposite state of mind is induced, there is a strong and involuntary tendency to the performance of movements of a directly opposite nature, though these have never been of any service." For example, a dog bristles at what it takes to be a stranger, holds its body high and stiff, its tail erect and rigid. It pricks its ears forward and stares but then realizes that the stranger is in fact its master and abruptly shifts to the opposite range of habitual actions, even though they aren't necessary, and may even be organismically counterproductive:

> Instead of walking upright, the body sinks downwards or even crouches, and is thrown into flexuous movements; his tail, instead of being held stiff and upright, is lowered and wagged from side to side; his hair instantly becomes smooth; his ears are depressed and drawn backwards, but not closely to the head; and his lips hang loosely. From the drawing back of the ears, the eyelids become elongated, and the eyes no longer appear round and staring. It should be added that the animal is at such times in an excited condition from joy; and nerve-force will be generated in excess, which naturally leads to action of some kind. Not one of the above movements, so clearly expressive of affection, are [*sic*] of the least direct service to the animal. They are explicable, as far as I can see, solely from being in complete opposition or antithesis to the attitude and movements which, from intelligible causes, are assumed when a dog intends to fight, and which consequently are expressive of anger. (51)

But, Vygotsky supposes, what happens in cases of mixed emotional states, such as are aroused by great art? Surely these would create in us *simultaneous* enact-

ments of this principle of antithesis? "It is now no longer likely to seem puzzling to us that tragedy, which simultaneously excites in us affects of an opposing nature, apparently works by the principle of antithesis and sends opposing
impulses to opposing muscle groups. It makes us as it were at once lift and
drop weights; it excites at once muscles and their antagonists" (*Psikhologiya*,
267, my translation). This is especially true of actors, particularly those trained
in various radical traditions, not just Brecht but Vsevolod Meyerhold, Erwin
Piscator, Antonin Artaud, Jerzy Grotowski. Rather than responding with isolated habitualized or stereotyped actions (hands to mouth and wide eyes for
shock, head thrown back for laughter, etc.), they respond with what Brecht
calls *der ganze Komplex* "the entire complex," or what Artaud calls "total creation" (93) and Grotowski calls the "total act" (123).[20] What the audience for
this sort of acting internalizes, again, is a Trojan Horse of antithetical feeling,
which instigates a potentially transformative rethinking of anesthetized contradictions.

This focus on the contradictory or antithetical somatic exchange between actors and spectators is a very different thematization of the epic theater than we
find in many studies of Brecht, including those of Benjamin and Doherty:

> Interruption, as we have seen, is also the epic theater's technique for repre-
> senting *Gesten* and making them quotable. "The more frequently we inter-
> rupt someone engaged in an action, the more gestures we obtain. Hence
> the interrupting of action is one of the principal concerns of epic theater."
> In epic theater, that mode of interruption resembles techniques of photo-
> graphic representation employed in psychotechnical testing. Interruption
> fixes, as if cinematographically, the "strict, frame-like enclosure of each ele-
> ment of a *Haltung* (i.e., each gesture)" . . . The frames of the gesture are like
> the frames of a strip of film, and hence they are also like the projections that
> hovered behind the action in the 1931 production of *Mann ist Mann,* which
> was designed by Caspar Neher. Those projections recapitulated elements of
> the action in telegraphic prose and, you will recall, in arithmetic. In epic
> theater, projections are gestic; they function as interruptions, and their own
> form is punctuated either paratactically or mathematically. Seen that way,
> the projections call to mind Benjamin's likening of the epic actor's presenta-
> tion of quotable gestures to the setting of type for emphasis: "he must be
> able to space [*sperren*] his gestures as the compositor spaces words" . . . That
> metaphor in turn recalls Brecht's assertion of the need for "footnotes" in
> dramatic writing, as well as his emphasis on the writer's desire to emulate
> the apparatus, a point I have said we should understand in relation to Benja-
> min's claims about the "training regimen" of Hemingway's prose, and hence
> in relation to his thoughts on *Haltung* as the interrupted action of a body in

motion. All of which underscore the mechanical aspects of writing, understood in terms of a text's capacity to represent *Gesten*. (Doherty, 474–75)

Doherty has here selected from the first version of "What Is Epic Theatre?" some of the most strongly structuralizing of Benjamin's interpretations of Brecht, making it seem as if for Benjamin epic theater was largely an abstract matter of forms or frames or spacings, rather than, say, a series of complex interactions. This is not entirely accurate: Benjamin does in passing recognize the importance to epic theater of the various relationships "between stage and public, text and performance, producer and actors"—"For the stage, the public is no longer a collection of hypnotized test subjects, but an assembly of interested persons whose demands it must satisfy" (Benjamin, 2). Indeed one of Doherty's quotations seems to take us to a rehearsal, where Brecht is pushing his actors to complicate their gestic movements: "The more frequently we interrupt someone engaged in an action, the more gestures we obtain. Hence the interrupting of action is one of the principal concerns of epic theater" (3). But of course that "we" is not Brecht running a rehearsal but people in general, indeed a kind of generalized or universalized principle of human behavior disguised rhetorically as an interactive intervention. In any case Benjamin's emphasis on the *quantification* of interruptions and gestures ("The more frequently we interrupt someone engaged in an action, the more gestures we obtain") comes out of his remarks on the *framing* of the gesture ("it has a definable beginning and a definable end . . . this strict, frame-like, enclosed nature of each moment of an attitude," 3), which in turn set up his discussion of the serial spatialization of gesticity, the likening of interruptions or "haltings" to cinematic frames on a strip of celluloid, "punctuated either paratactically or mathematically," or to typesetting, and thus to "the mechanical aspects of writing." Hence also, presumably, the temptation to use the literary text of *Mann ist Mann* to represent the estranging effect of the Brechtian *Gestus* (Benjamin, 2–3, 8–9, 12–13). For a depersonalizing or desomatizing critique, the truest form of any theatrical or literary effect is one that has been abstracted out of the realm of human interaction.

As we've seen, Brecht, too, is drawn to this depersonalizing mode all his life, from his early fascination with behaviorism to his partial assimilation to the vulgar materialism of Soviet Marxism. I am not arguing, in other words, that my somatic reading of Brecht rescues some "true" Brecht from a "false" Brecht propagated by Benjamin, Jameson, Doherty, and others. They are at least as right about their Brecht as I think I am about mine. What I'm arguing is that mine is not only *a* true Brecht but also a more radical true Brecht than theirs: more powerfully innovative, less dependent on phantom objectivisms, undialectical binaries, and other forms of bad theory.

Conclusion: The Somatics of Literature

So if, as I'm arguing, a desomatizing reading of *Mann ist Mann* (or of Brecht's theory of the estranging epic *Gestus* through *Mann ist Mann*) goes astray by relying too heavily on the written text of the play, by not paying sufficient attention to the somatic interaction of bodies on stage and bodies in the house, does this mean that the somatics of literature depends on the interactive presence of actual bodies, and therefore is not a somatics of literature at all but of, say, drama, or of "real" (embodied) life?

No. That would be a simplistic excluded-middle argument. The distinction I'm setting up in this book is not between the disembodied written text and the embodied performance of literature but between theorizations of literature based imaginatively on disembodiment and embodiment—between a depersonalized theorization of literature as abstract structure, both texts and performances conceived as sheer textuality from which felt human interactivity has been subtracted, and a somatic theorization of literature as felt interactive form, both texts and performances as imaginatively (proprioceptively) fleshed out by group ideosomatic and individual idiosomatic and counterideosomatic response.

These two theoretical poles are themselves excluded-middle arguments, of course—just more complex ones. The depersonalizing or desomatizing theorization of literature as abstract form or structure manages to construct the "real" (in the Kantian/Lacanian sense of unattainable and unimaginable) and therefore desirable pole of a postsocial textuality by excluding the Hegelian middle of human interactions with things, the projection of self onto objects and the incorporation of objects into the self, leaving a binary between an impossibly attractive posthuman transobjectivity and a shopworn, philosophically discredited, sentimentally liberal, embarrassingly declassé, and therefore (hopefully) "dead" subjectivity. My somatic theorization of literature excludes the twentieth century's avant-garde embarrassment about the self, the subject, feeling, community, interaction, and so on—all the liberal detritus of Victorian moralism—in order to set up a binary between the ideosomatic self-regulation of social groups (the "real" as constructed ideosomatically by precisely those regulatory collective forces) and the wistful dystopian (posthuman) illusions of depersonalized structuralism. Each approach is set up, obviously, to exclude the other—though I would argue that depersonalized structuralism has no conceptual equipment that would allow it to recognize the existence of, let alone the nature or socially constitutive importance of, ideosomatic regulation.

To put all that more simply: where the structuralist reads literature in terms of pure textuality, as if the writer and the reader did not exist, the somaticist reads literature in terms of human relationship, as if the text did not exist. The structuralist wants to convert the human beings involved in the creation of literature (writers and readers) into the mere structural functions of textuality; the somaticist sees the text as dead signs that the group must bring to life through the regulatory somatics of written communication. More simply still: the structuralist mentally subtracts human subjects even from an embodied performance; the somaticist (emotionally-becoming-)mentally adds human subjects even to a written text. Both "mathematical" operations, the structuralist's subtraction and the somaticist's addition, are actually performed proprioceptively, each theorist more or less unconsciously adjusting incoming sense data to fit his or her proprioception of the body politic. The structuralist constantly recreates a world stripped of human signification, human interaction, human feeling; the somaticist constantly recreates a world overdetermined by felt collective regulation, in the form of ideosomatic, idiosomatic, and counterideosomatic body language, estranging and deestranging *Gestes*.

I have not stopped along the way to document the historical instances of these opposing approaches, outside of Tolstoy, Shklovsky, Brecht, and their structuralist and vulgar-materialist critics, and do not propose to do so now. In any case it should not be difficult for anyone who knows anything about the history of literary theory to set up structuralist-somaticist binaries like the New Critics (W. K. Wimsatt and Monroe Beardsley's "The Affective Fallacy") versus reader-response (Norman Holland and David Bleich), or Tzvetan Todorov versus Julia Kristeva. What I want to do instead is to close this book with an example of practical somaticist criticism, taken from Scene 10 of *Mann ist Mann:*

> BEGBICK: Come and give us a kiss, Jippie.
> GALY GAY: I don't mind if I do, but I think you have got me a bit muddled with someone else.
> BEGBICK: Jippie!
> JESSE: This gentleman claims his head is not quite clear; he says he doesn't know you.

BEGBICK: Oh, how can you humiliate me so in front of this gentleman?

GALY GAY: If I duck my head in this pail of water I'll know you right away. *He sticks his head into the pail of water.*

BEGBICK: Do you know me now?

GALY GAY *lying:* Yes.

POLLY: Then you also know who you yourself are?

GALY GAY *slyly:* Didn't I know that?

POLLY: No, because you were out of your mind and claimed to be someone else.

GALY GAY: Who was I, then?

JESSE: You're not getting much better, I see. What's more I still think you are a public menace, because last night when we called you by your right name you turned as dangerous as any murderer.

GALY GAY: All I know is that my name is Galy Gay.

JESSE: Listen to that, you people, he's starting all over again. You'd better call him Galy Gay like he says, or he'll throw another fit.

URIAH: Oh bollocks. Mr Jip from Ireland, consider yourself free to play the wild man right up to the point where you get tied to a post outside the canteen and the night rain comes down. We who have been your mates since the battle of the River Chadze would sell our shirts to make things easier for you.

GALY GAY: No need for that about the shirts.

URIAH: Call him anything he wants.

JESSE: Shut up, Uriah. Would you care for a glass of water, Galy Gay?

GALY GAY: Yes, that is my name.

JESSE: Of course, Galy Gay. How could you be called anything else? Just take it easy, lie down. Tomorrow they will put you in hospital, in a nice comfortable bed with plenty of castor oil, and that will relieve you, Galy Gay. Tread delicately, all of you, our friend Jip, I mean Galy Gay, is unwell.

GALY GAY: Let me tell you, gentlemen, the situation is beyond me. But when it is a matter of carrying a cabin trunk, never mind how heavy it is, they say every cabin trunk is supposed to have its soft spot.

POLLY *ostensibly aside to Jesse:* Just keep him away from that pouch around his neck, or he'll read his real name in his paybook and throw another fit. (66–67)

Objectively, of course, what we have here is a series of black squiggles; but anyone who can read English projects onto those squiggles the somatized collective regulation that makes English a meaningful language, a shared channel of communication for hundreds of millions of people. Because we have been socialized to the English language through long ideosomatic interaction with other speakers of the language, we feel (somatically construct) not only the meanings of *just, keep, him, away, from, that,* and *pouch,* and of "just keep him away from that pouch," but of what Polly and the others are trying to do to Galy Gay as well.[21]

We can sense, in other words, as if it were happening to us—because, proprioceptively, it *is*—that the Widow Begbick, Polly, and the other soldiers are using group ideosomatic regulation manipulatively in order to restructure Galy Gay's understanding of reality, including his own identity. The "fact" that Galy Gay's name is Galy Gay or that my name is Doug Robinson is, after all, just as powerfully regulated by the group as is the meaning of each of the words in "just keep him away from that pouch around his neck," and of the sentence as a whole, and of the devious multilayered speech act Polly is performing with that line. While it is possible to resist that group pressure, as Galy Gay so far is continuing here to do successfully, it is extremely difficult. The Widow Begbick says, "Oh, how can you humiliate me so in front of this gentleman?" using the patriarchal ideosomatics of chivalry to shame Galy Gay into giving up his stubborn individualism in clinging to his old name rather than going along with the group. Jesse says "What's more I still think you are a public menace, because last night when we called you by your right name you turned as dangerous as any murderer," using a more legalistic form of group pressure to make Galy Gay conform, as if to the law. Uriah says, "Mr Jip from Ireland, consider yourself free to play the wild man right up to the point where you get tied to a post outside the canteen and the night rain comes down," using the veiled threat of physical violence and restraint to put group pressure on him, and "We who have been your mates since the battle of the River Chadze would sell our shirts to make things easier for you," using the ideosomatics of group camaraderie and sacrifice for friendship, and the normative *quid pro quo* expectation of gratitude. Jesse says "Tread delicately, all of you, our friend Jip, I mean Galy Gay, is unwell," pretending to accommodate himself (and to bring pressure on the others to join him in that accommodation) to Galy Gay's insanity by pointedly calling him by his "delusional" name and only "accidentally" calling him by his "real" name.

To anyone susceptible to ideosomatic group pressure—and the vast majority of us are—resisting the group *is* tantamount to insanity. We even say to ourselves and our friends, wonderingly, semi-ironically, when everyone around us flatly rejects some version of an event that we are absolutely sure is accurate: "Am I crazy, or are you all?" Even while resisting group pressure, Galy Gay here resorts to various evasive strategies, lying that he knows the Widow Begbick, returning Polly's question of whether he knows himself with another question, and so on; and in fact he can't hold out much longer. This passage comes in the middle of Scene 10, at the end of which he finally gives in and *becomes* Jeraiah Jip. The somatic discomfort of feeling insane, of feeling radically at odds with the group construction of reality, is too powerful, too disturbing. This is why brainwashing works. It is why mass movements are so hard to stop or even to redirect. It is why, when social reality changes drastically—after the Russian revolution for Viktor Shklovsky, say—most people do manage to adapt and come to feel uneasily sorry for those who don't (as, indeed, we do for the misfits in any social reality). It is why depersonalizing structuralist critics and theorists who idealize a posthuman world of pure objective structure do not teeter on the brink of insanity, as did Lev Tolstoy: despite their dystopian denial of group ideosomatic regulation, they continue to rely on it, and even to feel at home in it.

The reading of a play text like this works, in fact, not just because we may have seen the play performed or can imagine the play being performed but because, as Brecht recognizes (and exfoliates at length in "The Street Scene" [Willett, *Brecht,* 121–29]), we project ourselves mimetically (empathetically) into any narrated or dramatized scene like this—whether the narration or dramatization is realistic or unrealistic, Aristotelian or non-Aristotelian, identificatory or "quoted." The specific interactive relationship created in and through and around the narration or dramatization will channel or shape this mimetic projection in a variety of ways, obviously—far more complexly than Brecht's empathy versus estrangement binary can predict—but the important point to recognize is that the "reality" of the narrated or dramatized scene *is* created and channeled and shaped interactively, through the bodily economy of the group's somatic exchange, and indeed that this is the *only* way that reality is created and shaped.

Our somatic response to the Widow Begbick, Polly, Jesse, and Uriah in this passage emerges out of our construction of an imaginary (proprioceptive) somatic exchange, in which all these characters are imaginatively present to us in the body and are putting pressure on us to conform to group norms through imagined body language, and we are present to them in the body as well, and responding to their pressure with our own feelings and body language. Because we have been socialized to group regulation, to what Brecht calls infectious "living together," we know what it feels like to be subjected to this kind of body-language pressure, this barrage of chivalrous or legalistic or violent or psychiatric *Gestes,* and project what we know onto these black squiggles on the page. This is, in fact, how actors begin to turn written characters into embodied characters: they feel their way somatically, through their experience of similar pressures in their own lives, to a reconstruction of those pressures in their bodies through the playwright's words. But we don't have to be actors to undertake this sort of projective mimetic response; we don't even have to be aware of doing so. We do it because we are social beings, conditioned to construct this somatic exchange in every group that includes us, whether physically present or merely imaginatively reembodied. To the extent that we identify with Galy Gay, we project ourselves into "his" "body," which is to say, construct an imaginary proprioceptive body for him that is more or less coextensive with our own, and fill that body with our own somatic response to the manipulative group regulation we're imaginatively encountering. As Galy Gay in the end is successfully transformed into Jeraiah Jip, we coexperience with him the violence of his transformation, feel that we too are being turned into gung-ho soldiers expected to lead the charge against the fortress—and, especially in an estranging production, this empathetic coexperience becomes the Trojan Horse of antithetical feeling that, internalized as "our own" feeling, Brecht hopes will wreak its heuristic havoc on our anesthetized belief systems.

Let me close by noting once again what I mentioned in the preface: that the somatics of literature is neither liberal humanism (as it may seem to depersonalizing (post)structuralists) nor behaviorism (as it may seem to National Association of Scholars conservatives). My earlier suggestion that depersonalizing structuralism is partly driven by an embarrassment with subjective feeling as "the liberal detritus of Victorian moralism" may seem to imply that somatic theory, in embracing feeling and subjectivity, is a form of liberal humanism. In fact, somatic theory occupies a fairly broad excluded middle ground between the rationalist autonomy of liberal humanism (NAS conservatism) and either the depersonalized stimulus-response mechanisms of behaviorism or the depersonalized posthuman abstractions of structuralism or structuralist formalism. Somatic theory is far too heavily grounded in the regulation of the individual by the group to mesh very comfortably with liberal conceptions of friendly and mutually respectful cooperation among autonomous rational beings, but it is also too heavily grounded in (guided but ultimately more or less free) choice to mesh with behaviorist conceptions of robotic conditioning and control.

What makes the somatics of literature seem "liberal," and therefore theoretically conservative, is, again, a collectivized embarrassment with feeling and the body. The ideosomatics of patriarchal gender formation have too strongly associated feeling and the body with women, and therefore with physical and intellectual weakness and submissiveness, for traditional male comfort; and the ideosomatics of social class have too strongly associated "womanish" feeling with the middle class, with middle-class morality, for traditional avant-garde comfort. It doesn't even help that somatic theory is not only perfectly congruent with the ideological analysis of Hegelian Western Marxism but also *explains* the dissemination of ideological norms and orientations throughout a population far more coherently than any abstract structuralist Marxism. To many, the idea that Marxist ideological analysis might depend on the "inherently" liberal (middle-class, womanish, weak-minded, etc.) structures of feeling still seems categorically like a simple oxymoron.

That the supposedly "antipsychological" Viktor Shklovsky and the supposedly "antiemotional" Bertolt Brecht were able to fight their way free of these ideosomatic binaries, however, suggests that a somatic theory of literature may still be viable. As Brecht tells Bernard Guillemin in the 1926 "Conversation with Bert Brecht":

Q. And what else are you working at?
A. A comedy called *Mann ist Mann.* It's about a man being taken to pieces and rebuilt as someone else for a particular purpose.
Q. And who does the re-building?
A. Three engineers of the feelings.
Q. Is the experiment a success?
A. Yes, and they are all of them much relieved.
Q. Does it produce the perfect human being?
A. Not specially. (16)

In the end, Brecht insists, we are all engineers of the feelings.

▌ *Notes*

Introduction

1. It's interesting to note that while the formalist "estrangers" Shklovsky and Brecht were looked upon with suspicion under Stalin's regime, Tolstoy's utopian-Christian infection theory—specifically, his association of the perverse infectiousness of high modernism with the corrupt upper classes and of the "pure" (antimodernist and antielitist) infectiousness of "true" art with the honest toiling masses—was highly valued as an important precursor of the Marxist-Leninist-Stalinist "revolutionary" ideology.

2. On James and the formalists, see Erlich (181–82, n. 49), Emerson (645, n. 19), and Svetlikova, who writes: "the formalists depended more on a small fragment of James than they did on Tolstoy" (13), and "If we return to the articles of Shklovsky, the least careful reader among them, we will discover that even his theoretical reflections relied on a familiarity with psychological thought. The important thing is not whether he read, say, James attentively, in general whether he read him at all, or just heard about him from his more knowledgeable comrades. The important thing is that even his opinions depended to some degree on psychology" (54, my translations). For James and Brecht, see Doherty (460, n. 22) and, through Eisenstein and Benjamin, Hansen (318, n. 37). I return to James and Shklovsky in chapter 3 and to James and Brecht in chapter 5.

James's influence on the Russian formalists was partly channeled by the German aesthetician Broder Christiansen's *Philosophy of Art* (1909, Russian translation 1911); see Svetlikova (59) and Shukman (592, n. 4).

3. Brennan insists that, while affect may sometimes be transmitted mimetically—as it definitively is in somatic theory—the great transpersonal power of affect-transmission can only be explained through chemical entrainment:

> We shall return to this issue, but first, let us deal with a familiar objection to the notion of affective transmission: it might exist, but it works by sight rather than smell. Does it not spread, say, by the visual observation of a depressed person's physiognomy and body language? On the answer to this question hinges much of the argument of this book. Because what is interesting about the question is the resistance it reveals to the idea that a foreign body—something from without—can enter into one's own. If entrainment

is effected by sight, then on the face of it, our boundaries stay intact. We become *like* someone else by imitating that person, not by literally becoming or in some way merging with him or her. (10)

Brennan's problem here is that she is thinking purely of *conscious* imitation and does not know—because she has not read Damasio or the extensive literature influenced by his findings—that somatic mimesis also breaks down the imaginary boundaries between persons. In somatic theory we do not merely become like someone else through imitation; there is a kind of mimetic merging of personality, or what I would prefer to describe as a flowing of personality through us. Because she does not know about what Damasio calls the as-if body loop, she thinks that visually based mimesis is incapable of transmitting whole personal orientations through other bodies.

More important for my argument here is that chemical entrainment cannot explain the transmission of affect through *story* and thus cannot become the basis of a somatics of literature. If I tell you a story about falling off my bike and skidding three feet along the asphalt in my shorts and t-shirt, and you cringe and shudder, Brennan would have to insist that your ability to experience my affect is transmitted hormonally rather than through your as-if body loop's instantaneous sympathetic mimetic reconstruction of my body state. But what if I tell the story over the phone or in writing, and you *still* cringe and shudder sympathetically? How are the hormones carrying my "foreign body" into yours then?

For more on Brennan, see notes 1, 5, and 8 in chapter 1.

One   Tolstoy's Infection

1. For those who would complain that *zarazhenie* is simply the opposite of *vyrazhenie,* the inward (impression) movement of expression, and has nothing to do with disease, Caryl Emerson's stricture is important: "The epidemiological resonances of 'infection' and 'infectiousness' (*zarazhenie, zarazitel'nost*) are of course deliberate—for in Tolstoy's view, every important truth had to prove itself on the individual body" ("Aesthetics," 238).

For another interesting parallel to my approach here, see Dan Sperber's *Explaining Culture,* which he describes as an "epidemiological" model of social interaction, based on "the cumulative effect of countless processes of inter-individual transmission through imitation" (3). The imitation he means is, however, entirely cognitive, channeled not through feelings or the body-becoming-mind but through words and ideas, or what Richard Dawkins calls "memes":

Here you are, reading this page, which is a trace of my work. Observing a behavior or its traces gives rise to ideas, such as the ideas that are at this very moment coming to your mind. Sometimes, the ideas caused by a behavior resemble the ideas that have caused this behavior. This will be the case if I succeed in making myself understood.

Through a material process like the one just evoked, an idea, born in the brain of one individual, may have, in the brain of other individuals, descendants that resemble it. Ideas can be transmitted, and, by being transmitted from one person to another, they may even propagate. Some ideas—religious beliefs, cooking recipes, or scientific hypotheses, for instance—propagate so effectively that, in different versions, they may end up durably invading whole populations. Culture is made up, first and foremost, of such contagious ideas. It is made up also of all the productions (writings, artworks, tools, etc.) the presence of which in the shared environment of a human group permits the propagation of ideas.

To explain culture, then, is to explain why and how some ideas happen to be contagious. This calls for the development of a true *epidemiology of representations*. (1)

I am not exactly sure how the transmission of ideas can be regarded as a *material* process—any more than my conception of somatic mimesis is material. Both are based not on *material transmission* (unlike Teresa Brennan's theory of the chemical transmission of affect, for which see note 3 in the introduction) but on *imaginative reconstructions* of other people's words and ideas (Sperber's epidemiology of representations) or body states (my somatic theory). That somatic mimesis is a neurological event makes it "material," I suppose, but then everything in human life is a neurological event, rendering the term meaningless in its universal extension. For a discussion of the grounding of verbal language in body language, and thus, by implication, of Sperber's epidemiology of representations in an epidemiology of feelings, see my "Somatics of Language."

2. The famous passage is this one from 1901, in conversation with Paul Boyer: "I read all of Rousseau, all twenty volumes including his *Dictionary of Music*. I more than delighted in him—I worshipped him. At the age of 15, I wore a medallion with his portrait around my neck in place of my natal cross. Many of his pages are so close to me, that it seems I wrote them myself" (quoted in Barran, "Rousseau," 1–2). Barran's article is the best discussion in English of this connection between the two "misunderstood prophets," Rousseau and Tolstoy.

3. Martine de Courcel writes:

That is why he was with God, yet not *in* God, for he refused the mediation of Christ. He wrote in 1887 in the essay "On Life" that he was "obliged to make real all the truth in his own life and in the world's for himself, not by the mediation of another." He still thought the same in 1901 and wrote to a French Protestant minister that "the principal meaning of Christian doctrine is to establish a direct communication between God and man." Such is the meaning it had for him, but certainly not for the Christian churches;

for them communion comes through the sacraments that Christ instituted, while for Tolstoy "every man who takes this role [of priest or mediator] upon him prevents whomsoever he seeks to guide from communicating with God." (163)

4. "In 1905," de Courcel writes, "Tolstoy had an enormous audience both in Russia and abroad. To this public at large he was a revolutionary; actually, he was a perpetual dissenter—he even opposed revolution. Yet Stefan Zweig is nevertheless right to say that 'no nineteenth-century Russian revolutionary did so much to clear the way for Lenin and for Trotsky as the anti-revolutionary Count'" (298). As de Courcel goes on to show, while Tolstoy thought the Russian revolution was inevitable, and would probably be beneficial, he opposed it on the basis of his pacifist doctrine of nonviolence, and hoped for a "natural" revolution arising out of the mass conversion of Russians to "true" Christianity, namely, his own. For a useful summary of Lenin's six articles on Tolstoy between 1908 and 1911, see de Courcel, 305–12.

5. Tolstoy does seem to believe that the author's feeling physically *infects* the reader, leaps across the space between and invades the reader's body. In this, though he does not theorize the precise mechanism of this materialist transmission, he is closer to the chemical model for the transmission of affect developed by Teresa Brennan; see notes 3 in the introduction and 1 in chapter 1 for further discussion.

6. Literally *imagined:* as de Courcel writes, "Tolstoy passes into a kind of autistic spiritual state; for him, 'salvation is within you' means it is *in oneself,* so that the real proof of God's existence for Tolstoy is the fact that he *believes* in Him" (163).

7. Tolstoy also uses the term *infection* when speaking of his relations with Sof'ya in his diary of February 14, 1891: "I ya stal govorit' yey razdrazhitel'no i zarazil yeyo zloboy" (52:7), "And I began to talk to her irritably and infected her with my anger" (1:301).

8. By "somatic orientation" I mean not just a body state but a social feeling, or what Teresa Brennan calls an evaluative affect: "By an affect, I mean the physiological shift accompanying a judgment" (5). It is not, in other words, enough to feel something; it must be a socially directed feeling, an affective form of social pressure.

Brennan's interesting book is everywhere relevant to my somatic theory of literature, but to my mind its usefulness is limited by her lack of awareness of the work of Damasio's team, and of the scholars in a wide variety of fields Damasio has influenced. Indeed, she claims on her first page that no one has sought to explain the phenomenon of the transmission of affect, and on her second writes that "the transmission of affect is not understood or studied because of the distance between the concept of transmission and the reigning modes of biological explanation. No one really knows how it happens, which may explain the reluctance to acknowledge its existence" (2). It's true, of course, that the phenomenon isn't studied much and isn't widely understood, and that many psychological and sociological researchers are reluctant to acknowledge its existence, but Damasio's team began publishing on the phenomenon in the early 1990s, and the extent to which their research has revolutionized the field of affect regulation studies is clear from the work of Allan Schore.

9. Note that the Adolphs article Damasio is summarizing here is almost exclusively devoted to the "Neural Mechanisms for Recognizing Emotion" stated in its title; Adolphs raises the possibility that "knowledge of other people's emotions may rely on simulating the observed emotion" (171) *very* briefly, in eight lines. Damasio's "summary" of Adolphs's research the following year, in 2003, actually breaks the news.

10. For discussions of transference and countertransference in terms of somatic "affect regulation," see Schore, *Origin* (450–57) and *Repair* (22–32, 50–53, 71–73, 84–87); for projective/introjective identification, see Schore, *Repair,* ch. 3, esp. 64–65. Schore calls his integrative project regulation theory; it is based on the notion that the right-brain-to-right-brain synchronization of affect-based mother-infant communication ("attachment") is the foundation and model of all later affect regulation, both as the origin of the self and for later psychotherapeutic and other repair of the self. He draws heavily on Damasio and other neurological research into the social nature of affect regulation, with the result that regulation theory is thoroughly congruent with somatic theory; the major difference is that he is focused exclusively on social dyads (mother-infant, therapist-patient) and tends to neglect the importance of larger social groups for affect regulation.

11. Slingerland, applying Damasio's somatic-marker hypothesis to cognitive linguistics (specifically, to the conceptual-blending theory of Fauconnier and Turner), gives examples of this latter: "Dispassionate calculation makes it clear that we are likely to achieve a much better payoff investing $20 weekly in some conservative mutual fund rather than using that money to buy lottery tickets, but the reasoning processes of many are (incorrectly, in this case) biased by the powerfully positive somatic marker attached to the image of the multi-million-dollar payoff" (560), or the decision to drive rather than fly based on the negative somatic markers occasioned by a recent jet crash.

Slingerland also grounds somatic response in normativity, or what I call ideosomatics: "Somatic marking thus works by attaching emotional-normative weight to images" (560). This is an important expansion of Damasio's theory, but to the extent that Slingerland sees somatic markers as *exclusively* normative, his reading is unnecessarily restrictive. Our experience of the world also teaches us to mark idiosyncratic and even resistant or antinormative orientations somatically—what I call idiosomatics and counterideosomatics, respectively.

12. The original scientific publication of this thesis by the Damasio team was the 1999 article in *Nature Neuroscience* by Anderson et al.

Two   Tolstoy's Estrangement

1. But see also the 1953 article on Comenius' *Labyrinth of the World* by Dmitry Čiževsky (alphabetized in the Works Cited as Chizhevsky), which Ginzburg does not cite. Čiževsky calls the estrangement device "negative allegory":

> We are dealing here with a clearly defined artistic device. In many respects the use of this device resembles allegory: real things are represented by certain "substitutes." The basic difference between allegory and this device is that it is the purpose of allegory to reveal the real meaning of the things (even though this meaning may sometimes have a negative value), while the device under discussion aims at exactly the opposite: things are to be shown in their plain physical existence, stripped and drained of any meaning. One could term this device negative allegory or allegory which divests of meaning. (120)

Noting that Erich Auerbach calls it a *Scheinwerfertechnik* or "searchlight technique" (121, n. 94), he traces it back to what he takes to be its first use in Xenophanes, finds examples of it in Plato, Dio Chrysostom, Lucian, Seneca, Epictetus, and especially Marcus Aurelius (indeed his discussion of "negative allegory" in Marcus Aurelius sounds uncannily like Ginzburg's treatment more than four decades later). He says it is used sparingly by Christian writers like Tertullian and Augustine, but it begins to flourish again in the Renaissance and Reformation, in Sebastian Brant, Erasmus, Sebastian Franck, and J. V. Andreae. "The real flowering of the negative allegory," he writes, "did not come until the Enlightenment, when the right form for it was found (which, to be sure, we already encountered in Lucian and Dio). Reality is presented through the eyes of a foreigner or nonhuman creature; a suggestion of this may already be seen in the works of Swift" (125) and is found overwhelmingly in Voltaire (again, as in Ginzburg).

"The fact that this device has been used copiously in modern literature," Čiževsky notes at the end of his historical presentation, "from the romanticists to L. Tolstoj and Bernard Shaw, is beyond the scope of this study" (125). He briefly cites Shklovsky, but with an incorrect year and neither translation nor discussion of the key term *ostranenie:* "After 1920, V. Šklovskij gave the Russian term 'ostranenie' to this device; this word is also in use in American circles. Neither Šklovskij nor his disciples pay attention to the fact that this device, far from having been invented by L. Tolstoj, has just as long a history as all tropes and figures" (121, n. 94). Shklovsky never claims that the estrangement device was invented by Tolstoy, indeed remarks that he is only using Tolstoy because his works are well known; and he gives examples of estrangement from other and older sources as well (Boccaccio, Pushkin, Gogol, Russian folk tales and riddles). (I am grateful to Michael Denner for steering me to this article.)

Another interesting attempt to connect *ostranenie* with allegory may be found in Daniel Laferrière's 1976 article comparing Shklovsky's theory with its roots in the nineteenth-century Russian aesthetician Aleksandr Afanas'evich Potebnya (1835–91), who defines allegory (*inoskazanie,* lit. "differently narrating" or "differently telling") broadly enough to include the kind of felt imagistic connections generated when the poet Fyodor Ivanovich Tyutchev (1803–1873) translates two nouns in a Heinrich Heine poem with Russian nouns of the exact same genders. Citing the passage from *Kholstomer* that Shklovsky discusses as an example of estrangement in "Art as Device," Laferrière notes: "Yet, however well this passage demonstrates Šklovskij's notion of defamiliarization [*ostranenie*], it also superbly illustrates Potebnja's concept of the '*alle*goricalness' ('*ino*skazatel'nost") of the image. If we were to apply Potebnja's line of reasoning here, we would say that the image of an equine observer is allegorical, is 'something *other*' ('nečto *inoe*') than the image of an ordinary human observer. What for Šklovskij is 'made strange' would for Potebnja be 'made other'" (182). Except, of course, as Čiževsky would insist, in *ostranenie* the "making strange" also empties the allegory of all conventionalized meaning.

Cf. also Jameson, *Prison-House,* 54–58.

2. Cf. Gustafson here, who binarizes Tolstoy into the Stranger and the Resident and then insists that he was somehow both, without exploring the complicated ways in which both opposed reductions interrelate: "Tolstoy the Stranger lives his life separated from the life around him," Gustafson writes, and "Tolstoy the Resident lives to the fullest, assured that his life has meaning and purpose because he is participating in the activity of the world around him" (21). "Resident" and "Stranger" would appear to be thematic categories for Gustafson, convenient labels to affix to specific passages in Tolstoy's fiction, diaries, and letters, and thus mainly organizational strategies; he does not seem particularly interested in how such opposing tendencies could have coexisted in the same life.

3. Note Emerson's phrasing here: "the feeling remains." This is precisely the kind of decentered collective "feeling" that I am calling ideosomatic regulation. Another way of expressing the same vague transindividual certainty, as we see in chapter 5, uses the impersonal pronoun *one:* "one knows," "one feels," and so on. See also Riley, *Impersonal.*

4. Rudnev's opera image here is based on his reading of Natasha's depersonalized reaction to the opera in *War and Peace.* For an important discussion of the connections between Tolstoy's art and his art theory—one that does not, however, go as far as Rudnev—see Šilbajoris (alphabetized in the Works Cited as Shilbajoris):

For instance, Natasha's feelings of estrangement at the opera in Book Eight of *War and Peace* resemble almost perfectly Tolstoy's own description at the beginning of the essay [*What Is Art?*] of an opera rehearsal he saw and was disgusted by. The point emerges from such comparisons that while in reading the essay we are expected to confront the argument itself, in the fiction we need not judge that argument but are free to respond to the characters' human experiences in the context of their depicted lives. This may help us understand why it is that the art of Tolstoy seems so powerful, and the essay often so unacceptable. (11)

Šilbajoris here seems to imply that the argumentative form of Tolstoy's deperson-alization in *What Is Art?* disturbs us because argument requires generalization, indeed in this case universalization. I would add that equally problematic in Tol-stoy's depersonalized argumentation is its repressive idealization, its presentation of estrangement in the idealized guise of nonestrangement. He seems much less inclined to "defend" his estranged characters than he does his own reactions in *What Is Art?* by idealizing their estrangement as true spiritual connection; if he had, I suspect his fiction would be less esteemed.

5. This pattern is especially clear around the time of the writing of *The Kreutzer Sonata* (1891), the book that most violently expresses his disgust at all forms of sexuality, especially that between a husband and his wife. While he is writing the novel, he also works in the fields cutting hay, and records in his diary one evening his conversations with the peasants: "I spoke to them of the sin of sleeping with one's wife, and they agreed" (July 3, 1889; quoted in de Courcel, 201). Right about the time that the novel is published, however, Sof'ya records in her diary that "Lyovochka woke me with passionate kisses" (Sof'ya's diary, July 27, 1891, 158); she imagines that people will somehow know that they're having sex and worries about getting pregnant again, thinking that if people see her walking around with a big belly they "will mechanically repeat the joke circulating in Moscow society: 'there goes the real epilogue to *The Kreutzer Sonata*'" (Sofia's diary, December 25, 1890; quoted in de Courcel, 216).

6. "I'm every sort of onanist," Tolstoy writes in his diary on July 28, 1884 (1:223).

7. Which then, of course, immediately exerted a depersonalizing counterin-fluence, turning Kristeva's Bakhtinian thought into more structuralism: "By shift-ing our attention from the triangle of author/work/tradition to that of text/dis-course/culture, intertextuality replaces the evolutionary model of literary history with a structural or synchronic model of literature as a sign system. The most salient effect of this strategic change is to free the literary text from psychological, sociological, and historical determinisms, opening it up to an apparently infinite play of relationships with other texts, or semiosis" (Morgan, 1). With other *texts—*not *speakers* of texts, Kristeva's original concern.

8. Note that something like this same binary *stran-* logic seems to be operative in Western European languages as well, where the "strand" is a shore that is also a border or edge (one of its meanings in Old Norse) between here and away, the local and the foreign, the "own" and the alien—though, as I say, English *strange,* Spanish *extraño,* and French *étrange* are derived not from the same root but from Latin *extra* < *exter* "outside."

9. "Thus Tolstoy can despise the developmental 'historical view' and yet still posit a utopia up ahead, because, like Rousseau, he is convinced that humanity's task is not to move forward but to move back" (Emerson, "Aesthetics," 246). See also Barran, "Rousseau": "In order to understand *What is Art?*, we must read it as a political work containing both a critique of present civilization and a utopian outline of an ideal society" (1).

10. There is a similar dynamic at work in Tolstoy's attitude toward his loved ones: they are nearly intolerable to him while they are alive, but all his feelings of love and connection and gratitude surge within him upon their death. Thus when Tante Toinette (his distant relation Tat'yana Aleksandrovna Yergol'skaya, who had helped raise him and lived with him most of his life) dies in 1874, he writes his cousin Alexandrine that she had faded in life so that for several years "I avoided her and couldn't see her without a feeling of agony; but now that she's dead . . . my feeling for her has returned with a still greater force" (quoted in Shirer, 76). He has similar reactions to Turgenev and Dostoyevsky, whom he despises while they are alive and finds real love for after they are dead: "I am always thinking of Turgenev. I was intensely fond of him and sorry for him and now I do nothing but read him. I live entirely with him"; "How I should like to be able to say all I feel about Dostoyevsky. I never saw the man and never had any direct relations with him, and suddenly when he died I realized that he was the very closest, dearest and most necessary man for me" (quoted in Shirer, 100–102). He also seems to love his children more expressively after they are dead than he ever could while they were alive, and his anger at his surviving children for summoning doctors and pressuring him to let them operate on Sof'ya in the late summer of 1906—explicitly, as he put it, for not letting her die—may be another example of this same dynamic. Certainly, Tolstoy's last four years would have been much easier had Sof'ya died of her uterine tumor and peritonitis: then Tolstoy could have loved her idealized memory with all his heart.

Three   Shklovsky's Modernist Politics

1. Specifically, he does deal at length with Brecht's *Verfremdungseffekt,* but he leaves Brecht's debt to his own theorization of the *priyom ostraneniya* implicit. See Günther (137), however, for an argument that Shklovsky hints at this debt by illustrating Brecht's theory with an example from Tolstoy's story "Kholstomer," one of the prime examples he used of the *priyom ostraneniya* in "Art as Device."

2. I cite from the book: *Literaturnaya teoriya nemetskogo romantizma* [The literary theory of German romanticism], edited by N. Ya. Berkovsky, translated by T. I. Sil'man and I. Ya. Kopubovsky. Published in Leningrad, 1934, p. 126. [Shklovsky's note]

3. In her book *Istoki russkogo formalizma* [the sources of Russian formalism] Svetlikova quotes from Nikolay Sergeevich Trubetskoy's notes published in 2004:

"'Ostrannenie [*sic*]—Brik's term, Jan. 1969' (the date indicates a conversation with [Roman] Jakobson, who mentioned this). There and again dated in 1992 is the note: 'cf. [Yevgeny] Shvarts on Shklovsky' (referring to the place in 'I Live Restlessly' where he tells us that if Shklovsky liked some idea, he just took it and forgot who he got it from; Shvarts, 1990, 404–5)" (72, my translation). She goes on to explain that Brik was well known for his verbal creativity and invented several of the famous terms and phrases associated with other members of the formalist group.

On the other hand, this report that Brik coined the term and Shklovsky simply stole it isn't exactly a *fact*. Trubetskoy's note is his interpretation of the memory of something that happened sixty years before, dredged up by a man (Jakobson) who was always rather contemptuous of the term, calling it one of those formalist "platitudes galvaudées" that should not be taken too seriously (see Tihanov, "Politics," 667–68). The two men were somewhat uneasy friends, especially after Shklovsky criticized Jakobson for emigrating to Prague scant months before fleeing Russia himself for Berlin in 1922; he also carefully criticizes Jakobson in a letter in *Third Factory* (39–41).

4. For a different historical etiology of modernist estrangement in Shklovsky, Bakhtin, and others, based on the idea that Kantian epistemology introduced an estrangement from reality into all thought and all language, see Holquist and Kliger.

5. Bely writes, for example:

All of them amount to nothing in the face of a living language; living language is an eternally flowing, creative activity, which raises before us a series of images and myths; our consciousness derives power and confidence from these images; they are weapons with which we penetrate darkness. As darkness is defeated, images disintegrate and the poetry of words is gradually worn away; already we identify words with abstract concepts, though above all not in order to convince ourselves of the purposelessness of the images of language; we break down living language into concepts in order to tear them away from life, pack them into thousands of tomes and leave them to rest in the dust of archives and libraries. Then vital life, deprived of vital words, becomes madness and chaos for us; space and time begin to threaten us again; new clouds of the unknown, having drifted up to the horizon of what has been identified, menace us with fire and lightning, threaten to sweep humankind from the face of the earth. Then there follows a period of so-called degeneration; man comes to see that terms have not saved him. Blinded by imminent destruction, man in terror begins to cast a spell with the word over the unknown dangers; to his astonishment he recognizes only in words the means for real incantation; then beneath the crust of the worn-out words a bright stream of new word meanings gushes forth. New words are created. Degeneration is transformed into a healthy barbarism.

The cause of the degeneration is the death of the living word; the struggle with degeneration is the creation of new words. In all declines of culture, regeneration has been preceded and accompanied by a special cult of words; the cult of words is the active cause of new creation. (127–28)

Here are most of the key elements of Shklovsky's theory: the creative power of words, the collapse of creative language into "abstract" (Shklovsky follows Bergson in saying "algebraic") concepts, the resulting descent of life into madness and chaos (actually the opposite end of the symptomatological spectrum of depersonalization from the numbness that Shklovsky theorizes), and the regenerative power of new words.

6. The basic study of the Bergsonian paradigm in Russian formalism—especially Shklovsky, and especially "Art as Device"—is Curtis, who notes that while Shklovsky does not quote Bergson in "Art," "he does make two references to the article in which Yakubinsky links Bergson and the concept of automatization" (115).

7. For a recent attempt to situate Shklovsky's theory of estrangement in the historical context of World War I, see Tihanov: "The War was the propitious ground on which a materialist, substance-oriented view of the world grew strong and flourished amid and out of—ultimately as a protest against—the cacophony and chaos of annihilation" ("Politics," 684).

8. In the acknowledgments to *A Sentimental Journey*, Richard Sheldon describes the process thus: "It actually consists of three separate books: *Revolution and the Front*, written by Shklovsky in the summer of 1919 and published in 1921; *Epilogue: End of the Book 'Revolution and the Front*,' written in the latter part of 1921 and published early in 1922; and 'Writing Desk,' written in May 1922. To make *A Sentimental Journey*, Shklovsky used *Revolution and the Front* as Part One, added 'Writing Desk' as Part Two, divided *Epilogue* into two sections and spliced them into 'Writing Desk'" (xv). And further: "*A Sentimental Journey* was republished twice after Shklovsky returned to the Soviet Union: in Leningrad, 1924, and in Moscow, 1929. Part One, 'Revolution and the Front,' was omitted from the 1924 edition, and Part Two, 'Writing Desk,' was severely cut in the predictable places. The 1929 edition contains both parts, with deletions in Part One and still more drastic deletions in Part Two" (v).

9. El'za (or, in the book, "Alya") is not only the "third Heloise" (after the Heloises of the medieval *Letters of Abelard and Heloise* and Rousseau's *Julie, or the New Eloise*) but, as Richard Sheldon points out, the second Eliza: "It is an interesting coincidence that Laurence Sterne, whose novels *Sentimental Journey* and *Tristram Shandy* so deeply influenced Shklovsky, also wrote a book called *Journal to Eliza*, which is a highly autobiographical epistolary novel about unrequited love. The name Eliza serves the pun made on the names Elsa (El'za in Russian) and Héloïse" (introduction to *Zoo/ZOO*, xxvi, n. 17).

10. Trotsky's critique of formalism was balanced and intelligent, and most

theorists today would probably agree with it: "The form of art is, to a certain and very large degree, independent, but the artist who creates this form, and the spectator who is enjoying it, are not empty machines, one for creating form and the other for appreciating it. They are living people, with a crystallized psychology representing a certain unity, even if not entirely harmonious. This psychology is the result of social conditions" (171). But then, as we'll see, Shklovsky would have agreed with this as well—he was overwhelmingly interested in author and reader psychology, and his memoirs show his sensitivity to the shaping power of social conditions as well. For example, from *A Sentimental Journey:*

> A human being absolutely requires butter. When my niece Marina was sick, she kept asking for butter—even just a little on her tongue.
>   And I wanted butter and sugar all the time.

>> If I were a poet, I would write a poem about butter and set it to music. How much the greed for fat runs through the Bible and Homer! Now the writers and scholars of Petrograd understand that greed . . . Don't think that you don't need art theoreticians.

> A human being lives not by what he eats, but by what he digests. Art is needed as ferment. (*Sentimental,* 234–35, slightly edited in accordance with *Sentimental'noe* 228)

Or, as he says in the preface to the 1925 and 1929 editions of *Theory of Prose,* almost certainly in response to Trotsky's critique: "It is perfectly clear that language is influenced by socioeconomic conditions [*nakhoditsya pod vlyaniem sotsial'nikh otnosheniy,* lit. "exists under the influence of social relations"]" (*O teorii,* 5; *Theory,* vii; he goes on to argue there that "the word is not a shadow . . . the word is a thing," tacitly refuting Trotsky's claim that the word is "the phonetic shadow of the deed"). The infamous line from "Ullya, Ullya, Martians" (published in *Knight's Move*) that Trotsky cites—"Art has always been free of life. Its flag has never reflected the color of the flag that flies over the fortress of the City" (22)—does not deny the *shaping* power of social conditions over art, only the absolute social (or especially political and partisan) *determination* of art. Art is "free of life" not in the sense of being absolutely autonomous from it but in the sense of not being absolutely determined by it. Shklovsky's argument in that piece is close to Oscar Wilde's in "The Decay of Lying," that "Life imitates Art far more than Art imitates Life" (307). It is not that life has *no* impact on art but simply that art's impact on life is *stronger* than life's on art.

For discussion of Trotsky's critique of Shklovsky, see also Erlich (100–105).

11. But his irony is much more complex than this. He also describes himself as at odds with other people, going his own strange way despite the disastrous consequences ("I'm like a samovar used to drive nails," *Sentimental,* 165), and as just as happy merging with an alien identity as with the crowds: "It's pleasant to

lose yourself. To forget your name, slip out of your old habits. To think up some other man and consider yourself him" (151). He is at the time traveling with forged documents, with the identity of a dead man, to avoid capture by the Cheka for his participation in the anti-Bolshevik conspiracy.

12. I suggest later that Shklovsky moves from a somatic focus on author and reader psychology in his essays of the teens to a more "machinic" focus on abstract form in his essays of the early 1920s, but note that even in *Zoo* (1923) we find him warning against the depersonalizing effects of the machine age:

> Things have reshaped man—especially machines.
> Nowadays man only knows how to start them, but then they continue running without any help. They run and run, and they crush man. In science the situation is extremely serious.
> The certainties of reason and the certainties of nature have evaporated. Once there was a top and a bottom, there was time, there was matter. Now nothing is certain. Method reigns supreme. (34, letter 9)

See also letter 30: "An engine of more than forty horsepower annihilates the old morality" and "Speed puts distance between a driver and mankind" (116). This letter is filled with examples of the resulting depersonalization, like the gang that drove around Moscow in a big black automobile abducting and raping women. When they were caught, they confessed readily to both the crimes and their motivation: "We were bored" (119). Admitting ruefully that he loves automobiles himself and is "a man with knowledge of speed and no sense of purpose" (119), Shklovsky insists that "The speed of an engine and the blare of a horn knocked them [the gang members] off the track" (119).

13. See n. 2 in the introduction for sources.

14. Shklovsky adds parenthetically: "Note from Tolstoy's diary, February 29, 1897. Nikol'skoe. 'Chronicles,' December 1915, p. 354." Of course, in 1897 there *was* no February 29; more recent editions of Tolstoy's diaries have tacitly corrected that date to March 1 (see *Polnoe,* 53:141–42). Shklovsky also makes a few small errors in copying Tolstoy's diary entry into his essay: where Tolstoy writes *obtiral pyl'* "I was wiping dust," Shklovsky drops the *pyl'* (*obtiral* "I was wiping"); where Tolstoy writes *mozhno by vosstanovit'* "could be recovered," Shklovsky adds *bylo* (*mozhno bylo by vosstanovit'* "could have been recovered"), and where Tolstoy writes *tselaya slozhnaya zhizn'* "the whole complex life," Shklovsky drops *slozhnaya* (*tselaya zhizn'* "the whole life").

15. Rather than analyzing the obvious contradiction between Shklovsky's discussion of estrangement as a hypermimetic cure for estrangement and his aestheticist claim that "the perceptual process is self-purposive in art," Vygotsky simply takes the stray aestheticist claim to be Shklovsky's main point, riffing on what that claim might have meant had Shklovsky been Immanuel Kant writing two and a half centuries before about the purposelessness of the pleasant:

"The perceptual process is self-purposive in art," as Shklovsky asserts. And indeed that assertion of the self-purposiveness of the perceptual process, that definition of the value of art based on the sweetness it adds to our feeling, unexpectedly reveals all the psychological poverty of formalism and returns us to Kant, who formulated the principle that "that is pleasant which pleases us independently of its meaning." And from this formalist doctrine it follows that the perception of a thing is pleasant for its own sake, as are the beautiful plumage of birds, the color and form of a flower, the coloring of a seashell (Kant's examples). This elementary hedonism, a return to the long since abandoned doctrine of the pleasure and enjoyment we obtain in the contemplation of beautiful things, may in fact be the weakest part of the psychological theory of formalism. (*Psikhologiya,* 82, my translation)

16. In writing his dissertation, Vygotsky has a problem: he is basically on Shklovsky's side, is essentially exfoliating Shklovsky's theory of belabored form as a theory of artistic catharsis, and by the time the attacks on formalism begin in 1924, the dissertation is almost finished. If he simply says outright that he is working in the formalist mode, the dissertation will never be approved. So he conceals his reliance on Shklovsky as best he can. He airbrushes Shklovsky out of Part 4 and writes a new exaggeratedly weak attack on Shklovsky in chapter 3, so weak that only an idiot would not see through it—but then he assumes that most of the people reading it *will* be idiots, so he should be safe. He cannot remove all traces of formalism from his argument, of course; it is too heavily steeped in Shklovsky's theory for that. But he can downplay those traces to the extent that the formalist thread in the dissertation looks like an accident, a coincidence, a case of unplanned parallel thought. (Van Der Veer and Valsinger also speculate that the remaining traces of formalism in the dissertation may have been one reason why Vygotsky found it impossible to find a publisher for it [19].)

What Vygotsky does in Part 4, then, especially chapter 9, is to base his argument on Shklovsky but never mention his name. It is clear to anyone comparing Vygotsky's chapter with Shklovsky's "Art as Device," for example, that Vygotsky has taken his main sources for chapter 9 directly from Shklovsky's essay and indeed is paraphrasing whole sections without attribution. This sort of unattributed paraphrase is a significant academic sin in the West, of course; in a totalitarian society the situation is quite different. There it might even be taken to constitute a subtle act of political subversion, a courageous half-hidden celebration of Shklovsky's work—especially since Vygotsky has already, in his chapter 3 attack, quoted enough of Shklovsky by name to make it clear just whom he is paraphrasing here as the theoretical foundation for his own claims. Vladimir Sobkin and Dmitri Leontev show, in fact, that Vygotsky practiced this sort of virtual citing a good deal in his work (186–87). In *Thinking and Speech,* for example, he paraphrases without attribution important passages from a 1922 article entitled "On the Nature of the Word" by his good friend the banned writer Osip Mandel'shtam, then in internal exile in Voronezh. "This was not just an act of civic courage," Sobkin and Leontev write; "we believe this shows that Vygotsky understood that the days of the culture to which he himself belonged were numbered. And it was probably only because he felt confident that the editors and censors of the new regime were completely uneducated that he indulged himself in quoting these passages. Thereby he was both challenging and ridiculing the emerging totalitarian culture of the 1930s" (186). And that culture had already begun emerging by the mid-1920s. As Lidiya Ginzburg, a literary critic who was Shklovsky's student, wrote in her diary in 1927: "The merry times of laying bare the device have passed (leaving us a real writer—Shklovsky). Now is the time when one has to hide the device as far as one can" (quoted in Boym, "Estrangement," 250).

17. For an interesting study of Shklovsky's encounter with Lukács in the Soviet Union in the late 1930s—writing a balanced (but more negative than positive) reader's report of Lukács's book on the historical novel, not published in book form until 1955 in Hungary, see Tihanov, "Literature." Shklovsky's review reflects not only his attempts to sound like a good Stalinist and lingering traces of his recanted formalism but also rising Russian nationalism on the eve of the Second World War and Lukács's increasingly precarious status as a German-speaking and "cosmopolitan" foreigner in the Soviet Union—who did not discuss a single Russian author in his study of the historical novel.

18. "The relations of parts and the end of the whole remaining the same, what is the difference, whether land and sea interact, and worlds revolve and intermingle without number or end,—deep yawning under deep, and galaxy balancing galaxy, throughout absolute space,—or, whether, without relations of time and space, the same appearances are inscribed in the constant faith of man? Whether nature enjoy a substantial existence without, or is only in the apocalypse of the mind, it is alike useful and alike venerable to me. Be it what it may, it is ideal to me, so long as I cannot try the accuracy of my senses" (Emerson, *Nature,* 46–47). See also Frye, Bloom, Hartman, Woodman, Altizer, Stahl, and my *Apocalypses* (101–8).

19. In this formulation, clearly, the vulgar-materialist approach required of Vygotsky and the older Shklovsky by the Soviet censors is an institutionalized version of Thing 4. Another way of putting that, drawing on the cognitive thought of Lakoff and Johnson, is that a vulgar-materialist approach to literature, in requiring a focus on contents at the expense of form, relies on a CONTAINER metaphor. The contents (contained by the literary text) are things, either as material objects or as objective representations of material objects. For these objectivist thinkers a concern with form is a concern with the shape of the container—which may have important utilitarian consequences (it is hard to drink from a trash can) or trifling aesthetic ones (a tall or a short glass, a teacup or a beer mug, etc.: if all that matters is getting the liquid into your mouth, none of these formal differentials makes the slightest difference). The formalists' focus on form seems to them to imply that for the formalists there's nothing in the glass, or that it doesn't matter what's in the glass; all that matters to them is the shape.

For the formalists, of course, the Kantian idealism that makes the *Ding-an-sich* radically unavailable means that "contents" are an imaginative construct based on mental representations of sense data, psychological (and social/cultural/ideological/etc.) orientations, and so on. Obviously, the aesthetics of form will have a powerful shaping effect on all of that.

In an important sense, however, battling this out on the ground of content and form basically means fighting by rules invented by objectivists. The form/content binary inherently favors an objectivist approach by positing a CONTAINER that either contains an actual substance or is empty. From this point of view, the formalist approach inevitably looks like a small child's tea party: the child and her imaginary friends sitting around an imaginary table sipping imaginary tea.

Of course, this whole objectivist model requires for its successful operation the uncritical literalization of a metaphor: the assumption that a literary text *really is* a container containing things, the corollary assumption that the things contained are (very nearly) the real-world objects they represent. But these objectivizing assumptions are normative in Western culture, giving them the imprimatur of ideosomatic regulation, which *feels* like reality.

Cf. also Boris Eikhenbaum's remark that "the notion of 'content' is, in fact, correlative of the notion 'volume' and not at all of 'form'" (cited and translated by Peter Steiner, 17).

20. This idea was anticipated by Pavel Medvedev in *The Formal Method in Literary Scholarship* (60–61), a 1928 book rhetorically charged with the strident official Soviet antiformalism of the late twenties.

21. For an early anticipation of this reading, see the article on Potebnya and Shklovsky by Daniel Laferrière, who begins with the observation that Shklovsky's notion of estrangement is very similar to Potebnya's notion of allegory or "telling differently," except that Shklovsky thematizes the aesthetic phenomenology in terms of the strange, Potebnya in terms of the familiar. Still, Shklovsky recognizes that every image estranges, and Potebnya notes that in showing the reader something familiar, the image also brings about a *new* perception, a discovery. Laferrière begins to unpack this phenomenological complexity by noting that "Research in the psychology of recognition has established that what is familiar is always 'familiar to *me.*' That is, the feeling of familiarity ('sentiment du familier') is intimately bound up with the 'feeling of me-ness,' with the entire ego of the perceiver" (186). This should mean that anything that is unfamiliar should *not* be bound up with the perceiver's ego; but in Freudian psychoanalysis that which seems strange may in fact be "separated from the conscious part of the ego by the barrier of repression, and [may] therefore [*seem*] not to be connected to the ego from the viewpoint of consciousness" (186). What is repressed from the ego's conscious awareness (and therefore experienced as uncanny or strange—Laferrière notes that he is reading "repression" through the lens of the Freudian paradox of *heimlich/unheimlich,* lit. "homey/unhomey," usually translated "canny/uncanny,"

possibly paraphrasable as "familiar/strange" or "own/alien") poses a threat to the ego's stability and "is said to be 'ego-distonic'" (186):

> Pierre's [brief mystical] experience [in *War and Peace*], for example, is clearly ego-distonic because it goes right back to the origin of the ego and threatens the loss of a boundary between ego and non-ego. Insofar as Pierre's experience seems strange to us it is normally a complex of semantic material that is repressed from our consciousness, while insofar as his experience is familiar to us it is a complex of semantic material that has to do with our own past. Cholstomer's words are also ego-distonic because they attack the notion of possessiveness which an ego in Western society needs in order to survive its contact with other egos. Insofar as Cholstomer's speech is strange to us it constitutes a complex of semantic material that is normally repressed from our consciousness, while insofar as his speech is familiar it is a complex of semantic material that has to do with our own past.
>
> More generally speaking, defamiliarization [by which, following Lemon and Reis, he means specifically *ostranenie*] will always be ego-distonic because it makes us regress back through the barrier of repression to a child-like, naïve, uncategorizing way of perceiving the world, i.e., to a state where the ego was as yet undefended by prearranged ways of sorting out internal and external sense data. Such a state is always *strange* because much of the past (especially early childhood) is normally repressed and is alien to our adult way of experiencing the world. What Šklovskij neglects to investigate is the fact that such a state is also always *familiar*. After all, nothing should be more familiar than one's own personal past. Šklovskij says that the literary artist makes us see a stone as a stone, but he does not add that we all were once perfectly capable of seeing a stone as a stone—not as a weapon to be hurled by an enemy, not as an object coveted for a collection, not as a piece going into the construction of a wall, but as a simple stone, a momentary union of perceiver and perceived before the perceived became an object of fear and desire, before the perceiver became 'other' than the perceived. The great accomplishment of the literary artist is to present us with complexes of semantic material that harmlessly return us to early ego states. (186–87)

This last analysis suggests the Hegelian dialectic I teased out of Shklovsky's article earlier—though I'm not sure I would want to reduce that dialectic to "harmlessly return[ing] us to early ego states."

22. Note that Shklovsky tells us that the fragments of the cylinder that exploded in his hands did not remain in his body but slid out of their own accord (*Sentimental*, 218).

23. The distinction between "thinkings/feelings" (present emotional-becoming-mental activities) and "thoughts/felts" (stored records of past emotional-

becoming-mental activities) is suggested in a later book by Bohm entitled *On Dialogue* (53). It is striking that our standard term for a cognitive action, *thought,* is derived from the participial form of the verb *to think,* suggesting that it represents a past action, while our standard term for an affective action, *feeling,* is derived from the continuous form of the verb *to feel,* suggesting that it represents a current action. Bohm's suggestion that we speak also of "thinkings" and "felts" is useful in drawing attention to the continuously emerging impact of what we've learned (thought and felt and stored) from what we've done in the past on what we are thinking and feeling in the present—or, to use Damasio's terminology, to the power of somatic markers (feelings as reactivations of felts) to shape our emergent decision-making processes (thinkings). Bohm also understands these processes to be collective, transmitted from body to body like a virus.

24. Cf. Tihanov, who writes of Shklovsky's "ambiguous theory of estrangement, where the new was hailed as the saviour of the old (timeless). The drive toward rediscovering the substance of things, the desire to regain in art their true nature, indeed went hand in hand with a conservative epistemology of permanence and inalterability" ("Politics," 686).

25. Cf. Tihanov, who writes of Shklovsky's "(not always unintentional) subversion of the Formalist focus on the literariness of literature (in favor of a traditionalist attention to its social functions)" ("Politics," 672).

26. As I've noted, James M. Curtis tracks the formalist opposition of automatization/deautomatization back to Bergson, probably primarily through Lev Yakubinsky.

27. For a neuropsychoanalytical parallel, see Schore, *Repair:*

> Furthermore, the right hemisphere uses an expansive attention mechanism that focuses on global features (while the left uses a restricted mode that focuses on local detail; Derryberry & Tucker, 1994), a characterization that fits well with Freud's "evenly suspended attention." And, in contrast to the left-hemisphere's activation of "narrow semantic fields," the right hemisphere's "coarse semantic coding is useful for noting and integrating *distantly* related semantic information" (Beeman, 1998, p. 279), a function that allows for the process of free association. Bucci (1993) described free association as "following the tracks of nonverbal schemata," by loosening the hold of the verbal system on the associative process and giving the nonverbal mode the chance to drive the representational and expressive systems; that is, by shifting dominance from a left to right hemispheric state. (50)

I would add that "the left-hemisphere's activation of 'narrow semantic fields' " finds its apotheosis in mathematical/logical notation (the absolute algebraic "purification" of verbal language) and that "loosening the hold of the verbal system on the associative process and giving the nonverbal mode the chance to drive the representational and expressive systems" is perfectly congruent with Kristeva's theory of the survival of the maternal semiotic in the rule of the paternal symbolic. For Schore, the unconscious regulatory expressivity of right-brain-to-right-brain synchronization is grounded in the preoedipal mother-infant dyad, which remains all through life as the model of and foundation for affect regulation and repair of the self or affect dysregulation and disorders of the self.

28. For a rather ill-informed attempt to situate Shklovsky's aesthetic quasi-mysticism in the theological context of Christ's kenosis or self-emptying, see Bogdanov.

29. We might find a literary example of this kind of "simple" or "artisan" making in a modern wig factory in the letter to the narrator from May Kasahara in Haruki Murakami's novel *The Wind-Up Bird Chronicle:*

> *It takes me a few days to make one of "my" wigs. The time differs according to the grade of the product, of course, but you have to measure the time it takes to make a wig in days. First you divide the base into checkerboard squares, and then you plant hair into one square after another in order. It's not assembly line work, though, like the factory in Chaplin's movie, where you tighten one bolt and then the next one comes; each wig is "mine." I almost feel like signing and dating each one when I'm through with it. But I don't, of course: they'd just get mad at me. It's a really nice feeling to know, though, that someone out there in the world is wearing the wig I made on his head. It sort of gives me a sense of, I don't know, connectedness.* (447–48, emphasis in original)

30. In "Nature Vs. Art" Sher lodges some second thoughts about his own published translation, in the course of which he draws particular attention to the fact that *delan'ye veschi* is literally "the making of a thing"; but his ruminations do not lead him to question his own rendition of those two words as "the process of creativity." He is more concerned to critique Lee Lemon and Marion Reis's choice of "object" for *vesch'* "thing," which, Sher says, tends to push Shklovsky's remarks in the direction of science: "So, while Lemon and Reis's bias is clearly in favor of general perception ('object' as nature/science), my framework tends rather to emphasize the artistic context (object as artifact)." Ironically enough, in this essay alone Sher himself translates *vesch'* as "object" sixteen times, as "thing" only eight times; he also renders it as "artifact" twice and as "work" once. He translates *predmet,* the standard Russian word for "object," as "object" five times, as "thing" twice, and as "subject" once. Shklovsky also uses *ob'yekt* once, and Sher translates it "object."

31. Neither of the two technical terms for empathy has entered the vocabulary of educated Russians; they are both specialized lexical items known only to aestheticians: *vchuvstvovanie* (lit. "in-feeling," a morphological loan-formation from German *Einfühlung*) and *vzhivanie* (lit. "in-living"). To the extent that ordinary educated Russians use this concept at all, they tend to refer to it as *perezhivanie* (lit. "across-living") and its verb form *perezhi(va)t'(sya),* which also mean "experi-

ence" and "worry." Mikhail Bakhtin also uses the verb *soperezhivat'* "coexperience" (lit. "with-across-live") for empathy.

32. As Svetlana Boym puts it in "Estrangement as Lifestyle: Shklovsky and Brodsky," it revivifies life by transforming it into a kind of imitation of art, of the making of art:

> By making things strange, the artist does not simply displace them from an everyday context into an artistic framework; he also helps to "return sensation" to life itself, to reinvent the world, to experience it anew. Estrangement is what makes art artistic, but by the same token, it makes everyday life lively, or worth living. It appears that Shklovsky's "Art as a Device" harbors the romantic and avant-garde dream of a reverse mimesis: everyday life can be redeemed if it imitates art, nor the other way around. So the device of estrangement could both *define* and *defy* the autonomy of art. (245)

33. Note that in "Voskreshenie slova," Shklovsky tends to use *perezhivanie* "experience" for the somatic response that he will mostly call *oschuschenie* "sensation" in "Iskusstvo kak priyom." He defines artistic perception, for example, as "perception in which form is experienced" ("vospriyatie, pri kotorom perezhivaetsya forma"; "Resurrection," 42, translation modified in accordance with "Voskreshenie," 37), a formulation that anticipates the notion he borrows five years later from Broder Christiansen that in artistic perception what is sensed is the *deviation* of form from an existing linguistic canon. Another anticipation here of Christiansen's "nicht-sinnliche Form" or "nechuvstvennaya forma" or "nonsensuous/unfelt form" here is: "I eta neobkhodimost' bessoznatel'no chuvstvuetsya mnogimi" (41), "And this necessity"—of creating a new "tight" (*tugoy,* what he will call in "Iskusstvo kak priyom" *zatrudnyonny* "belabored") language—"is unconsciously felt by many people" (47).

But *oschuschenie* and its verb forms do occur in the earlier essay as well, as in this anticipation of the passage from "Art as Device" under discussion: "Nowadays the old art has already died, the new has not yet been born; and things have died [*veschi umerli*]—we have lost our sensation of the world [*oschuschenie mira*]; we are like a violinist who has ceased to feel [*osyazat'*] the bow and the strings, we have ceased to be artists in everyday life, we do not love our houses and clothes, and easily part from a life that we do not sense [*ne oschuschaem*]. Only the creation of new forms of art can restore to the human being experience of the world [*vozvratit' cheloveku perezhivanie mira*], can resurrect things [*voskresit' veschi*] and kill pessimism" ("Resurrection," 46, translation modified in accordance with "Voskreshenie," 40). My alterations in those quotations all reflect the fact that Richard Sherwood systematically translates *perezhivanie* "experience" as "sensation" and *oschuschenie* "sensation" as "awareness."

Note that Shklovsky also uses another noun derived from *oschuschat'/oschutit'* "to feel, to sense" in another early piece, his article on "Potebnya" from 1916, *os-*

chutimost' (the ability to be felt or sensed) and Roman Jakobson suggests the English translation "palpability" for it: "Poetic language is distinguished from prosaic language by the palpability [*oschutimost'*] of its construction. Either the acoustic, the articulatory, or the semasiological aspect of a word may be made palpable" (quoted in Laferrière, 181). This is a good translation, but it becomes misleading as a translation of *oschuschenie,* as in Laferrière's rendering of the first clause of Shklovsky's key paragraph in "Iskusstvo kak priyom": "in order to return *palpability* to life" (181). *Oschuschenie* is not the *ability* to be felt or sensed; it is the feeling or the sensation itself.

Laferrière (under the expanded name now of Rancour-Laferriere) makes a similar argument about Potebnya and Shklovsky and translation of *oschuschenie* as "palpability" in a 1992 article dedicated to the proposition that Shklovsky and the other Russian formalists completely ignored the "literary person": "the writer, the reader, the narrator, the protagonist, the characters, etc.—any literary entity, in short, which might conceivably utter the pronoun 'I' " (327). "To my knowledge," Rancour-Laferriere notes wryly, "texts do not desire, or postulate, or know, or assert, or tell stories, or have encounters, or have dialogues. Persons do these things" (335). I agree with that correction but, as my argument in this section (and this note) should make clear, emphatically disagree with Rancour-Laferriere's reading of the Russian formalists. All he's doing is repeating the stale truisms we have inherited from the depersonalized tradition of structuralist readings of Russian formalism. Shklovsky in particular offers a far more personalized literary theory than the structuralists thought, in lines like "We, the readers, sense the presence of something new [*my oschuschaem noviznu*], the presence of an object in a new cluster" ("Structure," 62; "Stroenie," 80). True, the reader isn't saying "I," but only a person can say "we." It is only readers who let their perception of Shklovsky's argument be focused by the structuralist lens that miss this.

34. For a useful discussion of this argument in "Pamyatnik," see Richard Sheldon's introduction to his translation of *Third Factory,* esp. xxxiii–xxxvi.

35. Shklovsky rarely mentions James by name; he mentions him in passing in "Art as Device," in connection with his discussion of the then widely accepted theory of the "law of the economy of creative powers" ("Art," 4). Before lodging an extremely minimal critique of this idea, that "to so present ideas that they may be apprehended with the least possible mental effort, is the desideratum towards which most of the rules above quoted point" (Spencer, *The Philosophy of Style,* quoted in "Art," 25)—a quotation that Shklovsky does not give us directly but quotes from Aleksandr Veselovsky's paraphrase (see Tihanov, "Politics," 682–83)—Shklovsky notes that Lev Petrazhitsky, with hardly even a glance at Spencer's law, "flings out of the road of his thought James's theory of the bodily basis of affect that has fallen across it" ("Iskusstvo," 10, my translation). This is all he gives us of James, but it is enough to suggest that he is at least casually familiar with *The Principles of Psychology* even in 1916.

Note that Sher translates *telesnaya osnova affekta* "the bodily basis of affect" as "the corporeal basis of the effect" ("Art," 4). This is surely just a slip of the eye, but it has the *effect* of diminishing in Shklovsky's work the importance of *affect*.

36. Boris Paramonov points out that Shklovsky's word for *silenced* here, *vygoloshen,* literally "out-voiced" or "exvocalized" (from *vy* "ex, outward direction" + *golos* "voice"), is a Russian coinage that points tacitly to Hegel's punning on *Bestimmung:*

> In the actual art work, precisely as in literary evolution, what is important is a sensation of the relationship of the parts, we could say the internal self-mediation of its structure. Mediation is definition, and/but definition means/ stands for the correlation or linking of any given elements, their interaction and interdifferentiation. In this way Shklovsky understands the work of art as a self-determining system: this is a dialectical understanding. He writes: "The material of the artistic work is invariably pedaled/treadled [*pedalirovan:* Sher shifts metaphors from foot to hand and gives us 'manipulated'], i.e. isolated [*vydelen* singled/picked out, lit. "done out"], 'out-voiced' " (. . . italics Shklovsky's). "Exvocalization" in German is "definition/determination" (*die Stimme* "voice," *bestimmen* "define, determine"). Shklovsky and Hegel speak the same language. (39)

37. Here is Christiansen's original German:

> Ich hebe nur eine Gruppe der nicht-sinnlichen Formen hervor, die wichtigste, soweit ich sehe: die Differenzempfindungen. Wird etwas als Abweichung von einem Gewohnten, von einem Normalen, von einem irgendwie geltenden Kanon empfunden, so löst es dadurch eine Stimmungsimpression von besonderer Qualität aus, die generell nicht verschieden ist von den Stimmungselementen sinnlicher Formen, nur daß ihr Antezedens eine Differenz, also etwas nicht sinnlich Wahrnehmbares ist. (118)

Note that Fedotov renders Christiansen's "(nicht-)sinnliche Form" ([non-]sensuous form) as "(ne)chuvstvennaya forma" ([un]felt form), which Benjamin Sher translates into English as "(non-)sensuous form" ("Relationship," 20–21). This is especially remarkable given that Sher not only does not have the German original in front of him; he does not even realize that Shklovsky is quoting from a Russian translation of a German original. Because Shklovsky miswrote Christiansen's first initial as Cyrillic *B*—neglected to convert Roman *B* (which in Cyrillic is [v]) into Cyrillic Б—Sher went looking for an aesthetician named *V.* Christiansen, and couldn't find one, and so for some reason added "S." and listed Christiansen in his bibliography as "S. V. Khristiansen." It is, obviously, important to my somatic reading of Shklovsky that Fedotov's Russian translation for these terms (which is all that Shklovsky saw, or could read) uses the participial form of the verb "to feel," so that what is characteristic of *eine sinnliche Form* is that it is *felt,* and what is characteristic of *eine nicht-sinnliche Form* is that it is *not* felt.

38. What this does not mean, as many have assumed, is that "we should understand emotion as an effect, rather than a cause, of behavior" (Doherty, 460, n. 22; for this correction, see also Hansen, 318, n. 37). As John Dewey explains in an 1895 article, James is describing not *emotion* as an effect rather than a cause of behavior, but *feeling*:

> I can but think that Mr. James' critics have largely made their own difficulties, even on the basis of his "slap-dash" statement that "we feel sorry because we cry, angry because we strike, afraid because we tremble." The very statement brings out the idea of *feeling* sorry, not of *being* sorry. On p. 452 (Vol. II) he expressly refers to his task as "subtracting certain *elements of feeling* from an emotional state supposed to exist in its *fullness*" (italics mine). And in his article in this REVIEW (Sept., 1894), he definitely states that he is speaking of an *Affect,* or emotional seizure. By this I understand him to mean that he is not dealing with emotion as a concrete whole of experience, but with an abstraction from the actual emotion of that element which gives it its differentia—its feeling *quale,* its "feel." As I understand it, he did not conceive himself as dealing with that state which we term "being angry," but rather with the peculiar "feel" which any one has when he is angry, an element which may be intellectually abstracted, but certainly has no existence by itself, as full-fledged emotion-experience. (15–16)

James leaves himself vulnerable to the misunderstanding that he is speaking of emotion rather than feeling by writing that "*our feeling of the same changes as they occur* IS *the emotion*" (and indeed by writing this in a chapter entitled "The Emotions"); what he seems to mean is that feeling is an emotion as well, but an emotion *about* emotion, a higher-level emotional-becoming-mental representation of the bodily expression.

39. In another *Knight's Move* piece, "Pounding Nails with a Samovar," Shklovsky argues specifically that the Soviet regime doesn't *have* this sort of canon; it only has propaganda, which "is ceasing to be felt [*perestayot oschuschat'sya*]. What is taking place is an inoculation against it, a certain immunity" (*Khod,* 81; *Knight,* 27). What he presumably means is that Soviet propaganda works intellectually and so not only fails to enlist somatic support (or to disseminate ideosomatic regulation) but actually generates somatic resistance, or *counterideosomatic response.*

An interesting comparative study might be done, in fact, of the somatics of Soviet propaganda and American advertising: where the latter proverbially sells the sizzle, the former tried to sell the steak, and failed miserably, arguably due to the counterideosomatic "inoculation" of which Shklovsky writes. Part of the study would need to focus on the transformation of Russian news propaganda after the fall of the Soviet Union. In the 1994 war against Chechnya, the news simply followed the old Soviet model and suppressed all information about it; by 1999, the Russian news agencies had learned from American advertising (and American news reporting, which is saturated with the ethos of advertising) to sell the sizzle, not the steak. Russian viewers were treated every evening to images of bombed-out apartment buildings (widely blamed on Chechens, though many now suspect the Russian government), teary interviews with survivors and the families of the bombing victims, and fresh-faced Russian soldier boys waving at the camera and calling "Hi Mom!" In response, Russians enthusiastically supported the invasion.

Americans often express concern about the antidemocratic tendencies of post-Soviet Russia, which do in fact exist. What they miss, however, is that the superior effectiveness of American-style (advertising-based) propaganda in the Russian news has been mobilizing widespread popular *support* for the president and his antidemocratic policies—and that the same thing has long been endemic in the United States as well, with especial egregiousness since 2000.

40. Here is Christiansen's German original:

Warum ist uns fremdsprachliche Lyrik, auch wenn wir die Sprache erlernt haben, niemals ganz erschlossen? Die Klangspiele der Worte hören wir doch, wir vernehmen Reim um Reim und fühlen den Rhythmus, wir verstehen den Sinn der Worte und nehmen Bilder und Vergleiche und Inhalt auf: alle sinnlichen Formen, alles Gegenständliche können wir erfassen. Was fehlt uns noch? Es fehlen uns die Differenzimpressionen: die kleinsten Abweichungen vom Sprachgewohnten in der Wahl des Ausdrucks, in der Kombination der Worte, in der Stellung, in der Verschränkung de Sätze: das alles kann nur erfassen, wer in der Sprache lebt, wer durch ein lebendiges Bewußtsein des Sprachnormalen von jeder Abweichung unmittelbar getroffen wird wie von einer sinnlichen Erregung. Das Normale eine Sprache reicht aber noch weiter. Jede Sprache hat ihren charakteristischen Grad von Abstraktheit und Bildlichkeit, die Häufigkeit gewisser Klangmischungen und gewisse Arten des Vergleichs gehören zu ihrer Gewohnheit: jede Abweichung davon empfindet nur in voller Stärke, wem die Sprache als Muttersprache vertraut ist; ihn aber trifft jedes Anderssein eines Ausdrucks, eines Bildes, einer Wortverbindung mit der Stimmung eines sinnlichen Eindrucks. Das ist der Grund, warum wir fremdsprachliche Lyrik niemals ganz verstehen: es fehlen uns hier zur Synthese des ästhetischen Objekts wesentliche Momente.

Dabei gibt es die Möglichkeit einer Differenzverdopplung und einer Differenzumkehrung. Eine bestimmte Distanz vom Gewohnten kann ihrerseits wieder Ausgangspunkt und Maß für Abweichungen sein, sodaß von hier aus nun jede R ü ck k e h r zum Gewohnten als Differenz empfunden wird. (118–19)

41. This passage appears in revised form in "Parallels in Tolstoy," in *Knight's Move* (73–74), an essay into which he condenses his most critical ideas from the first three chapters of *On the Theory of Prose*.

Four   Shklovsky's Hegelianism

1. See note 36 in chapter 3 for an example of Shklovsky's Hegelian pun.
2. Shklovsky's use of Tolstoy's diary entry might be contrasted in this sense with the Soviet-era Russian joke about the man standing in the doorway with an empty bag, trying to remember whether he's just been to the grocery store or not. Here the automatization of experience exemplifies a specific historical and economic situation, in which the empty bag and the man's empty memory together symbolize empty store shelves, which themselves symbolize Soviet economic failure. The man's memory has been emptied not just by "habit" or even "senility" (the joke was typically told of "senility Soviet-style") but by specific material conditions that cannot provide empirical evidence at the bottom of his shopping bag which might be used to confirm or refute his vague suspicions one way or the other.
3. As Brecht writes in the piece on Chinese acting: "The bourgeois theatre emphasized the timelessness of its objects. Its representation of people is bound by the alleged 'eternally human'. Its story is arranged in such a way as to create 'universal' situations that allow Man with a capital M to express himself: man of every period and every colour" (96–97) and, I'd add, every gender. It's perfectly obvious to Shklovsky that Man, the timeless universal Man who experiences reality-loss through automatization, has a wife—though "yes, of course," he would no doubt add if challenged on this, if his habitualized assumptions were made strange, if he were made to work harder with this material, "this happens to women too"; naturally, he might say, he never intended to exclude *them*.

Five   Brecht's Modernist Marxism

1. A much later example of the latter, the Western Marxist "de-realisticizing" of Brecht, might be found in Fredric Jameson's 1998 book on Brecht: "Brecht offered many 'definitions' of this term [*Verfremdungseffekt*], which seems to have migrated from the 'ostranenie' or 'making-strange' of the Russian Formalists via any number of visits to Berlin by Soviet modernists like Eisenstein or Tretiakov" (39). Jameson's stance on Shklovsky's influence on Brecht was much more cautious a quarter of a century earlier, in 1972: "it is particularly instructive to compare the theory of Shklovsky with that of Bert Brecht which bears the same name: the theory of the so-called 'alienation effect' (where the German *Verfremdung* literally means estrangement, like Shklovsky's Russian equivalent)" (*Prison-House*, 58).

2. Böckmann simply agrees with Willett without mentioning Shklovsky by name: Brecht's term, he says, "wohl von den russischen Formalisten übernommen wurde" (31, n. 16), "was adopted from the Russian formalists"; Grimm writes that "Zugleich scheint er von der russischen formalistischen Literaturkritik den bereits 1917 von VIKTOR ŠKLOVSKIJ geprägten Begriff der >Entfremdung< (ostranenije) übernommen und als >Verfremdung< in sein Theoriengebäude eingefügt zu haben" (33), "at the same time he seems to have adopted from Russian formalist literary criticism the concept of 'alienation' (*ostranenie*) coined by Viktor Shklovsky as early as 1917 and introduced it into his theoretical framework as *Verfremdung*." (Both translations are mine.)

3. In his translator's introduction to *Zoo,* Richard Sheldon also notes that, when the book was published in French translation in 1963, the translation was done by Pozner and its publication was sponsored by Louis Aragon and his wife Elsa Triolet, the sister of Lilya Brik. Shklovsky had fallen in love with Triolet and been rejected during his Berlin exile, and his correspondence with her formed the real-world basis of *Zoo* (xxiv). Seven of the letters in the book were written by Triolet, and when Maksim Gorky noticed that they were among the best writing in *Zoo,* he encouraged her to publish a book on Tahiti, which she did in 1925. In the 1930s she too began to write in French and won the Prix Goncourt in 1944 for *Le premier accroc coûte deux cents francs.*

4. Ungvári offers a rather confused account of this:

> The meaning of "ostranenija": to make rare, peculiar, strange. Its true meaning, of course, can only be understood by contrasting it with the term "becoming used to," since *ostranenija* stems from the word *strannoi* (strange), and recognizably refers to the Hegelian confrontation, that of the contradiction between becoming used to and recognizing something anew. Linguistically, of course, one would have to force the identification of "making strange" with "*Verfremdung.*" The Russian translator of Brecht, Victor Klujev expresses the term *Verfremdung* with *otchuzhdenije.* True enough, even in Soviet literary criticism there are those who favor the identification of the two concepts, but on the whole the matter of linguistic identification is beside the point. (222)

First, the nominative forms are *ostraneni(y/j)e* and *stranniy/j,* not *ostranenija* (a genitive) and *strannoi* (a genitive or dative). Second, it's a bit of a stretch to call the connection with Hegel "recognizable," since there is nothing in Shklovsky's argumentation or the morphology of his term that recognizably connects up with Hegel. The connection with Hegel is *speculative,* not "recognizable." Third, given that the roots *stran-* and *fremd* both mean strange, the linguistic connection between *ostranenie* and *Verfremdung* doesn't exactly need to be "forced." Fourth, the 1966 Kluyev book he cites—*Teatral'no-esteticheskie vsgladi Brekhta*—is a literary-critical study of Brecht, not a translation. (The translation, as we've seen, had been done six years earlier by Nedelin and Yakovenko.) And fifth, since he has been talking about *three* named concepts, *ostranenie, otchuzhdenie,* and *Verfremdung,* it's difficult to know which two concepts he thinks are identified "even in Soviet literary criticism"—presumably *ostranenie* and *Verfremdung,* since the pairing that immediately precedes this sentence, "*Verfremdung* with *otchuzhdenie,*" was standard and mandatory in Soviet literary criticism and thus wouldn't merit the "even."

5. This famous passage, for example:

> The bourgeoisie cannot exist without constantly revolutionising the instruments of production, and thereby the relations of production, and with them the whole relations of society. Conservation of the old modes of production in unaltered form, was, on the contrary, the first condition of existence for all earlier industrial classes. Constant revolutionising of production, uninterrupted disturbance of all social conditions, everlasting uncertainty and agitation distinguish the bourgeois epoch from all earlier ones. All fixed, fast-frozen relations, with their train of ancient and venerable prejudices and opinions, are swept away, all new-formed ones become antiquated before they can ossify. All that is solid melts into air, all that is holy is profaned, and man is at last compelled to face with sober senses his real conditions of life, and his relations with his kind. (29–30)

6. Note that Jameson also challenges the notion that Brecht is "doctrinaire," that he is "dogmatic," that he has a specific Marxist "message" that he is attempting to inculcate:

> But a serious (yet productive) question may precisely be raised here by the very nature of Brecht's Marxism as such: for on one view, what he learned from Korsch was not a set of doctrines and principles, which could serve as just such a framework, but, rather, an attitude hostile to system in general, the so-called "logical empiricism" of the Vienna circle, which was equally hostile to the dialectic (and to Hegelian versions of Marxism) and, while committed to a radical and Marxian politics, felt able to denounce abstract doctrine and belief in fully as thoroughgoing a way as the modernist littérateurs evoked above. Where, then, is Brecht's Marxism as a doctrine to be found in the first place? Where are his ideas? And even if, as Lukács so scandalously suggested in "What is Orthodox Marxism?" . . . , "Orthodox Marxism . . . refers exclusively to *method*"—a hint we will try to follow up below—there remains the matter of the ideational content Brecht's work is supposed to teach, since it is precisely didacticism that offered our other stumbling block. (24)

As Steven Helmling notes in his reading of Jameson's Brecht book, "Jameson dissolves the complaint of Brechtian 'doctrine' itself, daring any complainant to specify, on any issue, a particular Brechtian dogma, let alone a system of doctrine or a doctrinal cast of mind more generally. (Brecht's detractors make this point negatively when they dismiss Brecht as a *failed* dogmatist, his 'doctrine' falling short of systematic consistency, and lapsing into mere *plumpes Denken.*)"

7. I know of no evidence that suggests that Wilhelm Reich and Brecht knew each other, or knew of each other's work; but they both lived in Berlin at around the same time (Brecht from 1924 to 1933, Reich from 1930 to 1939), and both were Marxists (though Reich joined the German Communist Party and Brecht did not).

8. Carol Martin provides more detail:

> What Brecht saw Mei perform—the title of the "opera" was *Dayu shajia* (The Fisherman's Revenge)—could only give Brecht a small part of the system of signification of Chinese acting. Generally, *jingju,* the traditional style of acting that Mei mastered, stressed both techniques of representation and an inner technique of introspection. The four salient characteristics of traditional Chinese acting at the time of Mei were fluidity, plasticity, sculpturality, and conventionality. Conventionality, however, refers not only to form but also to *xie yi,* which has no exact equivalent in English but which can be understood as "essence." This characterization of traditional performance via Chinese painting has been used since the beginning of the 20th century.
>
> While Brecht was seeing "alienation," Mei was concerned with essence, specifically the four essences: life, movement, language, and decor (costumes, general setting). Mei's technique appeared to Brecht's Western eyes as form but was to Mei, at least in part, a transcendent kind of theatre refined from life into a higher plane of human movement, lyrical language, and theatrical visuality . . . Thus Mei, in the words of his contemporaries, was concerned with the "essence rather than the appearance of things" (78)

Citing Sun Huizhu to the effect that "while the external action is far removed from its natural appearance in real life—every little gesture, every utterance, is guided by convention and timed to music and rhythm—internally the actors are encouraged, however, to forget about 'acting' and to move as close as possible to their characters," Martin comments: "Following Sun's explanation, Mei's pantomime and his interior process were parallel but dialectical. Highly stylized and predetermined dance, gesture, and voice work place exterior demands on the actor. Yet, the actor has also to invent an interior reality to transform the distance between the artificiality of what he is doing into the reality of what he wants to convey. Brecht seems not to have been interested in Mei's explanations of the dual structure of exterior and interior processes in Chinese acting" (79).

9. Eric Bentley translates this as: "In the first place it is difficult, when watching the Chinese act, to rid ourselves of the feeling of strangeness that they arouse

in us because we are Europeans. One must be able to imagine they achieve the 'alienation effect' also in their Chinese spectators" (19).

10. Brecht was always susceptible to this sort of dogmatization of his own theory. Just one example, from the same theoretical domain as the Chinese acting essay, the problem of the estranging force of the foreign: "Similarly the Eskimo definition 'A car is a wingless aircraft that crawls along the ground' is a way of estranging the car" (Willett, *Brecht*, 145). Since the Eskimo definition is not "a way of estranging the car" for the Eskimo, only for non-Eskimos, and especially for non-Eskimos who are so familiar with cars as to be unconscious of that familiarity, Brecht's theorization of that definition as *generally* estranging seems to partake of Feeling 4. Once the estrangement effect becomes a stable property of an utterance—or, worse, of an unuttered sentence—it is an effect without an effect, an idealized estrangement that does not estrange.

This passage could be retheorized, however, as a description of deindividualized group estrangement, as an effect created not by an Eskimo speaking to a non-Eskimo, or by a non-Eskimo quoting an Eskimo to a non-Eskimo, but by *das Man*. That is to say, if estrangement is not a specific effect perpetrated by an individual on another individual, or on a group, but a group metaeffect that is circulated as part of the group's ideosomatic self-regulation, then "a way of estranging" without grammatical subject or object, without situational context, becomes an accurate description of the impersonal functioning of *das Man*. Then, too, the estrangement effect as a theatrical strategy—the sense in which Brecht typically speaks of it—might need to be retheorized as a secondary (re)*channeling* of that group metaeffect, an attempt to do deliberately what one has experienced "accidentally" or "randomly," which is to say, collectively, without individualized agency. (Since Brecht particularizes the Eskimo definition and "the car," this radical retheorization of his utterance gives him too much credit; he is, almost certainly, just museumizing the estrangement effect.)

For further discussion of the dialectical cycling of ideosomatic regulation through the outward identificatory movement of empathy and the inward critical movement of estrangement, see "Practical Work in the Theater" below.

11. Marcuse himself had pronounced approvingly on Brecht's concept of *Verfremdung* the previous year, in chapter 3 of his 1964 book *One-Dimensional Man*. Having read Tzvetan Todorov's 1965 French translation of key formalist texts, including Shklovsky's "Art as Device," Marcuse in his *An Essay on Liberation* (1969) pronounced somewhat less approvingly on Shklovsky's *ostranenie,* seeing it as ultimately powerless against alienation. For discussion, see Tihanov, "Politics," 689–91.

12. Cf. Günther on Brecht's incipient dialecticization of the empathy/estrangement distinction in this passage:

The *Gestus* of the showing and the citing effects a distancing in the relationship to the behavior and the expressions of the represented characters. But estrangement should not be misunderstood as a complete driving out of the quirks of the represented characters. It means not the absence of emotion but rather emotions "which need not correspond to those of the character portrayed." The conflict between empathy and distancing comes to a crisis and is thereby rendered conscious as an element of representation. The stress on the contradictory and the dialectical expressed in the distanced showings and citings of the epic theater can thus be understood as the counterpart to Bakhtin's dialogical principle. (139, my translation)

13. For discussion, see note 14 of chapter 3.

14. For a reading of Vygotsky's dissertation exclusively in terms of this behaviorism, all but ignoring the dialectical complexities of chapter 9 and especially chapter 11, see the two articles by West.

15. For some reason, when Fredric Jameson quotes this passage in his epilogue, having given Brecht's original German and then Willett's English translation—his practice throughout the book, though many of the translations are his own—he tacitly amends Willett, changing "we have to conclude that we are partaking in interests which really *were* universally human" (146) to "we must suppose that in doing so we are sharing interests that *are* actually universally human" (Jameson, 177; emphasis added to both quotations). Does this mean that Jameson believes that Brecht believed that these interests from a specific past historical context and specific social class really *are* universally human? Or is it merely a typo, like *Arbeit* for *Art* in his retyping into the book of Brecht's phrase as "eine Verallgemeinerung interessantester *Arbeit* statt" (176)?

16. Marx continues:

> An adult cannot become a child again, or he becomes childish. But does the naivete of the child not give him pleasure, and does not he himself endeavor to reproduce the child's veracity on a higher level? Does not in every epoch the child represent the character of the period in its natural veracity? Why should not the historical childhood of humanity, where it attained its most beautiful form, exert an eternal charm because it is a stage that will never recur? There are rude children and precocious children. Many of the ancient peoples belong to this category. The Greeks were normal children. The charm their art has for us does not conflict with the immature stage of the society in which it originated. On the contrary, its charm is a consequence of this and is inseparably linked with the fact that the immature social conditions which gave rise, and which alone could give rise, to this art cannot recur. (*German*, 47)

17. Western Marxism is generally conceptualized as arising out of the reinterpretations of Marx undertaken in 1923 by Lukács in *History and Class Consciousness* and Korsch in *Marxism and Philosophy* in opposition to the objectivizing tradition of the Second International and the Soviet Union, associated first

with Plekhanov, Kautsky, and Bernstein, and later (though problematically) with Lenin, and certainly with Stalin. As the distinction is normally presented, orthodox "Eastern" or Soviet Marxism (or "Marxism-Leninism-Stalinism") is grounded in a mechanistic and deterministic model according to which the "objective" material facts of economics (ownership of the means of production) and class position automatically determine both action and thought; the Western opposition, later including Gramsci and Brecht and the Frankfurt school, is characterized by a return to the Hegelian dialectic (as opposed to simple unidirectional determinism) as the true motor force behind historical movement and an insistence on the transformative power of art and ideology, or what Lukács called the subjectivity of class consciousness. Lukács was also the first to insist on the importance for Marx (the Hegelian thinker) of alienation, or what he renamed reification, which for him was the bourgeois illusion that social phenomena were in fact things: "Its basis is that a relation between people takes on the character of a thing and thus acquires a 'phantom-objectivity,' an autonomy that seems so strictly rational and all-embracing as to conceal every trace of its fundamental nature—the relation between people" (*History,* 83). This phantom objectivity dominated the Soviet condemnation of formalism in the late 1920s and early 1930s, of course—Shklovsky's Hegelian belief that the "thing" is a construct that can lose reality through automatization being read undialectically as sheer subjectivism—and continued to cause problems for Brecht upon his return to Germany after the war. Lukács and Korsch were vilified by the orthodox Marxists in the Soviet Union in the remaining months of Lenin's life, as Stalin and Zinoviev began to plot to take over after his death (in January 1924). By 1930 Lukács too had recanted and converted to Stalinism, thus laying the groundwork for the famous Lukács-Brecht debate (see Dusek), Lukács representing "conservative" Stalinist Marxism and socialist realism, Brecht representing the radical revolutionary Hegelian Marxism of the earlier Lukács and, of course, formalist modernism.

For the two Marxisms, see Gouldner, Kevin Anderson, and Perry Anderson. For Lukács, see Arato and Breines (Lukács and Western Marxism), Starosta, Rockmore, Tihanov *Master* and Neubauer (Lukács and Bakhtin), Sheppard (Lukács and Worringer), and Goldmann (Lukács and Heidegger). For Korsch, see Goode (Korsch and Western Marxism), Giles (81–112), and Kellner's commentary in *Korsch.* For Gramsci, see Boggs and Beilharz (Gramsci and Western Marxism), Haug, Morton, Jessop, and Brandist (Gramsci and Bakhtin).

18. For discussion of *das Man,* see my "Somatics of Literature," chapter 6.

19. Or this passage from "Interview with an Exile" (1934):

Our time has seen amazing developments in all the sciences. We have acquired an entirely new psychology: viz., the American Dr Watson's Behaviourism. While other psychologists were proposing introspective investigation of the psyche in depth, twisting and bending human nature, this philosophy based itself solely on the human psyche's outward effects: on people's behaviour. Its theories have something in common with American business life, with the whole of modern advertising. Salesmen all over the world are trained according to its principles to influence their customers' behaviour; they learn by rule of thumb how to provide new needs for their fellow men. (Example: a man goes into a showroom, mildly infected, and comes out, severely ill, in possession of a motor-car.) (67)

Brecht's point here is not that the theater should do exactly the same as Watson in the lab or as the car salesman making a sale but that in a behavioristic era the theater should *explore* the conditions, strategies, and consequences of the manipulation of human nature.

20. Artaud also speaks of "total spectacle" (86), which harks back to Gropius's and Piscator's concept of "total theater" (see Willett, *Art,* 151, 155–56), and insists that the Theater of Cruelty be addressed not to "psychological man" or "social man" but "only to total man" (123). While these are related concepts, however, they refer to acts performed by the whole troupe, overseen by the *metteur en scène,* not, like "total creation" and the "total act," by the single actor, of whom Artaud writes:

Moreover, these symbolical gestures, masks, and attitudes, these individual or group movements whose innumerable meanings constitute an important part of the concrete language of the theater, evocative gestures, emotive or arbitrary attitudes, excited pounding out of rhythms and sounds, will be doubled, will be multiplied by reflections, as it were, of the gestures and attitudes consisting of the mass of all the impulsive gestures, all the abortive attitudes, all the lapses of mind and tongue, by which are revealed what might be called the impotence of speech, and in which is a prodigious wealth of expressions, to which we shall not fail to have recourse on occasion. (94–95, emphasis in original)

Grotowski argues "that what the actor achieves should be . . . a total act, that he does whatever he does with his entire being, and not just one mechanical (and therefore rigid) gesture of arm or leg, not any grimace, helped by a logical inflection and a thought. No thought can guide the entire organism of an actor in any living way" (123). He also compares "a total reaction" with "a reaction guided by a thought." For Brecht and Artaud, see Friedrich "Deconstructed."

21. If we have been socialized to the German language, we feel the German original in much the same apparently "foundational" way: "Laß ihn nur nicht in seinen Brustbeutel langen" (149). If we have been socialized to both German and English, we can read the two texts comparatively, trying out how each makes us feel, juxtaposing the pressure one puts on us to create reality in one way with the pressure the other puts on us to create reality in perhaps a slightly different way, and so sitting in judgment on the translator. This is the dual proprioceptive stabilization that makes it possible for us as translation critics to speak of "equivalence": we create in our own mediatory proprioceptive bodies a felt convergence between two group linguistic stabilizations, the source-cultural and the target-cultural, and

use that convergence as a touchstone by which to evaluate the felt mesh between the two texts. Because this convergence is a somatic construct, of course, it will inevitably be constructed to some degree differently by different people: hence the endless arguments over the quality of a specific translation. Because that construct is nevertheless bilaterally *stabilized* by ideosomatic group regulation, however, it is unlikely that those arguments will be entirely erratic, aleatory, centrifugal, hit or miss. There will never be an infinite number of random subjective constructions of a stabilizing convergence between source-cultural and target-cultural proprioception. While it is unlikely that every translator or translation critic will agree as to the "accuracy" or "equivalence" or other measure of translation quality in regard to a specific translation, it is highly likely that a few issues or features will be agreed upon as the contested basis for the assessment.

Works Cited

Adolphs, Ralph. "Neural Mechanisms for Recognizing Emotion." *Current Opinion in Neurobiology* 12.2 (2002): 169–78.

Adolphs, Ralph, Daniel Tranel, and Antonio Damasio. "Impaired Recognition of Emotion in Facial Expressions Following Bilateral Damage to the Human Amygdala." *Nature* 372 (1994): 669–72.

———. "The Human Amygdala in Social Judgment." *Nature* 393 (June 4, 1998): 470–74.

Adolphs, Ralph, Hannah Damasio, Daniel Tranel, Gregory Cooper, and Antonio Damasio. "A Role for Somatosensory Cortices in the Visual Recognition of Emotion as Revealed by 3-D Lesion Mapping." *Journal of Neuroscience* 20 (2000): 2683–90.

Albert, Georgia. "Understanding Irony: Three *essais* on Friedrich Schlegel." *MLN* 108.5 (December 1993): 825–48.

Allee, Warder C., Alfred E. Emerson, Orlando Park, Thomas Park, and Karl P. Schmidt. *Principles of Animal Ecology.* Philadelphia: Saunders, 1949.

Altizer, Thomas J. J. *The New Apocalypse: The Radical Christian Vision of William Blake.* East Lansing: Michigan State University Press, 1967.

Anargyros-Klinger, Annie. "The Thread of Depression Throughout the Life and Works of Leo Tolstoy." Translated by Elaine Bolton. *International Journal of Psycho-analysis* 83.2 (2002): 407–18.

Anderson, Kevin. *Lenin, Hegel, and Western Marxism: A Critical Study.* Urbana: University of Illinois Press, 1995.

Anderson, Perry. *Considerations on Western Marxism.* London: New Left Books, 1976.

Anderson, Steven W., Antoine Bechara, Hannah Damasio, Daniel Tranel, and Antonio R. Damasio. "Impairment of Social and Moral Behavior Related to Early Damage in Human Prefrontal Cortex." *Nature Neuroscience* 2 (1999): 1032–37.

Arato, Andrew, and Paul Breines. *The Young Lukács and the Origins of Western Marxism.* New York: Seabury, 1979.

Artaud, Antonin. *The Theater and Its Double.* 1938. Translated by Mary Caroline Richards. 1958. Reprint, New York: Grove, 1979.

Austin, J. L. *How To Do Things With Words.* 1962. Reprint, Cambridge, MA: Harvard University Press, 1975.

Works Cited

Avineri, Shlomo. *Hegel's Theory of the Modern State.* Cambridge: Cambridge University Press, 1972.

Bai, Ronnie. "Dances with Mei Lanfang: Brecht and the Alienation Effect." *Comparative Drama* 32.3 (Fall 1998): 389–433.

Bakhtin, Mikhail. "Author and Hero in Aesthetic Activity." Translated by Vadim Liapunov. In Michael Holquist and Vadim Liapunov, eds., *Art and Answerability: Early Philosophical Essays,* 4–256. Austin: University of Texas Press, 1990.

———. "Discourse in the Novel." 1934–1935. In *The Dialogic Imagination: Four Essays,* 259–422. Edited by Michael Holquist. Translated by Caryl Emerson and Michael Holquist. Austin: University of Texas Press, 1981.

Barran, Thomas. "Anna's Dreams." In Liza Knapp and Amy Mandelker, eds., *Approaches to Teaching Tolstoy's Anna Karenina,* 161–65. New York: Modern Language Association of America, 2003.

———. "Rousseau's Political Vision and Tolstoy's *What is Art?*" *Tolstoy Studies Journal* 5 (1992): 1–12.

Bateson, Gregory. "Toward a Theory of Schizophrenia." In *Steps to an Ecology of Mind,* 201–27. 1972. Reprint, New York: Ballantine, 1985.

Beilharz, Peter. "The Decline of Western Marxism: Trotsky, Gramsci, Althusser." *Thesis Eleven* 75.1 (2003): 126–34.

Bely, Andrey. "The Magic of Words." In Thomas G. West, ed., *Symbolism: An Anthology,* 121–43. London: Methuen, 1980.

Benjamin, Walter. "What Is Epic Theatre? [First Version]." *Understanding Brecht,* 1–13. 1966. Translated by Anna Bostock. London: Verso, 1998.

Berg-Pan, Renata. "The Chinese Influence on the Dramaturgy of Bertolt Brecht." Ph.D. diss., Harvard University, 1971.

Bergson, Henri. *Time and Free Will: Essay on the Immediate Data of Consciousness.* 1889. Translated by F. L. Pogson. London: George Allen / New York: Macmillan, 1913.

Blake, William. *The Complete Poetry and Prose of William Blake.* Edited by David V. Erdman. Garden City, NY: Anchor/Doubleday, 1982.

Bloch, Ernst. "Entfremdung, Verfremdung." *Verfremdungen,* vol. 1, 81–90. Frankfurt: Suhrkamp, 1962. Translated by Anne Halley and Darko Suvin as "Entfremdung, Verfremdung: Alienation, Estrangement." *TDR/The Drama Review* 15.1 (Fall 1970): 120–25.

Bloom, Harold. *Blake's Apocalypse: A Study in Poetic Argument.* New York: Anchor/Doubleday, 1963.

Böckmann, Paul. *Provokation und Dialektik in der Dramatik Bert Brechts* ("Provocation and Dialectic in the Drama of Bert Brecht"). Krefeld: Scherpe, 1961.

Bogdanov, Alexei. "*Ostranenie,* Kenosis, and Dialogue: The Metaphysics of Formalism According to Shklovsky." *Slavic and East European Journal* 49 (2005): 48–62.

Boggs, Carl. *The Two Revolutions: Antonio Gramsci and the Dilemmas of Western Marxism.* Boston, MA: South End, 1984.

Bohm, David. *On Dialogue.* London: Routledge, 1996.

———. *Thought as a System.* 1992. Reprint, London: Routledge, 1994.

Bourdieu, Pierre. *Distinction: A Social Critique of the Judgement of Taste.* 1979. Translated by Richard Nice. London: Routledge and Kegan Paul, 1984.

———. *Language and Symbolic Power.* Edited by John B. Thompson. Translated by Gino Raymond and Matthew Adamson. 1982. Cambridge: Harvard University Press, 1991.

Boym, Svetlana. "Estrangement as a Lifestyle: Shklovsky and Brodsky." In Susan Rubin Suleiman, ed., *Exile and Creativity: Signposts, Travelers, Outsiders, Backward Glances,* 241–62. Durham: Duke University Press, 1998.

———. "Poetics and Politics of Estrangement: Victor Shklovsky and Hannah Arendt." *Poetics Today* 26.4 (Winter 2005): 581–611.

Brandist, Craig. "Gramsci, Bakhtin, and the Semiotics of Hegemony." *New Left Review* 216 (March-April 1996): 94–109.

Brecht, Bertolt. "Bei Durchsicht meiner ersten Stücke." In *Schriften 3,* 239–45. Vol. 23 of Brecht, *Werke.* Translated by John Willett as "On Looking Through My First Plays." In Brecht, *Man,* 272.

———. "Dialog über Schauspielkunst." In *Schriften 1,* 279–83. Vol. 23 of Brecht, *Werke.* Translated by John Willett as "A Dialogue About Acting." In Willett, *Brecht,* 26–28.

———. " 'Katzgraben'—Notate 953." In *Schrifte 5: Theatermodelle, 'Katzgraben' Notate 1953,* 399–490. Vol. 25 of Brecht, *Werke.* Translated by John Willett as "Notes on Erwin Strittmatter's Play *Katzgraben.*" In Willett, *Brecht,* 247–51.

———. "Kleines Organon für das Theater." In *Schriften 3,* 65–97, vol. 23 of Brecht, *Werke.* Translated by John Willett as "A Short Organon for the Theater." In Willett, *Brecht,* 179–205.

———. "Kurze Beschreibung einer neuen Technik der Schauspielkunst, die einen Verfremdungseffekt hervorbringt." In *Schriften 2,* 641–59. Vol. 22 of Brecht, *Werke.* Translated by John Willett as "Short Description of a New Technique of Acting which Produces an Alienation Effect." In Willett, *Brecht,* 136–47.

———. "Lohnt es sich, vom Amateurtheater zu reden?" In *Schriften 2,* 590–93. Vol. 22 of Brecht, *Werke.* Translated by John Willett as "Is It Worth Speaking About the Amateur Theatre?" In Willett, *Brecht,* 149–52.

———. *Man Equals Man and the Elephant Calf.* In John Willett and Ralph Manheim, eds., *Collected Plays: Two.* 1979. Reprint, London: Methuen, 1994.

———. *Mann ist Mann: Die Verwandlung des Packers Galy Gay in den Militärbaracken von Kilkoa im Jahre neunzehnhundertfünfundzwanzig.* In *Stücke 2,* 93–168. Vol. 2 of Brecht, *Werke.* Translated by Gerhard Nellhaus as "Man Equals Man." In Brecht, *Man,* 1–76.

———. "Rede im Rundfunk." In *Schriften 4: Texte zu Stücke,* 40–42. Vol. 24 of

Brecht, *Werke*. Translated by John Willett as "Introductory Speech to *Mann ist Mann*." In Willett, *Brecht*, 31–32.

———. "Verfremdungseffekte in der chinesischen Schauspielkunst." In *Schriften 2*, 200–210. Vol. 22 of Brecht, *Werke*. Translated into Russian by V. Nedelin and L. Yakovenko as "'Effekt otchuzhdeniya' v kitayskom stsenicheskom iskusstve." In *O teatre* (On the theater). Moscow: Izdatel'stvo inostrannoy literatury, 1960. Available at http://tafi.narod.ru/world_drams/breht/china.htm. (accessed November 3, 2005). Translated into English as "The Fourth Wall of China." *Life and Letters* (Winter 1936). Retranslated by John Willett as "Alienation Effects in Chinese Acting." In Willett, *Brecht*, 91–99. Retranslated by Eric Bentley as "On Chinese Acting." In Carol Martin and Henry Bial, eds., *Brecht Sourcebook*, 15–22. London: Routledge, 2000.

———. "Was arbeiten Sie? / Gespräch mit Bert Brecht." In Carl Wege, ed., *Brechts "Mann ist Mann": Materialien*, 281–85. Frankfurt am Main: Suhrkamp Verlag, 1982. Translated by John Willett as "Conversation with Bert Brecht." In Willett, *Brecht*, 14–16.

———. *Werke: Große kommentierte Berliner und Frankfurter Ausgabe.* 30 vols. Edited by Werner Hecht, Jan Knopf, Werner Mittenzwei, and Klaus-Detlef Müller. Berlin and Weimar: Aufbau-Verlag / Frankfurt am Main: Suhrkamp Verlag, 1988–94.

———. "Zu 'Der Flug der Lindberghs'." In *Schriften 4: Texte zu Stücke*, 87–88. Vol. 24 of Brecht, *Werke*. Translated by John Willett as "An Example of Paedagogics (Notes to *Der Flug der Lindberghs*)." In Willett, *Brecht*, 31–32.

Brennan, Teresa. *The Transmission of Affect.* Ithaca: Cornell University Press, 2004.

Bruns, Gerald L. "Toward a Random Theory of Prose." In Shklovsky, *O teorii/ Theory*, ix–xiv.

Burke, Kenneth. *Language as Symbolic Action: Essays on Life, Literature, and Method.* Berkeley: University of California Press, 1966.

Butler, Judith. *Bodies That Matter: On the Discursive Limits of "Sex."* New York: Routledge, 1993.

———. *Excitable Speech: A Politics of the Performative.* London: Routledge, 1997.

———. *Gender Trouble: Feminism and the Subversion of Identity.* 1990. Reprint, London: Routledge, 1999.

Carpenter, William B. *Principles of Mental Physiology, with Their Applications to the Training and Discipline of the Mind, and the Study of Its Morbid Conditions.* New York: Appleton, 1874.

Carter, Adam. "'Self-Creation and Self-Destruction': Irony, Ideology, and Politics in Richard Rorty and Friedrich Schlegel." *Parallax* 4.4 (October 1, 1998): 21–40.

Čiževsky, Dmitry. "Comenius' *Labyrinth of the World*: Its Themes and Their Sources." *Harvard Slavic Studies*, 1:83–135. Cambridge, MA: Harvard University Press, 1953.

Christiansen, Broder. *Der Philosophie der Kunst* ("The Philosophy of Art"). Hanau: Clauss and Fedderson, 1909. Translated into Russian by G. P. Fedotov as *Filosofiya iskusstva.* St. Petersburg: Shipovnik, 1911.

Cixous, Hélène. *"Coming to Writing" and Other Essays.* Edited by Deborah Jenson. Translated by Sarah Cornell, Deborah Jensen, Ann Liddle, and Susan Sellers. Cambridge, MA: Harvard University Press, 1991.

———. "The Laugh of the Medusa." In Elaine Marks and Isabelle de Courtivron, eds., *New French Feminisms,* 334–49. New York: Schocken, 1981.

Coleridge, Samuel Taylor. *Biographia Literaria, or Biographical Sketches of My Literary Life and Opinions.* Edited by Henry Nelson Coleridge. New York: Wiley and Putnam, 1847.

Curtis, James M. "Bergson and Russian Formalism." *Comparative Literature* 28.2 (Spring 1976): 109–21.

Damasio, Antonio R. *Descartes' Error: Emotion, Reason, and the Human Brain.* New York: Putnam, 1994.

———. *Looking for Spinoza: Joy, Sorrow, and the Feeling Brain.* New York: Harcourt, 2003.

———. *The Feeling of What Happens: Body and Emotion in the Making of Consciousness.* New York: Harcourt, 1999.

Darwin, Charles. *The Expression of Emotion in Man and Animals.* 1872. Reprint, Chicago: University of Chicago Press, 1974.

De Courcel, Martine. *Tolstoy: The Ultimate Reconciliation.* 1980. Translated by Peter Levi. New York: Scribner's/Macmillan, 1988.

Deikman, Arthur J. "Deautomatization and the Mystical Experience." *Psychiatry* 29 (1966): 324–38.

Deleuze, Gilles, and Félix Guattari. *Anti-Oedipus.* 1972. Translated by Robert Hurley, Mark Seem, and Helen R. Lane. Minneapolis: University of Minnesota Press, 1983.

Demetz, Peter. Foreword to *Brecht: A Collection of Critical Essays.* Englewood Cliffs, NJ: Prentice-Hall, 1962.

Denner, Michael A. "Accidental Art: Tolstoy's Poetics of Unintentionality." *Philosophy and Literature* 27.2 (October 2003): 284–303.

Derrida, Jacques. *Of Grammatology.* Translated by Gayatri Chakvravorty Spivak. Baltimore: Johns Hopkins University Press, 1976.

Descartes, Rene. *Meditations on First Philosophy. With Selections from the Objections and Replies.* Translated by John Cottingham. Cambridge: Cambridge University Press, 1986.

Dewey, John. "The Theory of Emotion. (2) The Significance of Emotions." *Psychological Review* 2 (1895): 13–32.

Doherty, Brigid. "Test and *Gestus* in Brecht and Benjamin." *MLN* 115.3 (2000): 442–81.

Dusek, Val. "Brecht and Lukács as Teachers of Feyerabend and Lakatos: The Feyerabend-Lakatos Debate as Scientific Recapitulation of the Brecht-Lukács Debate." *History of the Human Sciences* 11.2 (1998): 25–44.

Eaton, Katherine Bliss. *The Theater of Meyerhold and Brecht.* Westport, CT: Greenwood, 1985.

Elliott, J. E. "Schlegel, Brecht and the Jokes of Theory." *MLN* 113.5 (1998): 1056–88.

Emerson, Caryl. "Shklovsky's *ostranenie,* Bakhtin's *vnenakhodimost'* (How distance serves an aesthetics of arousal differently from an aesthetics based on pain)." *Poetics Today* 26.4 (Winter 2005): 637–64.

———. "Tolstoy's Aesthetics." In Donna Tussing Orwin, ed., *Cambridge Companion to Tolstoy,* 237–51. Cambridge: Cambridge University Press, 2002.

Emerson, Ralph Waldo. *Nature.* In *Nature, Addresses and Lectures,* 1–77. Vol. 1 of *The Complete Works of Ralph Waldo Emerson.* 1876. Reprint, Boston: Houghton Mifflin, 1903.

Erlich, Victor. *Russian Formalism: History, Doctrine.* The Hague: Mouton, 1955.

Ewen, Frederic. *Bertolt Brecht: His Life, His Art, His Times.* 1967. Reprint, New York: Citadel, 1992.

Fauconnier, Gilles, and Mark Turner. *The Way We Think: Conceptual Blending and the Mind's Hidden Complexities.* New York: Basic Books, 2002.

Feger, Hans. "Kierkegaard's Critique of Romantic Irony." *Harvard Review of Philosophy* 8 (2000): 109–31.

Felman, Shoshana. *The Scandal of the Speaking Body: Don Juan With J. L. Austin, or Seduction in Two Languages.* 1980. Translated by Catherine Porter, 1984. Rev. ed. Stanford: Stanford University Press, 2003.

Fiumara, Gemma Corradi. *The Mind's Affective Life: A Psychoanalytic and Philosophical Inquiry.* London: Routledge, 2001.

Foucault, Michel. "Nietzsche, Genealogy, History." Translated by Donald F. Bouchard and Sherry Simon. In Michel Foucault, *Language, Counter-Memory, Practice: Selected Essays and Interviews,* 139–64, ed. Bouchard. Ithaca: Cornell University Press, 1977.

———. *Surveiller et punir. Naissance de la prison.* Paris: Gallimard, 1975. Translated by Alan Sheridan as *Discipline and Punish: The Birth of the Prison.* New York: Pantheon, 1977.

Fradkin, Ilya. *Bertolt Brecht: Weg und Methode.* ("Way and Method"). Leipzig: Philipp Reclam, 1974.

Friedman, Howard S. "The Interactive Effects of Facial Expressions of Emotion and Verbal Messages on Perceptions of Affective Meaning." *Journal of Experimental Social Psychology* 15.5 (September 1979): 453–69.

Friedman, Howard S., Louise M. Prince, Ronald E. Riggio, and M. Robin DiMatteo. "Understanding and Assessing Nonverbal Expressiveness: The Affective Communication Test." *Journal of Personality and Social Psychology* 39.2 (August 1980): 333–51.

Friedman, Howard S., and Ronald E. Riggio. "Effect of Individual Differences in Nonverbal Expressiveness on Transmission of Emotion." *Journal of Nonverbal Behavior* 6.2 (Winter 1981): 96–104.

Friedrich, Rainer. "Brecht and Postmodernism." *Philosophy and Literature* 23.1 (1999): 44–64.

———. "The Deconstructed Self in Artaud and Brecht: Negation of Subject and Antitotalitarianism." *Forum for Modern Language Studies* 26.3 (July 1990): 282–95.

Frye, Northrop. *Fearful Symmetry.* Princeton: Princeton University Press, 1947.

Giles, Steve. *Bertolt Brecht and Critical Theory: Marxism, Modernity, and the Three-penny Lawsuit.* Bern: Peter Lang, 1997.

Ginzburg, Carlo. "Making Things Strange: The Prehistory of a Literary Device." *Representations* 56 (1996): 8–28.

Goldmann, Lucien. "Lukács and Heidegger." *Philosophical Forum* 23.1–2 (Fall 1991): 20–25.

Goode, Patrick. *Karl Korsch: A Study in Western Marxism.* London: Macmillan, 1979.

Gouldner, Alvin W. *The Two Marxisms.* New York: Oxford University Press, 1980.

Gray, Chris Hables, ed. *The Cyborg Handbook.* London: Routledge, 1995.

Green, Martin Burgess. *The Origins of Nonviolence: Tolstoy and Gandhi in Their Historical Settings.* University Park: Pennsylvania State University Press, 1986.

———. *Tolstoy and Gandhi, Men of Peace: A Biography.* New York: Basic Books, 1983.

Griffin, Susan. *Woman and Nature: The Roaring Inside Her.* New York: Harper and Row, 1978.

Grimm, Reinhold. *Bertolt Brecht.* Stuttgart: Metzler, 1963.

Grosz, Elizabeth. "Bodies and Knowledges: Feminism and the Crisis of Reason." In L. Alcoff and E. Potter, eds., *Feminist Epistemologies, 187–215.* New York: Routledge, 1993.

———. *Space, Time, and Perversion: Essays on the Politics of Bodies.* New York: Routledge, 1995.

———. *Volatile Bodies: Toward a Corporeal Feminism.* Bloomington: Indiana University Press, 1994.

Grotowski, Jerzy. *Towards a Poor Theatre.* Edited by Eugenio Barba. 1968. New York: Routledge/Theatre Arts, 2002.

Günther, Hans. "Verfremdung: Brecht und Šklovskij." In Susi K. Frank et al., eds., *Gedächtnis und Phantasma. Festschrift für Renate Lachmann,* 137–45. München: Otto Sagner, 2001.

Gustafson, Richard. *Leo Tolstoy: Resident and Stranger: A Study in Fiction and Theology.* Princeton: Princeton University Press, 1986.

Hamilton, William D. "The Genetical Theory of Social Behavior: I and II." *Journal of Theoretical Biology* 7 (1964): 1–52.

Works Cited

Hansen, Miriam Bratu. "Benjamin and Cinema: Not a One-Way Street." *Critical Inquiry* 25.2 (Winter 1999): 306–43.

Hartman, Geoffrey. *Wordsworth's Poetry, 1787–1814.* New Haven: Yale University Press, 1964.

Hatfield, Elaine, John T. Cacioppo, and Richard L. Rapson. *Emotional Contagion.* Cambridge: Cambridge University Press, 1994.

Haug, Wolfgang Fritz. "From Marx to Gramsci, from Gramsci to Marx: Historical Materialism and the Philosophy of Praxis." *Rethinking Marxism* 13.1 (2001): 69–82.

Hayot, Eric. *Chinese Dreams: Pound, Brecht, "Tel Quel."* Ann Arbor: University of Michigan Press, 2003.

Hegel, Georg Wilhelm Friedrich. *Phänomenologie des Geistes.* Vol. 2 of *Sämtliche Werke: Jubiläumsausgabe in zwanzig Bänden* (Collected works: Jubilee edition in twenty volumes). Edited by Hermann Glockner. Stuttgart: Fr. Frommans Verlag, 1951.

———. *System der Sittlichkeit.* Edited by Georg Lasson. Hamburg: Verlag von Felix Meiner, 1967. Edited and translated by H. S. Harris and T. M. Knox as *System of Ethical Life.* In *System of Ethical Life (1802/3) and First Philosophy of Spirit (Part III of the System of Speculative Philosophy 1803/4), 97–186.* Albany: SUNY Press, 1979.

———. *Vorlesungen über die Aesthetik.* Vols. 12–14 of Georg Wilhelm Friedrich Hegel, *Sämtliche Werke: Jubiläumsausgabe in zwanzig Bänden.* Edited by Hermann Glockner. Stuttgart: Fr. Frommans Verlag, 1953. Translated by T. M. Knox as *Aesthetics: Lectures on Fine Art.* 2 vols. Oxford: Clarendon, 1975.

Heidegger, Martin. *Sein und Zeit.* 1927. Reprint, Tübingen: Max Niemeyer Verlag, 1953. Translated by John Macquarrie and Edward Robinson as *Being and Time.* London: SCM Press, 1962.

Helmling, Steven. "Brecht Our (Post-)Contemporary." *Postmodern Culture* 10.2 (January 2000). Internet journal.

Holquist, Michael, and Ilya Kliger. "Minding the Gap: Toward a Historical Poetics of Estrangement." *Poetics Today* 26.4 (Winter 2005): 613–36.

Irigaray, Luce. *Elemental Passions.* Translated by Joanne Collie and Judith Still. London: Routledge, 1992.

———. *Sexes and Genealogies.* Translated by Gillian C. Gill. Ithaca, NY: Cornell University Press, 1993.

———. *Speculum of the Other Woman.* Translated by Gillian C. Gill. Ithaca, NY: Cornell University Press, 1985.

———. *This Sex Which Is Not One.* Translated by Catherine Porter. Ithaca, NY: Cornell Univ. Press, 1985.

Jahn, Gary R. "The Aesthetic Theory of Leo Tolstoy's *What Is Art?*" *Journal of Aesthetics and Art Criticism* 34.1 (Fall 1975): 59–65.

James, William. *Principles of Psychology.* 2 vols. New York: Holt, 1890.

———. *The Varieties of Religious Experience: A Study in Human Nature.* London: Longmans, Green, 1928.

Jameson, Fredric. *Brecht and Method.* London: Verso, 1998.

———. *The Prison-House of Language: A Critical Account of Structuralism and Russian Formalism.* Princeton: Princeton University Press, 1972.

Jennings, Lane Eaton. "Chinese Literature and Thought in the Poetry and Prose of Bertolt Brecht." Ph.D. diss., Harvard University, 1970.

Jessop, Bob. "Gramsci as a Spatial Theorist." *Critical Review of International Social and Political Philosophy* 8.4 (2005): 421–37.

Johnson, Mark. *The Body in the Mind: The Bodily Basis of Meaning, Imagination, and Reason.* Chicago: University of Chicago Press, 1987.

Kellner, Douglas, ed. *Karl Korsch: Revolutionary Theory.* Austin: University of Texas Press, 1977.

Korsch, Karl. *Marxism and Philosophy.* 1923. Translated by Fred Halliday. London: New Left Books, 1970.

Koss, Juliet. "Playing Politics with Estranged and Empathetic Audiences: Bertolt Brecht and Georg Fuchs." *South Atlantic Quarterly* 96.4 (1997): 809–20.

Kristeva, Julia. *Powers of Horror: An Essay on Abjection.* 1980. Translated by Léon S. Roudiez. New York: Columbia University Press, 1982.

———. "The System and the Speaking Subject." 1973. Reprinted in Toril Moi, ed., *The Kristeva Reader,* 24–33. New York: Columbia University Press, 1986.

Kuhn, Tom, and Steve Giles, eds. *Brecht on Art and Politics.* Translated by Laura Bradley, Steve Giles, and Tom Kuhn. London: Methuen, 2003.

Krystal, Henry. "Desomatization and the Consequences of Infantile Psychic Trauma." *Psychoanalytic Inquiry* 17.2 (1997): 126–50.

Lacan, Jacques. *Ethics of Psychoanalysis, 1959–1960.* Translated by Dennis Porter. New York: Norton, 1992.

———. *On Feminine Sexuality: The Limits of Love and Knowledge (Book XX: Encore 1972–1973).* 1975. Translated by Bruce Fink. New York: Norton, 1998.

Laferrière, Daniel. "Potebnja, Šklovskij and the Familiarity/Strangeness Paradox." *Russian Literature* 4.2 (1976): 175–98.

Lakoff, George. *Women, Fire, and Dangerous Things: What Categories Reveal About the Mind.* Chicago: University of Chicago Press, 1987.

Lakoff, George, and Mark Johnson. *Metaphors We Live By.* Chicago: University of Chicago Press, 1980.

———. *Philosophy in the Flesh: The Embodied Mind and Its Challenge to Western Thought.* New York: Basic Books, 1999.

Lemon, Lee T., and Marion J. Reis, eds. and trans. *Russian Formalist Criticism: Four Essays.* Lincoln: University of Nebraska Press, 1965.

Lukács, Georg. *The Young Hegel: Studies in the Relations Between Dialectics and Economics.* Translated by Rodney Livingstone. Cambridge, MA: MIT Press, 1975.

Marcuse, Herbert. *An Essay on Liberation.* Boston: Beacon, 1969.

———. *One-Dimensional Man: Studies in the Ideology of Advanced Industrial Society.* Boston: Beacon, 1964.

———. "Repressive Tolerance." In Robert Paul Wolff, Barrington Moore Jr., and Herbert Marcuse, *A Critique of Pure Tolerance,* 81–123. 1965. Reprint, Boston: Beacon Press, 1969.

Martin, Carol. "Brecht, Feminism, and Chinese Theatre." *TDR: The Drama Review* 43.4 (1999): 77–85.

Marx, Karl. "Introduction to a Critique of Political Economy." Translated by S. W. Ryazanskaya. Edited by C. J. Arthur. In Marx and Engels, *German,* 124–51.

———. *Ökonomisch-philosophische Manuskripte aus dem Jahre 1844.* In *Schriften und Briefe, November 1837—August 1844,* 465–588. Vol. 40 of *Karl Marx Friedrich Engels Werke.* Berlin: Dietz Verlag, 1985.

Marx, Karl, and Friedrich Engels. *The Communist Manifesto.* Calcutta: Radical Book Club, 1944.

———. *The German Ideology, Part One, with Selections from Parts Two and Three, Together with Marx's "Introduction to a Critique of Political Economy."* Edited by C. J. Arthur. Translated by Clemens Dutt and C. P. Magill. New York: International Publishers, 1970.

Medvedev, P. N. *The Formal Method in Literary Scholarship: A Critical Introduction to Sociological Poetics.* Translated by Albert J. Wehrle. Baltimore: Johns Hopkins University Press, 1978.

Mészáros, István. *Marx's Theory of Alienation.* London: Merlin, 1970.

Mitchell, Stanley. "From Shklovsky to Brecht: Some Preliminary Remarks Towards a History of the Politicization of Russian Formalism." *Screen* 15 (1974): 74–81.

Mollon, Phil. *Releasing the Self: The Healing Legacy of Heinz Kohut.* London: Whurr, 2001.

Moore, Stanley. "Rousseau on Alienation and the Rights of Man." *History of Political Thought* 12.1 (Spring 1990): 73–85.

Morgan, Thais E. "Is There an Intertext in this Text?: Literary and Interdisciplinary Approaches to Intertextuality." *American Journal of Semiotics* 3 (1985): 1–40.

Morton, Adam David. "A Double Reading of Gramsci: Beyond the Logic of Contingency." *Critical Review of International Social and Political Philosophy* 8.4 (2005): 439–53.

———. "Historicizing Gramsci: Situating Ideas In and Beyond their Context." *Review of International Political Economy* 10.1 (February 2003): 118–46.

Murakami, Haruki. *The Wind-Up Bird Chronicle.* Translated by Jay Rubin. New York: Vintage, 1998.

Muschg, Walter. *Von Trakl zu Brecht: Dichter des Expressionismus* (From Trakl to Brecht: Poets of Expressionism). Munich: Piper and Co., 1963.

Neubauer, John. "Bakhtin versus Lukács: Inscriptions of Homelessness in Theories of the Novel." *Poetics Today* 17.4 (1996): 531–46.

Nijenhuis, Ellert R. S. "Somatoform Dissociation: Major Symptoms of Dissociative Disorders." *Journal of Trauma and Dissociation* 1.4 (2000): 7–32.

Novalis. "Abteilung XII: Fragmente und Studien 1799–1800." In *Das philosophische Werk II,* 527–694. Vol. 3 of Richard Samuel, ed., *Novalis Schriften.* 5 vols. Stuttgart: Verlag W. Kohlhammer, 1960–88.

Paramonov, Boris. "*Formalizm: Metod ili mirovozzrenie?*" ("Formalism: Method or Worldview?"). *NLO* 14 (1996): 35–52.

Prophet, Becky B. "Aspects of Traditional Chinese Theatre in the Plays of Bertolt Brecht." Ph.D. diss., University of Michigan, 1986.

Rancour-Laferriere, Daniel. *Tolstoy on the Couch: Misogyny, Masochism, and the Absent Mother.* New York: New York University Press, 1998.

———. "Why the Russian Formalists Had No Theory of the Literary Person." *Wiener Slawistischer Almanach* 32 (1992): 327–37.

Reich, Bernhard. *Im Wettlauf mit der Zeit: Erinnerungen aus fünf Jahrzehnten deutscher Theatergeschichte* ("In the Race with Time: Memoirs of Five Decades of German Theater History"). Berlin: Henschelverlag, 1970.

Reich, Wilhelm. *Character-analysis.* 1933. Translated by Theodore P. Wolfe. New York: Noonday, 1949.

Riley, Denise. *Impersonal Passion: Language as Affect.* Durham: Duke University Press, 2005.

Robinson, Douglas. *American Apocalypses: The Image of the End of the World in American Literature.* Baltimore: Johns Hopkins University Press, 1985.

———. "Displacement and the Somatics of Postcolonial Culture." Unpublished book manuscript.

———. "The Somatics of Language." Unpublished book manuscript.

———. *The Translator's Turn.* Baltimore: Johns Hopkins University Press, 1991.

Rockmore, Tom. "Fichte, Lask, and Lukács' Hegelian Marxism." *Journal of the History of Philosophy* 30.4 (October 1992): 557–77.

Ross, Stephen David. *The Gift of Touch: Embodying the Good.* Albany: SUNY Press, 1998.

Rousseau, Jean-Jacques. *Emile or On Education.* Edited and translated by Allan Bloom. New York: Basic Books, 1979.

———. *Social Contract, Discourse on the Virtue Most Necessary for a Hero, Political Fragments, and Geneva Manuscript.* 1767. Translated by Judith R. Bush, Roger D. Masters, and Christopher Kelly. Vol. 4 of *The Collected Writings of Rousseau.* Hanover: University Press of New England, 1994.

Rudnev, Vadim P. "Poetika depersonalizatsii (L. N. Tolstoy i V. B. Shklovsky)." ("The Poetics of Depersonalization" [L. N. Tolstoy and V. B. Shklovsky]). *Logos* 11/12.21 (1999): 55–63.

Sacks, Oliver. *The Man Who Mistook His Wife for a Hat, and Other Clinical Tales.* New York: Harper and Row, 1985.

San Juan, Epifanio. "Antonio Gramsci on Surrealism and the Avant-garde." *Journal of Aesthetic Education* 37.2 (2003): 31–45.

Sayers, Sean. "Creative Activity and Alienation in Hegel and Marx." *Historical Materialism* 11.1 (2003): 107–28.

Scaer, Robert C. *Trauma, Dissociation, and Disease: The Body Bears the Burden.* New York: Haworth, 2001.

Schäfer, Heinz. *Der Hegelianismus der Bert Brecht'schen Verfremdungstechnik im Anhängigkeit von ihren marxistischen Grundlagen* ("The Hegelianism of the Brechtian Estrangement Effect in Its Reliance on Its Marxist Foundations"). Ph.D. diss., University of Stuttgart, 1958.

Schiller, Friedrich von. *Die Piccolomini.* In *Dramen II,* 313–405. In Gerhard Fricke and Herbert G. Göpfert, eds., *Friedrich Schillers Sämtliche Werke.* Munich: Carl Hanser Verlag, 1965.

Schlegel, Friedrich. "Fragmente." In Ernst Behler, ed., *Schriften und Fragmente: Ein Gesamtbild seines Geistes,* 81–113. Stuttgart: Alfred Kröner Verlag, 1956. Translated by Peter Firchow as *Philosophical Fragments.* Minneapolis: University of Minnesota Press, 1991.

Scholes, Robert. *Structuralism in Literature: An Introduction.* New Haven: Yale University Press, 1974.

Schore, Allan N. *Affect Regulation and the Origin of the Self: The Neurobiology of Emotional Development.* Mahwah, NJ: Erlbaum, 1994.

———. *Affect Regulation and the Repair of the Self.* New York: Norton, 2003.

Schumacher, Ernst. *Brecht: Theater und Gesellschaft im 20. Jahrhundert* ("Theater and Society in the Twentieth Century). Berlin: Henschelverlag, 1973.

Sheldon, Richard. Acknowledgements in Shklovsky, *Sentimental'noe/Sentimental,* v–vi.

———. Introduction to Shklovsky, *Zoo/ZOO,* xiii–xxxiii.

———. "Introduction: Viktor Shklovsky and the Device of Ostensible Surrender." In Shklovsky, *Tret'ya/Third,* ix–xlii.

Shelley, Percy Bysshe. "A Defence of Poetry." In Hazard Adams and Leroy Searle, eds., *Critical Theory Since Plato,* 538–51. 3d ed. Boston: Thomson Wadsworth, 2005.

Sheppard, Richard. "Georg Lukács, Wilhelm Worringer, and German Expressionism." *Journal of European Studies* 25.3 (1995): 241–82.

Sher, Benjamin. "Nature Vs. Art: A Note On Translating Shklovsky." Available at www.websher.net/srl/tran.html. (accessed July 25, 2005).

Šilbajoris, Rimvydas. *Tolstoy's Aesthetics and His Art.* Columbus, OH: Slavica, 1991.

Shirer, William L. *Love and Hatred: The Stormy Marriage of Leo and Sonya Tolstoy.* New York: Simon and Schuster, 1994.

Shklovsky, Viktor. *"Eschyo nichego ne konchilos'"* ("Nothing is Over Yet"). Edited by V. P. Konchetov. Vol. 5 of *Literaturnye memuary* (Literary memoirs). Moscow: Vagrius, 2002.

———. *Gamburgsky schyot.* ("The Hamburg Score/Rankings/Account." The phrase refers to a wrestling competition, hence *score* or *rankings,* but Richard

Sheldon is translating the book for the Dalkey Archive Press under the title *Hamburg Account*.) 1928. Reprint, Moscow: Sovyetsky pisatel', 1990.

———. "Iskusstvo kak priyom." 1917. Reprinted in Shklovsky, *O teorii* (1925), 7–23; (1929), 7–20; (1983), 9–25, and Shklovsky, *Gamburgsky* (1990), 58–72. Translated into German by Gisela Drohla as "Kunst als Kunstgriff." In Drohla, ed., Shklovsky, *Theorie der Prosa*. Frankfurt am Main: Fischer-Taschenbuch-Verlag, 1966. Translated into English by Lee T. Lemon and Marion J. Reis as "Art as Technique." In Lemon and Reis, *Russian Formalist Criticism,* 3–24. Re-translated by Benjamin Sher as "Art as Device." In Shklovsky, *O teorii/ Theory,* 1–14.

———. *Khod konya.* Berlin: Helikon-Verlag, 1923. Reprinted in Shklovsky, *Gamburgsky* (1990), 74–150. Translated by Richard Sheldon as *Knight's Move.* Normal, IL: Dalkey Archive Press, 2005.

———. *Literatura i kinematograf* ("Literature and the Cinematographer"). Berlin: Helikon-Verlag, 1923.

———. *O teorii prozy.* Moscow and Leningrad: Krug, 1925. Reprint, Moscow: Federatsiya, 1929. Reprint, Moscow: Sovyetskiy pisatel', 1983. Translated by Benjamin Sher as *Theory of Prose.* 1990. Reprint, Normal, IL: Dalkey Archive Press, 1998.

———. "Obnovlenie ponyatiya" ("Renewal of a Concept"). In Shklovsky, *Povesti o proze: Razmyshleniya i razbory* ("Tales on Prose"), 2 vols., 2:298–305. Moscow: Khudozhestvennaya literatura, 1966.

———. "O poezii i zaumnom yazyke" ("On Poetry and Trans-Rational Language"). *Poetica* II (Petrograd, 1919).

———. "Pamyatnik nauchnoy oshibke" ("A Monument to a Scientific Error"). *Literaturnaya gazeta* 4.41 (January 27, 1930). Available at http://magazines.russ.ru/nlo/2000/44/shklovs.html. (accessed December 20, 2005).

———. "Parodiyny roman: 'Tristram Shendi' Sterna." In Shklovsky, *O teorii* (1925), 177–205; (1929), 139–61. Translated by Benjamin Sher as "The Novel as Parody: Sterne's *Tristram Shandy.*" In Shklovsky, *O teorii/Theory,* 141–70.

———. *Sentimental'noe puteshestvie.* Berlin: Helikon-Verlag, 1923. Reprinted in Shklovsky, *Eschyo,* 15–266. Translated by Richard Sheldon as *A Sentimental Journey: Memoirs, 1917–1922.* 1970. Reprint, Normal, IL: Dalkey Archive Press, 2004.

———. "Stroenie rasskaza i romana." In Shklovsky, *O teorii* (1929) 68–90. Translated by Benjamin Sher as "The Structure of Fiction." In Shklovsky, *O teorii/ Theory,* 52–71.

———. "Svyaz priyomov syuzhetoslozheniya s obschimi priyomami stilya." 1919. Reprinted in Shklovsky, *O teorii* (1925), 24–70; (1929) 21–59. Translated by Benjamin Sher as "The Relationship Between Devices of Plot Construction and General Devices of Style." In Shklovsky, *O teorii/Theory,* 15–51.

———. *Tret'ya fabrika.* Moscow: Krug, 1926. Reprinted in Shklovsky, *Eschyo,* 333–94. Translated by Richard Sheldon as *Third Factory.* 1977. Reprint, Normal, IL: Dalkey Archive Press, 2002.

———. "Voskreshenie slova." 1914. Reprinted in Shklovsky, *Gamburgsky* (1990), 36–42. Translated by Richard Sherwood as "The Resurrection of the Word." In Stephen Bann and John Bowlt, eds., *Russian Formalism: A Collection of Articles and Texts in Translation,* 41–47. New York: Barnes and Noble, 1973.

———. "Vyshla kniga Mayakovskogo 'Oblako v shtanakh'" ("Mayakovsky's Book 'Cloud in Pants' is Out"). 1915. Reprinted in Shklovsky, *Gamburgsky* (1990), 42–45.

———. *Zoo. Pis'ma ne o lyubvi, ili Tret'ya Eloiza.* Berlin: Helikon-Verlag, 1923. Reprinted in Shklovsky, *Eschyo,* 267–332. Translated by Richard Sheldon as *ZOO, or Letters Not about Love.* 1971. Reprint, Normal, IL: Dalkey Archive Press, 2001.

Shukman, Ann, trans. "The Ode as an Oratorical Genre," by Yury Tynyanov. *New Literary History* 34.3 (Summer 2003): 565–96.

Shvarts, Yevgeny. *Zhivu bespokoyno . . . Iz dnevnikov* ("I Live Restlessly . . . From the Journals"). Edited by K. N. Kirilenko. Leningrad: Sovyetsky pisatel', 1990.

Siebers, Tobin. "Pushkin and Romantic Self-Criticism." *Anthropoetics* 9.2 (Fall 2003 / Winter 2004). Available at www.anthropoetics.ucla.edu/apo902/push-kin.htm. (accessed November 13, 2005).

Silberman, Marc. "A Postmodernized Brecht?" *Theatre Journal* 45.1 (March 1993): 1–19.

Slingerland, Edward G. "Conceptual Blending, Somatic Marking, and Normativity: A Case Example from Ancient Chinese." *Cognitive Linguistics* 16.3 (2005): 557–84.

Sobkin, Vladimir S., and Dmitri A. Leontiev. "The Beginning of a New Psychology: Vygotsky's Psychology of Art." In Gerald C. Cupchik and Janos László, eds., *Emerging Visions of the Aesthetic Process: Psychology, Semiology, and Philosophy,* 185–94. Cambridge: Cambridge University Press, 1992.

Stahl, Harvey. *William Blake: The Apocalyptic Vision.* New York: Wittenborn, 1974.

Starosta, Guido. "Scientific Knowledge and Political Action: On the Antinomies of Lukács' Thought in *History and Class Consciousness.*" *Science and Society* 67.1 (2003): 39–67.

Steiner, Peter. *Russian Formalism: A Metapoetics.* Ithaca, NY: Cornell University Press, 1984.

Striedter, Jurij. *Literary Structure, Evolution, and Value: Russian Formalism and Czech Structuralism Reconsidered.* 1969. Cambridge, MA: Harvard University Press, 1989.

Sun Huizhu. "Aesthetics of Stanislavsky, Brecht, and Mei Lanfang." In Faye Chunfang Fei, ed. and trans., *Chinese Theories of Theater and Performance from Confucius to the Present,* 170–78. Ann Arbor: University of Michigan Press, 1999.

Svetlikova, Ilona. *Istoki russkogo formalizma* ("The Sources of Russian Formalism"). Moscow: Novoe literaturnoe obozrenie, 2005.

Tatlow, Antony. *The Function of Brecht's Asian Images.* Bern: Peter Lang, 1978.

———. *The Mask of Evil: Brecht's Response to the Poetry, Theatre and Thought of China and Japan: A Comparative and Critical Evaluation.* Bern: Peter Lang, 1977.

Tatlow, Antony, and Wong Tak-Wai, eds. *Brecht and East Asian Theatre.* Hong Kong: Hong Kong University Press, 1982.

Terada, Rei. *Feeling in Theory: Emotion after the "Death of the Subject."* Cambridge, MA: Harvard University Press, 2001.

Thomas, Emyr Vaughan. "Wittgenstein and Tolstoy: The Authentic Orientation." *Religious Studies* 33.4 (1997): 363–77.

Thompson, Caleb. "Wittgenstein, Tolstoy and the Meaning of Life." *Philosophical Investigations* 20.2 (1997): 96–116.

Tihanov, Galin. "Literature and Arts—Viktor Shklovskii and Georg Lukács in the 1930s." *Slavonic and East European Review* 78.1 (2000): 44–65.

———. *The Master and the Slave: Lukács, Bakhtin, and the Ideas of the Time.* Oxford: Oxford University Press, 2000.

———. "The Politics of Estrangement: The Case of the Early Shklovsky." *Poetics Today* 26.4 (Winter 2005): 665–96.

Todorov, Tzvetan, ed. and trans. *Theorie de la litterature: Textes des formalistes russes.* Paris: Seuil, 1965.

Tolstoy, Lev. *Anna Karenina.* 1875–1877. Reprint. Vols. 18–19 of Tolstoy, *Polnoe.* Translated by Aylmer Maude as *Anna Karenina.* 1918. Reprint. In George Gibian, ed., *Anna Karenina: The Maude Translation, Backgrounds and Sources, Essays in Criticism,* 1–740. New York: Norton, 1970.

———. *Chto takoe iskusstvo?* In Tolstoy, *Polnoe,* vol. 30, *Proizvedeniya 1882–1898* ("Works, 1882–1898"), 25–203. Translated by Aylmer Maude as *What Is Art?* in *What Is Art? and Essays on Art,* 70–312. 1898. New York: Oxford University Press, 1950.

———. *Dnevniki.* In Tolstoy, *Polnoe,* vols. 50–58. Edited and translated by R. F. Christian as *Tolstoy's Diaries.* 2 vols. New York: Scribner's, 1985.

———. *Ispoved'.* In Tolstoy, *Polnoe,* vol. 23, *Proizvedeniya 1879–1884* ("Works 1879–1884"), 1–59. Translated by Aylmer Maude as *A Confession.* In *A Confession, The Gospel in Brief, and What I Believe,* 1–84. 1921. Reprint, London: Oxford University Press, 1974.

———. *Polnoe sobranie sochinenii v 90 tomakh* ("Complete Collected Works in 90 Volumes"). Edited by V. G. Chertkov. Moscow: Gosudarstvennoe Isdatel'stvo Khudozhestvennoy Literatury, 1928–58.

Tolstoy, Sophia. *The Diaries of Sophia Tolstoy.* Translated by Cathy Porter. New York: Random House, 1985.

Trivedi, Saam. "Artist-Audience Communication: Tolstoy Reclaimed." *Journal of Aesthetic Education* 38.2 (Summer 2004): 38–52.

Trotsky, Leon. *Literature and Revolution.* 1924. New York: Russell and Russell, 1957.

Works Cited

Ungvári, Tamás. "The Origins of the Theory of *Verfremdung.*" *Neohelicon* 7.1 (1979): 171–232.

Van Der Veer, Rene, and Joan Valsinger. *Understanding Vygotsky: A Quest for Synthesis.* Oxford: Blackwell, 1994.

Vygotsky, Lev. *Psikhologiya iskusstva.* Dissertation, 1925. First published in Russian, 1965. Reprint, Moscow: Iskusstvo, 1986. Translated by Scripta Technica as *The Psychology of Art.* Cambridge, MA: MIT Press, 1971.

Wellek, René. *A History of Modern Criticism: 1750–1950.* New Haven: Yale University Press, 1965.

Welton, Donn, ed. *Body and Flesh: A Philosophical Reader.* Oxford: Blackwell, 1998.

West, David W. "Lev Vygotsky's Psychology of Art and Literature." *Changing English* 6.1 (March 1999): 47–55.

———. "Psychologies of Art and Literature: A Comparison of the Work of I. A. Richards and L. S. Vygotsky." *Changing English* 8.1 (March 2001): 17–27.

Wilde, Oscar. "The Decay of Lying." In Richard Ellmann, ed., *The Artist as Critic: Critical Writings of Oscar Wilde,* 290–320. 1968. Reprint, Chicago: University of Chicago Press, 1982.

Williams, Raymond. *Marxism and Literature.* London: Oxford University Press, 1977.

Willett, John, ed. *Brecht on Theatre: The Development of an Aesthetic.* 1964. Reprint, New York: Hill and Wang, 1992.

———. *The Theatre of Bertolt Brecht: A Study from Eight Aspects.* 1959. 3d ed. New York: New Directions, 1968.

Wilson, Edward O. *Sociobiology: The New Synthesis.* Cambridge, MA: Belknap, 1975.

Wittgenstein, Ludwig. *On Certainty/Über Gewissheit.* Edited by G. E. M. Anscombe and G. H. von Wright. Translated by Denis Paul and G. E. M. Anscombe. Oxford: Blackwell, 1969.

———. *Philosophische Untersuchungen/Philosophical Investigations.* Translated by G. E. M. Anscombe. Oxford: Blackwell, 1953.

Wittig, Monique. *The Straight Mind and Other Essays.* Boston: Beacon, 1992.

Woodman, Ross Grieg. *The Apocalyptic Vision in the Poetry of Shelley.* Toronto: University of Toronto Press, 1964.

Wordsworth, William, and Samuel Taylor Coleridge. *Lyrical Ballads 1798.* Oxford: Woodstock Books, 1990.

Yan Hai-Ping. "Brecht's Theory of Alienation and Peking Opera." Available at www .totse.com/en/ego/literary_genius/peking2.html (accessed July 22, 2005).

Index